STUDIES IN TRADE LIBERALIZATION

Problems and Prospects for the Industrial Countries

STUDIES IN
TRADE LIBERALIZATION

Problems and Prospects for the Industrial Countries

Bela Balassa
The Johns Hopkins University

In collaboration with:
M. E. Kreinin, *Michigan State University*
R. J. Wonnacott, *University of Western Ontario*
F. Hartog, *University of Groningen*
S. J. Wells, *University of Salford, Lancashire*
S. B. Linder, *Stockholm School of Economics*
Kiyoshi Kojima, *Hitotsubashi University*
Douglas Dosser, *University of York*
W. B. Kelly, Jr., Washington, D.C.

The Johns Hopkins Press, Baltimore, Maryland

PREFACE

This volume presents studies on the problems and prospects of trade liberalization among industrial countries that were carried out in the framework of the Atlantic Trade Project sponsored by the Council on Foreign Relations and financed by the Ford Foundation. Another volume by Bela Balassa, director of the Project, aimed at the general reader, is included in the publication series of the Council.

The present volume is the result of a co-ordinated work program, and as such, it has involved the combined efforts of the project director and the individual contributors. It contains six country-studies, each of which considers the problems of trade liberalization from the point of view of a single country or of a group of countries (the United States, Canada, the European Common Market, the United Kingdom, Scandinavia, and Japan). It further includes special studies: one examines the implications of intercountry differences in fiscal and social security systems for trade and foreign investment; another deals with the trade-restraining effects of nontariff barriers.

The book represents a novel experiment both in choice of subject matter and in method—it inquires into the objectives and the effects of freeing trade barriers for particular countries and groups of countries on the basis of common principles and methodology. In so doing, it attempts to illuminate the questions under discussion from different points of view, while providing for the comparability of the results. No effort has been made, however, to attain uniformity in the country studies. The problems facing the individual countries often differ to a considerable extent; hence, their analysis can shed further light on the possibilities for multilateral trade liberalization. Finally, the subject matter chosen for the special studies reflects the recent preoccupation with international differences in fiscal and social security systems and nontariff barriers, and the effects of these differences on international trade and the flow of capital.

146787

The authors are indebted to the Council on Foreign Relations and to the Ford Foundation for sponsoring and financing, respectively, the research underlying these studies. Thanks are also due to various individuals at national and international organizations, universities, and business firms for their advice and constructive criticism on matters pertaining to the individual studies or to the project as a whole.

Some findings of the studies have been published in professional journals, including the *Economic Journal*, the *Manchester School of Economic and Social Research*, the *Review of Economics and Statistics* and the *Southern Economic Journal*. The publishers of these periodicals kindly gave permission for use of published material.

CONTENTS

vii

CONTENTS ix

LIST OF TABLES

xi

STUDIES IN TRADE LIBERALIZATION

Problems and Prospects for the Industrial Countries

CHAPTER I

INTRODUCTION

Bela Balassa[1]

The Purpose and Scope of the Studies

The purpose of the country studies is to evaluate the desirability and the possible effects of trade liberalization on the basis of political and economic objectives and to consider the choice among alternative trade arrangements in the Atlantic area. The alternatives under study include: (A) an Atlantic Free Trade Area; (B) periodical tariff reductions under the most-favored-nation clause; (C) a trade arrangement among the industrial countries other than the Common Market; and (D) European integration.

Periodical negotiations on across-the-board tariff reductions under the most-favored-nation clause would represent the continuation of "Kennedy Rounds." Another, more revolutionary, solution that has been proposed in recent years would be to establish a free trade area among the industrial countries (the United States, Canada, the countries of the European Common Market and the European Free Trade Association and Japan).[2] With some disregard to geography, the expression "Atlantic Free Trade Area" will be used in the following to denote the latter alternative.

Another alternative would be to aim at trade liberalization among the United States, Canada, and the EFTA countries (and possibly Japan) on a preferential basis or in the form of a free trade area. Suggestions to this effect were originally made for the eventuality that the Kennedy Round remained unsuccessful by reason of the intransigent position taken by

[1] The author is professor of political economy at The Johns Hopkins University and adviser to the economics department of the International Bank for Reconstruction and Development.

[2] Senator Jacob Javits, in a speech at the Savoy Hotel in London on November 8, 1965, called for "a treaty of free trade and economic co-operation with the U.K., other EEC and EFTA nations, Canada, New Zealand and Australia, and other industrialized countries of the OECD which agree to adhere to the new rules of trade of [a] Free Trade Area."

3

the European Common Market.[3] More recently, the establishment of a free trade area among these countries has been proposed as a genuine alternative, irrespective of the outcome of the Kennedy Round.[4] This is our alternative (C), while the last-mentioned alternative is integration in Western Europe. Needless to say, some of these alternatives can be combined; for example, an accommodation between the Common Market and EFTA may be accompanied by tariff reductions under the most-favored-nation clause.

In evaluating the economic effects of trade liberalization, the contributors have utilized estimates prepared by the director of the project concerning the potential impact of tariff reductions on trade flows and on the "revealed" comparative advantage of the industrial countries. A short discussion of the methods underlying the calculations is given in this chapter; the appendix to the chapter contains a detailed description of the methodology. Slightly different assumptions have been used in the U.S. chapter whose calculations in part antedate those of the other studies. Further, the Canadian chapter has utilized the results of a book-length study by Ronald and Paul Wonnacott, *Free Trade between the United States and Canada: the Potential Economic Effects.* The special treatment of the Canadian case is explained by the fact that the Canadian economy is, economically and geographically, a part of the North American region. Correspondingly, in the event of the elimination of tariff barriers, the key issue becomes the structural change in supply conditions that is expected to result from the rationalization of Canadian industry in the North American context.

The scope of the country studies is restricted to trade liberalization in regard to industrial materials and manufactured goods that have been in the center of trade negotiations in the postwar period. Foods and fuels are excluded because of the special character of their protection and the uncertainties re-

---

[3] Cf., e.g., *Trade Negotiations for a Better Free World Economy* (Washington, D.C.: Committee for Economic Development, 1966), p. 41, and Henry S. Reuss, *The Critical Decade* (New York: McGraw-Hill, Co., 1964), pp. 59–61.

[4] *A New Trade Strategy for Canada and the United States* (Washington, D.C., Canadian-American Committee, 1966). The Committee considers this scheme as a first step towards the eventual establishment of an Atlantic Free Trade Area.

lating to the prospects and the modalities of removing obstacles to their international exchange. On the other hand, by reason of the interdependence of trade and capital flows, the country studies also consider the possible implications of trade liberalization for direct foreign investment.

In addition to the topics examined in all of the country studies (Chapters 2 to 7), the individual chapters deal with particular questions that are of interest to one or several countries. Thus, given the relatively small share of foreign trade in the American economy, the U.S. study gives emphasis to inter-industry differences in regard to dependence on trade, and analyzes the impact of trade liberalization on individual industries and regions. Further, the preoccupation of American policy-makers with the possible effects of tariff reductions on employment has made it desirable to consider this question in some detail. Finally, the U.S. study incorporates the findings of a survey in the course of which American firms with interests abroad have been asked to indicate how the establishment of an Atlantic Free Trade Area would affect their foreign investment decisions.

Trade and other barriers have artificially split, into two parts, the North American economy. Notwithstanding these barriers, the United States looms large—as trader and investor—in the Canadian economy, which is by far the smaller of the two. This explains the emphasis on U.S.-Canadian relations in the Canadian chapter. Drawing on the conclusions of a larger study referred to earlier, the chapter focuses on the possible effects for Canada of a North American Free Trade Area, and subsequently considers the implications of freeing trade with Western Europe and Japan. In this connection, the role of Commonwealth preference in British-Canadian trade is also discussed.

Some special problems arise if countries which are themselves in the process of economic integration participate in efforts to liberalize trade on a multilateral basis. The discussion of these problems occupies an important part in the Common Market study that raises the question whether, and to what extent, the fitting together of the jigsaw puzzle of the Atlantic area is facilitated or hindered by the formation of larger pieces, such as the European Economic Community. In the chapter, attention is further given to several questions of special interest to the Common Market countries in regard to the freeing of trade with the United States. These include differences in firm size, government support to research and development, patent licensing, nontariff barriers, agriculture, and U.S. investments in Western Europe.

European integration is the focus of the British study. Following a discussion of changes in British attitudes towards integration in Western Europe, the chapter examines the U.K. trade pattern, and the impact of the division of Western Europe on the trade of the United Kingdom. Attention is further given to the changing role of the Commonwealth preference system and the declining importance of Commonwealth countries in Britain's trade. The study also includes a detailed survey of the prospects of individual industries in the event of the liberalization of trade, and considers the possible effects of multilateral tariff reductions on industrial location.

The countries of Scandinavia (Denmark, Norway, Sweden) are among the foremost proponents of multilateral trade liberalization; hence, the emphasis on the economic benefits of tariff reductions in the Scandinavian chapter. In turn, in the case of Japan, the *leitmotiv* is structural transformation in its implications for the structure of Japanese trade. Much consideration is given to Japan's dual trade pattern in her relations with developed and less developed countries, and to the need for eliminating quantitative restrictions that presently impinge on Japanese exports and imports.

A detailed discussion of the implications of differences in domestic fiscal and social security regulations and nontariff barriers for trade and capital movements follows in Chapters 8 and 9 of this volume. Chapter 8 provides a quantitative assessment of differences in fiscal and social systems among the industrial countries, and a qualitative appraisal of the effects of these differences on trade and factor movements. Separate consideration is given to direct taxes (corporation tax and the personal income tax), indirect taxes (turnover taxes and excises), government expenditures, and social security systems. An attempt is further made to appraise the net fiscal "burden" on capital, labor, and consumers, and the experience of the Common Market and EFTA is utilized to examine possible avenues of fiscal harmonization among the industrial countries.

The nontariff measures reviewed in Chapter 9 include government regulations, other than customs duties, that have a restrictive effect on international trade. The major forms of nontariff barriers are quantitative restrictions and state trading; government procurement; customs classification and valuation; and antidumping legislation and practices. Consideration is further given to the effects on trade of various internal regulations such as automobile road taxes and internal revenue taxes on distilled spirits.

Estimation of the Effects of Tariff Reductions on Trade Flows
For purposes of the country studies, estimates have been prepared on the possible effects of tariff reductions on the exports and imports of the industrial countries. The estimates reflect the assumption of unchanged production methods, and do not extend to the dynamic effects of trade liberalization. We have considered the effects on trade of (A) an Atlantic Free Trade Area, and (B) a 50 per cent across-the-board tariff reduction undertaken by the industrial nations. We have also indicated the implications of (C) a trade arrangement among the industrial countries other than the Common Market, and (D) European integration, although numerical calculations for these alternatives have not been made.

The year 1960 has been chosen as the base year for the estimates, under the assumption that the discriminatory effects of the European Common Market and the European Free Trade Association were not yet appreciable at that time. This choice has made it possible to consider the effects of trade liberalization in three parts: (1) the direct effects of tariff reductions; (2) the elimination (reduction) of potential discrimination against nonmember countries in the EEC and EFTA; (3) the indirect effects of trade liberalization operating through the "feedback" mechanism.

The direct effects of trade liberalization refer to changes in exports and imports that would take place following multilateral reductions in duties if no account were taken of the potential discriminatory effect of the Common Market and EFTA. The exports of nonmember countries would increase further as a result of the elimination of, or reduction in, EEC and EFTA discrimination through multilateral reductions in duties. Finally, if tariff reductions were carried out under the most-favored-nation clause, imports from nonindustrial countries would also rise and, assuming that these countries spend the entire increment in their foreign exchange earnings, there would be a feedback effect on the exports of industrial areas.

Estimates have been made for industrial materials (SITC classes 2 and 4, plus unwrought metals) and for manufactured goods (SITC classes 5 to 8, less unwrought metals). A 107 commodity category breakdown has been used in the calculations, corresponding to the three-digit groups of the Standard International Trade Classification except for unwrought metals, where a four-digit classification has been necessary. The results are given in two variants: *Variant I* assumes that the expansion of the exports of manufactures would necessitate a rise in prices by one-third of the tariff reduction in Western Europe where tight labor conditions prevail, while *Variant II* is calculated with unchanged European export prices. In all other exporting areas, constant export prices have been assumed throughout, and the same assumption has been made in regard to industrial materials irrespective of their origin.

"Revealed" Comparative Advantage

Aside from the impact of tariff reductions on trade flows, it is of interest to indicate how trade liberalization would affect the industrial structure of the participating countries. Since the reallocation of resources depends on comparative advantage, we would have to ascertain where the comparative advantage of the industrial countries lies in their trade with each other. I have elsewhere noted that efforts made to provide an explanation on the basis of prevailing theories of comparative advantage have had little success; neither do manufacturing censuses and industry studies furnish sufficient data for this purpose.[5] As an alternative solution, we have utilized information on "revealed" comparative advantage.

Since the commodity pattern of trade reflects relative costs as well as the influence of nonprice factors, such as goodwill, quality, and the availability of servicing and repair facilities, the "revealed" comparative advantage of the industrial countries may be indicated by their trade performance with respect

[5] Bela Balassa, "Trade Liberalization and 'Revealed' Comparative Advantage," *Manchester School* (May, 1965), pp. 90–123.

to individual industries. For one thing, comparative advantage will tend to determine the structure of exports; for another, it will bear influence on the ratio of exports to imports in particular industries.

Indicators of export performance and export-import ratios have been derived for the United States, Canada, the European Common Market, the United Kingdom, Sweden, and Japan in regard to seventy-four categories of manufactured products. As to the first, we have calculated the relative shares of individual countries in the world exports of various commodity categories by dividing the country's share in the exports of a given commodity category by its share in the total exports of manufactured goods, and expressing the result in index number form. Thus, for a given commodity category, an index number of 110 will mean that the country's share in the exports of this commodity group is 10 per cent higher than in the total exports of manufactures.

Relative shares have been calculated for the periods 1953–55 and 1960–62, which have been taken as representative of the mid-1950s and the early 1960s. Further calculations have been made with regard to changes in shares between the two periods in order to indicate developments over time. Finally, a combined indicator of export performance has been derived with the aim to give expression to relative shares in 1960–62, as well as to changes in shares as compared to the earlier period.[6]

In the case of export-import ratios, too, indices of relative level and relative growth have been calculated, and a combined indicator reflecting both has been derived.[7] In evaluating comparative advantage, however, more reliance has been based on export performance indices than on indicators of export-import ratios because the latter are affected by differences in tastes as well as by the idiosyncrasies of national protection. In fact, in some of the country studies only export performance indices have been utilized.

---

[6] Cf. Appendix Table 1.2. For the appropriate formulas and a detailed description of methodology, see the Appendix to this chapter.

[7] Appendix Table 1.3.

APPENDIX TABLE 1.1. THE SHARE OF FOREIGN TRADE IN VALUE ADDED IN
THE PRODUCTION OF TRADED GOODS, 1963

(PER CENT)

	Export share	Import share	Average share
United States	11.7	9.5	10.6
Canada	48.8	50.6	49.7
European Common Market	31.8[a]	34.2	33.0
	18.3[b]	20.9	19.6
European Free Trade Association	41.6[a]	50.5	46.0
	32.9[b]	41.5	37.2
United Kingdom	37.8[a]	44.7	41.2
	33.2[b]	40.0	36.6
Continental EFTA	46.7[a]	58.6	57.6
	32.6[b]	43.6	38.1
Japan	24.6	30.4	27.5

Sources: Value added (at market prices for France, Germany, and the United
States, at factor prices for others). Organization for Economic Co-operation and
Development, *General Statistics*, January, 1965. Our estimates for Sweden and
Switzerland. Foreign trade (exports and f.o.b. prices, imports at c.i.f. prices),
OECD, *Foreign Trade, Statistical Bulletins*, 1963. Our estimates for U.S. and Ca-
nadian imports at c.i.f. prices.

Notes:

[a] Total trade.

[b] Extra-area trade.

APPENDIX TABLE 1.2. INDICES OF EXPORT PERFORMANCE

SITC No.		U.S. Index	U.S. Rank	Canada Index	Canada Rank	E.E.C. Index	E.E.C. Rank	U.K. Index	U.K. Rank	Sweden Index	Sweden Rank	Japan Index	Japan Rank
512	Organic chemicals	109.9	27	418.8	4	116.7	26	69.4	55	39.0	50	51.3	51
513,4,5	Inorganic chemicals	126.7	21	186.5	12	96.1	48	94.0	38	41.0	49	62.7	46
531	Synthetic organic dyestuffs	50.0	50	—	72	128.8	13	145.7	14	1.6	73	30.9	63
533	Pigments, paints, varnishes	107.4	29	28.7	45	90.8	59	239.8	3	32.7	52	20.3	65
541	Medical and pharmaceutical	144.2	16	34.3	41	95.6	49	127.7	23	26.6	55	38.5	58
551	Essential oil and perfumes	187.3	8	10.2	60	114.2	28	84.4	44	5.5	67	7.0	70
553,4	Perfumery and cosmetics	128.0	20	17.9	54	93.1	56	160.5	11	44.2	45	42.2	56
561	Fertilizers, manuf.	87.6	33	240.7	8	127.9	15	6.8	75	2.5	71	107.0	35
571	Explosives and Pyrotecnics	72.6	44	6.5	65	95.5	51	217.3	4	113.8	21	73.4	45
581	Plastic materials	142.8	18	29.2	44	104.0	39	86.1	43	84.7	31	77.2	43
599	Chemical material and products	288.6	2	43.7	33	67.4	69	119.0	26	35.4	51	7.2	69
611	Leather	84.4	35	120.8	18	112.8	31	136.1	19	43.5	46	32.5	62
612	Manufactures of leather	57.5	34	200.2	11	125.2	20	105.2	32	74.1	33	94.2	39
613	Fur skins	221.1	4	92.6	20	96.8	47	87.6	42	47.7	42	7.3	68
621	Materials of rubber	26.5	63	36.6	40	112.9	30	136.8	17	155.4	15	139.0	26
629.1	Rubber tires and tubes	78.1	40	40.0	36	100.6	43	133.9	21	102.2	25	163.5	23
629.0	Other rubber articles	209.1	6	18.3	53	50.9	72	115.4	29	323.5	6	118.1	31
641	Paper and paperboard	76.0	42	1,430.2	1	29.4	73	28.9	71	502.3	2	47.3	53
642	Articles made of paper	118.9	23	50.5	30	95.6	50	118.0	28	87.6	29	135.4	28
651.2	Yarn of wool	0.7	74	5.5	66	157.7	2	98.1	34	13.8	64	54.8	50
651.3	Cotton yarn, unbleached	18.1	66	—	72	103.0	40	43.8	67	0.5	74	545.9	2
651.4	Cotton yarn, bleached	16.6	68	4.2	67	136.2	7	118.6	27	22.8	56	243.4	16
651.6	Yarn of synthetic fibers	124.7	22	40.4	35	105.1	37	80.9	48	8.6	65	107.1	34
652	Cotton fabrics	61.9	46	78.3	22	79.5	62	54.7	65	45.6	43	442.0	5
653.2	Woolen fabrics	1.0	73	21.1	49	120.6	23	200.1	6	4.5	70	137.9	27
653.5,68	Synthetic fabrics	50.3	51	18.7	52	92.4	58	21.4	72	43.5	47	469.9	3
653.0	Other woven textile fabrics	36.0	58	58.9	23	110.9	33	78.2	49	53.8	40	361.9	7
654	Tulle, lace, embroidery	37.5	55	10.0	61	111.4	32	88.6	40	22.4	58	312.6	11
655	Special textile fabrics	60.2	47	57.4	24	94.1	54	139.4	16	68.9	35	184.2	21
656.6	Blankets	14.5	69	6.7	64	127.1	16	63.0	60	22.5	57	250.3	14
656.0	Made-up textiles	165.5	11	33.5	42	79.5	63	74.2	52	51.7	41	157.2	24
657	Floor coverings	21.8	64	4.0	68	118.7	25	136.6	18	30.7	54	190.2	19
664	Glass	49.4	53	9.1	62	147.1	5	72.2	54	18.9	61	55.1	49
665	Glassware	102.4	30	2.9	69	115.8	27	66.4	57	102.8	24	77.5	42
666	Pottery	2.6	72	—	72	76.0	65	135.5	20	31.9	53	458.8	4
671	Pig iron	31.4	60	258.6	7	148.2	3	32.6	70	149.9	17	50.2	47
673	Iron and steel bars	17.3	67	40.0	37	133.3	10	59.1	62	114.8	20	99.9	37
674	Universals, plates, and sheets	49.8	52	172.3	14	125.1	21	82.5	46	91.8	27	126.5	30
675	Hoops and strips	37.1	57	—	72	135.2	8	57.6	63	227.2	8	103.1	36
676	Railway construction material	75.2	43	396.2	5	95.4	52	83.5	45	558.1	1	153.2	25
678	Tubes, pipes, and fittings	37.3	56	51.9	29	127.0	17	94.1	37	178.4	12	116.6	32

APPENDIX TABLE 1.2. (CONTINUED)

SITC No.		U.S. Index	U.S. Rank	Canada Index	Canada Rank	E.E.C. Index	E.E.C. Rank	U.K. Index	U.K. Rank	Sweden Index	Sweden Rank	Japan Index	Japan Rank
682.2	Copper, wrought	19.6	65	281.7	6	108.0	34	169.7	9	223.2	9	33.3	61
683.2	Nickel, wrought	174.7	9	160.4	16	60.5	71	180.4	8	116.6	19	2.0	74
684.2	Aluminum, wrought	78.6	39	214.6	10	119.5	24	110.9	31	101.2	26	33.9	60
685.2	Lead, wrought	48.5	54	852.7	2	128.6	14	97.2	35	411.7	4	45.2	54
686.2	Zinc, wrought	118.7	24	48.6	31	107.6	35	146.7	13	2.4	72	2.8	73
687.2	Tin, wrought	270.1	3	—	72	129.5	12	149.7	12	17.8	62	50.2	52
691.8	Manufactures of metal	81.5	37	46.8	32	101.8	42	111.9	30	106.6	23	128.7	29
711	Power-generating machinery	99.0	31	228.0	9	64.9	70	248.0	2	78.2	32	40.2	57
712.0	Agricultural machinery	139.4	19	476.9	3	87.3	61	76.5	51	151.2	16	11.8	67
712.5	Tractors	214.7	5	53.7	26	25.9	74	301.3	1	42.9	48	3.8	71
714	Office machinery	157.0	14	132.8	17	92.5	57	62.1	61	170.8	13	77.0	44
715	Metal working machinery	173.2	10	20.9	50	97.2	46	72.3	53	56.6	39	22.5	64
717.1	Textile machinery	85.9	34	26.8	47	113.9	29	128.7	22	21.1	59	83.4	41
718.9	Other machinery	143.6	17	40.0	38	93.4	55	99.5	33	149.9	18	35.4	59
722.1	Electric generators	113.6	25	52.6	28	99.9	44	120.7	25	91.7	28	98.2	38
722.2	Other electric machinery	109.3	28	57.1	25	94.9	53	92.1	39	72.7	34	309.6	12
731	Railway vehicles	200.2	7	30.9	43	71.5	68	65.5	59	166.8	14	215.8	18
732.1,6	Automobiles	28.8	62	17.8	55	162.5	1	124.7	24	317.8	7	42.7	55
732.2,5,7	Buses, lorries, trucks	110.4	26	17.1	56	87.9	60	205.1	5	183.7	11	385.0	6
732.0	Bodies, chassis, frames	164.4	12	37.7	39	79.2	64	140.7	15	63.8	36	226.9	17
733	Bicycles	52.8	49	53.3	27	98.7	45	191.9	7	62.5	37	113.3	33
734	Aircraft	331.4	1	169.0	15	72.0	67	55.9	64	4.7	68	3.5	72
735	Ships and boats	14.5	70	13.0	59	102.0	41	82.4	47	423.6	3	347.1	8
812	Sanitary, plumbing, heating	97.3	32	100.6	19	104.2	38	77.4	50	407.1	5	92.9	40
821	Furniture	63.5	45	43.1	34	134.7	9	88.3	41	210.8	10	57.7	48
831	Travel goods, handbags	31.6	59	8.2	63	124.7	22	42.6	69	59.0	38	321.9	10
841	Clothing	29.5	61	20.0	51	136.6	6	43.3	68	87.2	30	245.9	15
842	Fur clothing	77.5	41	88.6	21	122.6	18	163.7	10	109.7	22	262.7	13
851	Footwear	7.2	71	26.5	48	147.4	4	47.9	66	15.9	63	601.4	1
861	Scientific, medical, optical	159.6	13	184.8	13	75.7	66	68.5	56	45.1	44	189.7	20
862	Photographic and cinematographic	148.1	15	28.1	46	106.5	36	95.3	36	4.7	69	20.3	66
891	Musical instruments	80.0	38	13.4	58	130.7	11	66.3	58	19.1	60	329.5	9
897	Jewelry and goldsmith	83.5	36	14.5	57	126.5	19	15.8	73	6.8	66	169.1	22

Source: Bela Balassa, "Trade Liberalization and 'Revealed' Comparative Advantage," Manchester School, May, 1965, pp. 118–20.

APPENDIX TABLE 1.3. INDICES OF EXPORT-IMPORT RATIOS

SITC No.		U.S.		Canada		E.E.C.		U.K.		Sweden		Japan	
		Index	Rank	Index	Rank	Index	Rank	Index	Rank	Index	Rank	Index	Rank
512	Organic chemicals	324.3	15	1,478.6	3	83.0	55	68.3	60	37.3	37	46.4	59
513,4,5	Inorganic chemicals	113.3	34	109.1	9	106.6	33	123.4	39	16.2	57	184.8	50
531	Synthetic organic dyestuffs	109.1	36	0.0	51	121.5	19	201.1	26	1.2	72	20.7	66
533,4	Pigments, paints, and varnishes	545.4	10	7.3	72	66.9	66	773.6	8	14.2	60	45.2	60
541	Medical and pharmaceutical	169.6	24	16.7	32	82.6	58	686.0	9	13.1	62	43.1	61
551	Essential oils and perfumes	166.1	25	7.2	52	112.8	26	76.3	56	13.5	61	5.5	69
553	Perfumery and cosmetics	241.0	18	4.7	60	75.5	60	474.8	13	23.8	51	592.3	34
561	Fertilizers, manufactured	93.0	39	174.1	7	176.8	4	6.2	74	1.5	71	61.8	56
571	Explosives and pyrotecnics	63.1	48	2.0	64	146.0	12	6,627.5	2	31.9	45	495.0	37
581	Plastic materials	1,683.6	4	8.2	47	95.2	42	82.7	53	39.4	35	76.0	55
599	Chemical material and products	1,367.8	5	7.8	49	76.3	59	104.7	46	23.3	52	4.6	71
611	Leather	88.4	41	107.4	10	104.6	34	100.0	47	43.4	32	241.9	46
612	Manufactures of leather	49.5	56	80.2	12	165.8	8	64.7	61	59.3	21	307.9	43
613	Fur skins	163.1	26	46.1	17	108.8	30	64.1	62	34.0	42	87.4	54
621	Materials of rubber	1,379.8	3	16.8	31	112.2	27	109.9	44	49.5	25	313.1	42
629.1	Rubber tires and tubes	74.6	43	22.2	26	88.1	46	279.4	19	28.6	47	2,093.1	21
629.0	Other rubber articles	91.1	40	4.3	61	64.5	68	1,216.5	6	403.3	4	375.6	41
641	Paper and paper board	36.6	59	1,498.0	2	38.4	73	22.0	72	2,683.1	2	2,386.6	18
642	Articles made of paper	153.3	28	11.1	44	90.4	45	179.5	31	54.6	22	1,109.2	31
651.2	Yarn of wool	2.0	72	7.8	48	102.5	37	251.0	22	15.8	58	1,320.8	29
651.3	Cotton yarn, unbleached	50.3	54	—		110.1	28	22.1	71	0.2	74	∞	1
651.4	Cotton yarn, bleached	35.3	60	0.3	69	146.1	11	186.2	29	12.8	63	10,766.3	9
651.6	Yarn of synthetic fibers	504.6	11	35.6	20	72.0	62	219.9	25	2.7	69	1,121.2	30
652	Cotton fabrics	65.9	46	22.7	25	139.8	13	22.6	70	50.9	24	11,142.8	8
653.2	Woolen fabrics	1.1	73	11.7	42	64.1	68	424.5	16	4.1	68	449.4	38
553.5,6,8	Synthetic fabrics	152.0	29	7.0	53	72.0	63	26.2	69	17.6	56	674.5	33
654	Other woven textile fabrics	22.3	63	20.4	28	83.8	51	123.3	41	77.0	18	5,876.2	11
655	Tulle, lace, and embroidery	51.9	52	3.2	62	100.1	38	75.2	51	34.8	40	3,252.8	16
	Special textile fabrics	49.9	55	12.7	40	104.2	36	232.5	24	38.6	36	2,008.2	23
656.6	Blankets	50.7	53	1.9	65	84.6	50	119.1	42	40.6	33	3,581.6	14
656.0	Made-up textiles	156.0	27	6.9	54	104.3	35	56.9	64	45.1	30	2,193.5	20
657	Floor coverings	18.0	66	3.0	63	108.1	31	145.6	36	21.1	55	3,989.2	13
664	Glass	23.4	62	1.8	67	172.1	6	258.4	21	10.8	64	283.2	45
665	Glassware	103.9	38	0.5	68	129.6	17	73.5	58	155.3	7	417.4	40
666	Pottery	—	74	—	72	130.0	16	94.4	40	48.5	26	∞	2
671	Pig iron	68.3	45	622.4	21	114.4	24	84.7	51	131.5	10	11.5	68
673	Iron and steel bars	10.8	70	27.2	8	114.6	23	434.5	15	141.9	9	1,638.1	25
674	Universals, plates, sheets	150.9	30	170.8	72	82.8	57	276.6	20	40.1	34	5,018.8	12
675	Hoops, strips	53.1	51	—		87.1	48	2,756.0	4	175.9	5	125.8	53
676	Railway construction material	424.4	12	569.0	5	54.6	69	5,633.1	3	2,749.4	1	177.4	52
678	Tubes, pipes, and fittings	17.7	67	24.3	24	139.3	15	347.4	17	77.8	17	1,516.3	27

APPENDIX TABLE 1.3. (CONTINUED)

SITC No.		U.S. Index	U.S. Rank	Canada Index	Canada Rank	E.E.C. Index	E.E.C. Rank	U.K. Index	U.K. Rank	Sweden Index	Sweden Rank	Japan Index	Japan Rank
682.2	Copper, wrought	14.1	69	212.7	6	91.2	44	576.1	10	98.4	13	417.5	39
683.2	Nickel, wrought	2,671.2	2	26.9	22	87.8	47	77.1	55	21.8	54	2.8	73
684.2	Aluminum, wrought	61.0	50	89.9	11	154.4	9	95.3	48	47.1	28	13.5	67
685.2	Lead, wrought	40.6	58	35,212.1	1	93.4	43	234.2	23	105.3	12	2,442.3	17
686.2	Zinc, wrought	299.3	16	19.2	30	68.3	65	298.2	18	14.6	59	36.6	63
687.2	Tin, wrought	1,340.1	6	0.0	72	83.3	54	—	1	4.5	67	500.0	36
691.8	Manufactures of metal	62.9	49	8.6	45	121.0	20	187.2	28	74.7	20	787.4	32
711	Power-generating machinery	403.7	14	46.4	16	71.6	64	182.5	30	44.3	31	51.1	57
712.0	Agricultural machinery	119.0	32	52.4	15	107.6	32	168.4	5	168.1	6	184.2	51
712.5	Tractors	194.4	22	4.9	58	34.6	74	2,054.6	54	26.5	49	24.5	64
714	Office machinery	219.2	20	62.4	34	109.7	29	111.9	43	79.2	16	40.9	62
715	Metal-working machinery	780.9	8	15.2	39	98.8	39	144.0	37	34.6	41	5.0	70
717.1	Textile machinery	147.1	31	12.8	46	97.5	41	108.2	45	26.7	48	10,444.2	10
718.9	Other machinery	807.5	7	8.5	35	83.4	53	199.8	27	94.6	14	48.4	58
722.1	Electric generators	224.2	19	15.0	27	83.5	52	160.8	34	45.2	29	200.8	49
722.0	Other electric machinery	112.9	35	22.1	43	86.1	49	147.9	35	36.2	38	1,397.2	28
731	Railway vehicles	648.8	9	11.7	59	43.3	71	508.7	12	51.5	23	557.5	35
732.1,6	Automobiles	15.1	68	4.8	56	789.8	2	1,030.3	2	33.6	43	0.3	74
732.2,5,7	Buses, lorries, trucks	4,209.3	1	5.2	37	72.7	61	451.4	17	33.0	44	11,177.5	7
732.0	Bodies, chassis, frames	284.4	17	13.2	36	39.2	72	527.3	14	93.0	15	21,329.9	5
733	Bicycles	29.6	61	14.0	19	120.8	21	166.1	11	35.5	39	1,997.3	24
734	Aircraft	405.3	13	37.6	38	53.2	70	43.1	33	6.8	66	3.6	72
735	Ships and boats	104.0	37	13.0	23	124.1	18	89.1	66	153.9	8	222.7	48
812	Sanitary, plumbing, heating	212.2	21	24.8	33	82.9	56	127.2	50	412.4	3	2,083.2	22
821	Furniture	68.4	44	15.6	66	114.1	25	42.5	40	126.8	11	3,541.6	15
831	Travel goods, handbags	18.6	65	1.9	41	210.2	3	39.8	67	48.4	27	1,609.8	26
841	Clothing	18.7	64	12.0	13	175.8	5	83.6	68	76.1	19	32,751.2	4
842	Fur clothing	74.9	42	63.0	29	115.9	22	47.5	52	22.7	53	16,686.4	6
851	Footwear	3.6	71	20.1	18	895.4	1	58.5	65	10.4	65	194,489.9	3
861	Scientific, medical, optical	189.3	23	41.6	50	98.5	40	140.7	63	25.5	50	223.3	47
862	Photographic, cinematographic	114.5	33	7.7	57	139.5	14	70.0	38	2.2	70	22.7	65
891	Musical instruments	65.7	47	5.2	55	149.8	10	70.0	59	30.2	46	2,311.4	19
897	Jewelry and goldsmith	44.4	57	6.2		170.3	7	16.2	73	0.8	73	306.4	44

Source: Bela Balassa, "Trade Liberalization and 'Revealed' Comparative Advantage," *Manchester School*, May, 1965, pp. 121–23.

CHAPTER II

>>>>>>>>>>>>>>>>>>>>>>>>>>>>>>>>>>>

TRADE ARRANGEMENTS AMONG INDUSTRIAL COUNTRIES: EFFECTS ON THE UNITED STATES

Mordechai E. Kreinin[1]

<<<<<<<<<<<<<<<<<<<<<<<<<<<<<<<<<<<

Foreign Trade in the American Economy

This chapter is concerned with the effects on the American economy of alternative trade arrangements among the industrial countries. After a detailed consideration of the most sweeping proposal—an Atlantic Free Trade Area (AFTA)—its impact will be compared to that of three more modest alternatives; the continuation of tariff reductions under the most-favored-nation clause, an Atlantic Free Trade Area excluding the EEC, and European integration. The chapter begins with a discussion of the role of foreign trade in the American economy, followed by an analysis of the effects of AFTA on U.S. exports and imports. The third section is devoted to the impact of the three alternative proposals on the U.S. external position, while the final sections examine the implications of AFTA for foreign investments and for the domestic economy.

Despite the fact that the United States is a leading exporter of manufactured commodities, it is often described as a "closed economy." The term refers to the fact that, quantitatively, foreign trade accounts for a relatively small proportion of total economic activity. Because of its large size and the diversity of its resources, the American economy can satisfy consumer wants and national needs with a minimum of reliance on foreign trade. This is in contrast to other industrial economies in which foreign trade plays a significant, if not a dominant, role. In 1963, the ratios of total U.S. exports and imports to value added in the production of traded goods were 11.7 and 9.5 per cent, respectively. In the same year, the corresponding ratios were about 50 per cent in the countries

---

[1] The author is professor of economics at Michigan State University. He is indebted to Tracy Murray for computational help.

of the European Free Trade Association and in Canada, and 30 per cent in the Common Market countries and in Japan.[2]

To be sure, quantitative measures do not tell the entire story. To say that in 1963, United States merchandise imports ($17 billion) amounted to less than 10 per cent of value added in the production of traded goods is to understate the importance of these imports in several respects. American imports contain important primary commodities which cannot be produced domestically, but which are crucial for nu-

TABLE 2.1. U.S. EXPORTS AND IMPORTS RELATED TO DOMESTIC PRODUCTION AND CONSUMPTION, 1962

Sector	Domestic production (billion $)	Exports as per cent of production	Imports as per cent of apparent consumption[a]
Agriculture (1960)	30.1	11.4	7.4
Minerals (1960)	17.9	3.3	10.1
Manufacturing (1962)	399.3	4.2	2.7

Sources: (1) U.S. Department of Agriculture, Census of Agriculture, 1959, 1960 Sample; (2) U.S. Department of the Interior, Minerals Yearbook, III (1960); (3) U.S. Bureau of the Census, Annual Survey of Manufacturing, 1962; (4) U.S. Bureau of the Census, U.S. Commodity Exports and Imports as Related to Output, 1960 and 1959 (Washington, D.C., 1962).

Note: [a] Production plus imports minus exports.

merous productive processes. Their absence would have curtailed domestic production, lowered consumer satisfaction, and interfered with our ability to attain national goals. Over 70 per cent of U.S. agricultural imports are "complementary commodities," such as tropical products, which cannot be grown in the United States. And while most manufacturing imports compete directly with domestically produced substitutes, foreign trade widens consumer choice and expands the producer's horizon. Moreover, foreign competition provides an inducement for technological improvements.

However, even the quantitative importance of foreign trade cannot be judged solely by using broad aggregative measures, because its impact is not evenly spread over all sectors of the

[2] See Appendix Table 1.1. The appropriate comparison is between the value of trade and the value of production (consumption) rather than value added, but only the latter figures are available on a comparative basis. See, however, Table 2.1 on the relative importance of trade in three major sectors of the U.S. economy.

economy. This is indicated in Table 2.1 which relates exports and imports to domestic production and consumption in three main sectors of the economy. Exports appear to be the most important in agriculture, while imports are most significant in the case of mineral commodities. Of these three sectors, the specific concern of this paper is with manufacturing, since manufactured goods predominate in trade among the industrial countries and these commodities are likely to be in the focus of Atlantic Trade arrangements.

In 1962, the manufacturing sector as defined by the U.S. Census Bureau (divisions 20–39 in the Standard Industrial Classification), constituted somewhat less than one-third of GNP, with value added of $179.3 billion. Total shipments approximated $400 billion, while exports of manufactures amounted to $17 billion, and imports to $10.7 billion, providing 79 per cent of total merchandise exports, and 66 per cent of imports. Foreign trade comprised a small proportion of shipments in all of the twenty SIC industry divisions, and exports exceeded 10 per cent of production in the case of nonelectrical machinery only.[3]

But even these figures are too aggregative. Foreign trade among industrial nations is very specialized, and any one of the twenty SIC divisions may contain large variations which are not reflected in the industry averages. Published data on the relationship between trade and domestic output permits disaggregation to the four-digit SIC level. Of the 271 SIC industries for which comparable export and production figures are available, 221 industries have an export-output ratio below 10 per cent.[4] Only 50 industries have a ratio exceeding this level, and their total exports amounted to $7.1 billion. Thus, 18 per cent of the industries account for 45 per cent of total manufacturing exports. On the imports side, 196 out of the 233 comparable industries have an import-supply ratio of less than 10 per cent. The remaining 37 industries, which constitute 16 per cent of the total number, account for 39 of total imports.[5]

[3] See Appendix Table 2.1.

[4] U.S. Bureau of the Census, *U.S. Commodity Exports and Imports as Related to Output*, 1961–62 (Washington, 1964), pp. 2, 4.

[5] The Committee for Economic Development has identified 18 industries whose exports in 1960 exceeded 10 per cent of output, with a value of over $100 million; and 14 industries whose 1961 imports were more

There is, of course, no certainty that the industries most affected by Atlantic trade liberalization would be those which are now heavily engaged in foreign trade. On the import side, there are industries in which the ratio of imports to new supplies is low *because* of tariff protection. Likewise, exports are to some extent influenced by the level of protection in foreign countries, and *ceteris paribus,* the same argument applies here. And the impact of trade liberalization on individual industries will further depend on the structure of comparative advantage among the industrial countries.

Effects of an Atlantic Free Trade Area on United States Trade

Manufactured goods. While in the previous section we used the Bureau of the Census definition of manufactured products that permits direct comparisons of commodity trade with domestic production and consumption, we will now adopt the Standard International Trade Classification that is employed by the United Nations. The category of manufactured goods defined as SITC Sections 5–8, less unwrought metals, roughly corresponds to SIC divisions 22–28 and 30–39, although some items in divisions 24, 26, and 33 are excluded. In 1960, U.S. exports of these commodities amounted to $12.6 billion, of which the industrial countries took close to one-half. In turn, these countries supplied nearly nine-tenths of U.S. manufacturing imports that were valued at $5.9 billion.

The rise in U.S. imports of manufactured goods from other industrial countries was estimated for each of eighty-five SITC

---

than 10 per cent of new supply and exceeded $50 million. (Note that several of these commodity groups are not included in the manufactured goods category in U.N. trade statistics.)

Leading Exports: condensed and evaporated milk; flour and meal; milled rice; grease and inedible tallow; synthetic rubber; internal combustion engines; farm machinery; construction and mining machinery; metal-cutting machine tools; oil-field machinery; metal-forming machine tools; textile machinery; pumps and compressors; computing and related machines; aircraft and engines; aircraft parts, etc.; railroad and streetcar parts, etc.; photographic equipment.

Leading Imports: raw cane sugar and by-products; wine and brandy; distilled liquor except brandy; vegetable oil mill products; scouring and combing mill products; textile goods, n.e.c.; sawmill products; pulp mill products; paper mill products; rubber footwear; refined lead; nonferrous smelter; watches and clocks; lapidary work.

See *Trade Negotiations for a Better Free World Economy* (Washington, D.C.: Committee for Economic Development, 1964), pp. 38, 39.

groups. They add up to a total of $1,837 million, an increase of 35.6 per cent over imports in 1960. Eleven SITC categories, each of which would experience an increase in imports of $50 million or more, account for some 60 per cent of the total increase.[6] These estimates are products of the assumptions made concerning: (1) tariff rates for each SITC group; (2) the impact of the tariff reductions on import prices; (3) the responsiveness of imports and exports to price changes. They can vary to a considerable extent with changes in the assumptions, and should be regarded as a minimum value.[7]

A further source of uncertainty is introduced by the application of quantitative restrictions to Japanese exports of cotton textiles and twenty-eight other products to the United States. There is no way to know what effect the establishment of an Atlantic Free Trade Area would have on these arrangements. Nevertheless, it is of interest to make a rough estimate of the impact of quantitative restrictions on U.S. imports from Japan. The estimates are based on data provided on the expansion of "controlled" and "uncontrolled" imports by the U.S. Department of Commerce. (See Table 2.2.)

Had the "controlled" items increased by 170 per cent in the period 1957–62, as did their "noncontrolled" counterparts, the 1962 imports of these commodities would have been $581 million, as compared to actual imports of $388 million. As an

[6] The relevant categories are (with increases in imports indicated in million $): paper and paperboard ($137.3), miscellaneous woven textile fabrics ($110.3), pottery ($50.7), finished articles of iron and steel ($69.6), manufactures of metal ($127.2), nonelectrical machinery ($108.6), automobiles ($96.5), clothing ($143.4), footwear ($63.2), watches and clocks ($75.7), and miscellaneous manufactured articles ($105.7).

[7] As indicated in the Appendix to this chapter, we used the Ball-Marwah estimates of import demand elasticities (R. J. Ball and K. Marwah, "The U.S. Demand for Imports, 1948–58," *Review of Economics and Statistics* [November, 1962]) to indicate the responsiveness of U.S. import demand to changes in import prices. Further, we assumed that only one-half of the tariff reduction would be translated into lower import prices because the export prices of European producers would rise by the same magnitude in response to the increased demand for their products. Alternative estimates were prepared under the following assumptions: (a) the Ball-Marwah estimates were adjusted upwards by adding two standard deviations to the co-efficients, as the authors themselves suggested; (b) European prices were taken to remain constant; in (c), a combination of (a) and (b) were used. The relevant estimates are: (a) $2,388 million; (b) $2,640 million; (c) $3,432 million.

TABLE 2.2. UNITED STATES IMPORTS FROM JAPAN
(MILLION $, F.O.B.)

	Total	Cotton textiles	28 other voluntarily controlled products	Total controlled products	Total un-controlled products
1957	597	91	128	219	378
1962	1400	136	252	388	1012
Change 1957–62	903	45	124	169	634
Percentage change	151%	50%	100%	77%	170%

Source: U.S. Department of Commerce, special communication.

approximation, we may assume that the voluntary controls excluded $193 millions of imports from the United States, of which $102 millions were cotton textiles. In contrast, increases in the imports of these commodities in the framework of an Atlantic Free Trade Area would have to be adjusted downwards if quantitative restrictions remained in effect.

An imponderable which cannot be allowed for in numerical terms is the effect of establishing an Atlantic Free Trade Area on Japan's exports to the countries of Western Europe. Many Japanese exports are currently barred from Western European markets by various means. As these restrictions disappear, Japan would ship more to Western Europe, thus lessening her need to export to the United States. On the other hand, Japanese exports may undercut some American products in European markets. Indications are that the first of these effects may be stronger than the second, but the magnitude of the two effects cannot be estimated.

As regards the prospective expansion of U.S. exports of manufactured goods in an Atlantic Free Trade Area, we made separate estimates for each of the eighty-five commodity categories, and for each country of destination within AFTA. Added up, the projected increase in U.S. exports amounts to $1,535 million, 25 per cent of the 1960 exports.[8] Six SITC

[8] These estimates were made under the assumption that import demand in the other industrial countries is less responsive to changes in import prices than is the case in the United States. We also assumed that with exports accounting for a small percentage of U.S. production, U.S. exporters are able to supply increasing quantities at constant costs. In conformity with our estimate of changes in U.S. imports in an Atlantic Free Trade Area, an alternative calculation was made reflect-

categories, each of which would experience an increase in exports of $75 million or more, account for 40 per cent of the total.[9]

In addition to tariffs, some American exports are also subject to quantitative restrictions. These restrictions are the most extensive in Japan, and according to the estimates of the U.S. Department of Commerce, their removal would raise U.S. exports of manufactured goods by $75–$125 million. Additionally, there are few quotas remaining in Western Europe. In total, removal of the import quotas may raise American exports by $120 million.

Industrial materials. The industrial materials category includes agricultural and nonagricultural raw materials, fuels, vegetable oils and fats, and unwrought metals. United States exports of these materials to the other industrial countries amounted to $2.6 billion in 1960, as compared to imports of $1.5 billion. With few exceptions, tariffs are the main method of protection, but rates are considerably lower than in the case of manufactured goods. Also, import demand appears to be less responsive to price changes in the case of industrial materials than for manufactures. Correspondingly, the estimated increase in trade in industrial materials in an Atlantic Free Trade Area is considerably smaller than in the case of manufactured goods. Under the assumptions outlined in the Appendix, we estimated U.S. exports of industrial materials to rise by 2.6 per cent or $67 million, and imports by 6.2 per cent, or $95 million.[10]

Trade in industrial materials would be affected further by the removal of quantitative restrictions. In 1958, the United States imposed import quotas on lead and zinc. Canada is the only major exporter of these products in the projected Atlantic

---

ing a greater responsiveness of import demand to price changes. (The alternative estimate is $1,996 million.)

[9] The categories are (with increases in exports in million $): miscellaneous chemicals ($83.9); conveying and excavating machinery ($90.3); other industrial machinery ($140.2); electrical machinery other than electrical generators ($91.2); buses, lorries, and trucks ($104.6); aircraft ($103.3).

[10] Again, the results are sensitive to the assumptions made. For alternative estimates, derived by using a more detailed commodity breakdown, see Bela Balassa, *Trade Liberalization among the Industrial Countries: Objectives and Alternatives,* Chap. IV.

Free Trade Area, while the rest comes mainly from Latin America. The Department of Commerce estimates that the removal of the quotas would raise imports by $45 million. The quotas were abolished in fact in 1965, but the effects of this measure on imports is not yet discernible.

In turn, the countries of Western Europe and Japan maintain tight restrictions on coal imports. An unpublished report by Robert Nathan and Associates, commissioned by the United States Department of the Interior in 1963, estimated that by 1970 the United States could increase its coal exports by $300—or $700 million over 1962 values. Of this figure, about 90 per cent would be destined to AFTA countries.[11] But, given the energy policy of the European countries, we assumed that these quotas would be maintained in an Atlantic Free Trade Area.

Elimination of discrimination by Europe's regional groupings.
The United States would further increase her exports following the establishment of an Atlantic Free Trade Area because this would entail the elimination of discrimination on U.S. exports by the European Economic Community and the European Free Trade Association. This discrimination has been due to the reduction of internal—and the maintenance of external—duties in the two European regional groupings. In the absence of a reduction in tariffs against outsiders, the effects of tariff discrimination on the exports of the nonparticipating countries would be fully felt by the end of the 1960s, when all duties on intra-area trade in the EEC and EFTA will have been eliminated. The removal of discrimination through the establishment of an Atlantic Free Trade Area would, then, result in a comparable benefit.

In an article published several years ago,[12] I attempted to identify the American export commodities which would be severely hurt by the EEC. The resulting list of industrial products was relatively short, but no quantitative estimate was made. Since then, an abundant literature has appeared on the

[11] It is interesting to note that most, if not all, of this coal would be mined in the depressed areas of West Virginia and central Pennsylvania.

[12] M. E. Kreinin, "European Integration and American Trade," *American Economic Review* (September, 1959), pp. 615–27.

effects of the Common Market on imports from nonmember countries,[13] subsequently, L. B. Krause presented a quantitative estimate of the diversionary impact on American exports.[14] Based on the calculations described in the Appendix, we estimate the gain to U.S. exports from the elimination of discrimination at $438 million in the case of the EEC and at $139 million in the case of EFTA.

Summary. Table 2.3 summarizes the estimates of the study, indicating increases in U.S. exports of $2,299 million and imports of $2,170 million in an Atlantic Free Trade Area.

TABLE 2.3. ESTIMATED CHANGES IN U.S. TRADE IN AN ATLANTIC FREE TRADE AREA

Source of change	Imports	Exports
Elimination of tariffs on manufactured products	$1,837	$1,535
Elimination of quotas on manufactured products	193	120
Elimination of tariffs on industrial materials	95	67
Elimination of quotas on industrial materials	45	—
Elimination of European discrimination	—	577
Total	$2,170	$2,299

Note: Estimates have been prepared on the basis of 1960 trade data. For the method of estimation, see the Appendix to this chapter.

American merchandise exports in 1960 totaled $17.5 billion, placing the projected increase at 13 per cent of the total. Merchandise imports in the same year were over $14.5 billion, and the anticipated increase of $2.2 billion constitutes 15 per cent of the total.[15] AFTA would appear to have a small net favorable effect on the United States trade balance to the tune of $130 millions: namely, less than 5 per cent of the 1960 surplus on merchandise trade.

It should be added that the estimates presented are of a

[13] See, for example, the papers by Erik Thorbecke, Bela Balassa and L. B. Krause on "Problems of Regional Integration," *American Economic Review,* Papers and Proceedings (May, 1963), pp. 147–96.

[14] Lawrence B. Krause, "The European Economic Community and the United States Balance of Payments," W. S. Salant (ed.), *The United States Balance of Payments in 1968* (Washington, D.C.: The Brookings Institution, 1963), pp. 95–118.

[15] But, given the low share of trade in GDP, the estimated expansion of trade would hardly exceed one-half of one per cent of the U.S. gross domestic product. Improvements in welfare, resulting from the reduction in the cost of protection, would be even smaller.

"static" character. They are concerned with the relation between the removal of trade restrictions and the increase in the volume of trade under the assumption of unchanged production methods. But the elimination of restrictions on the flow of goods also increases the size of the constituent markets and thereby contributes to the growth of productivity. It enables industries to realize economies of scale, intensifies competition, and reduces investment risks. Other things being equal, the smaller the country the more likely it is to benefit from these so called "dynamic" factors. Presumably, a country of the size of the United States can enjoy the economies of large-scale production in practically all industries without Atlantic integration, although foreign competition is likely to have beneficial effects on U.S. industries, too. Economies of scale are of importance for the smaller European countries, however, and the establishment of an Atlantic Free Trade Area may accelerate their rate of economic growth. This, in turn, is likely to increase their imports from the United States, and in the long run exert a favorable influence on the American trade balance.

Effects of Alternative Trade Arrangements on United States Exports and Imports

Continuation of tariff reductions under the m.f.n. clause. As an alternative to AFTA we considered the possible effects of tariff reductions undertaken by the industrial countries that are unilaterally extended to other members of GATT. We assumed here a 50 per cent reduction in duties that was the original target of the Kennedy Round of negotiations. No account was taken of possible exceptions to this rule, although industrial countries reportedly plan to exempt textiles, some metals, and a few technically advanced products from the negotiations.

Correspondingly, changes in U.S. trade with the industrial countries would be one-half of the magnitude estimated in the event that an Atlantic Free Trade Area were established. But, in the case of tariff reductions under the m.f.n. clause, U.S. imports of manufactured goods and industrial materials from the nonindustrial countries would also rise. Assuming that the expansion of exports could be supplied at constant prices, we estimate increases in U.S. imports from nonindustrial areas at 1 per cent for industrial materials, and 15 or 21 per cent for manufactured goods, depending on the assumptions made in regard to the responsiveness of import demand to price changes. In absolute terms, the relevant estimates are $18 million for the former and $109–$146 million for the latter category. On the other hand, U.S. exports to the nonindustrial countries would rise as their increased exchange earnings lead to larger purchases abroad.

An Atlantic Free Trade Area excluding the EEC. In recent years, attention has been given to the possibility that the United States would attempt to reach an agreement on free trade in industrial materials and manufactured goods with Canada, the EFTA countries, and Japan if the Common Market were not amenable to tariff reductions. It is of interest therefore to consider the implications of this alternative.

Applying the assumptions made in the case of AFTA, we estimated that the removal of tariffs and quotas on trade among the industrial countries other than the EEC would raise United States exports and imports by $1,467 million and $1,360 million respectively. A "truncated" AFTA, however, would retain the EEC discrimination against the U.S., which was estimated to cost $438 million in exports. But American exports would benefit from discrimination against the EEC by other AFTA countries. This gain is estimated at $0.6 billion. In total, an AFTA without the EEC would raise American exports by $1.6 billion, and U.S. imports by $1.4 billion.

While these results point to an improvement in the U.S. trade balance in an Atlantic Free Trade Area that excluded the EEC, balance-of-payments considerations do not offer an appropriate guide for choice among alternative trade arrangements. Rather, the importance of the Common Market countries in U.S. trade, as well as the political implications of alternative trade arrangements, point to the undesirability of establishing a "truncated" Atlantic Free Trade Area.

European integration. We indicated that U.S. exports are discriminated against in the European Common Market, as well as the European Free Trade Association. The merging of the two groups would increase discrimination against the United States, and augment the potential decline in U.S. exports. No attempt was made to estimate the magnitude of this discrimination. Neither did we estimate the dynamic effects that are likely to benefit U.S. exports as a result of the acceleration of the rate of economic growth in Western Europe following the fusion of the EEC and EFTA.

Effects of an Atlantic Free Trade Area on U.S. Foreign Investment

The establishment of a free trade area does not directly affect the freedom of capital movement. But the elimination of barriers to trade is likely to have indirect repercussions on the movement of productive factors, primarily capital, the most mobile factor of all. Two questions are involved in assessing the magnitude of these repercussions: First, how would trade liberalization affect foreign investment decisions? And second, how would the anticipated changes in overseas investments affect the United States balance of payments?

The basic reason for investing abroad can usually be traced back to the profit motive—Americans tend to invest in foreign countries when the profit prospects from such investments exceed those anticipated from alternative uses of funds. But numerous and diverse factors contribute to this basic motive. They include the need to develop particular resources or to obtain raw materials not readily available in the domestic market; desire to reduce transport, distribution and service costs; ability to take advantage of special tax treatment; need to gear the product-line to specific markets, and to cater to the nationalistic feeling of the consumer and his acceptance of the product; and desire to circumvent tariffs and other trade restrictions, discriminatory (as in the EEC) or otherwise. Although the last-mentioned factor is the most direct avenue through which the AFTA would exert its influence on foreign investment decisions, all other factors would also come into play; and these influences may not all operate in the same direction.

The basic theoretical tenet, that factor and commodity movements are partial substitutes for each other,[16] would lead

---

[16] By this, we mean that if commodity trade is restricted by governmental or other actions, its place would be taken—in part—by movement of capital and other factors. Conversely, restrictions placed on

one to expect a reduction in capital outflow from the United States if free trade were established among the major trading nations. This is particularly true in an Atlantic Free Trade Area, involving the elimination of discrimination against American exports in the EEC and EFTA. These markets could then be served more effectively from the United States. But the theory is based on a simplified model, and cannot account for the counter-forces that may arise. First, there is a historical pattern whereby firms are induced to invest abroad as they become familiar with foreign markets through exports. The general widening of business horizons attendant upon the reduction in trade barriers may lead businessmen to increase their foreign investments. Here, the desire to cater to specific market needs and to take advantage of low factor costs may loom increasingly important. Also, foreign investments would become more attractive under an AFTA, since each facility could then serve a larger region, thereby enjoying economies of scale. Indeed, a survey conducted by the National Industrial Conference Board[17] among U.S. firms that have operations abroad showed that costs in domestic plants are generally lower in cases where the foreign plant's capacity is less than one-tenth of the U.S. plant; costs become nearly equal as the 10 per cent level is reached, while costs in foreign operations are lower than in the United States in 85 per cent of the cases when the output of plants abroad exceeds one-half of that in the domestic plants. Finally, the expansion of trade, including the need to sell more in the U.S., may induce American enterprises to expand their overseas facilities for producing raw materials, and to seek new sources of supply.

Because of the hypothetical nature of the problem posed here, it is not possible to resolve it by reliance on past data. Yet it is of interest to shed light on the relative strength of the conflicting influences outlined above. In order to gain such an insight, a questionnaire was sent to over 2,000 producing firms listed in the *1964 Directory of American Firms Operat-*

---

international factor mobility would tend to stimulate commodity trade. See R. A. Mundell, "International Trade and Factor Mobility," *American Economic Review* (June, 1957), pp. 321–35.

[17] See T. R. Gates and F. Linden, *Costs and Competition: American Experience Abroad* (New York: The National Industrial Conference Board, 1961).

ing in Foreign Countries.[18] The respondents were asked to indicate how an Atlantic Free Trade Area would affect their foreign investment decisions and the disposition of their foreign earnings. (The questions related only to direct investments.)

On the face of it, the universe selected would appear to impart a downward bias to the flow of foreign investments. If only the firms already operating abroad are queried, possible new entrants into foreign productive activities are excluded out of hand. It turned out, however, that the *Directory* includes many firms which are merely doing foreign business rather than engaged in direct overseas production. At most, only one-fifth of them have direct control over manufacturing facilities. In all probability, the universe included most American firms with a horizon wide enough to contemplate foreign investments.

Altogether, 191 replies were received, of which 22 did not answer the questions for various reasons. The 169 usable questionnaires represent close to one-half of the companies with direct production interests abroad.[19] Although they cannot be regarded as a representative sample in a statistical sense, they do offer a qualitative view of the factors affecting foreign investment decisions under the projected AFTA.

It is possible to divide the 169 valid replies as follows: 82 firms stated that an Atlantic Free Trade Area would not affect their over-all foreign investment position; 46 responding companies expected either to contract their foreign manufacturing operations or to avoid an otherwise contemplated expansion in the event of an AFTA; finally, 41 firms anticipated an expansion of their foreign production facilities to follow the establishment of an AFTA. These categories cannot be distinguished on the basis of products or product lines, since many industries are represented in all three.

Equally significant to the quantitative breakdown are the reasons, arguments, and general discussion contained in the replies, which yield important insights into business thinking.

---

[18] New York: World Trade Academy Press, 1964. (The questionnaire is reproduced in M. E. Kreinin.)

[19] The National Industrial Conference Board Study, *Cost and Competition: American Experience Abroad,* is based on the experience of 147 firms with foreign production facilities.

Since several of the respondents did not advance any reasoning for their answer, the qualitative analysis is based on fewer than the total number of replies.

No change. For the most part, companies which expect that AFTA would have no effect on their over-all investment position stated that tariffs and related obstacles were insignificant elements in their competitive posture. Some are resource-oriented industries, and must produce where raw materials are; others produce perishable commodities; but many emphasized transport cost as the overwhelming impediment to trade, dwarfing tariffs in importance. Following are a few illustrative responses:

A manufacturer of heating, plumbing, and air conditioning equipment states:

Generally speaking, our products are heavy and the freight element is more important than duties, tariffs, . . . We believe that a possible 'Atlantic Free Trade Area' would have little effect on our operations.

A chemical producer wrote:

Since transportation costs are large in relation to the selling prices of our products and since raw materials are in general available within each country involved in your study or are close at hand, local manufacture is imperative to meet local competition.

Similar responses were given by a score of other firms producing a variety of commodities. But the majority of the respondents in this category did not specify a reason at all. Most of these companies also indicated that AFTA would not affect the disposition of their foreign earnings.

However, seven firms under this classification emphasized that the "no effect" reply applied only to their over-all foreign investments position. They do expect considerable changes in the product-mix of their facilities as well as in their overseas locations, both aimed at the attainment of lower costs. Two of them anticipate consolidation of a few plants into one large and more efficient facility, from which several markets can be supplied. It appears that Canada would be a main "loser" from such a transformation. Three examples of these responses are presented below:

We would contract in the EEC and expand in Japan on the basis of free market into EEC from Japan and lower manufacturing costs in Japan. This would not affect the total of our foreign investment but would reallocate it. (Printing Machinery)

Rather than expand existing manufacturing facilities in Canada, which necessarily supply a restricted market, consideration would be given to the most advantageous area in which to produce any additional volume or even relocate present operations. (Chemicals)

Our product line—largely variable resistors, switches, and microelectronic components and circuits—is easily transported and contains a relatively small percentage of material costs in relation to capital and labor costs. Without an Atlantic Free Trade Area we would tend to build general purpose plants in countries having large, growing markets. With an Atlantic Free Trade Area we would probably build specialized plants in countries with cheap production costs. For example, those products using high capital and low labor inputs would be made in specialized plants in a low cost capital area such as the U.S. But products requiring a large labor input would be made in specialized plants in low cost labor areas such as Ireland or Hong Kong. *Thus an AFTA would cause us to be more resource-oriented and less market-oriented* in selecting investment sites. (Electronic Components)

Contraction. Of the 46 firms which expect "contraction" if the Atlantic Free Trade Area were created, some indicated that they would actually reduce their foreign operations. But many stated that existing facilities would remain intact, "because cost to get out is too great," but the contemplated expansion programs would be avoided. Several firms wrote that in the event that the Atlantic Free Trade Area were established, they would consolidate their foreign manufacturing operations. Western Europe, for example, could then be served from one or two locations, thus eliminating the need for plants in many individual countries now made necessary by the tariff. Respondents often stressed that an AFTA would lead to economies of scale and more efficient production, as facilities are consolidated in a way dictated by costs consideration. More rational production patterns would then follow.

The reason given for these changes was invariably clear-cut, and directly traceable to the tariff. The elimination of tariffs under an AFTA would increase the competitiveness of American exports, making it unnecessary to produce abroad. Thus commodity trade would partly replace capital movements. A few direct quotations to that effect will serve to illustrate the point:

We could supply our Canadian market at less expense from our U.S. factories if tariffs were eliminated. We would prefer to serve our customers in the EFTA area and the other countries of Western Europe outside of EEC from our plant in Holland. (Hydraulic Cylinders)

Re. Japan—now contemplating establishment of Japanese manufacturing facilities because duty and freight preclude extensive sales *ex* U.S.A. Would establish only a sales office in Japan if 30 per cent duty were eliminated. (Valves)

If we had not established manufacturing facilities in Holland recently (1960) an AFTA might well cause us to avoid such an undertaking. (Sewing Machines)

The high duties on our machines in England forces us to manufacture there. (Cutting Machines)

In a long product-line business, many of the low-volume items would be manufactured in U.S.A. for economy reasons—hence diminishing the development of facilities in Canada. (Pens)

With tariff eliminated it would almost surely be more economical to supply our Canadian requirements for electrical appliances from U.S. plants. We will shortly consider the establishment of common market plants for both appliances and machinery. Tariff is a major cost factor and might make it practical to supply the common market from existing U.S. and Scottish plants. Elimination of common market tariff on appliances and machinery would improve our competitive position on both products from present plants and would encourage greater sales effort. (Textile Machinery)

By being able economically to concentrate manufacturing of trackless equipment in the United States, removing that product line from France and Great Britain, it would eliminate the major production in France and leave manufacturing facilities free in Britain to absorb the remainder of manufacturing done in France. With elimination of tariffs going into Common Market countries, the desirability of manufacturing capability in France would disappear. The trend in the Common Market countries appears to be towards higher prices, wages, and costs generally as against an apparently better control of economic factors in Britain. (Industrial Machinery)

We could probably service our Canadian needs, or at least a large portion of those needs, from our manufacturing facilities in the United States. (Records)

Elimination of duties and import restrictions would eliminate the need for local manufacture thus permitting higher volume and resultant cost reductions in other plants which could supply the area. (Household Appliances)

These responses apply to most foreign areas of manufacture. The EEC is often mentioned, probably because of the tariff discrimination. But the most frequently mentioned area of contemplated contraction is Canada, a market which can be readily serviced from stateside locations. In addition to easy accessability and low transport costs, costs of production there are similar to those prevailing in the United States. Thus, a producer of electronic components stated:

Time, distance, shipping costs, etc., are no real problem in dealing with Canadian business. If duties were eliminated, we would deal with Canada on the same basis as a '51st State.' This would not be true in the EEC, EFTA, or Japan where we feel we would still have to maintain manufacturing facilities—although they might well be planned to be less independent of U.S. components, etc., than is the case at present.

Most respondents in this category also indicated that they would increase repatriation of foreign earnings, because less would be needed for expansion purposes:

More remittance back here simply because if none or slower expansion of manufacturing abroad—less need to reinvest profits. (Elastic Fabrics)

Finally, a great majority of the firms expecting contraction plan to expand their marketing and warehousing facilities abroad, in order to support intensified sales efforts from the United States.

Expansion. Unlike the cases of "contraction," many of the 41 firms which expect to expand their foreign production facilities in the event of AFTA did not give unambiguous reasons. The "relevant" reasons can be classified into two groups: cost considerations, and market considerations.

The expansion of trade following the establishment of AFTA, and the intensification of competition in international markets, would force firms to locate in least-cost areas. Since products manufactured in the United States would not always be competitive, some of the production would have to move abroad. In three of the cases so explained, involving relatively labor-intensive products, the foreign expansion was deemed necessary in order to sell in the American market. As American manufacturers lose the protective tariffs, they would not be able to compete against lower-cost imports. Consequently, they would set up or expand production facilities in low-cost areas, from which they would supply the United States. These reasons are documented in the following quotations:

Due to lower labor costs, the cost of manufacturing in our plants in Great Britain is less than in U.S.A., and we therefore would be more competitive or obtain a greater profit. (Electric Instruments)

Unless there was a significant change towards equalizing labor rates, labor productivity, and governmental "subsidies" on export trade, much of our United States production would not be competitive with other countries. (Clothing)

Lower European production costs will require increased facilities abroad, both as a defensive measure with respect to domestic market, and to permit expansion of foreign sales. (Typesetting Machines)

With completely free trade between the United States and the markets indicated, it will be very difficult in our industry to compete with countries which are currently exporting to the United States due to the dramatically lower wages and salaries presently existing in these countries. (Electronic Components)

With the elimination of even the present rather inadequate protection which the U.S. special steel industry now has against the taking over of the U.S. market by lower cost foreign producers, there would be even greater inroads made by foreign producers in taking over a large share of this U.S. market. Accordingly, there would be reduced incentive for additional investment in manufacturing plants in the United States until such time as wage levels in foreign countries, such as Japan and the Common Market, more nearly approach those in the United States. This would seem to be a long time off. At the same time, there would be encouragement to expand our present foreign joint ventures to at least participate in enterprises whose expansion in the specialty steel field would thereby be greatly encouraged. There would, at the same time, seem to be little incentive to proceed with any investment in Canada, since the market could be probably more efficiently served from the United States or foreign countries. (Steel Products)

The second reason can be articulated as follows: AFTA would lead to the expansion of trade. Once a company increases its exports, it is drawn to set up production or assembly and conversion facilities abroad, so as to be close to its customers, to provide better services, to gear its product lines to local demand, and at times to satisfy the nationalistic feelings of its customers (or of the local government). The following citations illustrate this argument:

Such an AFTA would give us considerable opportunity to further expand distribution in the areas concerned, by initially establishing warehousing and sales organizations. As these develop, consideration could be given to further plant expansion, either of our present plants, or in the areas wherein warehousing proved to be successful. (Floor-covering Accessories and Supplies)

We find it advisable to have our production facilities close to our customers. Geographically our present plants are well located to handle major markets. Increased opportunity for more trade in given areas would require more capacity at existing locations. (Abrasives)

Our products, metal office furniture, in most cases are not of sufficient value to justify overseas shipment (given their bulk and unit price). Thus, overseas manufacturing subsidiaries are necessary in order to enter markets outside this hemisphere. Given a FTA, we assume that very shortly European plants and U.S. plants would be invading each other's markets. Thus, we would consider going abroad. (Metal Office Furniture)

Decisions on location are primarily based on geographical proximity to our customers. (Containers and Packages)

Although free trade between nations looks good on paper, we feel that the nationalistic approach is still the best. The French will buy from the French, Japan from Japan, Germany from Germans, etc. (Engine Bearings)

Of the various geographical areas, the EEC is mentioned most frequently as the site of possible expansion, followed closely by the EFTA countries. This reflects their potential as important markets, but it is also a result of the lower production costs prevailing there. Although Canada and Japan are also mentioned frequently as possible locations for expansion, several firms indicated that they would contract or liquidate their Canadian operation, along with expansion elsewhere, because the Canadian market could (in the event of AFTA) be better supplied from the United States:

For example, some of our products are produced less expensively in Europe than at our United States plants, so we would probably import these items if there were no restrictions. For other products, exactly the reverse is true. In one case, we might have to increase our investment in France, while in another, we might decrease our investment in Canada. (Equipment)

There would be little reason for two plants so close together— one in north central U.S. and the other in southern Canada.

Therefore, the Canadian manufacturing facilities would probably be liquidated. (Industrial Equipment and Electronic Components)

If there were no tariff between Canada and the United States, a number of our manufacturing operations in that country would not have been built. (Chemicals)

Only one company indicated the reverse:

We could supply part of the U.S. market from the Canadian plant. This is impractical now because of the U.S. duties on the products imported from Canada. At present there is no (or little) duty on these products sent to Canada from our U.S. plant. (Pharmaceuticals)

Although the firms in the "expansion" category expect to use some new U.S. capital, the main sources of funds for the new plants would be reinvested foreign earnings, followed closely by foreign borrowing. Consequently, many responding companies expect a slow-down in the repatriation of earnings to the United States:

Availability of new foreign investment opportunities would probably result in reinvestments in these new areas, rather than repatriation to the U.S. (Fibre Containers)

With less fear of currency fluctuations, we would probably tend to leave more money abroad—assuming a reasonable flowback for dividends after initial expansion costs. (Office Furniture)

With increased opportunity for further expansion, it is possible that a larger proportion of foreign earnings would be reinvested abroad. (Gloves)

We would expect that there would be a rapid increase in the manufacture of our products in the countries indicated with a corresponding lessening of our manufacturing activities in the United States. It would require reinvestment of our earnings abroad to support this expansion of our foreign activities. (Electrical and Electronic Components)

Summary. It would appear that the forces leading to expansion and contraction are both powerful, making it difficult to determine the net effect. On balance, however, judging from the strength and lucidity of the reasoning offered by the respondents as well as from their numbers, AFTA may result in a small net contraction of total foreign investments—primarily in Canada (because of its accessibility to stateside facilities). But more important than the over-all effect would be the rationalization of production, involving consolidation of facilities and of product lines, changes in the composition of investments, and shifts in location. Here the main "loser" would be Canada. Firms in all three categories, including those contemplating expansion, indicated that they are likely to contract their Canadian operations or avoid expansion in that country.

But what would be the effect of a shift in American investments from Canada to Western Europe on the United States balance of payments? The answer to this question will depend on the rate of return on U.S. investments, the division between repatriated and reinvested earnings, as well as the foreign trade activity of U.S. subsidiaries in the two areas. On the basis of data relating to the years 1950–59, A. G. Homan estimated that over a fifteen-year period, an American investment of $1 million would have a net effect on the U.S. balance of payments of plus $1.0 million in Western Europe, and minus $0.1 million in Canada.[20] According to Homan's results, then, the projected shift in the location of U.S. subsidiaries in an Atlantic Free Trade Area would tend to improve our payments balance.

These conclusions are reinforced if we consider the differential impact of U.S. investments in Canada and in Western Europe on American exports. It would appear from replies to the questionnaire that the main reason for the shift from Canadian to other locations is the ability of U.S. firms to supply the Canadian market from their domestic plants in the absence of the tariff. On the other hand, increased sales from European locations cannot be expected to fully replace U.S. exports. On balance, then, a shift in U.S. investments from Canada to Western Europe would tend to have a favorable effect on the U.S. balance of payments. It should be noted, however, that this may be counteracted to some degree by feedback from Canada. To the extent that Canadian imports from the United States depend on the availability of U.S. dollars, the increased imports of certain types of goods will result in lower purchases of American products.

[20] A. G. Homan, "Some Measures and Interpretation of the Effects of the Operations of U.S. Foreign Enterprises on the U.S. Balance of Payments" (August 23, 1962), mimeographed.

*Effects of Atlantic Free Trade Area on the Domestic
Economy of the United States*

Employment. In recent years, a considerable amount of information has become available on the relationship between foreign trade and domestic employment.[21] Of these studies, the most comprehensive one is that of Salant and Vaccara. For each of 72 selected manufacturing industries, the authors estimate the following effects of million $ increases in imports: (1) the direct impact on employment in a given industry; (2) the indirect effect on employment in all other industries that provide inputs for the industry in question; (3) the effect of liberalization on employment in industries connected with the process of importation, such as ocean freight and insurance; (4) the direct and indirect effect of higher foreign incomes and dollar earnings on American exports and employment.[22] The four components are then combined to obtain the net short-run employment effect of trade liberalization in each industry. Of the 72 industries, the net decrease in employment is largest for apparel products, where a million dollar increase in imports would result in the loss of 175 jobs; in turn, for grain milling a net increase of five jobs is shown. A summary of the main findings is given in Table 2.4.

For several reasons, however, the estimates of Salant and Vaccara are inappropriate for purposes of this study. First, some of the assumptions made[23] may result in an overstatement of the employment effect of trade liberalization. Second, the authors used 1953 data, and "in most of the cases studied,

[21] For example, see the following: (1) W. Salant and B. Vaccara, *Import Liberalization and Employment* (Washington, D.C.: The Brookings Institution, 1961); (2) *Domestic Employment Attributable to U.S. Exports, 1960,* and *Employment in Relation to U.S. Imports, 1960* (Washington, D.C.: U.S. Department of Labor, Bureau of Labor Statistics [BLS], 1962), mimeographed; (3) *The Relationship Between Imports and Employment* [an analysis of 27 import-competing industries and 2 industry case studies] (Washington, D.C.: U.S. Department of Labor, April, 1962), mimeographed; (4) B. Vaccara, *Employment Implications of Trade with the Common Market* (September, 1962), mimeographed.

[22] Items (1) and (2) are usually negative, and were found to be of roughly equal magnitude. On the other hand (3) and (4) are positive.

[23] E.g., the supposition that imports replace domestic production of equal magnitude.

TABLE 2.4. EMPLOYMENT EFFECTS OF IMPORT LIBERALIZATION
IN 72 INDUSTRIES

(number of employees per million $ increase in imports)

	First quartile	Median	Third quartile
1. Gross decrease (direct and indirect)	94	115	135
2. Gross increase associated with shipping of imports	0	1	2
3. Gross increase associated with exports	19	26	50
4. Net decrease	57	86	104

Source: W. Salant and B. Vaccara, *Import Liberalization and Employment,* (Washington, D.C.: The Brookings Institution, 1961), p. 215.

liberalization undertaken in 1960 would cause smaller . . . effects on employment . . . than is indicated by the estimates."[24] Third, the 72 selected industries do not fully represent the products covered by AFTA; on the other hand, they include several food items which are not considered in this study. Finally, the estimates are based on the industry distribution of actual foreign trade, which may not correspond to that of the estimated changes in trade.

Neither could the Bureau of Labor Statistics' estimates, contained in *Employment in Relation to U.S. Imports* and *Domestic Employment Attributable to U.S. Exports,* be utilized for our purposes.[25] Instead, we used the 1960 employment matrix which was prepared by the Bureau of Labor Statistics.[26] For each of some 200 industries in the economy, the matrix shows the number of jobs required, directly and indirectly, to produce $1 million of output in 1960. The indirect requirements are further subdivided into six major sectors (agriculture, mining, manufacturing, transport, trade, and all others), but they contain no estimate for the replacement of capital goods. In order to use the BLS figures, we

[24] *Import Liberalization and Employment,* p. 236.

[25] The data relate to all trade, including trade in agricultural products. The two pamphlets indicate the direct and indirect effects *on* each two-digit industry, but they do not show the employment consequences of output changes *in* each industry. While for the direct impact the two figures are identical, the indirect effect caused by each industry is not given, and we cannot estimate them for each industry. Consequently, it is not possible to separate out the sectors which do not concern us.

[26] I am grateful to Dr. Jack Alterman of BLS for making the matrix available.

allocated them, and the increases in trade shown for the 85 SITC groups, among the two-digit SIC industries.

Appendix Table 2.2 presents estimates of the employment changes in each industry obtained by applying the BLS coefficients to the estimated changes in trade under AFTA. The total gain in employment resulting from the expansion of exports is 227.5 thousand jobs, with three industry divisions, chemicals, nonelectrical machinery, and transportation equipment accounting for over one-half of the total. The employment loss caused by the expansion of imports would be 238.5 thousand jobs, with textile mill products, apparel, and miscellaneous products accounting for over one-third of the total. Both the gain and the loss are almost equally divided between direct and indirect effects. On balance, the table shows a net loss of 11,000 jobs as a result of AFTA.

Several adjustments must be made in the aggregate estimates. First, according to Salant and Vaccara, the increase in imports would require on the average an additional worker per $1 million for handling the merchandise, yielding a gain of 2.2 thousand jobs. Second, allowance must be made for employment attributable to the replacement of plant and equipment consumed. The figures provided in the BLS reports relate to total (including agriculture) exports and competitive imports; they show 9.5 and 10.8 workers respectively per $1 million of trade. From these exports and imports, we obtain a gain of 21.8 thousand jobs, and a loss of 23.3 thousand jobs attributable to plant and equipment used. Inclusion of these adjustments yields a net loss of 10,000 jobs. This estimate abstracts from any prospective expansion in employment resulting from the increase in the volume of trade. But in any event, it is an insignificant number compared to a total labor force of over 70 million or even to the 16.7 million employed in the manufacturing sector of the economy.

Individual industries. Because of data constraints, this final section is limited to manufactured products, namely SITC Sections 5–8, exclusive of unwrought metals. The disaggregative approach employed in Section 2 makes it possible to identify the individual industries which are likely to experience an increase, or a decline, in their output in an Atlantic Free Trade Area. Within the estimated increase of the exports of manufactured goods of $1.5 billion, six industries would show increases amounting to at least $80 million. In turn, eleven industries, with imports of $50 million or more, account for about 60 per cent of the total increase of imports of manufactured goods of $1.8 billion.[27]

TABLE 2.5. ESTIMATED INCREASES IN U.S. EXPORTS AND IMPORTS OF MANUFACTURED GOODS ACCORDING TO SITC INDUSTRIES

(MILLION $)

SITC No.	Exports Industry description	Estimated increase
599	Miscellaneous chemical materials and products	83.9
718.9	Other machinery	90.3
718.4	Construction and mining machinery n.e.s.	140.2
722–6, 9	Other electrical machinery	91.2
732.0	Bodies, chassis, and frames	104.6
734	Aircraft	103.3
	Total	613.5

SITC No.	Imports Industry description	Estimated increase
641	Paper and paperboard	137.3
653	Other woven textile fabrics	110.3
666	Pottery	50.7
673	Iron and steel bars	69.6
691.8	Manufactures of metal n.e.s.	127.0
722–6, 9	Other electrical machinery apparatus	108.0
732.1, 6	Automobiles	96.5
841	Clothing	143.3
851	Footwear	63.2
864	Watches and clocks	75.7
899	Manufactured articles n.e.s.	105.1
	Total	1,086.4

Source: See text.

These two lists indicate the competitive strength of the United States in several machinery categories, and her weakness in some labor and material-intensive items. Industries producing machinery and equipment would derive further gains from the elimination of discrimination in the EEC and EFTA. To provide a more accurate picture, however, the net effects of AFTA (derived by substracting the estimated increase of imports from that of exports) on individual industries need to be indicated.

[27] See Table 2.5. The data do not include the expansion of exports due to the elimination of EEC and EFTA discrimination.

Before turning to these figures, it should be recalled that the disaggregative estimates were obtained by applying fairly uniform elasticities to the tariff rates and to the 1960 trade figures. Under this "mechanistic" approach, the changes in trade of a particular industry depend on its trade position at a given point of time, and on the level of tariff protection it enjoys. In actual fact, however, that change is a function of the level of protection and the degree of comparative advantage (or disadvantage) enjoyed by the industry. The latter can be indicated by utilizing the indices of "revealed" comparative advantage shown in Appendix Tables 1.2 and 1.3.

On the basis of these indices, the following picture emerges in regard to the United States: (1) This country enjoys a comparative advantage in most chemical materials and products, with the exception of dyestuffs, fertilizers, and explosives; (2) The United States is also in a strong competitive position in most machinery items, particularly in aircraft, railway vehicles, tractors, metal-working machinery, and office machinery—on the other hand, it appears to be at a comparative disadvantage with regard to ships, boats, bicycles, and automobiles; (3) In various material-intensive products the United States finds itself at a disadvantage. The latter applies particularly to such items as manufactures of leather, materials of rubber, most (but not all) textile products, glass and pottery, simple forms of steel, and wrought copper and lead. But this country maintains a strong position in some synthetic articles, made-up textiles, and wrought tin and nickel; (4) Among "other manufactures," the United States holds a competitive edge in various types of precision instruments, such as scientific, medical, and optical equipment, as well as photographic and cinematographic equipment. On the other hand, it is at a comparative disadvantage in regard to clothing, footwear, and leather goods.

In turn, then, Table 2.6 presents estimated net changes in the export performance indices for industries whose trade balance would change by at least $20 million as a result of AFTA. It appears that major increases would be concentrated in the various machinery groups and certain chemical specialities. On the other hand, potential declines are relatively large in material-intensive products and certain labor-intensive goods such as clothing and footwear. At the same time,

TABLE 2.6. MAJOR UNITED STATES INDUSTRIES AFFECTED BY AFTA

(A) Main Gainers

SITC No.	Description	Direct effects of AFTA on trade flows (net)	Increase in exports due to EEC and EFTA	Index of export per-formance
512	Organic chemicals	20	25	110
599	Chemical material and products	74	31	289
711	Power-generating machinery nonelectric	26		99
714	Office machinery	24	10	157
715	Metal-working machinery	59	23	173
718.9	Other machinery	189	58	144
732.0	Bodies, chassis, and frames	86	27	164
734	Aircraft	89	37	331

(B) Main Losers

SITC No.	Description	Direct effects of AFTA on trade flows (net)	Increase in exports due to EEC and EFTA	Index of export per-formance
531	Synthetic organic dyestuffs	− 22		50
641	Paper and paperboard	−113		76
653	Other woven textile fabrics	− 90		36
657	Floor coverings and tapestries	− 20		22
664	Glass	− 23		49
666	Pottery	− 50		3
682.2	Copper, wrought	− 27		20
691.8	Manufactures of metals, n.e.s.	− 67		81
732.1, 6	Automobiles	− 52		29
841	Clothes, except fur clothing	−129		29
851	Footwear	− 62		7

Source: Appendix Table 1.2, and text.

the "gainers" register above 100 on the export performance index, while the prospective "losers" are well below 100.

It should not be expected, however, to find a correspondence between the estimated expansion of trade and the export performance indices *within* the two groups of "gainers" and "losers." For one thing, tariffs differ from commodity to commodity; for another, the absolute change in trade is affected by the size of the industry. At the same time, data on domestic production and consumption are not available according to the breakdown employed in trade statistics. Thus, in order to examine the domestic implications of the trade changes, it is necessary to convert the SITC groups of Table 2.6 to their SIC components. However, such a conversion is possible only on a high level of aggregation. Since significant domestic effects would be revealed only at a very disaggregative level, a "reversed" method was used in order to identify two groups of industries: the "export group" which stands to derive a benefit, and the "import-competing" group, which would lose in an Atlantic Free Trade Area. We first selected detailed SIC groups that are heavily involved in foreign trade, and then checked the probable effect of AFTA by placing them in the SITC groups to which they belong.[28]

Appendix Tables 2.3 and 2.4 present the two lists of industries selected under the above criteria. In addition, there would be indirectly affected industries; namely, industries heavily involved in supplying those listed in the tables. We attempted to identify them by using the 1958 O.B.E. Interindustry Relations study.[29] But that study is too aggregative for the purpose at hand, with the manufacturing sector broken into 52 two- or three-digit SIC industry groups. The same shortcoming applies to the data provided by Salant and Vaccara, who supplied estimates on the indirect effects of trade liberalization in a 40-industry breakdown, of which only 24 are in the manufacturing sector.[30]

Although the indirect effects of import liberalization often exceed half of the total effects, they are spread over a number

[28] The criteria used in the selection were the following:

Export Industries: (a) Four- or five-digit SIC industries that export at least $50 million, and whose exports constituted at least 5 per cent of production in 3 out of the 5 years (1958–62); (b) industries that export at least 10 per cent of production, and whose exports exceed $10 million in 3 out of 5 years. The SIC industries so selected must belong to an SITC group where the expected net increase in export to AFTA is at least $20 million or more.

Import-competing Industries: (a) four- or five-digit SIC industries that import at least $25 million, and whose imports constitute at least 5 per cent of new supply in 3 out of 5 years; (b) industries that import at least 10 per cent of new supply, and whose imports exceed $10 million in 3 out of 5 years; (c) for very heavily protected industries (where low imports might have been caused by a high level of protection), imports must exceed $5 million (3 per cent of new supplies) in 3 out of 5 years. The SIC industries so selected must belong to an SITC group where the expected net increase in imports from AFTA amounts to $20 million or more.

[29] See M. Goldman, M. Martimont, and B. Vaccara, "The Interindustry Structure of the United States—A Report on the 1958 Input-Output Study," *Survey of Current Business* (November, 1964), pp. 10–29. The study was prepared by the Office of Business Economics (OBE).

[30] Salant and Vaccara, *Import Liberalization and Employment*, Appendix Tables F–1 and F–2 (pp. 340–61).

of industries. Therefore, in any one case, only rarely does one industry suffer (or enjoy) a concentrated indirect impact. On the other hand, an industry can appear as an indirect loser (or beneficiary) several times (namely, as a result of trade expansion in several industries), and the total may be of significant proportions. Bearing in mind these limitations, I have tentatively concluded from the 1958 O.B.E. study that "primary iron and steel manufacturing" (SIC Nos. 331, 332, 3,391, 3,399) would be a major indirect gainer, while the "fabrics, yarn and thread mill" industries (SIC Nos. 221–224, 226, 228) would be main indirect losers.

As a next step, the Census of Manufactures was used to identify the geographical regions in the United States which may be strongly affected by AFTA.[31] Considering only the direct effects, and allowing for some aggregation dictated by the availability of data, it appears that the East North Central,[32] and Pacific[33] regions stand to gain the most from the expansion of exports. In terms of both employment and value added, there is an above-average concentration of industries included in Table 2.6 in these regions. On the other hand, New England[34] and the mountain[35] states would suffer most from the establishment of an Atlantic Free Trade Area.

Conclusion

The results of this chapter indicate that the effects of the proposed Atlantic Free Trade Area on trade and employment in the United States would be rather small. This is hardly surprising since foreign trade accounts for a small proportion of the U.S. gross domestic product, and hence even large percentage changes in trade flows would have little impact on the American economy. The United States is therefore likely to derive the greatest economic benefits from increased

[31] For a study of the geographical origin of American exports in 1960, see *Current Industrial Reports*, U.S. Bureau of the Census, Series M. 161 (60)–1, released May 4, 1960.

[32] Includes the states of Ohio, Indiana, Illinois, Michigan, and Wisconsin.

[33] Includes the states of Washington, Oregon, California, Alaska, and Hawaii.

[34] Includes the states of Maine, New Hampshire, Vermont, Massachusetts, Rhode Island, and Connecticut.

[35] Includes the states of Montana, Idaho, Wyoming, Colorado, New Mexico, Arizona, Utah, and Nevada.

competition in the event of the elimination of tariffs. Furthermore, trade liberalization is considered desirable because of its implications for the cohesion of the Atlantic alliance.

Nor can a choice among alternative trade arrangements be made on the basis of purely economic considerations. It should be noted, however, that the relatively extensive U.S. trade with the Common Market countries speaks for the inclusion of the EEC in any Atlantic trade grouping. Moreover, the balance of payments of the United States stands to benefit from the elimination of, or reductions in, EEC discrimination through multilateral reductions in tariffs.

While the over-all effects of trade liberalization on the American economy are likely to be relatively small, some U.S. industries would be affected to a considerable degree. The principal gainers appear to be organic chemicals, other chemical specialities, as well as a variety of nonelectrical machinery, and aircraft. In turn, imports would rise more than exports in the case of textile products, paper and paperboard, automobiles, and a few other products. Finally, on balance, the East North Central, and Pacific regions stand to benefit from trade liberalization while New England and the mountain states may suffer adverse effects.

APPENDIX TABLE 2.1. U.S. EXPORTS AND IMPORTS RELATED TO THE VALUE OF DOMESTIC PRODUCTION AND CONSUMPTION, 1962

SIC No.	Industry	Value of shipments (billions $)	Exports as per- centage of value of production	Imports as per- centage of apparent consump- tion
20	Food and kindred products	66.9	2.5	2.9
21	Tobacco manufactures	4.5	2.6	0.0
22	Textile mill products	15.1	2.0	4.6
23	Apparel and related products	16.1	0.9	2.3
24	Lumber and wood products	8.4	2.3	6.8
25	Furniture and fixtures	5.5	0.5	0.5
26	Paper and allied products	15.7	2.9	6.8
27	Printing and publishing products	15.6	1.0	0.4
28	Chemicals and allied products	29.4	7.5	1.7
29	Petroleum and coal products	17.2	2.6	4.3
30	Rubber and plastic products, n.e.c.	8.5	2.0	1.4
31	Leather and leather products	4.3	1.2	4.3
32	Stone, clay, and glass products	11.5	1.9	2.2
33	Primary metal products	34.0	2.6	4.1
34	Fabricated metal products, n.e.c.	22.3	2.7	0.9
35	Machinery, except electrical	28.4	13.0	2.0
36	Electrical machinery	27.6	4.6	1.8
37	Transportation equipment	51.3	5.5	1.4
38	Instruments and related products	6.6	8.0	3.5
39	Miscellaneous manufactured products	10.4	1.7	3.9
	All manufactures	399.3	4.2	2.7

Sources: Value of production: U.S. Bureau of the Census, *Annual Survey of Manufactures,* 1962.

Foreign trade: U.S. Bureau of the Census, *U.S. Commodity Exports and Imports as Related to Output, 1962 and 1961.* Washington, 1964.

APPENDIX TABLE 2.2. EMPLOYMENT EFFECTS OF TRADE LIBERALIZATION IN THE UNITED STATES

SIC No. / Industry	Job requirements per million $ of final demand	Changes in trade (million $)		Changes in employment (per 1,000 Jobs)	
		Imports	Exports	Imports	Exports
22 Textile mill products	144.75	202.5	63.0	34,089	9,119
23 Apparel and related products	178.18	165.7	31.6	29,524	5,630
24 Lumber and wood products	114.32	29.9	9.5	3,418	1,086
25 Furniture and fixtures	117.86	9.5	2.8	1,120	330
26 Paper and allied products	68.29	141.9	42.8	9,690	2,923
27 Printing and publishing products	94.96	11.5	12.8	1,092	1,215
28 Chemicals and allied products	111.06	116.3	340.6	12,916	37,827
29 Petroleum products	71.67	0	30.1	0	2,157
30 Rubber and plastic products n.e.c.	88.61	58.0	29.8	5,139	2,641
31 Leather and leather products	114.54	49.9	10.1	5,716	1,157
32 Stone, clay, and glass products	87.55	126.2	31.0	11,049	2,714
33 Primary metal products	78.19	209.0	232.0	19,860	18,140
34 Fabricated metal products n.e.c.	97.41	108.1	104.0	10,530	10,131
35 Machinery, except electrical	92.93	91.0	490.5	8,457	45,582
36 Electrical machinery	94.30	132.2	129.6	12,466	12,221
37 Transportation equipment	98.65	151.3	349.9	14,926	34,518
38 Instruments and related products	102.77	129.0	90.1	13,257	9,260
39 Misc. manufactured products	103.49	193.8	66.2	20,056	6,851
19 Ordnance and accessories		9.2	1.0	} 1,057	} 227
99 Other		1.0	1.2		
Not assigned (use arithmetic average)	103.3	234.0	230.4	24,172	23,800
Total		2170.0	2299.0	238,531	227,529

Source: See text.

APPENDIX TABLE 2.3. MAJOR U.S. EXPORT INDUSTRIES TO BE AFFECTED DIRECTLY BY AFTA

SIC No.	Industry	Production (million $)		Exports (million $)		Exports as a percentage of production	
		1960	1962	1960	1962	1960	1962
2221, 2262	Man-made and silk broad-woven fabrics	1,384.7	1,559.7	85.5	84.6	6	5
2815	Intermediate and tar products, dyes, pigments	1,012.6	1,049.5	81.3	86.4	8	8
2818	Industrial organic chemicals n.e.c.	3,116.3	3,453.8	189.2	192.9	6	5
2861	Gum and wood chemicals	182.6	180.8	62.2	41.7	34	23
28730, 28790, 28184	Agricultural insecticide chemicals and formulations	507.4	626.8	90.2	119.1	18	19
28993, 28185, 28198, 9 2899	Misc. chemical preparations, n.e.c.	1,650.3	1,785.0	293.8	331.2	18	19
34431, 3	Heat exchangers and steam condensers; steel-power boilers and parts	442.9	463.6	49.2	132.8	11	29
3511, 3519	Steam engines, turbines, turbo-generators, and parts; Internal combustion engines, n.e.c.	1,837.9	1,866.4	220.0	248.6	12	15
3531, 2	Construction and mining machinery and equipment			789.9	839.2	33	35
3533	Oil field machinery and equipment	506.6	551.4	159.6	142.9	32	26
3537	Industrial trucks and tractors	389.5	394.4	40.7	40.1	10	10
3541	Metal-cutting machine tools and parts	746.8	831.2	127.8	205.1	17	25
3542, 35485	Machine tools, metal-forming, and parts	400.5	417.3	88.8	124.0	22	30
35481-4	Metal-working machinery, except machine tools	582.3	610.5	130.5	157.2	22	26
3584, 3551-5, 8	Machinery and parts for food products, textiles, wood-working, pulp and paper industry, printing trades and special industry	2,770.2	3,028.7	497.8	596.6	18	20
3561	Pumps and compressors	1,106.7	1,147.3	142.2	157.0	13	14
3562	Ball and roller bearings and parts	836.2	937.9	55.7	62.2	7	7
3567	Industrial furnaces and ovens and parts	214.6	194.2	23.1	32.9	11	17
3569	General industry machinery and equipment, n.e.c.	246.8	608.0	23.1	72.2	9	12
3571	Computing and related machines	1,279.2	1,637.5	169.7	270.6	13	17
3585, 35811	Refrigerators and refrigeration machinery, except household	1,683.1	1,852.7	145.8	155.0	9	9
3717 (2, 3)	Trucks and motor coaches	2,742.6	3,087.9	382.1	253.7	14	9
372	Aircraft and parts	11,488.5	11,999.9	1,759.0	1,987.4	15	17

Source: U.S. Bureau of the Census, U.S. Commodity Exports and Imports as Related to Output, various issues.

APPENDIX TABLE 2.4. MAJOR U.S. IMPORT-COMPETING INDUSTRIES TO BE AFFECTED DIRECTLY BY AFTA

SIC No.	Industry	Production (million $)		Imports (million $)		Imports as a percentage of apparent consumption	
		1960	1962	1960	1962	1960	1962
2231	Wool, broadwoven fabrics and blankets	677.7	690.3	80.5	75.9	11	10
2271, 2	Carpets and rugs, woven and tufted	770.1	925.3	49.2	48.0	6	5
2279	Carpets, rugs, and mats, n.e.c.	53.7	44.2	5.8	4.8	10	10
22992	Textile goods, n.e.c.	49.2	45.3	135.4	181.1	73	80
2381, 2259	Dress and work gloves, except leather	147.1	176.6	22.6	23.6	13	12
26211	Newsprint	248.9	265.6	688.7	695.8	75	73
2815	Intermediate coal tar products, dyes, pigments	1,012.6	1,049.5	27.8	41.9	3	4
3151	Leather gloves	55.1	45.2	12.6	25.3	19	36
3211, 32313	Flat glass	754.8	679.7	50.8	51.7	6	7
3262	Vitreous china table kitchenware	49.0	47.8	23.4	24.8	33	35
3263	Earthenware food utensils	62.2	50.2	13.0	13.6	17	21
33152	Steel nails and spikes	132.7	138.7	39.0	40.0	23	23
33312, 33412, 33512	Refined copper and alloys (copper alloys, rolled, drawn, etc.)	1,783.1	2,045.6	180.7	122.2	11	6
3421	Cutlery	177.1	207.4	10.2	11.6	6	5
3871	Watches and clocks	386.7	405.1	62.6	67.7	14	14
3872	Watch cases	28.1	25.6	5.3	5.6	16	18
3913	Lapidary work	46.0	48.5	91.6	103.4	70	76
3914	Silverware and plated ware	203.6	215.4	29.9	27.7	13	12
3941	Games and toys, n.e.c.	568.5	690.5	34.7	41.4	6	6
3942	Dolls	198.3	200.9	9.1	20.0	4	9
3949	Sporting and athletic goods, n.e.c.	661.9	654.9	26.8	34.7	4	5
3961, 39112	Jewelry (including costume), except platinum and carat gold	311.4	318.3	28.6	33.1	9	10
3962	Feather, plumes, and artificial flowers	60.2	55.1	39.5	43.8	40	44
3963	Buttons	73.5	76.8	6.8	6.5	9	8
3995	Umbrellas, parasols, and canes	33.9	34.1	3.9	5.7	12	15

Source: U.S. Bureau of the Census, *U.S. Commodity Exports and Imports as Related to Output,* various issues.

CHAPTER III

TRADE ARRANGEMENTS AMONG INDUSTRIAL COUNTRIES: EFFECTS ON CANADA

Ronald J. Wonnacott[1]

Canada's Position in World Trade

For historical and political reasons, the North American economy has been split lengthwise into quite unequal parts; the smaller portion (Canada) has a population about one-tenth—and an economy about one-fourteenth—the size of the larger portion (the United States). The problem is not just this imbalance between the two parts. Canada cannot by any economic definition be regarded as a single natural region; instead, it is made up, economically and demographically, of a thin slice along the long northern edge of North America.

This split, of course, has not been a complete rupture. It is true that tariffs applied by both countries to many commodities have prevented the economic intercourse that would have occurred otherwise. However, despite this and the conscious attempts (such as the Commonwealth preference system) to divert Canadian trade elsewhere, the bulk of Canadian trade is still with the United States. As indicated in the last two columns of Table 3.1, about 56 per cent of Canadian exports and 67 per cent of Canadian imports are traded with the United States.[2] Canada's next-to-largest trading partner by a substan-

[1] The author is professor of economics at the University of Western Ontario. He owes a special debt to Paul Wonnacott and Klaus Skarabis. The third section of this chapter draws heavily on a more detailed study of U.S./Canadian free trade in manufacturing completed in collaboration with Paul Wonnacott to be published by Harvard University Press under the title *Free Trade between the United States and Canada: the Potential Economic Effects*. Klaus Skarabis was responsible both for the estimates on resource response in the second section, and for developing the technique for making these estimates (see appendix to this chapter). Finally, Donald Angevine cheerfully assisted with a number of the tables.

[2] Given the differences in the size of the two economies, this trade is of far less consequence to the larger U.S. economy. (It accounted for about one-fifth of United States trade in 1963.)

TABLE 3.1. STRUCTURE OF CANADIAN TRADE

(MILLION $)

	Food, beverages and tobacco		Industrial materials		Fuels		Manufactured goods		Commodity totals	
	Exports to	Imports from	Exports to	Imports from	Exports to	Imports from	Exports to	Imports from	Exports to	Imports from
United States	347	332	1,497	377	316	128	1,453	3,153	3,613	3,990
European Economic Community	161	26	170	10	1	1	118	276	450	313
United Kingdom	274	30	469	41	0	2	197	410	940	483
Continental EFTA	24	9	79	20	—	—	29	80	133	109
Japan	96	7	156	2	7	—	18	112	277	121
Other developed countries	47	77	68	21	1	—	124	16	240	114
Less developed countries	141	224	108	127	1	370	259	61	507	782
Soviet-type economies	261	3	14	2	—	—	2	18	277	23
Total	1,351	708	2,560	600	326	501	2,199	4,126	6,436	5,935

Source: United Nations, Commodity Trade Statistics, 1963.

tial margin is Britain; this trade exceeds that between Canada and all countries in the Common Market combined. Yet, important as trade with the United Kingdom may be, it is rather small in comparison with Canada's trade with the United States. And it would be even less important without Commonwealth preference.

The other striking characteristic of Table 3.1 is the imbalance in Canada's trade in each product grouping. A deficit of about $2 billion in manufactured goods is offset by an even greater surplus in food and industrial materials. This pattern holds true for Canadian trade with almost all areas, especially with the United States; the only exception is Canada's trade balance with the less developed countries, where the pattern is reversed.

The key question in any Canadian move toward free trade is, "What would be the impact of further integration with the U.S. economy?" Loss of Commonwealth preference, and the opening—rather than the closing—of EEC markets are two other questions of considerable interest. Yet these are of secondary importance for Canada, and cannot be analyzed without first examining how free trade would affect the place of Canada in the North American economy. This makes an analysis of Canada's prospects easier in one respect, yet more difficult in another. It is easier because the "two-country" model provides a more reasonable first approximation than for almost any other pair of countries; it is more difficult because the restructuring of industry that would follow free trade has received little attention in traditional international trade theory, nor have techniques to handle this problem been developed.

For example, an examination of relative Canadian costs in manufacturing in the recent past may provide interesting background information, and perhaps some clues to the question of what Canadians may have produced efficiently despite the restraints imposed by the limited Canadian market. However, current cost figures of this kind provide a seriously inadequate indication of what Canada might produce efficiently under free trade, and are a doubtful basis for projecting free trade export capability; accordingly, Canada's present trade deficit in manufacturing cannot be extrapolated into free trade circumstances.

The reason is that *present* Canadian manufacturing costs

and supply reactions will become irrelevant under free trade. While manufacturing costs in Canada are now generally higher than in the United States, at least part of this higher cost may be traced to protection. Canadian producers have been restricted from exploiting the larger United States markets by the U.S. tariff; at the same time, the Canadian tariff has protected them from United States competition in the Canadian market. Hence, both tariffs have induced them to restrict themselves to the relatively limited Canadian market, with the result that their costs have remained high.

A related consideration is that the Canadian tariff and the Commonwealth preference system have provided an inducement to U.S. firms to establish subsidiaries in Canada. But, because of the smallness of the Canadian market, these firms have not been able fully to employ the efficient production methods used in the United States. In addition, the endeavor by oligopolistic firms to gain a foothold in Canada has resulted in a seriously over-serviced Canadian market.[3] As a result, the subsidiary typically produces in Canada on an inefficient scale many or most items in the product range offered by the parent in the U.S. market.

Accordingly, present techniques and costs in Canada would not be relevant in free trade circumstances, and a complete reorganization of Canadian production to cut costs would be necessary. Canadian prices would be forced down by the increased competition from U.S. imports coming into Canada duty free; lower prices of some industrial materials would reduce the costs of material using Canadian industries; and finally, scaling up by Canadian industry would be made practical by the opening of the large markets south of the border.

Geography ensures some irreducible degree of economic insulation between the North American economy and the rest of the world; no matter how tariffs may be reduced, the two major oceans will provide North American industry with some natural protection. However, within North America there is no such protection for either the U.S. or Canada; in fact, Canadian consumers are often nearer to U.S. than to Canadian producers, and vice versa.

[3] On this point, see H. Edward English, "Industrial Structure in Canada's International Competitive Position," *Canadian Trade Committee,* 1964.

The elimination of tariffs would provide Canadian industry with enormous new opportunities; it would also force it into a crisis situation. Because of the relative size of the two economies, almost the entire burden of reorganization in the North American area would fall on Canada. U.S. firms already service over 90 per cent of the entire North American market, and hence are operating at a scale appropriate for this market. However, Canadian firms will suddenly find their market greatly increased. A rationalized North American system implies U.S. specialization in roughly 90 per cent of internationally traded goods, but Canadian specialization in only about 10 per cent. As a consequence, Canadian industry will be forced to move rapidly from high-cost production of full lines for domestic consumption to low-cost production of selected items for North American consumption.

In determining the extent to which past export performance can be used as a basis for projecting export capability under free trade, the Canadian tariff holds the key. In sectors—particularly manufacturing—in which this tariff is high, Canadian industry is unlikely to be able to match foreign competition without a reorganization sufficient to transform its entire cost structure. On the other hand, tariffs on industrial materials are low; these industries already have engaged in international competition, and their export capabilities may be estimated from information on existing trade and tariffs. The second section will examine prospective changes in trade in industrial materials, while subsequent sections will deal with trade in manufactured goods—first, in the context of a free trade area between the United States and Canada, and later in an Atlantic context. Alternative trade arrangements will next be considered, whereas the concluding section will provide an evaluation of the suggested alternatives for trade liberalization among the industrial countries.

Projected Changes in Canadian Exports and Imports of Industrial Materials

We have distinguished two groups of industrial materials: raw materials, and partially manufactured goods. Most raw materials can be imported into Canada duty free; even protected items have a low tariff, so that the duty collected on Canadian imports of all raw materials is less than 1 per cent of their value. Consequently, freeing trade will not subject this sector to suddenly increased foreign competition. Its ability to prosper without protection in the past implies that it will be in a competitive position in free trade circumstances. It therefore seems valid enough to assume that present Canadian production techniques, costs and supply responses, are appropriate in estimating trade changes resulting from the elimination of the low remaining tariffs on these materials.

Changing trade patterns in partially manufactured goods[4] are also computed in this way. It is quite true that the assumption that present Canadian costs and supply response would remain the same becomes less satisfactory for this category of goods, since Canadian protection of semi-manufactures is considerably higher than the protection of raw materials. For this reason, these tentative estimates indicate only what might occur, to the degree that rationalization of these Canadian activities proves unnecessary.

There are two ways of computing increased Canadian exports of a commodity. The first is to apply some reasonable estimate of the elasticity of demand for Canadian exports to the average price change that results from foreign tariff reduction. The advantage of this procedure is that it is the simplest to apply. Its major disadvantage is the assumption of one (representative) elasticity of demand for Canadian exports; there are strong *a priori* grounds for expecting that import elasticities will vary between countries. Even if *domestic* demand and supply elasticities are the same in all countries, the elasticity of demand for imports will vary inversely with the share of imports in domestic consumption. Since the share of imports in domestic consumption differs greatly between the United States, the United Kingdom, and the other industrial countries, this should, if possible, be taken into account. Moreover, account should be taken of the effects on trade flows of eliminating Commonwealth preference.

An indirect method, which has been used by Robert Stern[5] to analyze U.S. export potential conforms to these requirements, and has been employed, in modified form, in this

---

[4] Using the definition of the Canadian trade classification.

[5] "The U.S. Tariff and the Efficiency of the U.S. Economy," *American Economic Review*, Papers and Proceedings (May, 1964), pp. 459–70.

study.[6] On the basis of reasonable assumptions of domestic demand and supply elasticities in the industrial countries, each country's import demand elasticity is computed from information on the share of imports in domestic consumption.[7] This yields a different import demand elasticity for each of Canada's trading partners, to which the appropriate tariff cut by each country can be applied. The same method has been applied in the case of Canadian imports.

The major problem, then, is deciding upon the domestic price elasticities of demand and supply to be used for each commodity. In the absence of direct estimates for the commodities under consideration, reasonable ranges were used within which the actual values for the respective elasticities are most likely to lie.[8] The selection of an upper and a lower bound on supply as well as demand elasticity produces four sets of estimates for the expected changes in trade flows. Large absolute values for both demand and supply elasticity in combination produce the largest price elasticity of demand for imports—and thus the largest change in imports; similarly, small absolute values for both demand and supply elasticity result in the smallest estimated import changes. Only these two bounding estimates will be presented; the first is derived from applying lower bound demand and supply elasticities (referred to as Assumption Set 1), and the second is derived by applying upper bound demand and supply elasticities (Assumption Set 2).

Exports. Only about 27 per cent of Canada's exports of industrial materials incur a duty abroad; it is only this group of exports that would change as tariffs in receiving countries are eliminated. In the raw material category, about two-fifths of Canadian exports are dutiable; available statistics indicate that only the U.S.—by far the largest importer—levies duties

[6] It should not be inferred that this approach is without error. For example, the assumptions of homogeneous products and negligible transport costs are involved. Hence, one cannot generalize that this indirect method is preferable to the other direct method in all instances.

[7] For the precise technique used, see the appendix to this chapter. In a few cases, it was necessary to work with import and production values rather than quantities, since there was no information on the latter.

[8] Relatively low demand elasticities (−.1 to −.25) were used for industrial materials. It was also assumed that the elasticities of supply of resource industries are low (0 to .25).

of any significance on Canadian raw materials. In the semi-processed category, about 30 per cent of Canadian exports are subject to duties.

The estimated changes in Canadian exports that would result from the establishment of an Atlantic Free Trade Area (AFTA) were computed on a detailed product basis, using assumed elasticities and trade flows.[9] These estimates were then aggregated and are presented in Table 3.2.[10] The two most

TABLE 3.2. PROJECTED INCREASES IN CANADIAN EXPORTS OF INDUSTRIAL MATERIALS IN AN ATLANTIC FREE TRADE AREA

(IN MILLIONS OF CANADIAN DOLLARS, BASE YEAR 1958)

	Assumption sets	United States	United Kingdom	Other industrial countries	Total
Raw materials	(1)	2.6	—	—	2.6
	(2)	11.8	—	—	11.8
Partially	(1)	29.5	− .6	.7	29.6
manufactured goods	(2)	119.1	−1.4	2.8	120.5
Total	(1)	32.1	− .6	.7	32.2
	(2)	130.9	−1.4	2.8	132.3

Source: See text.

notable results are: (1) The only substantial increase in Canadian raw material exports would be to the United States, since this is the only industrial country which now levies significant duties on Canadian exports of resource; (2) Canadian exports of partially manufactured goods to the United Kingdom would actually decline. This is because there are

[9] There are some interesting results for specific commodities. It is no surprise that increased exports to the United States are projected in the large Canadian export sector of base metals. On the other hand, the impact of trade liberalization on forestry products is not important, due to low or zero tariffs that already exist in this sector. (There is no tariff now, for example, on newsprint.)

One surprise is the large projected increase in exports of artificial abrasives. Canada is now the largest exporter of these commodities to the United States. But imports represent only a very small proportion of U.S. domestic consumption. To the extent that tariff elimination reduces U.S. price, any small increase in U.S. consumption and decrease in U.S. domestic supply would tend to increase presently small Canadian exports by a large proportion.

[10] It should be noted that these figures were not estimated by examining Canadian export possibilities, but rather by analyzing the import position of the countries with which Canada trades.

many items which are subject to tariffs in the U.K. market, but are admitted duty free from Canada, due to Commonwealth preference. If British tariffs against other AFTA countries were removed, their increased exports would displace both U.K. domestic supplies *and* Canadian exports. Thus, for example, Canadian exports of base metals and wood products to the U.K. would be reduced.

Imports. Canadian imports are simpler to treat than exports, since no consideration needs to be given to the country with which Canada trades. The Canadian tariff on dutiable raw material imports (6.4 per cent) is higher than the tariff (of 6.2 per cent) that must be paid by Canadian exports which are subject to duty abroad. The opposite is true, however, if average tariffs on all items—dutiable and nondutiable—are considered. Canadian resource protection, therefore, is less than resource protection in the countries to which Canada exports because tariffs are levied on fewer import items, and not because the tariffs levied are any lower. On the other hand, in the semi-processed category, Canadian protection substantially exceeds the protection other countries impose against Canadian exports.[11]

Estimated changes in trade flows as a result of AFTA are shown in the first column of Table 3.3. Changes in import

TABLE 3.3. ESTIMATED CHANGES IN CANADIAN EXPORTS AND IMPORTS OF INDUSTRIAL MATERIALS COMBINED

(IN MILLIONS OF CANADIAN DOLLARS, 1958 BASE)

Raw	Assumption sets	Imports	Exports	Trade balance
Raw materials	(1)	.9	2.6	1.7
	(2)	3.3	11.8	8.5
Partially	(1)	3.5	29.6	26.1
manufactured goods	(2)	14.1	120.5	106.4
Both	(1)	4.4	32.2	27.8
categories	(2)	17.4	132.3	114.9

Source: See text.

[11] The difficulties in interpreting tariff averages of this kind are well-known, and should be kept in mind. The higher the tariff, the more it will restrict trade flows, and as a consequence, the less its weight will be in the averaging process.

flows would occur chiefly in items in which there are now substantial imports, despite Canadian protection. These include coal, along with semi-processed iron, and wood products.

Combined effects of balance of payments. When export and import projections are compared in Table 3.3, the conclusion is quite clear. Regardless of the assumptions made about demand and supply elasticities, elimination of tariffs would improve the Canadian balance of trade in these items, with increases in exports exceeding those in imports. This is true both for raw materials and partially manufactured goods. The largest possible net improvement is estimated at about $130 million, and the smallest net improvement about $15 million.[12] These two limits suggest a possible improvement in the Canadian current account in the range of $50–$100 million. This improvement would represent 1 per cent of the total 1958 current account of about $7 billion, and a 5 to 10 per cent reduction in the current account deficit of over $1 billion in that year.

In summary, the two reasons for this unambiguous result are: (1) Canada is already a large exporter in the raw materials and semi-processed items analyzed in this study, but not a large importer; (2) the proportion (25 per cent) of Canadian exports that is dutiable is considerably greater than the proportion (15 per cent) of Canadian imports that is dutiable.

Implications of a U.S.-Canadian Free Trade Area
for Canada's Trade in Manufactures

We encounter greater difficulties in projecting Canadian performance in manufactured goods. The method—used for industrial materials—of estimating changes in exports from tariff reductions and present supply and demand conditions is inappropriate, since Canadian supply responses in manufactured goods would be transformed by the removal of tariffs. Consequently, it is necessary to consider industrial costs, not as they now exist but as they *would* exist under free trade. Although such a comparison with all trading partners is not

---

[12] In both cases, extreme values of the export and import projections have been compared.

feasible, reasonable estimates can be made in the most critical area, i.e., cost differences between Canada and the United States.[13]

The Canadian adjustment to free trade will be considered under two headings: (1) effects on the North American economy of reciprocal U.S.-Canadian free trade; (2) third-country effects. Of these two effects, the adjustment with the United States must be viewed as by far the more critical. In terms of both geography and resources, the two countries are tied together, but their association with other countries is limited by the major oceans. Canada's natural free trade markets are concentrated in the United States; at the same time, Canadian industry would face the stiffest competition from the United States.

Past Canadian export performance has been severely limited by high Canadian manufacturing costs. Canadian costs differ from those in the U.S. for four reasons: (1) Restricted from free access to U.S. markets by the U.S. tariff, and protected in their domestic market by the Canadian tariff, Canadian manufacturers have been limited to a small domestic base. Their limited production runs have not afforded the large-scale economies enjoyed by U.S. industry, which produces for a market of 10–15 times the size.[14] This problem has been made even more acute by the fact that the small Canadian market is not concentrated geographically, but is widely dispersed; (2) intermediate products are often more expensive in Canada than in the United States, because of tariff protection and lack of economies of scale; (3) there are a number of inherent reasons why costs have been higher in Canada, and would permanently remain higher regardless of changes in commercial policy. Production in certain regions in Canada would involve heavier transport charges, and capital

[13] Unless otherwise specified, the source of all estimates in this section is Ronald J. Wonnacott and Paul Wonnacott, *Free Trade between the United States and Canada: the Potential Economic Effects,* Harvard University Press, 1967.

[14] *Costs and Competition: American Experience Abroad* (New York: The National Industrial Conference Board, 1961), p. 164, cites economies of scale and the low cost of intermediate products as the two most important reasons that provide an advantage to U.S. establishments. For empirical estimates of inefficiencies of market size in Canada, see Wonnacott and Wonnacott, *Free Trade between the United States and Canada,* Pt. III.

costs in Canada would almost certainly remain higher than in the United States; (4) on the other hand, labor costs are lower in Canada than in the United States.

To the extent that manufacturing costs are currently higher in Canada than in the U.S., it may be inferred that the current Canadian cost disadvantages (1), (2), and (3) more than offset the Canadian advantage of lower wage rates (4). But current cost conditions would not continue to apply in free trade circumstances; specifically, cost differences (1) and (2), traceable to the existence of North American tariff barriers, would tend to be eliminated with U.S.-Canadian free trade. The ability of Canadian industry to compete would instead depend upon remaining cost differences (3), on changes in wage differentials (4), *and* on the speed and ease of the reorganization of Canadian industry to eliminate cost differences (1) and (2). The key question is whether higher Canadian capital and other costs would be offset, or more than offset, by the Canadian wage advantage.[15]

U.S. free trade cost advantages. Capital costs. These costs may now differ between Canada and the United States for several reasons: (1) The limited scale of Canadian production means that capital cost per unit of output is greater in Canada. Even though similar capital equipment may be used in similar processes in the two countries, shorter Canadian production runs mean that overhead capital charges cannot be spread over as large a number of units of output. (2) Machinery and equipment is often more expensive in Canada because of the Canadian tariff protecting domestic production of machinery. (3) Costs of new plant construction vary because of different material costs, and lower Canadian wage rates. (4) There are heavier costs of carrying debt in Canada, because of prevailing higher interest rates. (5) The cost of raising equity funds may be higher in Canada than in the United States.

The capital cost problem in Canada is much more complex than the traditional theory of international trade would suggest. In analyzing costs in the capital-scarce country (Can-

---

[15] It should not be assumed, however, that the present wage advantage would continue indefinitely. To the degree that Canadian industry is successfully rationalized, Canadian wages and/or the value of the Canadian dollar would adjust to the new free trade circumstances (see pp. 70–71, para. 3, below).

ada), conventional explanations focus on effects (4) and (5) above. Important as these are, the other effects should also be recognized. Effects (1) and (2) are now of critical importance in explaining high Canadian capital costs; however, these effects would tend to disappear with free trade. North American free trade would mean that Canadian production need no longer be limited to the Canadian market; hence, higher Canadian capital costs (1) attributed to this restriction would tend to disappear. Moreover, the elimination of both Canadian and U.S. tariffs on machinery and construction materials would mean that present cost differences noted under (2) would also tend to be eliminated. The other capital cost differences (3 to 5) would remain, however, and each may be considered in turn.

Construction costs. Since construction wages in Canada are roughly 35 per cent lower than in the U.S., total costs of construction in Canada could be as much as 9 per cent lower. However, this will not have a major effect on manufacturing costs in Canada, and would make the total costs of industrial production lower by 0.6 per cent at most. At any rate, as noted below, the Canadian wage advantage would diminish with time under free trade conditions.

Interest rates. It is not surprising that interest costs in Canada have historically been higher than in the United States; any impediments to the free flow of capital from a capital export area (the U.S.) to a capital import area (Canada) will normally be reflected in a continuing interest premium in the import area.

Many of the barriers to free capital flow between regions or countries are difficult to define. Some are psychological; others are geographical, as is evident from the persistent difference in the rate of return in California and New York. In the U.S.-Canadian case, one major economic impediment to free capital flow may be specified: the risk involved for an American investor in Canada who may find his interest and principal return affected by a future revaluation of the Canadian dollar. This risk would be eliminated only if the two countries formed a common currency area; it would not disappear with free trade, nor would the related interest premium in Canada be eliminated.

The Canadian prime bank rate[16] runs about 0.9 per cent higher than in the U.S.,[17] while the Canadian interest rate on industrial bonds[18] has been about 1.2 per cent higher than the equivalent U.S. rate.[19] Applying each of these differentials to the debt of each type outstanding in manufacturing yields an estimated impact on total costs of roughly .13 per cent. Summing these higher debt costs with the (negligible) effects of lower labor costs in construction would raise manufacturing costs by about .07 per cent in Canada as compared to the United States.

Equity costs. It might be expected that the international flow of equity funds would be influenced by the same factors as the flow of debt: if a U.S. investor provides funds for Canadian expansion through the purchase of Canadian equities, he runs the risk of a change in the exchange rate, and the consequent revaluation of his equity and dividend. This exchange risk, along with any other barriers to the free flow of capital, might be expected to increase the cost of raising equity funds in Canada.[20] Assuming that the (after-tax) premium on equity return is similar to that on debt, average costs in Canada could be as much as 1.08 per cent higher for this reason. Combined capital cost effects are shown in Table 3.4.

Clearly, equity effects dominate other capital cost differences (i.e., debt costs and construction costs). There are two reasons for this: (1) the importance of equity funds in financing manufacturing; (2) the effects of the corporate income tax—firms have to increase their before-tax earnings by about double the desired increment in after-tax profits. Nevertheless, even including possible equity effects, the combined influences of differences in capital costs on total costs in Canadian

[16] As quoted by the Bank of Nova Scotia.

[17] Bank rate on short-term business loans for nineteen U.S. cities, as quoted in the *Federal Reserve Bulletin.*

[18] See McLeon, Young, and Weir, "Ten Industrial-Bond Rates for Canada."

[19] Moody's AAA United States Industrial Bond Rate.

[20] Suppose two shares—one Canadian and one U.S.—have identical expected returns. If the Canadian share sells at a lower price, this indicates that sale of a new issue will be at less satisfactory terms in Canada. In this sense, raising equity capital is more costly. Or, to put it another way, a firm raising equity capital in Canada has to generate higher expected returns. This is strictly parallel to the well-known inverse relationship of interest rates and bond prices.

TABLE 3.4. FACTOR COSTS IN CANADA AND THE UNITED STATES, 1958

Industry	Capital costs Effects on total costs of higher capital costs in Canada as compared to United States	Average hourly wage (production workers)	
		Canada	U.S.
	per cent	(Canadian dollars)	(U.S. dollars)
Textiles and knitting mills	1.26	1.29	1.54
Apparel and related products	.35	1.09	1.51
Lumber and wood products	.79	1.46	1.74
Pulp and paper products	1.07	1.94	2.18
Printing and publishing	.48	1.93	2.60
Electrical machinery and apparatus	1.07	1.73	2.21
Chemical products	1.58	1.80	2.47
Petroleum and coal products	4.11	2.29	2.98
Rubber and plastics products	1.11	1.69	2.27
Leather and leather products	.76	1.15	1.60
Nonmetallic mineral products	1.27	1.77	2.19
Metallic products and nonelectrical machinery	1.38	1.91	2.55
Transportation equipment	1.00	1.91	2.66
Miscellaneous manufactures	.73	1.65	2.17
Average, all manufacturing	1.15	1.65	2.19

Source: R. J. Wonnacott and Paul Wonnacott, *Free Trade between the United States and Canada: the Potential Economic Effects, Harvard University Press, 1967.*

manufacturing are not of large order—except perhaps in the capital-intensive petroleum and coal products industry. Otherwise, total costs are affected by just over 1 per cent, and in several instances by substantially less.

Moreover, this estimate is likely to be too high. The most important component—equity effects—was computed by assuming that the U.S.–Canadian differential return on equity was similar to the differential return on debt. This is suggested by the similarity in barriers to capital flows (such as exchange risk) that apply to either type of investment. However, the exchange risk on equity—but not debt—may be partly offset by a compensating revaluation of exports by Canadian firms producing for the U.S. market.[21] Furthermore,

[21] This is a complex issue, and the results depend on import content as well as export patterns of the goods such firms produce.

the absence of a capital gains tax in Canada has undoubtedly had the effect of diverting funds from debt to equity investment, thus reducing equity costs in Canada. For this reason, the difference in equity costs between the two countries may be less than the difference in debt costs, and even the relatively modest estimates in the first column of Table 3.4 are likely to overstate the importance of higher Canadian capital costs.

Other U.S. cost advantages. There are several additional reasons that free trade costs might be higher in Canada than in the U.S. The influence most often cited is higher transport costs, both on acquiring inputs and in marketing final output. Both the major North American markets and the major sources of manufactured inputs are centered in the United States rather than Canada. This appears to provide U.S. locations with a decided cost advantage; however, the statement is subject to important qualifications.

The major Canadian center of industry is the Windsor-Montreal axis; major U.S. markets and supply sources are concentrated in the Chicago-Boston-Washington triangle. Whereas it is true that a firm locating in this latter area would have a slight market and supply advantage over a Canadian firm in the Windsor-Montreal area, industry locations in other regions of the U.S. are *not* more attractively situated, and in some instances are less attractive in terms of transport costs. Given the U.S.-Canadian geographical configuration—and especially the extension of Ontario into the U.S. industrial and market heartland—it cannot be concluded that each U.S. location is preferred in terms of transport costs to all Canadian locations. Instead, conclusions must be restricted to a regional dimension: (1) any Canadian region is generally at a slight disadvantage vis-à-vis its adjacent U.S. region; (2) the major differences in transport costs are interregional rather than international—with distant regions in either Canada and the U.S. at a disadvantage vis-à-vis the core region in either country.

There is an additional disadvantage that Canadian locations might face in competing for industry in a free trade area. External economies may accrue to firms that locate close to competitors. For example, apparel firms seem to be attracted to New York—precisely because the existence of the industry there means low costs for any new firm. External economies are impossible to measure, and they are more important in some industries than in others. But if the relative size of an industry in each region[22] is used as an index of these effects, the conclusions are much the same as for transport costs: Ontario and Quebec would be less attractive than the Chicago-Boston-Washington area, but about as attractive generally as other U.S. areas. In terms of external economies, the other Canadian regions (especially the Prairie and Maritime provinces) are the least attractive locations.

This does not imply that the distant Canadian regions necessarily would be adversely affected by free trade. There is no doubt that they would face disadvantages, but they must contend with these under protection as well as under free trade. In analyzing the effect of free trade on these regions, one should not compare their prospects with those of regions which do not face their spatial disadvantages; instead, their prospects under free trade must be compared with their prospects under protection. The most appropriate precedent is provided by U.S. regions: within the U.S. free trade area, distant regions (such as the Upper Midwest) have successfully overcome spatial problems (similar to those of the Canadian Prairie provinces) by specializing in selected industries with low transport cost–value ratios.

A final possible deterrent to the growth of industry in Canada under conditions of free trade might be differences in federal tax treatment of industry in the two countries. While U.S. tax reductions now give the U.S. an edge, it is not clear at the time of this writing whether or not Canadian taxes will also be reduced. In any case, taxes are an instrument of policy, and can be adapted to changing economic circumstances. Hence, unlike transport costs, they do not impose a permanent cost differential between two countries.

The Canadian labor cost advantage. The lower Canadian wage rate presently provides the major cost advantage for manufacturing firms in Canada, vis-à-vis their U.S. competitors. As Table 3.4 indicates, 1958 average U.S. wages in manufactur-

---

[22] More precisely, the employment of that industry in the Standard Metropolitan Area of heaviest concentration.

ing exceeded those in Canada by one-third, if both are expressed in terms of the respective national currencies.[23] This means that Canadian costs would be lower than those in the U.S. if labor productivities were equalized but relative wages remained the same, and the U.S. and the Canadian dollar were at parity. This cost advantage varies widely, depending on the wage difference and labor intensity of specific industries. On the one hand, the present Canadian wage advantage represents a total cost advantage of 7 or 8 per cent in the labor-intensive leather and apparel sectors; at the other extreme, the Canadian cost advantage is as low as 1 to 2 per cent in the petroleum and pulp and paper industries in which wages account for a small proportion of total costs.

It should be emphasized that these calculations depend on the assumption that labor productivity in the two countries would become equal in free trade conditions.[24] The observation that average labor productivity in Canada is now lower than in the U.S. provides no useful guideline on this issue; this is due in whole or in part to the limited scale of Canadian production resulting from Canadian and U.S. protection. Hence, it does not follow that in a tariff-free North American economy, labor productivity would be lower in Canada. In terms of inherent characteristics of intelligence, responsibility, and flexibility, it is difficult to argue that there is much difference in the labor force of the two countries, or that the Canadian worker now employed in Detroit is any less efficient than his U.S. counterpart. Comparative studies show little difference in the efficiency of labor in Canada and the U.S.;[25] hence, with identical capital equipment and similar

[23] In fact, the Canadian dollar was at a premium of 2.3 per cent in 1958, and at a discount of 7.8 per cent in 1966.

[24] A further assumption is that present wage differences would be maintained under free trade, and that wage differences also reflect differences in fringe benefits. Indeed, wages and fringe benefits tend to be correlated; moreover, available evidence suggests that differences in fringe benefits have a small impact on wage costs.

[25] John H. Young, "Some Aspects of Canadian Economic Development" (unpublished Ph.D. dissertation, Cambridge University, 1955), pp. 71–73 and 86–87; Mordechai Kreinin, "The Leontief Scarce-Factor Paradox," *American Economic Review* (March, 1965), p. 131; National Industrial Conference Board, *Costs and Competition*, p. 54. For a further discussion (esp. on the issues raised in the Second Annual Report of the Canadian Economic Council), see Wonnacott and Wonnacott, *Free Trade between the United States and Canada*, Chap. 2.

production runs, labor productivity in comparable activities will tend to be the same in the two countries.

Net cost differences and potential effects on U.S.-Canadian trade. According to our results, in comparison with the United States, Canada would have a labor cost advantage, and a smaller capital cost disadvantage under free trade. The impact of transport costs is basically a regional rather than a national one; Ontario and Quebec are almost as well situated as the major U.S. industrial areas, while both are at a substantial advantage vis-à-vis distant regions in either country. This means that any detailed comparison of costs should embrace a regional dimension which is outside the scope of this study.[26] However, useful conclusions can be drawn if the most heavily industrialized areas in the two countries are compared—i.e., Ontario and Quebec *vs.* the Chicago-Boston-Washington triangle. The net effect of the above influences is to leave nine of the thirteen industries at a total cost advantage in Canada, ranging up to 10 per cent. In two industries, neither country would enjoy an advantage, while in the remaining two, the United States has a cost advantage ranging up to 10 per cent.[27] In addition to this, at the time of this writing, there is a 7.5 per cent discount on the Canadian dollar. Depending on the import content of production, this would provide an advantage to Canadian locations of up to 7.5 per cent on total costs. This would imply an expansion of manufacturing in Canada, and high levels of employment and exports. However, the resulting pressure on the Canadian labor force and the balance of payments imply a shift upwards in the Canadian dollar and/or the relative Canadian wage level. This upward shift would eliminate the absolute advantage (in terms of lower costs) in many Canadian industries, leaving lower costs only in industries of comparative advantage.[28] Finally, it should be empha-

[26] For a full regional matrix of costs, see Wonnacott and Wonnacott, *Free Trade between the United States and Canada.* In this study, other cost factors (e.g., proximity to resources) are also analyzed.

[27] On the tripartite division of industries see the last column of Table 3.5.

[28] The degree of equalization of factor prices that might result from free trade has been analyzed in Wonnacott and Wonnacott, Chap. XI. It is sufficient to note here that in the event of successful Canadian rationalization, Canadian real wages should rise toward the U.S. level.

It should be recognized that upward shifts in Canadian wages would take place during the period of rationalization, concurrent with im-

sized that our results depend on the assumption that rationalization and cost reductions will in fact take place in Canadian industry in response to the liberalization of trade.

Implications of an Atlantic Free Trade Area for Canadian Manufacturing Trade with Third Countries

Whereas the major effects of free trade on Canada would come from changes within North America, there would also be substantial effects on Canada's trade with third countries. But, given the expected transformation of the Canadian econ-omy, there is no satisfactory method for analyzing Canada's changing trade with third countries in specific quantitative terms. It is only possible to take account of the major influences that would determine changing Canadian trade patterns, and outline the broad dimensions of change.

The effects of transition to an Atlantic Free Trade Area on Canadian trade with third countries will be described by partitioning the change into three stages:

1. Suppose that factor costs (of labor, capital, etc.) were similar in Canada and the U.S. In these circumstances, what would be the likely effect on Canada's trade *with third countries* of the elimination of trade barriers *between Canada and the United States only,* and the complete rationalization and economic integration of the two economies?

2. Retaining the assumption of equal factor costs, what would be the further effect of tariff elimination in the Atlantic area, i.e., what would be the effect of the elimination of North American tariffs against third countries, and the elimination of third country tariffs against North America?

3. How are these conclusions affected by relaxing the assumption of factor price equality, used as a basis for estimating effects in stages (1) and (2) above? How do present factor cost differences in the two countries affect Canada's

---

provements in Canadian labor productivity. The process of adjustment involves a number of complex issues which have been dealt with in the volume on *Free Trade between the United States and Canada,* but cannot be detailed within the limits of this chapter. For example, the inter-industry pattern of comparative advantage depends on whether the international adjustment takes the form of a shift in relative wages, or the exchange rate, or both. This in turn depends on a number of policy decisions; for example, would the Canadian dollar be fixed or will it be free to fluctuate?

competitive position vis-à-vis the United States in third markets?

Before proceeding further, it is essential to consider the issue of Commonwealth preference, and in particular the mutual preference between Canada and the United Kingdom. In the course of shifting to Atlantic free trade, the U.K. will lose its preference in Canadian markets, and Canada will lose its preference in U.K. markets.

If North American integration in stage (1) were to take the form of a Canada-U.S. free trade area, these preferences might be retained in whole or in part in this initial stage; in such a case they would be completely eliminated only by Atlantic free trade, in stage (2). On the other hand, if Canada and the U.S. were to form a customs union (with a common tariff vis-à-vis the rest of the world), U.K. preference in Canadian markets would be eliminated in this first stage; it is extremely likely in these circumstances that the reciprocal Canadian advantages in U.K. markets would also be cancelled. For estimating purposes, the simpler assumption of a customs union is used in this study, with tariffs in both countries at present U.S. rates.[29]

Effects of U.S.-Canadian integration on Canada's competitive position in third markets. Assuming free trade between Canada and the United States, Canadian industry would be forced onto a competitive footing with present U.S. industry, with costs comparable to the level now prevailing in the United States. It has been established in the previous section that this sort of reorganization would be feasible; Canadian manufacturing would not be likely either to disappear, nor to contract substantially under competitive pressure. A continuing Canadian industry, operating at U.S. cost levels, should be in a position to emulate more closely U.S. export performance in third countries. Furthermore, it would be roughly as vulnerable to imports from these third countries.

[29] It should *not* be inferred from this discussion either that a partitioned move to free trade is being recommended, or that a North American customs union would be in any way preferred to free trade as the first step if such a staging were to be undertaken. It simply makes it easier to think about the problem in this way, and to estimate changes in trade flows accordingly. The entire loss of Canadian–U.K. preference is then viewed as occurring in the formation of the customs union (stage 1), rather than being spread in some undefinable way over stages 1 and 2.

Not only are more competitive Canadian cost levels implied by this change. In addition, the loss of preference in U.K. markets would reduce Canadian exports, and loss of preference in Canadian markets would reduce British exports to Canada. Furthermore, in moving into the present U.S. tariff situation, Canadian tariffs vis-à-vis third countries would change.

It would be extremely difficult to estimate any of these effects individually. However, the direction of their collective effect should be reasonably clear. By moving—in terms of both domestic costs and tariff treatment—from the present Canadian position into what amounts to the present U.S. situation, any change in the Canadian trade balance in manufactured goods would be towards the present U.S. position. Accordingly, one means of inferring the direction of change in the Canadian export-import balance in each item is to compare the present Canadian balance with the present U.S. balance.[30] The direction of this change is shown for each industrial sector in the first column of Table 3.5.[31]

The preponderance of positive signs in this column is a reflection of the fact that U.S. industry now enjoys a more favorable export-import balance than Canadian industry; hence, Canada's competitive performance in third markets

[30] Adjusted by an appropriate scale factor representing the relative trade volume of the two countries. Specifically, the index of the direction of change in Canadian performance is the sign of:

$$(X_{US} - M_{US})Z - (X_{Can} - M_{Can})$$

in which X represents exports to third countries by the subscripted country, and M represents imports by the subscripted country from third countries. Z is a scale factor used to deflate the absolute U.S. trade balance to a level appropriate for comparison with that of Canada, i.e.:

$$Z = \left[\frac{X_{Can} + M_{Can}}{X_{US} + M_{US}} \right].$$

[31] It is reasonable to argue that, as a result of cost reductions, Canadian performance should *more closely* match that of the United States; however, it cannot reasonably be argued that it would *fully* match the U.S. performance. For example, Canada is likely to continue to specialize more heavily than the United States in resource-intensive products, and as a consequence somewhat less heavily in other products. Hence, only the direction of change is shown, but not its magnitude.

TABLE 3.5. EFFECTS OF TRADE LIBERALIZATION ON THE CANADIAN EXPORT/
IMPORT BALANCE IN MANUFACTURED GOODS WITH INDUSTRIAL
COUNTRIES OTHER THAN U.S.

Industry	Stage 1 Effects of moving onto a competitive footing similar to that of the United States	Stage 2 Further effects of freeing trade with other countries	Combined effects of (1) and (2)	Stage 3 Canadian cost advantage (+) or disadvantage (−) vis-à-vis the U.S., (assuming rationalization)
Textile and knitting mills, apparel and related products	+	−	+	+
Lumber and wood products	+	−	+	+
Pulp and paper products	−	−	−	*
Printing and publishing	+	+	+	+
Electrical machinery and apparatus	+	−	+	+
Chemical products	+	+	+	*
Petroleum and coal products	+	+	+	−
Rubber and plastics	+	+	+	+
Leather and leather products	+	−	−	+
Nonmetallic mineral products	+	−	+	−
Metal products and non-electrical machinery	+	+	+	+
Transport equipment	+	+	+	+
Miscellaneous	+	−	+	+

Source: R. J. Wonnacott and Paul Wonnacott, *Free Trade between the United States and Canada:
the Potential Economic Effects.*
* Either + or −, depending on the regions in each country that are compared.

would tend to improve if Canadian firms were producing in a
North American market on an equal footing with U.S. firms
and at similar cost levels. The explanation is simple. Canadian
costs are now higher than in the U.S. largely because of scale
effects; hence, Canadian firms often have difficulty competing
against U.S. imports, even in the protected Canadian market.
It is even more difficult to compete in third markets in which
they do not receive preferred treatment.[32]

To the extent that Canadian costs come down with the
rationalization of North American industry, and both import-competing and export industries in Canada more
closely match U.S. performance, the Canadian export-import
balance in manufactures would tend to improve. Such a result
implies that the negative effects on export-import balance of

[32] Canadian exports, of course, get preference over U.S. exports in
Commonwealth markets; but even this often provides less of an edge
over their U.S. competitors than they receive in the Canadian market.

loss of Canadian preference in U.K. markets would be more than offset by the positive[33] effects of Canadian rationalization and cost reduction.[34]

Effects of tariff elimination between North America and third countries. Since Canadian industry has been viewed as having passed in stage (1) into a situation similar to that of U.S. industry, it might be expected to respond to tariff reductions with third countries in much the same way. Projections on changes in the trade balance following the liberalization of trade have been derived from the chapter on the United States by M. E. Kreinin. The change for each Canadian industry should be in the same direction as that for the corresponding U.S. industry, although the magnitude of the change will differ because of the differing size of production and trade in the two countries.[35] The direction (sign) of this change is shown in column 2 of Table 3.5. In this case, the pattern is decidedly mixed; in some categories, imports would expand more rapidly than exports, while in others the reverse would be true.

Only the direction of change is shown in columns 1 and 2 of Table 3.5, since the numerical estimates do not warrant more precise interpretation. However, since roughly comparable estimates for both columns have been derived in the process, the net effect may be computed for each industry; this is shown in column 3.

In many instances, the signs in columns 1 and 2 are similar. It is more revealing to consider the instances in which these two effects operate in different directions. Of the six such instances, five of the signs in the composite column retain the sign appearing in column 1. This implies that under the assumptions made in this study, the major potential

[33] The adjectives "positive" and "negative" are used in this discussion as purely descriptive terms, signifying the sign of the change in the index in Table 3.5. No normative significance should be implied.

[34] And the U.K. loss of preference in Canadian markets.

[35] On the assumption that the Canadian trade response will be similar to that of the U.S. except of smaller absolute dimension, the effect on the Canadian balance of trade in any item would be:

$$(\Delta X_{US} - \Delta M_{US})Z$$

in which ΔX_{US} and ΔM_{US} represent respectively the change in U.S. exports to, and imports from, third countries estimated by Kreinin, and Z is the scale factor defined in the n. 30 on p. 72 above.

change in Canadian export performance with third countries would come, not as a result of tariff reductions with third countries (stage 2), but as a result of the improved competitive posture of Canadian industry following North American integration (stage 1).

Effects of U.S.-Canadian cost differences on Canada's competitive position vis-à-vis the United States in third markets. The computations in stages 1 and 2 were based on the assumption that total costs (including factor costs and transport costs) would be the same under free trade for producers in both Canada and the United States. But it is evident from the discussion in the third section that this assumption must be relaxed. Under the assumption that labor productivity in Canada reached the U.S. level while present wage differences were maintained, Canadian producers would have a cost advantage in many industries, with lower Canadian wage costs more than compensating for higher transport and capital costs. This cost advantage (+) or disadvantage (−) is shown (by industry) in the last column of Table 3.5, with an asterisk representing those ambiguous cases in which costs may be lower in either Canada or the U.S., depending on which regions in the two countries are compared.

Since there are no instances in which the signs in both of the last two columns of this table are negative, Canadian industrial sectors can be divided into two groups. (1) Those sectors in which the two indices differ in sign; in these cases there is no clear indication of the likely expansion or contraction of the industry; (2) those cases in which both indices point to Canadian expansion. A majority (eight out of thirteen) of the sectors fall in the latter category, indicating an improvement in Canadian export performance in manufactured goods under the assumption of unchanged wage rates and exchange rates.

The ability of Canadian industry to compete is further increased by the cost advantage provided by the current discount on the Canadian dollar. But, as we have noted earlier, in the process of adjustment wages will rise and/or the exchange rate will appreciate in Canada. Correspondingly, the results in Table 3.5 do not show the eventual pattern of specialization in Canadian industry but provide an indication of the competitive position of the rationalized Canadian industry under the stated assumptions. Still, it can be inferred that Canada will have comparative advantage in *some* of the eight industries in which both indicators point to expansion. It should be added, however, that the experience of the industrial countries indicates the predominance of intra-industry as against inter-industry specialization. Thus, Canadian specialization is more likely to occur *within* industrial categories, rather than *between* them. In particular, Canadian firms are likely to specialize in resource- and labor-intensive subsectors of the above industries.[36]

Two special issues.

1. *Elimination of Commonwealth preference.* Placing Canada in circumstances similar to the United States (in stage 1) involves, among other things, eliminating Canadian preference in the United Kingdom, and U.K. preference in Canada. It may be of interest to indicate the commodities most likely to be affected by this one change alone.

The largest Canadian export to the U.K. in 1963 was $162 million of wheat, a commodity outside the limits of this study. However, there are a number of other Canadian exports in the range of $25–$100 million. These include industrial materials such as pulp, shaped wood, iron ore concentrates, nonferrous metal ores, and unwrought copper and aluminum, which were considered in the second section. Major Canadian exports of manufactured goods are chemicals, machinery, transport equipment, and wood products.[37] The largest of these

[36] Cf. Wonnacott and Wonnacott, *Free Trade between the United States and Canada,* Chap. 11.

[37] In 1963, selected Canadian exports of manufactures to the United Kingdom and Canadian preference in U.K. markets were:

SITC No.			Canadian exports to U. K. (million $)	U. K. average m. f. n. tariff rate (per cent)
5		Chemicals	27.6	15.0
6		Basic manufactures		
	631	Veneers, plywood, etc.	18.3	14.5
	641.1	Newsprint	63.7	0
	641.2–9	Other paper and paperboard	30.2	18.0
7		Machinery, transport equipment	33.8	20.0

Sources: Exports: United Nations *Commodity Trade Statistics,* 1963. Tariffs: Political and Economic Planning *Atlantic Tariffs and Trade* (London, 1962).

items—newsprint—enters the United Kingdom duty free from all sources. Others are dutiable if they come from non-Commonwealth countries, while Canadian exports are not subject to tariff. Such Canadian exports would clearly be sensitive to the elimination of preferences; this is especially true in machinery and transport equipment in which Canada now receives strongest preferential treatment. Other non-Commonwealth sources of supply not only exist, but are now servicing the British market over relatively high tariffs.

U.K. exports to Canada include only one major raw material item (wool), along with a wide range of manufactured goods including motor vehicles, power machinery, and textiles.[38] Canadian preference rates on these latter manufactured items range between 0–15 per cent; corresponding tariffs on imports from non-Commonwealth sources are often higher, and range between 0–25 per cent. For example, autos enter Canada from the U.K. duty free under preference, but pay a 17.5 per cent tariff from other countries.[39] Wherever these two rates vary substantially, U.K. exports to Canada would be vulnerable if preference were to disappear; other non-Commonwealth sources of supply exist and are competing successfully in the Canadian market despite the discrimination they now face. Accordingly, British exports would suffer as a result of the elimination of Commonwealth preference.

2. *Elimination of EEC discrimination.* The potential effect of an Atlantic free trade area on Canada is not only the net change it would bring in Canada's *present* trading position; in addition, by preempting the Common Market scheme, an AFTA would prevent the trade diversion of Common Market imports from Canada to EEC sources that is now taking place.

By far the largest Canadian export to the EEC is food grains, especially wheat ($112 million in 1963). This area of Canadian vulnerability, however, is outside the scope of this study. Some other Canadian exports (e.g., synthetic rubber, and unwrought copper and nickel) receive duty-free access to the Common Market, and do not face discrimination. A num-

[38] In 1963, U.K. exports to Canada totaled $20–$30 million in each of these categories.
[39] The United States is an exception. Under the recent bilateral agreement between the United States and Canada, auto producers in both countries receive (conditional) duty-free access to the other.

ber of exports are, however, discriminated against; among them, aluminum is the most important.[40] Still, the trade affected by EEC discrimination is only a small proportion of Canadian exports.

Some Implications of Alternative Proposals

In this section the implications of three other proposals will be considered: partial tariff reductions by all AFTA countries through successive rounds of tariff bargaining under the most-favored-nation clause; a North Atlantic free trade area in which the European Economic Community does not participate; and finally, European integration in a free trade area excluding the United States, Canada and Japan.

Successive rounds of tariff reductions under m.f.n. There are three reasons why such an alternative would be less satisfactory than the Atlantic Free Trade Area from the Canadian point of view. In the first place, Common Market discrimination against Canadian exports would be completely preempted by AFTA, but only partially prevented by the limited tariff-cuts likely to follow multilateral trade negotiations. Second, partial

---

[40] Canadian-manufactured exports to the Common Market in 1960 (the last year prior to the introduction of substantial discrimination by internal EEC tariff reductions) were as follows:

SITC No.			Canadian exports to the EEC (million $)	Approximate EEC tariff (per cent)
5		Chemicals	8.5	12
6		Basic manufactures	129.7	
	682	Copper[a]	23.7	0
	683	Nickel[a]	28.8	0
	684	Aluminum[a]	50.1	10
		Other basic manufactures	27.1	13
7		Machinery and transport equipment	27.2	
	714	Office machines	5.0	14
	721	Electrical machinery	6.5	16
		Other machinery and transport equipment	15.7	14
8		Miscellaneous manufactures	2.3	

[a] Mostly unwrought.

Sources: Trade Flows: *United Nations Community Trade Statistics.* Tariffs: Political and Economic Planning, *Atlantic Tariffs and Trade.*

tariff elimination would result, at best, in only a partial reorganization of industry; Canadian resources could not be efficiently allocated if barriers to trade (such as U.S. tariffs) remained. Third, even in the event that successive "Kennedy Rounds" resulted in the complete elimination of tariffs, it would be a less efficient route to this goal than an AFTA treaty.

The reason for this last conclusion is that the major problem for Canadian industry is reorganization. And the key is entry into the U.S. market. The question is, "On what terms?" To facilitate long-run planning by business, it is imperative that these terms be clarified as early as possible, in order to keep expectations clear and stable. A treaty commitment to eventually eliminate tariffs keeps elements of uncertainty at a minimum; but a succession of bargaining rounds leaves the outcome of each round, as well as the over-all result, in considerable doubt. Thus, Canadian firms might become caught up in a series of costly reorganizations, rather than once-and-for-all revamping their facilities. In the latter case, Canadian resources might eventually be allocated efficiently but the reallocation process would involve additional costs.

Furthermore, the uncertainty surrounding the eventual outcome of these bargaining rounds might prevent Canadian industry from being reorganized. If the tariff reductions achieved in the Kennedy Round are within the limits that may reasonably be assumed at the date of this writing (between 25 and 50 per cent), Canadian industry may attempt to continue with present techniques. This degree of tariff reduction might be insufficient either to induce or to enforce Canadian reorganization, while the lack of guarantees on further reductions in duties would remove the incentive for change that would exist under an AFTA treaty. Correspondingly, potential benefits to Canada could go unrealized, with remaining inefficiency in the Canadian production structure reflected in a continued lower real income in Canada, as compared to the United States.

Any empirical projection of Canadian trade performance requires a key assumption about the extent of Canadian industry rationalization. Since there is no indication whatsoever of the degree of reorganization and cost reduction that would occur in Canada in the event of successive tariff reductions under m.f.n., there are no clear guidelines for judging the impact on Canadian merchandise trade. However, the improvement in Canadian performance will certainly be less than that envisaged in the third and fourth sections since the analysis there was based on the assumption of a fully rationalized Canadian industry, operating in a completely unrestricted free trade area.

It should be emphasized that this should *not* in any way be construed as an argument against the current negotiations. This discussion simply suggests that, on purely economic grounds, another alternative would be preferable to rounds of tariff reductions. But the establishment of an Atlantic free trade area may not be feasible for some time, while the Kennedy Round has succeeded and others may follow. Furthermore, there are three political advantages for Canada in successive rounds of tariff reductions under m.f.n.: (1) Canadian opinion may be mobilized behind a gradual program, but may not accept a drastic change such as AFTA would entail; (2) the Commonwealth preference system might be retained, although the extent of preferences would decrease; (3) the less-developed countries would automatically benefit from tariff reductions under the most-favored-nation clause. This is in marked contrast to the discrimination they would face if a North American free trade area or an AFTA were to be established.

Free trade among industrial countries excluding the Common Market. From the Canadian point of view, there are two major disadvantages of excluding the EEC countries from AFTA. First, the impending Common Market discrimination against Canadian exports would continue. Second, gains from reciprocal tariff reductions with the EEC countries would be foregone. The first of these effects on Canadian exports has already been discussed. The second can be analyzed by comparing the effects of a free trade area excluding the EEC with the effects of a full AFTA. The direction of the initial effects (in column 1, Table 3.5) generated by U.S.-Canadian free trade would be similar in either case. However, the effects of further free trade between North America and other countries (column 2) would be different, since the list of other participants would be more restricted. As before, Canadian performance under these conditions was projected by referring to U.S. estimates—in this case, U.S. figures which exclude EEC participation.[41] The results were almost identical to those shown in Table 3.5.

European integration. This proposal would involve the integration of the EEC and EFTA into a broader European common market; Canada, the U.S., and Japan would be excluded. In comparison with AFTA, two major Canadian disadvantages may be identified.

First, Canadian exports would face discrimination in European markets, with a resulting diversion of European purchases from Canadian sources to European sources. This would apply not only to Canadian exports to the present EEC, but also to Canadian exports to areas like Scandinavia and the United Kingdom.[42] Second, and more important, Canada and the United States would not be reducing their tariffs mutually; hence, Canadian industry would continue to operate under its present levels of efficiency, and the potential gains that might result from the rationalization of North American manufacturing would be foregone. On the other hand, integration in Western Europe might give an impetus to establishing a free trade area in North America.

Economic Alternatives and the Question of Political Independence

In purely economic terms, there is a strong Canadian case for initially undertaking free trade with the U.S. alone.[43] It is

[41] Specifically, the estimating equation in the n. 35 on p. 74 was used; the estimates used for ΔX_{US} and ΔM_{US} were those figures in the U.S. chapter on changing flows in which the EEC was not included.

It should be noted that elimination of Commonwealth preference is formally taken into account in this sort of procedure. (See the fourth section, above.) However, since the elimination of tariffs would be confined to a smaller number of countries, the attendant loss of Commonwealth preference would also be less comprehensive. Thus, for example, Canada would lose its present preferred position in the U.K. over the U.S., but retain its preferred position over France. In fact, Canadians may find it easier to understand the implications of the proposal by simply viewing it as a redefinition of the Commonwealth preference system to include the United States, AFTA, and Japan.

[42] Two Canadian problems would be involved in this case—loss of present preference in the U.K. market, *and* the new discrimination (or reverse preference) against Canadian exports.

[43] Along the lines suggested in *A Possible Plan for a Canadian-U.S. Free Trade Area,* Canadian-American Committee, 1965.

true that third country benefits would be foregone during the interim period; nevertheless, there are a number of special advantages in such a scheme.

The key to the future for Canadian manufacturing is success in getting onto a competitive footing with U.S. industry; this holds true for any of the above free-trade schemes which include Canada and the United States. However, it may be easier for Canadian industry to manage this adjustment, if only Canada and the United States eliminated tariffs. If Europe and Japan are included, there is no guarantee that Canada will not be bypassed in the process of international rationalization. The Canadian advantage vis-à-vis the U.S. is in terms of lower wage costs. But if the free trade area includes other countries with even lower wages, they might very well preempt many of the labor-intensive activities that might otherwise locate in Canada.[44] This possibility is strongly implied by the evidence on possible trends in capital movements shown in the survey described in Chapter 2 of this volume.

It is also evident that rationalization would involve large elements of risk for Canada. If only the United States and Canada were included, the Canadian problem would involve adjustment to present U.S. cost levels; these can fairly reasonably be regarded as fixed by Canadian producers attempting to get onto a competitive basis, since opening the relatively small Canadian market is unlikely to provide U.S. firms with many economies of scale or other opportunities to cut costs that they

[44] To be more precise, it is necessary to distinguish three categories of labor-intensive activity that Canada would attract under free trade with the U.S. only. The first is the set of activities which would go elsewhere (e.g., Japan) under AFTA; the second is a set which could go either to Japan or Canada under AFTA, but because of inertia would tend to remain wherever they are initially established; the third is the set which should go to Canada in any case. In a world of perfect information, the argument in the text can apply only to Set 2. Set 3 will come to Canada in any case, and there is little point in temporarily establishing Set 1 in Canada only to lose it later when the free trade area is broadened; indeed, this may involve substantial costs.

However, information is never perfect, especially when the adjustment process depends on (unknown) future changes in wage and exchange levels; hence, it is quite possible Canada might simply be overlooked as a location by businessmen preoccupied with the more critical issue of deciding which activities should be located in the U.S., which in Europe, and which in Japan. In this case, the second (and perhaps even the third) set of activities might not be established in Canada.

do not already enjoy. But if Europe and Japan are included, many new dimensions of uncertainty are involved, and Canadian industry will have to adjust to compete with present European and Japanese as well as U.S. producers.[45] The chief obstacle of such a scheme is its possible political implications, and in particular the fear that Canada might drift into political union with the U.S. It is not now true, as it may perhaps have been at one time, that almost all Canadians are strongly opposed to closer political ties with the U.S. However, the best evidence[46] is that a majority oppose such a move, and current Canadian policy is now aimed at maintaining Canadian independence.

But a fundamental point is often missed in public debate: various forms of economic integration would have quite different political implications.

1. A free trade area would result in minimum loss of political autonomy. It would entail the elimination of tariffs, and a consequent increase in trade flows between the two countries. In a sense, with markets more heavily concentrated in the United States, Canadian vulnerability to loss of these markets would be increased. However, in another respect Canadian vulnerability would be reduced, since for the first time Canada would acquire a treaty commitment from the U.S. not to raise tariffs against Canadian goods. Such a treaty obligation should be viewed by Canada as a necessary condition for entering a free trade arrangement, as the only guarantee that the restructuring of Canadian industry can take place under firm and stable long run expectations.

2. If the two countries were to form a customs union, a greater loss of autonomy would be involved. The necessity of adopting a common tariff policy with third countries would inevitably restrict each country in this policy dimension; furthermore, given the relative size and bargaining power of

[45] From strictly the Canadian point of view, there is one other possible advantage of co-operating with the U.S. as a first step in a general move toward free trade. It may be argued that if only the U.S. is involved, Canada may be more likely to receive special treatment of the kind suggested by the Canadian-American Committee in their plan calling for U.S. tariff reductions of 20 per cent per year, but Canadian reduction of only 10 per cent. See their Report, *A Possible Plan for a Canadian-U.S. Free Trade Area*, 1965.

[46] See, for example, the survey undertaken by *MacLean's Magazine*, June 6, 1964.

the two countries, Canadian loss of control over tariffs would greatly exceed that of the United States. In addition, a customs union would leave no flexibility whatsoever for continued Canadian participation in the Commonwealth preference system; nor would it allow each country to independently determine the level of its tariffs on trade with less developed countries.

3. Further loss of autonomy would be involved in the formation of a common currency area. The management of a single currency would involve setting up a single North American central bank or, as a bare minimum, extremely close monetary co-ordination between the central banks of the two countries. In either case, the relative size of the two economies implies a more rigid limitation of freedom of action by the monetary authorities in Canada than in the U.S. Furthermore, since monetary policy and debt management are so closely related, monetary co-ordination would severely restrict Canadian fiscal freedom—for example, in incurring budget deficits.

The conclusion is that various types of economic integration involve loss of political autonomy of varying degrees, but that of all these schemes, free trade would involve minimum political implications. Moreover, there is no automatic escalation process involved in a free trade area; EFTA was designed as a free trade area, with a minimum of political overtones, and it has remained that way; on the other hand, the Common Market was designed to eventually include political integration, and moves in this direction can now be observed. Whether or not a U.S.-Canadian free trade would lead to some form of political union, or even to a more advanced form of economic integration, would still depend on what the public in both countries viewed to be desirable. Trade dependence does not inevitably lead to political union; were this so, the two countries would long since have been united. At the same time, it should be recognized that closer economic integration may influence people's political views—either to corrupt or enlighten, depending on whether one prefers the old or new set of preferences.

In politics, the public's view of reality may be of more consequence than reality itself. The idea that trade inevitably leads to political integration has become very important in Canadian politics. In a recent election campaign, diversion of

Canadian trade away from the United States and towards the United Kingdom was an important plank in the platform of one of the major political parties. That party's subsequent success in the election may, at least in part, have been the result of the intellectual simplicity and emotional attraction of such a program.

It is the traditional Canadian fear of being pulled, by some sort of undefined centripetal force, into the U.S. orbit that has inclined Canadians toward a wider free trade arrangement, including the counterbalance of the United Kingdom and continental Europe. Moreover, current opinion in Quebec seems to favor the inclusion of France.

It may be concluded that Canadian political and economic considerations in regard to alternative trade arrangements are in conflict. Politically, Canadians prefer the counterbalancing effect of tariff reductions by a broad grouping of nations, such as an Atlantic Free Trade Area. However, from an economic point of view, the transition to multilateral free trade might best be accomplished by a first step of North American integration. This would provide most of the potential free trade gains, while keeping adjustment risks at a minimum.

CHAPTER IV

TRADE ARRANGEMENTS AMONG INDUSTRIAL COUNTRIES: EFFECTS ON THE COMMON MARKET

F. Hartog[1]

Political Aspects

In considering the implications of Atlantic trade liberalization for the European Common Market, some special problems arise, since we deal with a group of countries which are themselves in the process of economic integration. Thus, on the one hand, there is no necessary uniformity in the attitudes of these countries towards Atlantic co-operation, and, on the other, their ideas on the question are likely to be influenced by their experience with European integration. Correspondingly, a compromise has to be found between a country-by-country approach, and the study of the Common Market as a unit. We will start out with the second approach, and will introduce considerations relating to individual countries at a later point.

In the present section, the relationships between political and economic considerations will be examined. Subsequently, we will focus on the main influences that appear to play a role in the case when integration takes place in an area, the constituent parts of which are themselves composed of national units. In the third section, the possible consequences of Atlantic trade liberalization for the manufacturing industries of the EEC countries are discussed, while questions relating to nontariff barriers, agriculture, and U.S. investments in the Common Market are dealt with separately. Finally, the concluding

[1] The author is professor of economics at the University of Groningen. He is indebted to H. Kraaijeveld, of The European Institute, University of Amsterdam, who contributed to the final drafting of the last three sections and the composition of the tables, and to P. G. Dekker and J. C. Reuyl of the Institute of Economic Research, University of Groningen, who assisted him in research and made some of the calculations underlying the study.

87

section considers alternative trade arrangements in the Atlantic area from the point-of-view of the EEC countries.

There is little doubt that problems of trade liberalization cannot be discussed in purely economic terms. The decision to liberalize trade is influenced by political factors, and in its turn, it affects the political sphere. At the same time, political and economic factors may reinforce one another, or political influences may hamper the liberalization of trade. These relationships will be considered in the European context, and references will also be made to the implications of the European experience for the Atlantic area.

It is significant that the idea of a united Europe in its original form was purely political. It was born as a Pan-European movement, aiming at a European federation, in the 1920s. At that time, it had no appeal for the masses, and was restricted to a small group of intellectuals and a few political leaders.

In the years following World War II, the European idea received new impetus. It was a response to the nationalism which had led to the war, and—to use Toynbee's famous phrase—the dwarfing of European countries by the two giants, the United States and the Soviet Union. At the Congress held in The Hague in May, 1948, leading statesmen of Europe came together to discuss the objectives and problems of European unification. This Congress had two important consequences: national movements for European unity established close co-operation, and the governments of the principal Western European countries set up the Council of Europe at Strasbourg. In subsequent years, the groundwork was laid for further advances in the field of European integration. European-minded politicians—among them, Konrad Adenauer, Alcide de Gasperi, Robert Schuman, and Paul-Henri Spaak—had a dominant influence over their respective countries. Moreover, public opinion has come to favor, to a greater or lesser degree, the idea of European unity.

Thus, historically speaking, three stages can be distinguished in the development of the European idea: it had originated in the intellectual sphere, it was subsequently adopted by politicians, and later, it exerted an influence on public opinion. From the results of the Gallup poll (reproduced in Table 4.1), it appears that the idea of European

TABLE 4.1. PERCENTAGES FOR AND AGAINST EUROPEAN
INTEGRATION, 1960
GALLUP POLL

	Germany	Belgium	France	Italy	Nether-lands	Luxem-bourg
For	81	65	72	60	87	27
Against	4	5	8	4	4	5
No answer	15	30	20	36	9	68
	100	100	100	100	100	100

Source: P. M. G. Levy, "Opinion publique et l'Europe," *European Yearbook,* Strasbourg, Council of Europe (1962), p. 185. Also in *Sondages,* Revue française de l'opinion publique (1963), No. 1.

integration is approved by a large majority in all of the EEC countries. It should be noted, however, that this inquiry was undertaken at the time when the six countries had already started on the road towards integration. Thus, the favorable attitude taken towards European unity has been influenced by the experience of the Common Market. In so far as this is the case, the public support for European integration appears as a *result* as well as a *cause*.[2] One may make a distinction therefore, between the original European idea, and the more or less "derived" common market idea.

After the launching of the idea of a united Europe at the end of the 1940s, it took some years before the political and the economic aspects of European co-operation were combined. "Political" Europe was located in Strasbourg, and "economic" Europe in Paris, where the Organization for European Economic Co-operation concentrated its activities on the liberalization of intra-European trade and payments. But it soon became clear that the separation of the political and economic approaches could advance the cause of European unification only to a certain point. The Council of Europe did not produce concrete plans for European integration, and the OEEC did not progress beyond the removal of restrictions on trade and payments.

The initiatives for European economic integration did not

[2] Ernst B. Haas gives an interesting view of this development, when he describes the evolution—within the group of six—in the gradual acceptance of the European Coal and Steel Community by the major political parties, employers' associations, and trade unions during the first years of its existence. See E. B. Haas, *The Uniting of Europe* (Stanford University Press, 1958), Chaps. 8–11.

come from either of the existing organizations. Benelux had already come into existence as a customs union in 1948. A further important step was taken in 1950 when Robert Schuman proposed the integration of the coal and steel industries of France, Germany, and any other European states that wished to join this group. However, besides France and Germany, only Italy and the Benelux countries were willing to participate.

The establishment of the Coal and Steel Community meant a deepening of economic co-operation in the European area, but this was accomplished at the expense of division in Western Europe. At the same time, the composition of the ECSC can in part be explained by reference to geographical and historical factors. To begin with, the six countries more or less form a geographical entity. Also, their economies were greatly affected by the devastation of World War II, and the integration of their coal and steel industries appeared to facilitate the task of rebuilding and reconstruction. Moreover, the French were worried about the implications of transferring the Ruhr industry from the Allied Ruhr Authority to Germany, while the Germans considered the establishment of the Coal and Steel Community as an important step in regaining their national sovereignty. For the rest, it may safely be said that the essentially political objective of Franco-German reconciliation was the main motivating influence.

Subsequently, it was proposed to establish a European defense community that would be guided by a European political authority and an assembly elected by direct suffrage. This political approach received a setback in 1954 when the French parliament rejected the EDC Treaty. Correspondingly, in the following years, the economic aspects of European integration were emphasized: in 1955, the Messina Conference of Foreign Ministers decided to study the possibilities of creating a Common Market and an Atomic Energy Community. Since the forces setting in motion the establishment of the Common Market largely coincided with those which led to the creation of the ECSC, it was only natural that the same group of countries took this step. While Britain participated in the earlier stages of the negotiations, for the sake of avoiding limitations on her national sovereignty she subsequently decided against becoming a member.

Later developments in the Common Market, and in the

sphere of European integration, are too well-known to be recounted here. It should be added, however, that the period since the EEC's establishment has provided ample evidence of the interdependence of economics and politics. The negotiations on British entry, the controversy concerning the common agricultural policy, and the discussions on the role of the EEC Commission and on the ways and means of political co-operation all provide evidence of this interdependence. The experience of the Common Market, then, shows the need for considering the political implications of trade liberalization in the Atlantic area.

In this connection, a few words should be said about attitudes towards Atlantic arrangements among the EEC countries. It is well known that France is opposed to political solutions in the Atlantic area because she fears that the United States would have the dominant voice in such a scheme. On the other hand, smaller countries—especially the Netherlands—favor wider arrangements, since the probability of their being dominated by one or two nations decreases thereby. As Duncan points out, small states are naturally inclined to favor larger groupings in order to increase their maneuverability.[3] But the small country–large country dichotomy should not be carried too far, since the German position is rather different from the one taken by France. In addition to defense, the Germans want American support for the eventual reunification of their nation. The question should further be raised as to how Britain's participation might affect the position taken by the EEC towards Atlantic arrangements. While it is often assumed that Britain would take a pro-American stance, this assumption may not be realistic. Rather, the establishment of a powerful Europe may lead to an emphasis on particular European objectives. The outcome will then depend on the relative strength of the centrifugal and the centripetal forces.

Regional Arrangements and Their Implication: the Jigsaw Puzzle

The Atlantic area may be compared to a huge jigsaw puzzle, when the question is how the fitting together of separate elements is facilitated or hindered by the formation of larger

[3] G. A. Duncan, "The Small State and International Economic Equilibrium," *Economia Internazionale* (November, 1950).

pieces like the European Common Market. At the same time, the experience of the Common Market may give some indication of the main influences which will affect the outcome. Among the positive influences, the demonstration effect and the leverage effect can be distinguished.

As regards the *demonstration effect,* the point should be stressed that through regional economic co-operation, experience is gained which can be used profitably in the building of larger structures. The EEC benefited from two experiments in European economic integration, the Benelux and the European Coal and Steel Community, for example. Such experience relates to the process of decision-making, as well as to the reactions of business and labor to the broadening of the market. Thus, the lack of frictions in the increase of mutual trade and specialization in the Common Market provides a reason for optimism in regard to the adaptation of business enterprises to trade liberalization in the Atlantic area.

Regional economic co-operation may also pave the way for broader forms of trade liberalization through the *leverage effect.* Nonmember states, who have important economic interests in trade relations with the partner countries, will want to escape discrimination against their exports that the establishment of a union entails and are induced to search for solutions which would broaden the area of economic integration. Following the formation of the EEC, the United Kingdom first proposed creating a large European free trade area, and later applied for entry into the Common Market. In the meantime, the European Free Trade Association was created, in large part to increase the bargaining power of European countries outside the EEC and to facilitate the merger of the two groups at a later date. The American proposal for the Kennedy Round of tariff negotiations can also be considered an answer to the Common Market's establishment, and an effort to decrease discrimination against American products in the EEC.

So far, we have considered the positive influences of the EEC as an extension of trade liberalization. There are also several negative factors. One of these is the element of time, which is needed for the enlargement of the scale of European production. It is often argued that the Common Market should first be *consolidated,* and industry has to adapt itself to the requirements of the larger market of the EEC before it can face the competition of American enterprises. In a narrower interpretation, the consolidation argument might be applied to new European industries, like the computer industry. This is a modern version of the infant-industry argument, and as such, it has a certain validity. On the other hand, the general argument for consolidation is open to criticism.

As a consequence of the mutual preferential treatment within the EEC, some imports are shifting from the United States to member countries. If, at a later stage, trade restrictions between the U.S. and the Common Market are liberalized, part of this trade will shift back to the old channels. This makes the two-step adaptation more costly than a direct realization of wider division of labor. At present, while the process of European adaptation is still under way, it would be easier to graft upon this process an adaptation to trade liberalization in the Atlantic area. On the other hand, should consolidation on a European scale be achieved first, business interests might raise objections to reopening the process of reorientation that has a cost in the form of uncertainty and changes in the structure of production.

More important as a negative influence is the possibility that a union may become *inward-looking*. In the Common Market, the framing of common policy has given rise to such tendencies in certain areas. While the co-ordination of economic policies enhances the effects of trade liberalization, and accentuates the personality of the Common Market by focusing attention on internal problems, it may come into conflict with the interests of outsiders. These considerations apply especially to common agricultural policy, and to relations with the overseas-associated territories. We will return to these questions at a later point.

Lastly, the compromises which are reached in the process of integration may make the admission of new partners difficult. The subtle equilibria, which are achieved by taking into account the objectives of the individual member countries, are easily upset if new members are admitted. This was apparent in the course of the negotiations on British entry into the Common Market. And it must be feared that the entrance fee, in the form of adherence to common regulations, may become higher as the co-ordination of economic policies proceeds.

In conclusion, various influences appear to be at work as far as the external relations of the Common Market are concerned. The consolidation argument particularly relates to industrial imports, while the protectionist consequences of common policy pertain to agricultural imports. Contrary to these negative forces on Atlantic trade liberalization, the leverage effect is a positive factor, and so is the experience gained in regard to the beneficial effects of integration. And while the structure of production in the EEC may become more rigid in the process of its consolidation, conflicts among national states may hinder an outward-looking attitude to a lesser extent after this consolidation will have been completed. Also, it may be easier for other countries to deal with one negotiating partner than with six countries. But an optimistic conclusion can be reached only if economic arguments are not misused for political purposes, so as to serve as a pretext for the unwillingness of certain countries to enlarge the Common Market on political grounds.

Economic Effects of Atlantic Trade Liberalization for the EEC

It is expected that the removal of trade barriers among the countries of the Atlantic area will improve the division of labor between them. This improvement is usually considered to be caused by static and dynamic factors. In a static sense, a reallocation of productive resources will take place; in a dynamic sense, the enlargement of national markets permits the exploitation of large-scale economies and provides a challenge for increasing productivity by intensifying competitive pressures.

Static effects. The static effects of trade liberalization can be estimated on the basis of data on trade flows, import duties, and reasonable assumptions on import demand and export supply elasticities. As indicated in Chapter I of this volume, two alternative estimates have been prepared, reflecting the assumptions made in regard to the responsiveness of export supply to price changes in the individual countries. Under Variant I, it was assumed that by reason of the high share of exports in domestic production and full-employment conditions in Western Europe, the export prices of manufactured goods in European countries would rise by one-third of the tariff reduction, while exports would be supplied at constant prices in the other industrial countries. In turn, under Variant II, constant export prices are assumed everywhere. The latter assumption applies also to industrial materials under both variants.

TABLE 4.2. ESTIMATED EXPANSION OF COMMON MARKET
TRADE IN AN ATLANTIC FREE TRADE AREA

(MILLION $)

	Variant I[a]			Variant II[a]		
	Exports	Imports	Balance	Exports	Imports	Balance
Trade with industrial countries, 1960						
Industrial materials	554	2,096	−1,542	554	2,096	−1,542
Manufactures	6,689	4,226	+2,463	6,689	4,226	+2,463
Together	7,243	6,322	+ 921	7,243	6,322	+ 921
Direct effects of AFTA						
Industrial materials	18	45	− 28	18	46	− 28
Manufactures	1,421	1,047	+ 374	1,802	1,197	+ 605
Together:	1,439	1,093	+ 346	1,820	1,243	+ 577
of which, United States	561	473	+ 88	706	473	+ 233
Canada	58	21	+ 37	68	21	+ 47
United Kingdom	322	233	+ 89	409	296	+ 113
Continental EETA	452	337	+ 115	580	424	+ 156
Japan	46	29	+ 17	57	29	+ 28
Elimination of EEC and EFTA discrimination[b]	297	814	− 517	297	814	− 517

Source: See Appendix to Chap. 1.
Notes: [a] *Variant I* assumes increases in European export prices of manufactured goods by one-third of the tariff reductions, while constant export prices are assumed elsewhere. The latter assumption pertains to all exporting areas under *Variant II*.
 [b] The country breakdown of the relevant figures are: *Exports:* United Kingdom, $78 million; Continental EFTA, $219 million *Imports:* United States, $311 million; Canada, $11 million; United Kingdom, $198 million; Continental EFTA, $275 million; Japan, $19 million.

The estimates relating to the Common Market are summarized in Table 4.2. It appears that depending on the variant chosen, the direct effects of the establishment of an Atlantic free trade area would entail a 20 to 25 per cent rise in the combined exports of industrial materials and manufactured goods from the Common Market to the other industrial countries, while the corresponding figures for imports are 17 to 20 per cent. The differences in the estimates are due to international differences in regard to the composition of exports and imports, the height of tariffs, and the responsiveness of import demand and export supply to price changes. Among these, the relatively small share of industrial materials in the exports and their large share in the imports of the EEC countries appears to be the principal influence. In 1960, the base year of the estimates, industrial materials accounted for less than 8 per cent of Common Market exports as against one-third of imports. Tariffs and the elasticity of import demand being much lower in the case of industrial materials than for manufactured goods, this circumstance tends to favor the balance of trade of the Common Market countries in the event of trade liberalization among the industrial nations.

The abolition of EEC and EFTA discrimination in an Atlantic free trade area points in the opposite direction. While Common Market discrimination has been estimated to entail a decrease in imports from nonparticipating countries of $814 million, discrimination in the European Free Trade Association would reduce EEC exports by $297 million. By "undoing" discrimination, the establishment of an Atlantic free trade area would thus involve a deterioration in the balance of trade of the Common Market countries in the amount of $517 million. This change would approximately offset the improvement in the balance of trade, due to the direct effects of AFTA. The conclusions are hardly affected if tariff reductions are extended to nonindustrial countries in the framework of the Kennedy Round, since the Common Market would benefit through the feedback of higher imports by these countries who are assumed to spend the entire increment in their foreign exchange earnings.

Aside from the effects of multilateral trade liberalization on the total exports and imports of the participating countries, interest attaches to the impact of tariff reductions on their industrial structure. (For this purpose, we may utilize the indices of "revealed" comparative advantage shown in Appendix Tables 1.2 and 1.3). Table 4.3 lists the twenty commodity groups in regard to which the Common Market has had the best export performance. According to these data, the EEC countries have a comparative advantage in the production of automobiles, nondurable consumer goods, glass, and some nonferrous metals. Should we also consider export-import ratios, the situation changes to the extent that nonferrous metals would place lower on the list. Nevertheless, by reason of the distorting effects of intercommodity differences in tariffs on export-import ratios, the following discussion is based on revealed comparative advantage as shown by export performance indices.

Among the member countries of the Common Market, we

TABLE 4.3. RANKING OF EXPORT PERFORMANCE INDICES FOR THE
TWENTY LEADING COMMON MARKET EXPORT INDUSTRIES

SITC No.	Product	Rank number
732.1.6	Automobiles	1
651.2	Yarn of wool	2
671	Pig iron	3
851	Footwear	4
664	Glass	5
841	Clothing	6
651.4	Cotton yarn, bleached	7
675	Hoops and strips of steel	8
821	Furniture	9
673	Iron and steel bars	10
891	Musical instruments	11
687.2	Tin, wrought	12
531	Synthetic organic dyestuffs	13
685.2	Lead, wrought	14
561	Fertilizer, manufactured	15
656.6	Blankets	16
678	Tubes, pipes, and fittings	17
842	Fur clothing	18
897	Jewelry	19
612	Leather manufactures	20

Source: Appendix Table 1.2.

find that Belgium has comparative advantages in the production of glass and wrought metals, while automobile manufacturing is concentrated in Germany and France, and Italy leads in regard to nondurable consumer goods.[4] To provide a more systematic appraisal of the position of individual countries in regard to the commodities in the production of which the EEC has comparative advantage, two kinds of calculations were made: first, we calculated the percentage share of the twenty leading Common Market export industries in the exports of manufactured goods of each of the member countries; second, we averaged the ranks of the twenty industries by using the percentages of exports for individual countries as weights (Table 4.4). As expected, a high share under the former method corresponds to a low average rank number for the second. Whichever method is employed, Belgium appears to be in the best position in the export of commodities in the case of which the Common Market has a comparative advan-

[4] Information on the comparative advantages of the individual countries has been obtained as a by-product of the calculations reported in Appendix Table 1.2.

TABLE 4.4. POSITION OF COMMON MARKET MEMBER COUNTRIES IN
REGARD TO THE TWENTY LEADING EEC EXPORT INDUSTRIES

Country	Combined share, the twenty export industries as a percentage of total exports of manufactures	Average weighted rank numbers for twenty leading export industries
Belgium	32.3	22.4
France	25.9	35.4
Germany	21.9	37.3
Italy	24.0	33.6
Netherlands	10.1	44.4

Source: Table 4.3 and international trade statistics.
Note: For explanation, see text.

tage while the Netherlands is at the opposite end of the scale. The ranking is not determinate for the three larger countries—Germany, France, and Italy.

The indices of revealed comparative advantage give some idea of the pattern of specialization in the individual countries. The expansion of world demand for the commodities in regard to which the Common Market—or its member countries—has a comparative advantage is a different question. To this effect, we calculated a correlation between indices representing the increase in the exports of the industrial countries between 1953–55 and 1960–62 for the 74 commodities included in Appendix Table 1.2 on the one hand, and the export performance indices on the other. The results show a slight positive correlation for the Common Market taken as a whole, while among the individual countries, for Germany and France there is a positive, and for the other three countries a negative relationship between the two variables. But the results do not permit reaching definite conclusions, since the degree of association is slight and the coefficients are not significant in the statistical sense.[5]

Next, we may consider the implications of multilateral tariff reductions for the encroachment in EEC markets by the

[5] The results shown by rank correlation coefficients are: Common Market, +0.07; Germany, +0.15; France +0.03; Netherlands, −0.06; Belgium, −0.16; Italy, −0.17. None of these coefficients is significant at the 5 per cent confidence level.

other industrial nations. It may be assumed that competition would be particularly felt by partner countries who have a large share in intra-EEC trade in commodities where outsiders have a comparative advantage, since they can expect a replacement of their exports by the products of the latter. Table 4.5 shows the weighted share in intra-EEC exports of the

TABLE 4.5. INDICATORS OF COMPETITIVE POWER OF THIRD COUNTRIES IN REGARD TO COMMODITIES TRADE WITHIN THE COMMON MARKET

	United States	United Kingdom	Japan
Combined weighted share in intra-EEC exports of twenty highest-ranking items			
Belgium	9.0	10.7	17.1
France	19.3	10.8	16.5
Germany	27.0	11.5	16.9
Italy	21.5	14.6	29.3
Netherlands	12.5	11.0	32.3
EEC, together	19.8	11.4	19.8
Unweighted average of tariffs for same items			
EEC average	12.7	15.5	17.0

Source: Appendix Table 1.2, and international statistics on tariff and trade.

twenty commodity groups in regard to which the United States, the United Kingdom, or Japan has a comparative advantage. Calculations were made for the Common Market taken as a unit, as well as for the individual member countries; in all cases, the rank numbers of the twenty commodity groups have been used as weights. The results have been compared to the unweighted average of EEC tariffs on the items in question to indicate the degree of existing protection against the outsiders in question.

Both the share and the tariff figures point to the conclusion that the United Kingdom is the least formidable competitor for the Common Market countries; there is no over-all difference in this respect between the United States and Japan. Among the member countries, France and Germany will face American competition principally in machine-building and in plastic materials. In turn, Japanese competition is concentrated on light industry and on the production of labor-intensive electrical machinery, and will affect chiefly the intra-EEC exports of Italy and the Netherlands. Italian producers will also have to compete in the markets of the partner countries with British exports of high-quality woolen textiles.

But would increased competition by third countries create serious problems of adjustment in Common Market industries? To answer this question, we should consider the effects of tariff reductions within the Common Market itself. While French and Italian producers had feared that the establishment of the EEC would entail the demise of some national industries, this has not happened in fact. Rather, tariff reductions have led to increased intra-industry specialization in machining and in intermediate products at higher levels of fabrication through changes in the product composition of individual firms. Moreover, in the case of consumer goods, the intensified exchange of national products is observed, while the structure of production in the member countries has hardly changed.[6]

These considerations indicate the inapplicability of the traditional theory of international trade to industries characterized by product differentiation. While according to this theory, tariff reductions would give rise to a shift of resources from import-competing to export industries with attendant frictions and adjustment difficulties, in the Common Market countries the adjustment has largely taken the form of changes in product composition within individual industries and has led to an increased exchange of consumer goods, machinery, and various intermediate products. It is hardly surprising, therefore, that frictional unemployment and bankruptcies have been at low levels. The number of bankruptcies has declined from 16.2 thousand in 1956 to 15.5 thousand in 1960, and again to 14.8 thousand in 1962. In the same year, unemployment fell below one million, while it was three million in 1956.[7]

The experience of the Common Market with tariff reduc-

---

[6] Evidence on the predominance of intra-industry specialization in Common Market industries is provided in Bela Balassa, "Tariff Reductions and Trade in Manufactures among the Industrial Countries," *American Economic Review* (June, 1966), pp. 466–73.

[7] Data have been taken from OECD statistics and national sources. Needless to say, decreases in unemployment have been associated with the buoyancy of the national economies of the Common Market countries which may be explained in part by the effects of the creation of the EEC.

tions on manufactured goods permits us to be optimistic in regard to the effects of multilateral trade liberalization in an Atlantic context. In the presence of product differentiation, the gradual dismantling of tariff barriers would tend to promote intra-industry exchange and specialization in narrow varieties of industrial goods. These conclusions do not apply, however, to standardized products where cost differences are of importance, and they also have to be modified in regard to some technologically progressive industries. We will return to the latter problems in the following discussion of the dynamic effects of trade liberalization.

Dynamic effects. Aside from the static effects of trade liberalization which follow under the assumption of unchanged production methods, important benefits can be obtained in the form of improvements in the methods of production. These improvements follow as a result of the application of large-scale production methods, and in response to greater competition on the part of foreign firms. At the same time, the dynamic benefits of trade liberalization are not necessarily evenly distributed among the participating countries. In the following, we will deal with the latter problem. In this connection, we will consider the implications of differences in firm size, research expenditures, patents, and vertical integration for international competitiveness.

In some of the member countries, fears have been expressed regarding the advantages American firms have over enterprises in the Common Market by reason of their larger size. Indeed, the *Fortune* survey based on sales figures for the year 1964 indicates that 287 out of the 500 largest enterprises of the world are American, and only 74 come from the Common Market.[8] Similar relationships are obtained if individual branches of industry are considered. But will size be a decisive factor in competition between the U.S. and the EEC? Before the establishment of the Common Market such fears had been expressed in regard to German firms. However, as a result of mergers in the other member countries, intercountry differences in firm size have since decreased.

Their larger size often provides advantages to U.S. firms over national enterprises in Western Europe in applying mod-

[8] *Fortune*, July and August, 1965.

ern production methods; however, in a large majority of the cases, economies of scale could be fully exploited on the Common Market level. Another advantage of size that has received much attention is the ability to engage in research on a large scale. Here we find that the proportion of firms undertaking research, and the share of research and development expenditures in sales tends to increase with the size of the firm, although this relationship does not continue indefinitely.[9]

Differences in firm size and in government support of research and development expenditures may explain that spending on research is a considerably higher proportion of the Gross National Product in the United States than in European countries. This relationship is hardly affected if, in order to avoid the difficulties related to the valuation of these expenditures, the ratios of manpower engaged in research and development to total employment are compared (see Table 4.6). At

TABLE 4.6. EXPENDITURE ON RESEARCH AND DEVELOPMENT IN THE MAJOR INDUSTRIAL COUNTRIES, 1962

	Manpower engaged in R. and D. per 1000 of working population	Expenditure on Research and Development		
		total million $	per capita $	as a percentage of GNP
United States	10.4	17,531	93.7	3.1
Belgium	3.5	133	14.8	1.0
France	3.8	1,108	23.6	1.5
Germany	3.9	1,105	20.1	1.3
Netherlands	4.5	239	20.3	1.8
United Kingdom	6.1	1,775	33.5	2.2

Source: C. Freeman and A. Young, The Research and Development Effort in Western Europe, North America, and the Soviet Union, Paris, Organization for Economic Co-operation and Development, 1965. See Tables 1–3.

the same time, the United States industry enjoys the benefits of the larger *absolute* size of research and development expenditures.

The U.S. is also in the lead in regard to government financing of research and development undertaken by the business

[9] On this point, as well as on the implications of research and government procurement for technological change, see Bela Balassa, *Trade Liberalization among the Industrial Countries: Objectives and Alternatives,* Chap. 5.

sector; the relevant proportion is 55 per cent in the United States, less than one-half in the United Kingdom, one-third in France, and only 15 per cent in Belgium, Germany, and the Netherlands.[10] Government support of research provides special advantages in aircraft production, and in some of the newer branches of manufacturing industry, especially computers and other electronic products. Indeed, as Table 4.7

TABLE 4.7. INDUSTRIAL DISTRIBUTION OF EXPENDITURE ON RESEARCH AND DEVELOPMENT, 1962

(PER CENT)

Industry	United States	Belgium	France	Germany	United Kingdom
Aircraft	36.3	0.8	27.7		35.4
Vehicles	7.4		2.6	19.2	3.0
Nonelectrical machinery	8.2	8.0	6.4		7.3
Electrical machinery	21.6				21.7
Instruments	3.9	19.4	25.7	33.8	2.3
Chemicals (industrial oil)	12.6	39.6	16.8	32.9	11.6
Metals	2.6	13.3	3.2	6.6	4.1
Other	7.4	18.9	17.6	7.5	14.6
	100.0	100.0	100.0	100.0	100.0

Source: C. Freeman and A. Young, The Research and Development Effort, Table 5.

indicates, a large proportion of research and development expenditure is in these industries.

The question arises whether the Common Market countries should leave the research-intensive industries to the United States. This does not appear to be desirable, since the EEC countries would thereby be excluded from technologically progressive industries that are of importance for their continuing industrial development. In some industries, such as electrical machinery and chemicals, the EEC firms are large enough to undertake research on an appropriate scale. On the other hand, they are at a considerable disadvantage in the case

[10] National Science Foundation, Basic Research, Applied Research and Development in Industry, 1962 (Washington, 1965), p. 107; C. Freeman and A. Young, The Research and Development Effort (Paris, Organization for Economic Co-operation and Development, 1965), p. 45.

of computers and aircraft. Here, a co-ordinated policy that aims at the fusion of national firms and provides government support to research and development could help. Another possibility is the importation of know-how in the form of patents and licenses. We now turn to this question.

Patent licensing—directly, and indirectly through subsidiaries—is one of the ways in which advances in technology may spread from one country to another. While the corresponding payments make for a negative patent balance in the recipient countries (see Table 4.8), the net effect on their

TABLE 4.8 ESTIMATED "TECHNOLOGICAL" BALANCE OF PAYMENTS, 1963
(MILLION $)

Country	Transactions with all countries			Transactions with United States		
	Receipts	Payments	Balance	Receipts	Payments	Balance
United States	577	63	514	—	—	—
France	53	125	−72	14	60	−46
Germany	50	135	−85	10	52	−42
Netherlands	36	43	−7	4	16	−12

Sources: C. Freeman and A. Young, *The Research and Development Effort*, Table 6; *Le Monde*, February 8, 1965; Nederlandsche Bank, unpublished.

balance of payments is generally favorable, because the application of foreign patents tends to increase their exports of technically advanced products and to reduce their imports of these commodities. More important, the importation of foreign technology will often be cheaper than the cost of duplicating the research undertaken by foreign firms. Finally, some of the results of basic research may be transmitted to other countries without requiring payment, and the transfer of the results of applied research may be accomplished in the form of co-operation in producing military goods.

The degree of vertical integration in the individual countries is a further consideration. In U.S. industries, vertical integration—from raw materials to the finished product—has made more headway than in the Common Market countries, the exception being Germany.[11] To some extent, this is an aspect of firm size, since the financial power of the large firm allows for the purchase of raw-material-producing sources. At

[11] In the latter case, the system of cumulative turnover taxes has contributed to vertical integration.

the same time, the availability of domestic raw materials provides an advantage to the vertically integrated firms, especially at times when these materials are in a short supply. Examples are nonferrous metals in the United States and Canada, and paper in Canada and Scandinavia.

While the advantages of vertical integration in the production of nonferrous metals are of importance chiefly in times of shortages, the advantages of the Scandinavian paper industry are more pervasive. In this case, prices of exported raw materials are kept artificially high, providing thereby a disincentive to paper production in the Common Market countries. Given the cartel policy followed in Scandinavia, reductions in tariffs would not establish conditions of competition; rather, an agreement on raw material prices would be necessary in order to remove distortions in competitive conditions. One may add that the Common Market paper industry would also be helped through the importation of woodpulp from other sources of supply such as the Soviet Union.

We may conclude that the advantages of size in trade between the United States and the European Common Market do not apply across-the-board but are limited to some technologically progressive industries. In these industries, differences in firm size, government-financed research, and government procurement are indeed advantages of American firms. To counteract these advantages, the application of a policy of research and development appears to be desirable on the Common Market level. This objective would also be served through the co-ordination of government procurement policies, and in some cases, the fusion of national firms. Moreover, in a few instances, a *décalage* in tariff reductions may be necessary in order to strengthen European firms before they confront American competition.

Nontariff Barriers, Agriculture, and Direct Foreign Investments

In this section, various problems are brought together that affect, in one way or another, economic relations between the United States and the Common Market. These include questions relating to nontariff barriers to trade; the implications of the common agricultural policy of the EEC for the nonparticipating countries in general and for the United States in particular; and the controversy about U.S. direct investments in Common Market industries.

Nontariff barriers. After the removal of quantitative restrictions in the framework of the OEEC in the early 1950s, the emphasis shifted to the restrictive effects of tariffs on international exchange. In turn, periodical reductions in tariffs have increasingly put into focus the existence of nontariff barriers which distort competitive conditions and often obstruct the flow of trade. The measures in question include, among other things, disguised subsidies in the form of government-financed research (open subsidies are prohibited by GATT regulations), preferential treatment of national goods and transportation facilities, customs valuation and classification procedures, and indirect taxes.

In the previous section, note was taken of the advantages that American firms derive from government-sponsored research in some technologically progressive industries. It was also suggested that these advantages can be at least partly offset by instituting a European policy of research. Emphasis was given to countervailing measures of this character, since evidently the U.S. government cannot be prevailed upon to reduce, or to altogether stop, its activities in the field of research and development. Neither would this be desirable since ultimately European consumers, too, enjoy the fruits of this research.

Reference was also made to the effects of government procurement on competitiveness. The American firms have certain advantages in this respect, since military procurement reduces the risk of the introduction of new products and often provides a basis for civilian applications. But again, despite the implicit subsidy element in these purchases they can hardly be objected to as long as all suppliers, domestic as well as foreign, are competing under equal conditions. This is not the case in the United States, however; under the "Buy American" Act, domestic suppliers receive preferential treatment. Depending on the purchasing agency, these suppliers enjoy the benefit of a preferential margin of varying magnitude over foreign producers. Moreover, the shipping of products in American bottoms under foreign aid regulations, and the compulsory use of American airlines by government

employees, entails discrimination against foreign transportation facilities. But one should not assume that it is only
the United States which favors domestic producers through
government procurement policies. While procurement regulations are rarely subject to legislation in European countries,
Common Market governments often give preferential treatment to their domestic suppliers.

On the other hand, the protective effects of customs valuation and classification procedures are greater in the United
States than elsewhere. The U.S. has not adopted the Brussels
tariff nomenclature, and the rather detailed and cumbersome
tariff classification employed provides a certain degree of "administrative" protection. Note should finally be taken of the
American selling-price issue: for a variety of coaltar-based
chemicals, the U.S. tariff is calculated on the basis of the
American selling price rather than the import value. Since the
former exceeds the latter by two or three times, the degree of
tariff protection is accordingly raised.

Differences in indirect taxes are more difficult to evaluate.
To the extent that rates of indirect taxes and the regulations
on their refunding on the occasion of exportation differ
internationally, these taxes have the effect of implicit tariffs
and subsidies. More generally, intercountry differences in tax
systems influence international trade as well as the movement
of the factors of production. But these questions can hardly be
analyzed in the framework of the present chapter, and the
reader is referred to Chapter 8 for a detailed discussion. In
turn, Chapter 9 considers the problem of nontariff barriers
other than indirect taxes in great detail.

Agriculture. While agriculture is excluded from the scope of
the studies in the present volume, some remarks on the agricultural policy of the Common Market will be useful to
indicate certain aspects of policy co-ordination in the Community. In this connection, it should be recalled that so far the
two main areas of action in the EEC have been the reduction
of tariff barriers on industrial goods and the establishment of
a common policy on agricultural products. The latter policy at
present applies to a few commodities only, although the general outline is reasonably clear.

At first sight, the common agricultural policy appears as a

simplification of national policies. The various instruments of protection that were used by the individual member countries are replaced by a single instrument—variable duties levied at the frontier. But this instrument is apparently being used to restrict imports to an amount that cannot be supplied from within the Common Market. Thus, while in the past national surpluses and deficits led to trade with third countries, under the new system producers in partner countries are given precedence, and the domestic prices adopted provide an incentive for the expansion of production in the surplus countries. In particular, the new wheat price has been set between the relatively low French and the high German price so that it will exceed the c.i.f. import price of $70 per ton by about $40. Now, the regulation of the wheat supply, which is higher in France than in Germany, on a common wheat price is bound to have an expansionary effect for the Common Market taken as a whole. It is also expected that the degree of self-sufficiency of the EEC will increase in regard to other temperate-zone products.

Aside from increasing the cost of food to the consumer, the Common Market agricultural policy entails a misallocation of resources, inasmuch as it obstructs the movement of labor into industrial occupations where productivity is higher, and the possibilities for technological improvements are greater. Moreover, this policy places obstacles in the way of enlargement of the EEC through the participation of other European countries, such as the United Kingdom, and created difficulties for the successful conclusion of the Kennedy Round. It provides, then, an example of the co-ordination of national policies being carried out in a protectionist direction, since the balancing of national interests makes it difficult to alter the outcome.

American direct investments in the Common Market. U.S. direct investments in Western Europe increased to a considerable extent in the postwar period. Between 1950 and 1964, the value of these investments grew sevenfold, from $1.7 billion to $12.1 billion; in the meantime, Western Europe's share in American direct foreign investments rose from 14.7 to 27.2 per cent. Within Western Europe, more-or-less parallel changes occurred in the Common Market and the

United Kingdom in the first half of the period, but an increasing share of U.S. investments went to the EEC countries after the establishment of the Community. This shift can best be seen from data on new investments: between 1957 and 1964, the amount of new investments grew from $212 million to $889 million in the Common Market as against a change from $332 to $377 million in the United Kingdom (Table 4.9). If

TABLE 4.9. AMERICAN DIRECT INVESTMENTS ABROAD
(MILLION $)

	The value of investments at the end of the year		The flow of new investments	
	1957	1964	1957	1964
All areas	25,394	44,343	3,845	3,793
Western Europe	4,151	12,067	581	1,752
Common Market	1,680	5,398	212	889
Belgium	192	452	24	86
France	464	1,437	49	188
Germany	581	2,077	114	289
Italy	252	845	7	199
Netherlands	191	587	18	127
United Kingdom	1,974	4,550	332	377
Scandinavia	202	551	8	72
Switzerland	59	944	7	328
Other European	226	624	22	96

Source: U.S. Department of Commerce, Survey of Current Business, various issues.

we also consider that nearly one-half of all new investments were financed by undistributed earnings in the United Kingdom compared to a proportion of one-eighth in the EEC, it will be apparent that the second half of the period saw an important reorientation of American direct investment within the European area. It should be added that as a result of the tax privileges enjoyed by companies with Swiss registration, Switzerland's share in American direct investments has also increased to a considerable extent.

These shifts can be explained by the attractiveness of the rapidly growing Common Market economies that are in the process of integration. In fact, a survey conducted by the McGraw-Hill Book Company, Inc. indicates that the availability of large markets provides the principal inducement for the establishment of subsidiaries by American firms. Forty-eight per cent of the firms questioned gave this as a motivating factor, while 20 per cent mentioned superior earnings possibilities; 10 per cent, better competitive conditions; 6 per cent, lower wages. It is interesting to note that the existence of tariff discrimination was rarely mentioned as a reason for investment in the EEC—only 16 per cent of the respondents referred to it in the course of the survey.[12] But the rapid expansion of U.S. direct investments has come under criticism in some of the Common Market countries, especially France. It has been charged that the encroachment of American capital into the European economy will bring some important industries under American domination, and ultimately will interfere with the national sovereignty of the member countries. The data do not reveal the existence of such domination, however. The share of American investments in the total fixed-capital stock in the EEC hardly exceeds 2 per cent, and it is below 4 per cent in the manufacturing sector.[13] At the same time, the share of these investments in French industry is lower than the average for the Common Market, while it well exceeds the average in Belgium and the Netherlands— countries which welcome foreign investments. These conclusions are confirmed by projections on plant and equipment expenditures in EEC manufacturing industries. While expenditures by U.S. companies have been estimated to rise from $682 million in 1964 to $1,100 million in 1966 in the Common Market taken as a whole, the relevant figures for France are $176 million and $225 million.[14]

The question remains whether U.S. capital may play a preponderant role in some European industries. In fact, much of American capital went into three industries: of the total of $6.5 billion invested in Common Market manufacturing at the end of 1964, the value of American investment in transportation equipment (chiefly automobiles) was estimated at $1.8 billion, and in chemicals at $1.1 billion. In the same year, American investments in petroleum-refining were valued at $3.1 billion.[15] But the U.S. share does not reach one-fourth in

[12] *Foreign Operations of U.S. Industrial Companies, 1960–61* (New York: McGraw-Hill Book Co., Inc., Department of Economics, 1960), p. 4.

[13] *Der Volkswirt*, March 22, 1963, and October 30, 1964; U.S. Department of Commerce, *Survey of Current Business*, various issues.

[14] *Survey of Current Business*, September, 1965.

[15] *Ibid.*

the EEC automobile industry, and this share is less than one-fifth in France. Nor can we speak of American domination of the chemical industry. Here again, France has a relatively small part of the total U.S. investment. On the other hand, in the case of petroleum refining, government intervention has been necessary to reduce the share of American capital.

In the smaller countries of the EEC, U.S. investments have been considered desirable by reason of the beneficial effects of the inflow of capital, technological know-how, and managerial skills. A similar position had been taken in Germany and Italy, although more recently objections have been levied against the increasing role played by U.S. firms in some technologically progressive industries, such as computers and other forms of electronics. It is hardly surprising that—aside from aircraft—these are the same industries in which American exporters have superior competitive power. In fact, these industries show the interaction of exports and foreign investment: American firms which possess certain advantages in the field of research and development may increase their sales in the Common Market countries from their domestic plants, or they may establish foreign subsidiaries for this purpose. It should be clear that the remedy is the same in both cases. Positive measures need to be taken to counteract the discriminatory advantages of American firms and to strengthen European enterprises.

The effect of American investments on the balance of payments of Common Market countries is a related issue. In recent years, the repatriated earnings of U.S. firms in Western Europe averaged 7–8 per cent of the value of investments, while payments for royalties, license fees, and management fees amounted to 3–4 per cent, and imports of U.S. goods to 15–16 per cent.[16] At first sight it would then appear that American investments would be "amortized" in balance-of-payments terms in about four years. But such a calculation would not take into consideration the replacement of imports and the expansion of exports by U.S. subsidiaries in Western Europe.

It is difficult to say to what extent the sales of U.S. subsidiaries may replace exports from the United States. This is certainly the case of new products such as carbon black and

[16] *Survey of Current Business,* September and December, 1965.

synthetic rubber, while the amount of replacement may be rather small in the automobile industry in which the specifications of passenger cars differ greatly between the United States and Western Europe. Import replacement may be quite important also in chemicals, and for electrical and nonelectrical machinery. In this connection, note that sales by U.S. subsidiaries were about twice the book value of U.S. direct investments in Western Europe in 1964, and hence import replacement would amount to 20 per cent of the book value of investments if only one-tenth of these sales replace imports from the United States. It should be added that U.S. subsidiaries account for about 5–6 per cent of Common Market manufacturing exports to the United States, while the corresponding figure for exports to other countries is 6–7 per cent. These percentages are considerably larger than the share of these subsidiaries in Common Market manufacturing. At the same time, the relevant figures are the highest in France: 7.2 per cent in the first case, and 8.3 per cent in the second.[17]

One may conclude that through import replacement and increases in exports the manufacturing subsidiaries of American companies are likely to favorably affect the balance of payments of the EEC countries. If we also consider the contribution of American investments to production improvements and technological change, the verdict will generally be a favorable one. This conclusion does not exclude, however, the taking of specific measures to strengthen European enterprise in what the French call *les industries de pointe*. But the emphasis should be put on positive measures rather than on raising obstacles to the inflow of U.S. capital.

A final point: could a certain equilibrium in foreign investments be established by increasing the flow of European capital to the United States? In the view of the present writer, this would certainly be a desirable objective; however, its attainment encounters considerable difficulties. In 1950, the value of European direct investments in the United States exceeded that of American investments in Western Europe. But the situation changed in the years following, and in 1964 European holdings in the United States amounted to only about one-half of the value of U.S. direct investments in Euro-

[17] *Survey of Current Business*, November, 1965, and United Nations, *Commodity Trade Statistics, 1964*, New York, 1965.

pean countries. Given the differences in the availability of capital and the attraction presented by the fusion of national markets in Europe, this trend is likely to continue. On the other hand, for the world as a whole increased investment in the less developed countries would appear to be a desirable alternative, since the latter have much lower capital-labor ratios, as well as less technological and managerial know-how than either the United States or Western Europe.

Alternative Solutions for Trade Liberalization in the Atlantic Area

In conformity with the discussion in Chapter I of this volume, we will consider here the possible effects of alternative trade arrangements for the Common Market countries. These alternatives are four in number: an Atlantic Free Trade Area, 50 per cent tariff reductions under the most-favored-nation clause, an Atlantic Free Trade Area with the exclusion of the Common Market, and European integration, i.e., some form of accommodation between the EEC and EFTA. As a background to this problem, some discussion of actual trade data is in order.

Appendix Table 4.1 indicates the high degree of integration reached by the Common Market countries. In 1963, intra-area trade accounted for two-fifths of the total trade of the EEC, as compared to a proportion of about 30 per cent in 1957. Intra-EEC trade is of greatest importance for the smaller member countries; it amounts to 50–60 per cent of the trade of Belgium and the Netherlands, as compared to about 30 per cent in the case of France, Germany, and Italy. These differences are explained in part by the close trade relations of Belgium and the Netherlands. However, the disparity does not disappear if adjustment is made for trade between the two countries.

Among nonparticipating countries, the United States is a more important trading partner for the EEC member states than the United Kingdom, the Netherlands being the only exception to this rule. Aside from political considerations, her close trade ties with the U.K. may explain the unqualified Dutch support for British entry. At the same time, the Common Market countries generally trade more with Continental EFTA economies than with the United States. Trade with

Continental EFTA is of especial interest to Germany: in 1963, 23.4 per cent of German exports found markets in Continental EFTA countries, while the latter provided 13.7 per cent of German imports. Switzerland and Austria are especially important as trade partners of Germany. France and Italy also have close trade relations with Switzerland, while the share of Continental EFTA is the smallest in the trade of Belgium and the Netherlands.

Should we consider the European Free Trade Association as a whole, it will be apparent that its importance for the Common Market far overshadows that of the United States. In 1963, 21.3 per cent of EEC exports went to the European Free Trade Association, and 6.9 per cent to the United States, while the relevant proportions are 15.3 per cent and 12.5 per cent for imports. At the same time, trade with Canada and Japan does not exceed 1 per cent of total EEC trade in either direction.

The data on actual trade flows point to the conclusion that the main interest of the Common Market lies in reaching an accommodation with the European Free Trade Association, the United States being the second most important trade partner. This conclusion hardly changes if we take into account the possible effects of trade liberalization among the industrial countries. From Table 4.2 it appears that over one-half of the expansion of EEC trade due to the direct effects of an Atlantic Free Trade Area would take place with the EFTA countries, about 40 per cent with the United States, and less than one-tenth with Canada and Japan taken together. In addition, the removal of discrimination associated with the division of Western Europe into two trading blocs would entail an increase of Common Market exports to EFTA by $297 million and an increase in imports of $473 million. By comparison, the removal of EEC discrimination against American exports would permit an increase of Common Market imports from the United States in the amount of $311 million.

It would seem, then, that the importance of trade with EFTA and with the United States would make the Atlantic Free Trade Area the most desirable trade arrangement for Common Market countries. Various considerations militate against this alternative, however. To begin with, in the course of the negotiations on the establishment of an all-European

free trade area, in EEC circles objections were raised against
the possibly cumbersome regulations on the origin of products
that the establishment of a free trade area would entail.
Secondly, there is a desire to maintain some degree of tariff
protection against U.S. exports in technologically progressive
industries, while no such need exists in competition with
EFTA countries. Third, the degree of policy co-ordination that
may appear desirable in a free trade area is likely to be easier
to attain in a European than in an Atlantic context. Finally,
as we have seen, the foremost trading interests of Common
Market countries lie in Western Europe.

But while these considerations would speak in favor of a
European trade arrangement, progress should also be made on
another front: multilateral reductions in tariffs on manufactured goods and industrial materials. Notwithstanding the
footdragging one observes on the part of the French, multilateral trade liberalization is a highly desirable objective of
the Common Market since it would provide benefits in the
form of the expansion of exports, the cheaper availability of
imports, and increased competition. Both economic arguments and considerations of political feasibility thus speak for
a policy aimed at European integration and tariff reductions
under the most-favored-nation clause. Such a policy would
also avoid the danger of a United States-proposed trade
arrangement among the industrial countries which excluded
the Common Market. Aside from discriminating against the
EEC, an arrangement of this kind would likely create considerable tensions within the Atlantic alliance.

Tariff reductions under the most-favored-nation clause
would also lead to larger imports from less developed countries. However, there is little danger that the lowering of tariff
barriers against the products of these countries would appreciably affect the balance of payments of the Common Market
countries. It is reasonable to assume that less developed countries spend all increases in their foreign exchange earnings,
and it can be expected that much of the increased imports by
the EEC would find a counterpart in the form of larger exports.

More difficult is the problem of labor-intensive industries, in
the case of which imports from less developed areas may
importantly affect domestic output and employment in the

Common Market. Here it is necessary to provide for a certain *décalage* to permit orderly transition for the industries that are adversely affected. But arguments for such a *décalage* should not be misused for keeping out the products of low-wage countries. Inasmuch as the comparative advantage of the latter increasingly lies in simple manufactures, developed countries will have to accept these imports in order to permit an acceleration of economic growth in less developed areas.

At the same time, the EEC countries face a special problem in their trade with less developed economies by reason of the preferential treatment accorded to the associated countries and territories. It will be recalled that at the insistence of the French, the export products of the latter have been granted free entry into the Common Market. This arrangement represents a continuation, in a different form, of the preferential system that existed between France and her overseas territories. Moreover, a special fund was created and financed by contributions of the member countries, to provide for an expansion of investment in the associated countries and territories.

It is understandable that the French wanted to maintain the privileges accorded to their former territories in the Common Market, although their EEC partners raised some objections against their sharing in the burden of financing. They have, however, accepted the modalities of the agreement as proposed by France, since the French regarded this as a *condition préalable* for the establishment of the Common Market. Since that time, the partner countries have tried to "water down" the preferences accorded to the overseas associates in the form of tariff reductions on overseas products, and have also attempted to enlarge the geographical scope of the association. In this regard, the accession of Nigeria represents an important step. While Nigeria originally opposed British entry and expressed its unwillingness to associate itself with the Common Market, it has since applied for association despite the fact that Britain has remained outside the Community.

The accession of Nigeria indicates a possible avenue of the transformation of the association agreement. But there is little chance that competing producers in Latin America would receive similar privileges, and several of the African countries do not want to participate for political reasons. Nor is it advisable to divide less developed countries according to zones of influence and to establish preferential arrangements (e.g., between the Common Market and Africa, and between the United States and Latin America). Such agreements would not fail to lead to political frictions and would entail inefficiencies in resource allocation. At the same time, the abolition of tariffs and excise taxes on tropical products undertaken by all the industrial countries would lead to an expansion of exports from less developed areas. One may conclude, therefore, that from the point of view of relationships with developing countries, the abolition of trade barriers on tropical products and multilateral tariff reductions on other products is the most desirable alternative. But such an action would also remove existing preferences that presently benefit the countries and territories associated with the Common Market, and would have adverse political repercussions. It is suggested here that the associates could be compensated in the form of larger aid through the special fund. Such a solution could also be applied to Commonwealth countries in the case Britain were to enter the EEC.

APPENDIX TABLE 4.1. INTERNATIONAL TRADE OF THE
COMMON MARKET COUNTRIES, 1963
(EXPORTS, F.O.B.; IMPORTS, C.I.F.)

| | Belgium | | | | Netherlands | | | | Germany | | | |
| | Imports | | Exports | | Imports | | Exports | | Imports | | Exports | |
	(million $)	(per cent)	(million $)	(per cent)	(million $)	(per cent)	(million $)	(per cent)	(million $)	(per cent)	(million $)	(per cent)
United States	472	9.2	411	8.5	649	10.9	303	4.1	1,987	15.3	1,051	7.2
Canada	54	1.1	44	0.9	47	0.8	31	0.6	186	1.4	133	0.9
Common Market	2,684	52.6	2,942	61.2	3,082	51.5	2,647	54.1	4,342	33.5	5,452	37.4
United Kingdom	421	8.2	278	5.8	431	7.2	477	9.7	612	4.7	555	3.8
Continental E.F.T.A.	291	5.7	397	8.3	399	6.7	560	11.5	1,784	13.7	3,404	23.4
Japan	36	0.7	35	0.7	39	0.7	38	0.8	130	1.0	199	1.4
Other developed countries	231	4.5	195	4.1	168	2.8	257	5.2	824	6.3	1,234	8.5
Less-developed countries	796	15.6	423	8.8	1,013	17.0	600	12.3	2,639	20.3	2,087	14.3
Communist countries	124	2.4	84	1.7	139	2.3	855	1.77	495	3.8	454	3.1
Total	5,109	100.0	4,809	100.0	5,967	100.0	4,898	100.0	12,999	100.0	14,569	100.0

APPENDIX TABLE 4.1. (CONTINUED)

	France				Italy				EEC, Consolidated			
	Imports		Exports		Imports		Exports		Imports		Exports	
	(million $)	(per cent)	(million $)	(per cent)	(million $)	(per cent)	(million $)	(per cent)	(million $)	(per cent)	(million $)	(per cent)
United States	901	10.3	421	5.2	1,028	13.7	476	9.6	5,037	12.5	2,562	6.9
Canada	80	0.9	53	0.7	84	1.1	49	1.0	451	1.1	310	0.8
Common Market	3,126	35.9	3,091	38.2	2,475	32.9	1,792	36.3	15,709	39.0	15,924	42.6
United Kingdom	520	6.0	397	4.9	463	6.1	270	5.5	2,447	6.1	1,977	5.3
Continental E.F.T.A.	536	6.1	916	11.3	704	9.3	685	13.8	3,714	9.2	5,962	16.0
Japan	40	0.5	45	0.6	91	1.2	42	0.8	336	0.8	359	1.0
Other developed countries	532	6.0	555	6.9	603	8.0	435	8.8	2,358	5.8	2,676	7.2
Less-developed countries	2,713	31.1	2,314	28.6	1,639	21.8	907	18.3	8,800	21.8	6,331	17.0
Communist countries	276	3.2	287	3.6	444	5.9	292	5.9	1,478	3.7	1,202	3.2
Total	8,724	100.0	8,079	100.0	7,531	100.0	4,948	100.0	40,330	100.0	37,303	100.0

Source: United Nations, Commodity Trade Statistics, 1965.

CHAPTER V

>>>>>>>>>>>>>>>>>>>>>>>>>>>>>>>>>>>>>

TRADE ARRANGEMENTS AMONG THE
INDUSTRIAL COUNTRIES: EFFECTS
ON THE UNITED KINGDOM

Sidney J. Wells[1]

<<<<<<<<<<<<<<<<<<<<<<<<<<<<<<<<<<<<

Historical Perspective

Postwar attitudes in Britain. In this chapter, we consider the implications for the United Kingdom economy of various proposals for trade liberalization. The first section is devoted to an examination of British attitudes towards integration in Western Europe. The second section examines the place of the United Kingdom in the world economy, and the implications for the United Kingdom balance of trade and capital account of alternative proposals for trade liberalization, while the next section deals with the possible consequences of lowering trade barriers for various commodity groups and industries in Britain. In the final section, we look briefly at the dynamic consequences of integration and in the light of economic and political realities try to assess for the United Kingdom the merits of the alternative policies.

During the early postwar period, successive British governments supported various endeavors for co-operation in the Atlantic area and in Western Europe, of which NATO and the OEEC were the most important. But Britain opposed participation in any scheme which seemed to interfere with her relationship with the United States on the one hand and the Commonwealth on the other. As the late Sir Winston Churchill was reported to have told General de Gaulle: "If we have to choose between you [meaning Europe] and the open sea, we choose the open sea." And this approach typified the attitude

[1] The author is professor of economics at the University of Salford, Lancashire. He is indebted to Miriam Camps, Andrew Shonfield, John Pinder, and Asa Briggs for comments.

121

of most Britishers as late as 1959. Thus, while Britain played a leading role in the establishment of the OEEC, the British government was opposed to all attempts at giving the organization direct powers of its own. Also, largely because of its supranational aspects, Britain was unwilling to participate in the European Coal and Steel Community. Various influences led to a change in the British position in subsequent years, however.

The deterioration of the competitive position of the United Kingdom was one of these influences. Also, with the passing of time, and especially following the Suez crisis, it was becoming apparent that the countries participating in the European Coal and Steel Community were earnest in their desire to integrate their economies and that exclusion from the Common Market would unfavorably affect the British economy. Miriam Camps, in her account of changing British attitudes to Europe, reports that by the spring of 1956 British attempts to dissuade the Six from going ahead with the establishment of a customs union had given place to beginning "to think seriously about ways of coming to terms with the Common Market."[2] At this stage, "coming to terms" did not mean joining the Community. Rather, the British government was thinking in terms of negotiating (but within the OEEC rather than directly with the Six) a European Free Trade Area in industrial products. This policy led to the long drawn-out OEEC negotiations for a European Free Trade Area under the chairmanship of Mr. Maudling. Throughout these discussions, the British objective was to minimize the impact of the trade discrimination inherent in the Common Market on U.K. exports, while allowing Great Britain's special trading relationship with the Commonwealth to continue.[3] One direct result of the failure of the Maudling negotiations was the decision of the British government to go ahead in the spring of 1959 with a plan, already tentatively discussed with the Swedish government, for establishing a free trade association, consisting of those countries of Western Europe which did not

[2] Miriam Camps, *Britain and the European Community 1955–63* (Princeton, N.J.: Princeton University Press, 1964), p. 51.

[3] For a full account of these discussions, and of the subsequent Brussels negotiations which followed Britain's application to join the EEC, see M. Camps, *Britain and the European Community 1955–63*.

wish to participate in the EEC for one reason or another. The very fact that the United Kingdom joined with Sweden (albeit after some hesitation) in sponsoring the Association suggests that, at the time, the British government had no thought of applying for membership in the EEC. Rather, the argument appears to have been that future accommodation between the EEC and EFTA would hold the best hope for trade liberalization in Western Europe.

There had been four major reasons for the unwillingness of the British government to accept the Treaty of Rome. First, there was the Commonwealth problem; secondly, the systems of agricultural protection practiced among the Six and envisaged for the Community appeared incompatible with the British method of support prices; thirdly, there was a reluctance to enter into an agreement that would limit national sovereignty; and finally, after 1959, there was the additional factor that Britain's accession to the Treaty of Rome would have broken up the European Free Trade Association.

Toward Europe. By the autumn of 1960, however, a change of attitude in Britain toward the Community was slowly becoming apparent. Whereas hitherto the Commonwealth and other issues had been considered decisive in opposing the entry into the EEC, these were now regarded not so much as objections as obstacles to be overcome. More and more people became alarmed at the exclusion of Britain from the rapidly growing markets of the Community. The political arguments in favor of Britain's entry were considered to be of even greater importance. It was argued that outside of the Community, Britain's influence would be peripheral in more than a geographic sense, while inside Britain could wield considerable influence in both the political and the economic spheres. A nationwide Gallup poll survey taken in July, 1960, showed that 49 per cent of those interviewed answered in the affirmative when asked the question: "If the British government were to decide that Britain's interest could best be served by joining the Common Market, would you approve?" It was not, however, until July, 1961, that Prime Minister Macmillan informed the House of Commons of Britain's intention to apply for membership in the Community.

The Brussels negotiations for entry continued through

1962. Agriculture proved less of a stumbling block than had been thought: the question of restrictions on national sovereignty received little discussion in the British press. Among the EFTA countries, Denmark and Norway announced that they too would apply for membership in the Community, while Britain showed less concern for arrangements with the neutral member countries of EFTA. Thus, the Commonwealth problem emerged as the chief obstacle to agreement.

With the progress of the negotiations, however, the British government had made clear that it was prepared to make concessions in this respect. But whatever concessions Britain was prepared to offer in economic questions were made irrelevant by the decision of the French government to demand the breaking off of the negotiations after the Nassau Agreement on nuclear weapons between Prime Minister Macmillan and President Kennedy. At his press conference on January 14th, 1963, General de Gaulle made it clear that he did not believe that Britain was yet ready "to transform itself enough to belong to the European Community without restriction and without reservation." The formal break in the negotiations soon followed de Gaulle's statement.

After Brussels. After de Gaulle's veto in January, 1963, the British government was virtually without a trade policy. All of its plans had been based upon a successful conclusion to the Brussels negotiations; during 1962, the European Free Trade Association had been allowed to freewheel, and no efforts had been made to cement Commonwealth trade relations with the United Kingdom. In the absence of a firm government lead, the weeks following the Brussels debacle saw a number of proposals (some more carefully thought out than others) for future British policy. Some urged that the U.K. should negotiate agreements with its trading partners on the basis of reciprocity—even if such agreements ran counter to GATT.[4]

A few days after the January veto, in a letter to the London *Times,* Professor James Meade advocated one more attempt by Britain and her EFTA partners to persuade the EEC to accept

---

[4] See, for example, the speech of the late W. Manning Dacey (then adviser to Lloyds' Bank), to the Folkestone Chamber of Trade on January 25, 1963.

the idea of a European free trade area. He also suggested that Britain should give its full support to the Kennedy Round negotiations, taking advantage of President Kennedy's new liberal trading policy. But should these attempts fail, Meade argued that the correct policy would be to negotiate preferential tariff reductions with Britain's trading partners, while refusing to extend these to EEC countries unless they were willing to reciprocate. Such an arrangement would, of course, have been against the present rules of GATT, according to which tariff concessions agreed to between any contracting parties should be extended to all other contracting parties.

Suggestions for renouncing Britain's obligations in the GATT met with no official favor in 1963. Instead there was much talk in official circles of "strengthening EFTA" and of "cementing Commonwealth ties." But there was a dearth of discussion on how these objectives might be achieved.

For some two years after the Brussels breakdown, the question of a renewed attempt by the U.K. to enter the Common Market was not a political issue. In the general election of 1964, little attention was paid to problems of long-term trade policy, and once more, the matter of Britain's seeking to enter the EEC was barely mentioned. The Conservatives generally paid lip-service to this issue, while leaders of the Labor government, formed after the October, 1964 General Election, appeared to be opposed to entry on terms likely to be acceptable by the Six.

Early in 1965, however, changes occurred in the attitudes of both Labor and Conservative parties. The leading article in *The Economist* of February 20 (p. 745) took as its text, "The Compass Swings Back to Europe," and made the point that Britain's most recent economic crisis "had cast doubt on either party's power to restore the country's impetus by purely national reforms." *The Economist* claimed to see "a purposeful continuity in the reluctant British crawl towards Europe." This continuity was becoming "the major fact of British politics."

In April, an unofficial but influential group of Conservative MPs published their ideas on the future of Anglo-European relations in a pamphlet entitled *One Europe*. The group, which included nine former ministers, urged that "the Conservative party should declare that it is its policy to join Europe by whatever means is best, upon its being returned to power."[5] The election in July, 1965, of Edward Heath as leader of the Opposition further strengthened the pro-European group in the party. On the Labor side, a number of younger politicians and writers expressed support for entry into the Common Market, and the Labor government itself showed increased interest in participating in the Community. By early 1966, it became apparent that the government sought an accommodation with the Common Market through entry, rather than through a fusion of EEC and EFTA.

Various factors have contributed to these developments. To begin with, there seemed to be little chance of strengthening relationships with Commonwealth countries, while EFTA provided neither adequate competition to improve the performance of British industry, nor sufficient markets to permit realizing large-scale economies in the technologically advanced sectors of U.K. manufacturing. At the same time, the Common Market countries are more important trading partners for Britain than her EFTA partners. Thus, despite the discriminatory effects of the division of Western Europe into two trading blocs, in 1963 only 12.3 per cent of U.K. export trade was with EFTA, as against 17.6 per cent with the EEC. In the same year, 11.2 per cent of imports came from EFTA countries, as against 16.5 per cent from the Common Market.

Britain in the World Economy

The U.K. trade pattern. Marked changes in the geographical pattern of U.K. trade have taken place since 1953. Table 5.1 shows that in 1963 industrial countries accounted for 54.6 per cent of British exports, as compared with 44.3 per cent in 1953. In particular, there was an increase in the share of Continental Europe in U.K. exports from 31.2 per cent to 40.8 per cent. In the same period, the share of the Common Market in British exports rose more than that of EFTA—from 13.2 to 17.6 per cent, as against 11.0 to 12.3 per cent.

Similar developments are shown on the import side. Whereas in 1953 industrial countries supplied 43.9 per cent of

[5] *One Europe,* ed. Nicholas Ridley, MP (London: Conservative Political Centre, 1965).

U.K. imports, by 1963 their share had risen to 54.1 per cent. Particularly important was the increase in the share of EEC countries in British imports. In 1953, this was 11.2 per cent; by 1963, it had risen to 16.5 per cent. In turn, the EFTA countries accounted for 10.5 per cent of U.K. imports in 1953, and for 11.2 per cent in 1963. At the same time, the share of nonindustrial areas—including that of Commonwealth countries—declined.

TABLE 5.1. CHANGING PATTERN OF U.K. TRADE, 1953–63.
(EXPORTS, F.O.B; IMPORTS, C.I.F.)

	Exports			Imports		
	1953	1958	1963	1953	1958	1963
Value to/of total trade million $	7,150	8,890	11,410	8,190	9,400	11,930
Share of area in exports/ imports	100	100	100	100	100	100
North America	12.4	14.6	12.6	15.3	17.3	17.8
Western Europe	31.2	29.8	40.8	28.2	30.6	35.0
of which EEC	13.2	13.2	17.6	11.2	14.2	16.5
of which EFTA	11.0	10.0	12.3	10.5	10.1	11.2
Japan	0.7	0.6	1.2	0.4	1.1	1.3
Industrial countries	44.3	45.0	54.6	43.9	49.0	54.1
Nonindustrial areas	54.6	52.4	41.9	53.2	47.5	42.0
of which Australia, N. Zealand, S. Africa	18.5	17.3	13.5	17.6	12.6	10.6
Eastern trading area	0.8	2.3	3.3	2.9	3.4	4.3

Source: International trade, statistics.

In spite of these changes in the geographical distribution of U.K. trade, in 1963 the nonindustrial areas still accounted for 42 per cent of British exports and imports. Thus, although the immediate growth prospects for Britain's trade are the most favorable in Western Europe, the United Kingdom is also vitally concerned with developments in nonindustrial nations, and particularly the Commonwealth countries, which account for about one-third of British trade.

The United Kingdom grants duty-free or low-duty entry to all imports from the Commonwealth. But since the general (nonpreferential) British tariff on foodstuffs and raw materials, which account for the bulk of U.K. imports from the Commonwealth, is low, the extent of preferences accorded to Commonwealth products is generally small or nonexistent. Moreover, since the mid-1930s, Commonwealth preferences have declined in real value in part because of the rise in prices, which has reduced the *ad valorem* equivalent of specific duties, and in part because of the reduction in the general level of tariffs. A study by Political and Economic Planning has shown that by 1957 the margin of preference had fallen to 9 per cent on those goods actually receiving preferences, and to little over 4 per cent on all Commonwealth imports.[6]

In turn, most African Commonwealth countries which have recently gained independence give no preferences to British exports while those granted by India, Malaya, and Pakistan are very limited. Australia, New Zealand and Canada, however, give preferences on a wide range of products. Lesser preferences are given by the Republic of South Africa, which maintained preferential relationship with the United Kingdom despite its withdrawal from the Commonwealth. In the case of these countries, preferential margins are generally greater on iron and steel, motor vehicles, textiles, and clothing, and smaller on chemicals and on most types of machinery.[7]

A study by the Board of Trade has shown that in 1961 one-half of British exports to the Commonwealth preference area entered the importing countries duty free.[8] The margin of preference enjoyed by the United Kingdom on imports receiving favored treatment was 12 per cent; on all imports into the area from the U.K. the average margin was 6–7 per cent. This margin is somewhat wider than that granted by the U..K to imports from countries enjoying preferences in its market. The margins are larger than average for Canada, Australia, and New Zealand—which themselves offer greater preferences to Britain—and also larger for the Caribbean countries than they were in the Afro-Asian Commonwealth countries.

Another link which binds the U.K. and many Commonwealth countries (with the exception of Canada) is the sterling system. The participating countries keep the values of their currencies stable in terms of sterling, and normally hold a high proportion of their international reserves in the form of sterling. Further, in the years of capital scarcity—notably in the early postwar years—they have enjoyed preferential ac-

[6] *Commonwealth Preference in the United Kingdom* (London, 1960).

[7] See *The Commonwealth and Europe* (London: Economist Intelligence Unit, 1960).

[8] "Commonwealth Preference: Tariff Duties and Preferences on U.K. Exports to the Preference Area," *Board of Trade Journal*, June, 1965.

cess to the London capital market. Since the United Kingdom acts as "banker" to the whole sterling area, variations in non-British member countries' balances of payments are reflected in the U.K. gold reserves. In the past, this often acted as an equilibrating mechanism, inasmuch as the United Kingdom enjoyed favorable terms of trade and buoyant export receipts at times when the terms of trade and export receipts of the rest of the sterling area were relatively unfavorable.

In recent years, however, instead of this "scissors" effect of balance-of-payments changes in the United Kingdom and the rest of the sterling area, the balance of payments of the two areas has tended to move in the same direction. Also, the overseas sterling countries are less willing than hitherto to hold the bulk of their foreign exchange reserves in sterling. Between 1957 and 1962, the reserves of the overseas sterling area rose by $1 billion, but of this 80 per cent was accounted for by increases in their holdings of gold and nonsterling currencies. This reluctance to hold sterling is in part a reflection of the political independence attained by many sterling-area countries, and also reflects a growing tendency on the part of these countries to buy from countries other than the United Kingdom. Finally, sterling-area countries are now less dependent upon the United Kingdom for their capital requirements than they were in the earlier postwar years.

Effects of Integration on British Trade and Foreign Investment

Integration and the balance of trade: some estimates. In this section, estimates will be presented of the probable impact of trade liberalization on British trade in manufactured goods and industrial materials. We will consider the alternatives of establishing an Atlantic Free Trade Area or reducing tariffs by 50 per cent under the most-favored-nation clause. In order to avoid complications caused by the present (as yet incomplete) trade discrimination due to the establishment of the EEC and EFTA, the year upon which the estimates are based is 1960. These estimates try to isolate the static effects of tariff changes; they take no account of the dynamic consequences of trade liberalization on production methods and on competition in the domestic economy.

The effects of tariff reductions on trade will depend on the level of tariffs, the rate of tariff reductions, the geographical and the commodity composition of trade, and the responsiveness of demand and supply to price changes. Among the industrial countries, the British tariff is one of the highest: nonpreferential tariffs average 16.5 per cent on manufactured goods, as compared to 13.2 per cent in the United States, 14.6 per cent in Canada, 12.2 per cent in the Common Market, 9.1 per cent in Continental EFTA, and 17.1 per cent in Japan. But the United Kingdom levies lower duties on imports from the Commonwealth countries and from her EFTA partners.

In line with the assumptions indicated in the Appendix to Chapter 1, we have further assumed that in Britain a 1 per cent fall in import prices would be accompanied by a 3.1 per cent increase in the amount of manufacturing imports, whereas a lower elasticity would pertain to industrial materials. As regards export prices, *Variant I* assumes that the prices on manufactured goods would rise by one-third of the tariff reductions in Western Europe while no change would take place in other areas. Prices of industrial materials are assumed to be unaffected by trade liberalization; this assumption was applied to all products under *Variant II*.

Further, it has been assumed that there would be no net change in the U.K. trade balance with Continental EFTA partners in the event of multilateral tariff reductions. Any change in the British trade balance with Canada, too, is likely to be small. Canada's exports of industrial materials are not subject to tariffs in the United Kingdom, and duties on manufactured goods are generally low. Accordingly, on balance, Canada is likely to lose following multilateral reductions in duties because there would be some switch to non-Commonwealth sources of supply. In turn, British gains in the Canadian market have been assumed to be fully offset by the loss of preferences.

The estimates on the possible effects of trade liberalization for British exports and imports are shown in Table 5.2. First, there are the direct effects resulting from tariff reductions; second, the consequences for the United Kingdom of the lessening of discrimination in EEC and EFTA; and third (in the case of m.f.n.-type tariff reductions), the feedback effects for British exports of the increased export earnings of nonindustrial countries.

TABLE 5.2. TRADE CONSEQUENCES FOR U.K. OF TARIFF REDUCTIONS

(MILLION $)

	1960 value of trade in industrial materials and manufactures	Variant I				Variant II			
		Direct effects	Discrim- inatory effects	Feedback	Combined effects	Direct effects	Discrim- inatory effects	Feedback	Combined effects
Atlantic Free Trade Area									
U.K. imports	2,897	+544	+141	—	+685	+631	+141	—	+772
exports	2,701	+452	+198	—	+650	+579	+198	—	+777
Net change in trade balance		− 92	+ 57	—	− 35	− 52	+ 57	—	+ 5
50 per cent m.f.n. tariff reductions									
U.K. imports	5,461	+334	+ 82	—	+416	+378	+ 82	—	+460
exports	2,701	+226	+ 99	+101	+426	+289	+ 99	+101	+489
Net change in trade balance		−108	+ 17	+101	+ 10	− 89	+ 17	+101	+ 29

Note: For explanation, see Appendix to Chap. 1.

In the case of Variant I, the direct effects of an Atlantic Free Trade Area were estimated to cause U.K. exports of manufactures and industrial materials to rise by 16.7 per cent of their 1960 value ($452 million), and imports by 18.8 per cent ($544 million). The deterioration in the U.K. trade balance would be of the order of $92 million under Variant I as compared to $52 million in the case of Variant II. The elimination of discrimination in EEC and EFTA would, however, lead to an improvement in Britain's trade balance since the discriminatory effects of the EEC on U.K.'s exports are greater than the corresponding effects of EFTA on imports into Britain.

These changes would be cut in half if industrial countries reduced tariffs by only 50 per cent. But their imports from nonindustrial areas would also increase in this case, while the latter are assumed to spend the entire increment in their export earnings. This "feedback" is likely to be greater than the increase in British imports from nonindustrial countries, so that the extension of tariff reductions under the most-favored-nation clause would tend to improve the British balance of trade. But, at any rate, the estimated changes in the U.K. trade balance are rather small.

Separate estimates have not been prepared for a trade arrangement among the industrial countries that excluded the EEC, or for the case of European integration. Nevertheless, the calculations on the geographical breakdown of the expansion of U.K. exports and imports can provide an indication of Britain's interest in these arrangements. It would appear, then, that an accommodation with the Common Market would bring larger benefits for Britain than a trade arrangement with the United States, Canada, and Japan. The United Kingdom would carry out over one-half of the estimated increase in trade with the EEC, and would further gain from the elimination of Common Market discrimination.

Trade discrimination—the evidence. Estimates on the potential effects of trade discrimination in the EEC and EFTA have been made on the basis of the 1960 U.K. trade-pattern. But by the end of 1964, countries in both groupings reduced tariffs on their mutual trade to 30 per cent of the 1960 level. It is possible, therefore, to consider the actual experience of these countries with trade discrimination.

It appears that the United Kingdom increased her share in the import markets and all EEC and EFTA countries, the only exception being Norway. Between 1960 and 1964, the British share in Common Market imports rose from 5.1 to 5.8 per cent, and in EFTA imports, from 10.9 to 11.8 per cent. In the same period, the EEC share in the U.K. import market increased from 15.3 to 16.6 per cent, while the EFTA share rose from 10.7 to 11.3 per cent. But these changes relate to trade as a whole, and it is more meaningful to compare trade flows in those products that are subject to high tariffs.

Table 5.3 compares the performance of particular commodity groups in EEC and U.K. markets by expressing changes in the import shares of these product groups as a proportion of changes in the share of all manufactures. The table shows that within the Common Market there was considerable variation in export performance as between British industries. There is no correlation, however, between the height of tariffs and export performance. On the other hand, EFTA countries have tended to gain at the expense of EEC producers in British markets and, more often than not, these gains have been associated with high British tariffs. Nevertheless, in a number of instances the EEC has done well relative to the EFTA in the U.K. market, in spite of high tariffs: leather manufactures, synthetic yarns, and agricultural machinery are examples.

It should be added that the performance of U.K. exports in the EEC is complicated by the fact that in the process of establishing a common external tariff, the relatively low Benelux and German tariffs have on the whole been rising, and the higher Italian and French tariffs falling. Although in a few cases, such as automobiles and tractors, much of the increase in British exports has taken place in the markets of France and Italy, it does not seem to have been true that the U.K., in general, fared best in those EEC country markets where tariffs were falling. In other words, the "alignment effect" has not been strong.[9]

Perhaps one explanation for the relatively small discriminatory effects of the Common Market on U.K. exports is the fact that the period to 1963 was one of fairly rapidly rising domes-

[9] For a discussion of the implications of the alignment of EEC tariffs with the Common External Tariff, see S. J. Wells, "Trade with Europe," in the symposium on the U.K. balance of payments, *Scottish Journal of Political Economy*, February, 1966.

TABLE 5.3. EFFECT OF DISCRIMINATION ON COMMODITY
TRADE IN WESTERN EUROPE, 1960–63.

Commodity	EEC import market		U.K. import market	
	EEC tariff	Relative change in U.K. share 1960–63[a]	U.K. tariff	Relative change in share of EEC compared with change in share of EFTA in U.K. import market 1960–63[b]
All manufactures	—	100.0	—	100.0
Inorganic chemical elements	9	84.3	14	109.6
Organic chemicals	14	106.0	25	99.8
Pigments, paints, etc.	14	91.8	14	115.5
Medical and pharmaceutical products	13	155.3	15	124.6
Essential oils, and perfumery materials	6	105.5	9	114.5
Fertilizers, manufactured	6	37.5	23	23.0
Leather	8	77.3	14	36.8
Manufactures of leather	14	53.2	20	150.5
Dressed furs, etc.	7	81.4	18	69.5
Rubber manufactures	16	68.4	22	100.9
Rubber tires	16	51.0	25	68.0
Veneers, plywood, etc.	13	97.6	15	363.3
Wood manufactures n.e.s.	13	110.3	12	33.4
Paper and board	10	136.0	6	77.7
Articles of pulp and paperboard	18	65.7	17	38.3
Wool yarn	8	128.3	15	21.4
Cotton yarn, bleached	13	neg.	17	6.8
Yarn of synthetic fibers	15	259.4	22	198.5
Cotton fabrics	14	82.1	20	66.4
Woolen and worsted fabrics	18	83.3	22	72.7
Synthetic fabrics	19	72.9	24	34.8
Made-up articles of textiles	22	94.0	25	42.4
Glass	11	86.4	16	21.1
Glassware	20	112.6	22	89.6
Pottery	23	92.4	14	86.6
Power generating machinery	12	97.8	18	95.2
Agricultural machinery	13	204.5	15	179.8
Tractors	16	111.3	15	51.7
Office machinery	11	117.3	13	104.3
Machine tools	8	105.1	17	134.0
Textile machinery	12	81.2	16	67.8
Electrical machinery	13	75.2	20	103.3
Private cars	20	137.2	25	12.8
Commercial vehicles	19	103.4	25	44.3
Aircraft	10	196.6	16	194.3
Sanitary, plumbing fittings, etc.	17	177.1	19	32.0
Furniture	17	128.6	21	66.1
Travel goods	15	94.0	18	64.9
Clothing	19	97.8	26	57.7
Footwear	20	76.4	24	68.3
Scientific instruments	14	86.6	29	90.7
Photo and cine supplies	16	67.2	13	49.4
Watches and clocks	11	59.3	29	94.0

Notes: [a] Change in U.K. percentage share of EEC import market in each commodity as compared with the change in U.K. share in all manufactures = 100.

[b] Change in EEC percentage share of U.K. import market in each commodity divided by change in percentage share of EFTA in U.K. market in commodity in relation to change in all manufactures.

Source: International trade statistics.

tic costs within the EEC. Moreover, rapid growth has created supply bottlenecks within the Community, particularly in regard to engineering goods, and United Kingdom exporters took advantage of these opportunities. Finally, it should be remembered that tariff changes in the period under consideration have been relatively small.

Integration and the flow of capital. It is customary to distinguish between short- and long-term movements of capital. The former are highly volatile, and tend to be greatly influenced by interest-rate differentials and speculative factors. In the case of the United Kingdom, the magnitude of these flows has been difficult to assess, largely because of the inclusion of part of the short-term capital flow in the "balancing item" of the U.K. balance-of-payments estimates. But whatever difficulties there may be in accurately measuring short-term capital movements, there can be no doubt that these are of considerable magnitude and have greatly influenced U.K. domestic policies. The imposition of a 7 per cent bank rate in September, 1957, and the general tightening of financial policies at that time, were prompted in large part by speculative movements against the pound in the autumn of that year. And, while there was also a severe balance-of-trade crisis in November, 1964, the large outflow of short-term funds played an important role in the decision of the newly elected Labor government to raise the bank rate and impose monetary discipline shortly after taking office.

It is uncertain whether the lowering of tariffs would have any influence on short-term money movements into, and out of, the United Kingdom. The basic question to be answered is whether a change in U.K. trade policy is likely to have an effect upon foreign residents' confidence in the pound. This, in turn, depends on the extent to which trade liberalization is likely to strengthen—or weaken—the competitiveness of British industry. This author's view, which is supported by the majority of businessmen, is that freer trade is likely to have a salutary impact upon the behavior of managers and workers.

In so far as the removal of tariffs would benefit the more enterprising and efficient industries and firms and help to cut away the deadwood of British industry, there would be a clear case for arguing that trade liberalization might ultimately strengthen sterling. But any reallocation of resources in the British economy is bound to take time, and while it is taking place, the reduction of the tariff might lead to a substantial increase in imports, thereby placing serious strain upon the balance of payments. Now it is precisely these periods of deterioration in Britain's overseas position that have, in the past, led to speculative movements against sterling. The very fact that so many countries hold sterling, and that these short-term sterling liabilities are three times as large as the United Kingdom's short-term assets, counsels against the taking of any "risks" with the balance of payments.

But this conclusion should not stand in the way of trade liberalization. In the first place, whether achieved through the formation of a free trade area or by means of GATT multilateral negotiations, trade liberalization is certain to be a gradual process that permits adaptation of British industry to new conditions of world trade. Secondly, during this transitional period, advantage might well be taken of drawing and standby facilities provided in the IMF, and the lines of the credits made available to Britain in November, 1964, by European and American banks. Finally, it should be remembered that the underlying cause of foreign distrust in the pound has been a lack of confidence in the strength of the British economy. There could be no clearer demonstration to the outside world that structural changes were being undertaken in Britain than a general dismantling of protection.

As regards the choice among alternatives, the participation of the U.K. in some kind of free trade area—Atlantic or European—with an institutional framework is more likely to provide opportunities for mutual help to countries in balance-of-payments difficulties than tariff reductions under the most-favored-nation clause. In turn, from the point of view of the U.K. balance of payments, the worst alternative would be a hardening of the present economic differences between the Six and other industrial countries. It would become increasingly difficult to mount an international banking support operation on the lines of the November–December, 1964, and September, 1965, arrangements if the Six and the other industrial countries went their separate ways.

Long-term capital movements can take the form of either portfolio or direct investment, and the decision to invest can be taken by the government, an individual, or a firm. In the case of the United Kingdom, by far the most important form of investment outflow has been private, almost all of it having been undertaken by firms (as distinct from individuals). In 1962, direct investment accounted for over 80 per cent of total private investment. In that year, of total direct investment of $594 million, just over 50 per cent took place in the overseas sterling area.

Direct investment has been of increasing importance in recent years, and this is the type of investment with which this chapter is mostly concerned. The question at issue here is how the lowering of tariff barriers will influence a firm's decisions as to whether or not to expand in a foreign country. There appears to be a *prima facie* assumption that the general raising of tariffs will tend to increase the flow of direct investment, and the lowering of tariffs to decrease it. But in the case of the United Kingdom in recent years, it is by no means obvious that the picture is as simple as that.

While the desire to get behind a tariff wall or to circumvent quantitative restrictions has been one of the primary motives for direct investment abroad by British firms, the desire to obtain access to raw materials, to be close to an expanding market, and to enjoy the incidental benefits of participation in rapidly growing areas may have been more important. In the early postwar years, the Commonwealth countries and especially Canada and Australia were the most attractive outlets for U.K. overseas investment, whether portfolio or direct. Since 1960, however, there has been a shift in the flow of U.K. investment funds away from the Commonwealth and towards Europe. While the tariff discrimination in the EEC might have contributed to this shift, other reasons are likely to have been more important. In the first place, the relatively slow growth of the economies of many Commonwealth countries, together with political uncertainties associated with the attainment of independence in many developing parts of the Commonwealth, have made private investment in these countries much less attractive. Secondly, incomes in Western Europe rose at a rapid rate throughout the postwar period, and the fusion of the national markets of the EEC countries provides further attractions to the inflow of foreign capital.

Firms setting up subsidiaries and branches in continental

Europe might also gain from the technical feedback of knowledge. This feedback may be felt in two ways: first, firms operating overseas obtain direct access to knowledge of new products, techniques, and managerial methods; second, they often derive an impetus to greater efficiency as the result of working in a more competitive environment than at home. Thus, of the U.K. firms operating on the Continent, some 39 per cent have indicated that they have gained from their overseas activity in the form of new ideas on organization and production methods. Just under 50 per cent of these firms claimed that conditions on the Continent were more conducive to efficiency than those of the United Kingdom.[10] Other firms have been known to choose a site on the Continent rather than in Britain in order to take advantage of relatively cheap continental (especially Dutch and Italian) labor, but with the rapid increase in wages after 1960 this must have been a factor of declining significance for explaining the increase in U.K. investment in recent years.

Further evidence that the desire to get behind a tariff wall is only part of the explanation for direct investment is provided by the fact that British investment in the EEC kept rising steadily during 1961 and 1962 when it appeared likely that tariffs between the U.K. and the Common Market would be removed. Neither did the failure of the Brussels negotiations cause a rush of direct investment by U.K. firms to get behind the common external tariff. The increase in the flow of U.K. investment into the Continental EFTA countries is a further consideration. While in 1960 direct investment by U.K. firms in EFTA amounted to $10.9 million, it rose to $44.5 million by 1963. Thus, freer entry of British manufactures has not slowed down, but rather accelerated, the flow of funds into the Continental EFTA countries.

For all of these reasons, it would be hazardous to speculate on the effect of the alternative trade arrangements upon direct investment. The removal of tariffs within Western Europe and within North America would, of itself, reduce the incentive to set up factories abroad, while Atlantic integration might increase the flow of direct investment. At the same time, some U.S. direct investment which is at present taking place in the

[10] J. H. Dunning, "Does Foreign Investment Pay?" *Moorgate and Wall Street*, Autumn, 1964.

EEC would probably be diverted to the U.K., if both the U.K. and the EEC belonged to the same trading area. In contrast, a flow in the opposite direction might occur if the EEC were excluded from an Atlantic Free Trade Area.

Industry Survey

Comparative advantage: some estimates. Whether the U.K. participates in an Atlantic or European free trade area, or whether liberalization takes the form of multilateral m.f.n. tariff reductions, changes will occur in the U.K. production pattern. Some firms may fail to withstand foreign competition in the home market, while others will gain from wider opportunities abroad. In the following section, we will consider possible changes in the British industrial structure as indicated by the indices of "revealed" comparative advantage shown in Appendix Tables 1.2 and 1.3, and in Table 5.4.

Section A of Table 5.4 lists the commodity groups in which export performance vis-à-vis other industrial nations has been especially good. British comparative advantage, as indicated by export performance indices, is less marked for commodities of the second group, and indeterminate for those of the third group. Finally, the United Kingdom had a poor export performance in commodities listed in Section D of the table.

A further indication of comparative advantage is provided by column 3 of Table 5.4, which provides an index of the U.K. export-import ratio. At the same time, the correlation between the two indicators is less for the United Kingdom than for most other industrial countries.[11] This result is explained by the distorting effects of high tariffs on selected commodities that have greatly reduced imports, and raised the corresponding export-import ratios. The largest differences between the two indicators are shown for iron and steel products, glass, synthetic and wool yarn, rubber products, automobiles, railway vehicles, aircraft and drugs.

To begin with, the U.K. tariff on steel products is considerably higher than that of other industrial countries, amounting generally to 10–15 per cent as compared to 5–10 per cent in the United States and the Common Market. In turn, enameled glass

[11] Cf. B. Balassa, "Trade Liberalization and 'Revealed' Comparative Advantage," *Manchester School,* May, 1965.

TABLE 5.4. "REVEALED" COMPARATIVE COST ADVANTAGE
OF U.K. MANUFACTURES[a]

	U.K. tariff	Export index	Export/ import index
A. Where comparative advantage is clearly marked			
Tractors	22	301.3	2054.6
Power generating machinery	19	248.0	182.5
Pigments, paints, varnishes	16	239.8	773.6
Explosives, fireworks	17.5	217.3	6627.5
Commercial vehicles	28	205.1	1030.3
Woolen fabrics	22	200.1	424.5
Bicycles	22	191.9	527.3
Fur clothing	25	163.7	83.6
B. Where there appears to be advantage			
Synthetic dyestuffs	21	145.7	201.1
Special textile fabrics	25	139.4	232.5
Materials of rubber	14	136.8	101.9
Floor coverings	23	136.6	145.6
Leather	14	136.1	100.0
Pottery	25	135.5	94.4
Rubber tires and tubes	27	133.9	279.4
Textile machinery	18	128.7	144.0
Medical and pharmaceutical	17	127.7	686
Private cars	30	124.7	508.7
Electric generating machinery	24	120.7	199.8
C. Where comparative advantage is indeterminate			
Cotton yarn, bleached	18	118.6	186.2
Articles made of paper	18	118	179.5
Other rubber manufactures[b]	22	115.4	1216.5
Manufactures of leather	20	105.2	64.7
Machinery[c]	17	99.5	108.2
Yarn of wool	17	98.1	251.0
Lead, wrought	10	97.2	234.2
Cine and photo supplies	17	95.3	140.7
Tubes, pipes, and fittings	18	94.1	347.1
Inorganic chemicals	14	94.0	123.4
Electrical machinery[d]	21	92.1	160.8
Furniture	20	88.3	127.2
D. Where there appears to be a disadvantage			
Yarn of synthetic fibers	24	80.9	219.9
Sanitary, plumbing, heating	20	77.4	89.1
Agricultural machinery	14	76.5	168.4
Made-up textiles	31	74.2	56.9
Metal-working machinery	10–19	72.3	111.9
Glass	19	72.2	258.4
Organic chemicals	27	69.4	68.3
Scientific instruments	33	68.5	58.5
Glassware	21	66.4	73.5
Office machinery	16	62.1	81.1
Iron and steel bars	14	59.1	434.5
Steel hoops and strips	10	57.6	2756.0
Cotton fabrics	23	54.7	22.6
Footwear	25	47.9	47.5
Clothing	26	43.3	39.8
Travel goods, handbags	18	42.6	42.5
Synthetic fabrics	22	21.4	26.2
Jewelry	20	15.8	16.2
Fertilizers, manufactured	16	6.8	6.2

Notes: [a] This Table does not include commodities in the case of which differences between indicators of export performance and export-import ratios are large.

[b] Excluding tires.

[c] Other than textile machinery.

[d] Other than generating machinery.

Source: Appendix Table 1.2 and 1.3, national tariff statistics.

rods and tubes are subject to a duty of 20 per cent; the tariff on unmarked glass is 15 per cent, and on mirrors 20–30 per cent. Duties on synthetic yarn are also high—16 per cent plus a specific duty of 7.5d. per lb., while producers of wool yarn are protected by a 7.5–10 per cent tariff on pure wool yarns, rising to over 16 per cent where the yarn contains silk or man-made fibres. Finally, U.K. duties on rubber products and automobiles are among the highest among industrial countries. The duty on imported rubber belting is 33.3 per cent; on rubber clothing and gloves 20–24 per cent; on automobiles 23 per cent.

In the case of railway vehicles and aircraft however, the differences between the two indicators are explained by influences other than tariffs. The British government has deliberately followed a policy of encouraging the British Railways (virtually a monopoly buyer) to place orders for locomotives and rolling stock with British manufacturers. The British aircraft industry is heavily subsidized by the government, and political factors are of importance in determining the purchasing policies of the nationalized British Overseas Airways Corporation and British European Airways. Finally, the high export-import ratio on medical and pharmaceutical supplies is explained by the policy of the National Health Service that until recently favored the use of domestically-produced drugs in British hospitals.

All the cases mentioned so far have been ones where the export-import index has been higher than the index of export performance. The reverse is true, among others, on power-generating machinery, leather and leather products, fur clothing, and various chemical products. In these cases, domestic industry appears to have fared well in third markets, but has had a less favorable record meeting foreign competition at home.

Prospects. We can now use some of the data on "revealed" comparative advantage to examine the possible effects. Among the commodity groups which have done especially well in terms of both indices are tractors, paints, explosives, commercial vehicles, woolen fabrics, and bicycles. Commodities at the opposite end of the scale are synthetic fabrics, jewelry, manufactured fertilizers, travel goods, clothing, footwear, and cotton fabrics. At the same time, we often find marked differences within industries—for example, wool textile fabrics have a better record than wool yarn, and there are considerable discrepancies within the chemicals sector.

One of the interesting facts shown by Table 5.4 is the contrast in performance between different branches of the U.K. textile industry. While cotton goods are listed in Section D of Table 5.4, Britain has a marked comparative advantage in woolen fabrics. But substantial differences are shown within the wool manufacturing sector, also. Despite high tariffs, high-quality British worsteds have done well in the industrial countries, but this cannot be said of cheaper woolen goods where Italian producers predominate.

The U.S. duty on woolen and worsted fabrics was raised several times in recent years, and now stands at 49.8 per cent. Thus, free entry into the United States for British wool textiles may provide important gains to Britain. There is evidence that the woolen industry is well poised to take advantage of tariff liberalization. There has recently been a considerable amount of concentration in the industry, which has enabled firms to obtain access to additional finance for installing modern machines. Large firms have always employed the most up-to-date machinery; 27 per cent of the looms used in the industry are automatic, a ratio which is considerably higher than elsewhere in Europe. But in the past, smaller firms have been unable to afford the expensive machinery necessary for higher productivity.[12]

In contrast to the wool industry, the performance of the British cotton textile industry has been rather poor, although cotton yarns have fared better than fabrics. Domestic producers of textile fabrics have been exposed to low-cost competition from India, Pakistan, and Hong Kong, but imports from these countries would not rise as the result of the U.K. joining an Atlantic or a European free trade area. Nevertheless, the British tariff on cotton products is higher than that of most European countries, so that trade liberalization would probably entail losses in domestic markets to foreign producers. At

---

[12] The smallest economic unit of large-package spinning frames might cost as much as £150,000. See *Growth of the United Kingdom Economy to 1966*, National Economic Development Council, (London: Her Majesty's Stationery Office, p. 123).

the same time, the British experience in EFTA suggests that trade in cotton yarn is particularly sensitive to changes in tariffs.

Table 5.4 also shows that the United Kingdom is at a comparative cost disadvantage in man-made textiles. In spite of high tariffs on both yarn and fabric imports, the industry appears to have been unable to hold its own against imports. Trade liberalization would expose the British man-made textile industry to competition from other industrial countries and especially from Japan, and the removal of duties is likely to lead to substantially increased imports. As for the U.K. textile industry as a whole, trade liberalization is likely to encourage closer integration, both horizontal and vertical, in all branches of textiles, especially in cotton. As a result, the disappearance of small, inefficient firms would almost certainly be accelerated.

In clothing and footwear, too, the U.K. appears to have a marked comparative disadvantage. The only industrial countries where the duties on clothing are higher than Britain are Portugal and the United States; in footwear, only Austria and Portugal impose higher duties. In view of the substantial increase since 1958 of the share of overseas suppliers in the U.K. market for these products, the outlook for both the clothing and footwear industries in the event of a general tariff reduction is unfavorable indeed. And while the better-quality fashion sector is optimistic about prospects of expanding sales in North America and the Common Market, it seems unlikely that this expansion would be sufficient to compensate for losses in the lower-quality sector on the home market. At the same time, the advantages of freer trade are likely to be reaped by the relatively few large and efficient firms which already have thriving export sales. As for footwear, imports from the EEC account for some 40 per cent of all footwear imports into the United Kingdom—and Italy accounts for two-thirds of imports from the Community. The removal of the present 25 per cent U.K. tariff on footwear is likely to strengthen the Italian position to a considerable extent. Japan is not at present a significant exporter of footwear to Britain, but given free entry she will be a formidable competitor also.

No clear pattern can be discerned in performance of the U.K. engineering industry. Tractors and power machinery are among the star performers; metal-working machinery (including machine tools) and office machinery are in Section D of Table 5.4. Farm tractors hold an exceptionally (and increasingly) large share of the EEC import market, in spite of an average EEC tariff of 16 per cent. Sales of tractors to the EEC countries in 1963 amounted to nearly $60 million— about one-fifth of the total value of U.K. tractor exports. However, the gains of the United Kingdom have been largely in France where the tariff on U.K. imports has been falling. Rationalization of agriculture, which is rapidly taking place on the continent of Europe, has created a demand for larger tractors of 50 h.p.; this is the type of vehicle that the large British firms are well fitted to supply.

Among other types of farm machinery, the most important British exports are combine harvesters, followed by pick-up balers. International Combine Harvesters dominate the world market in the former, and at present it seems unlikely that freer trade would enable U.K. exports to increase much. In contrast to tractors and harvesters, small firms catering to a local market in implements are at a distinct advantage, especially where there are wide variations in soil conditions and farm techniques. There are large numbers of small but highly efficient firms producing implements in the Common Market, and these are unlikely to be displaced by competition from Britain, especially as duties on such implements are generally low.

The performance of the United Kingdom office machinery industry has been disappointing, particularly as this includes electronic computers and other statistical machines, world demand for which is rising at a rapid rate. Similar considerations apply to metal-working machinery, and within this industry, to machine tools. That the United Kingdom is a net importer of machine tools is not necessarily a symptom of lack of efficiency; neither, by itself, is the fact that imports have in recent years risen considerably. What is a matter of concern, however, is that the U.K. tends to export simpler machines and to import more complex models. Thus, the unit value of machine-tool exports is considerably lower in the United Kingdom than in the United States, Germany, and France.[13] Per-

[13] See *Times Review of Industry and Technology,* October, 1964.

haps the present structure of British industry is not conducive to better performance; of the three-hundred-odd firms in the industry, only about twenty are said to be "of significant size." At the same time, in the mid-1950s, expenditure on research accounted for only 0.7 per cent of the value of sales.

The electrical industry occupies a midway position in Table 5.4; generating machinery, however, appears to have been more successful than other sectors of the industry. The British cable industry has also done well in export markets; its share in world exports is exceeded only by that of the United States. Production is in the hands of three or four large producers, and the industry seems confident of its ability to hold its own, both at home and overseas. Prospects for British home appliances are less bright. U.K. duties on these products are generally high—20 per cent on radios and cooking apparatus, 15 per cent on vacuum cleaners, food mixers, and other domestic equipment—and trade liberalization is expected to lead to increases in imports unmatched by the rise of exports.

The British motor vehicle industry has fared extremely well in foreign markets in recent years—especially in Western Europe where there has been a marked rise in the United Kingdom share in EEC imports. In fact, despite relatively high tariffs, the British automobile industry has expanded its sales faster in the EEC than in EFTA. Both the passenger and commercial vehicle branches of the British industry have been successful. It should be noted, however, that the U.K. duty on imported motor vehicles is very high, so that tariff reductions would be followed by increases in imports. In turn, foreign competition is likely to lead to a reduction in the number of models, and may also necessitate concentration in the British automobile industry.

The fortunes of several industries are closely linked to the motor vehicle industry. Table 5.4 suggests that the United Kingdom has a comparative cost advantage in producing tires. In view of the "international" nature of this industry, it is particularly difficult to estimate the effect on trade of the removal of tariffs which are generally high (an average of 20 per cent in the EEC, 27 per cent in the U.K., and 19 per cent in the United States). And while the removal of tariffs may bring about a more rational division of labor in the world rubber-tire industry, there is no reason to believe that the proportion of world output produced in the United Kingdom would change to an appreciable extent. Finally, manufactures of rubber products other than tires also appear to enjoy a comparative advantage in Great Britain. This is especially true of quality rubber products—e.g., rubber moldings for the motor industry and webbing upholstery.

The chemical industry has had varied export performance. According to Table 5.4, the United Kingdom has a comparative advantage in pigments, paints and varnishes, and a disadvantage in manufactured fertilizers. Fertilizer production in the United Kingdom is protected by a 16 per cent tariff—easily the highest of any country in the Atlantic area—pointing to losses to the industry in the event of trade liberalization. British pharmaceutical producers, too, receive more protection than their American competitors, but as in the case of rubber tires, the industry is highly internationalized, and it is not easy to foresee future prospects.

In the manufacturing industry as a whole, it seems clear that considerable adjustments are possibly forthcoming in the British economy following the liberalization of trade; but from the evidence available, it appears likely that adjustments would take the form of greater specialization within industries, rather than the demise of entire industries. It would seem, too, that present trends toward larger-scale production units are likely to be strengthened, particularly where large amounts of financing are necessary.

Industrial location. Further consideration should be given to the regional problem of the United Kingdom, which arises from the fact that in certain areas (notably Northern Ireland, Scotland, and Northern England), employment, income per capita, and growth rates of output have been lower than in the Midlands and the Southeast. While this question has received a great deal of attention in recent years, little consideration has been given to the effect of trade liberalization upon the subject. Trade liberalization may affect areas of high unemployment and low incomes in at least two ways. First, if industries which are likely to gain from integration are heavily concentrated in depressed areas, freer trade will have a beneficial effect upon their growth prospects; but if, on the other hand, a relatively high proportion of less well-placed industries are located in these areas, trade liberalization will have a harmful effect upon their prospects. Second, closer integration with particular geographical areas, especially with Europe, might have important implications for the export prospects of certain regions. Integration with Europe, for example, might favor southeastern England at the expense of Northern Ireland and Scotland.

As regards the first consideration, some of the industries most likely to be adversely affected by multilateral tariff reductions are, in fact, in areas of already relatively high unemployment. Only 2.3 per cent of those engaged in the manufacturing industry in the United Kingdom in 1958 were in Northern Ireland, but 6.3 per cent of those engaged in textiles were employed there. Within textiles, the cotton and man-made fiber industries predominate in Northern Ireland; these are sectors whose prospects are rather poor in the event of trade liberalization. Furthermore, over 4 per cent of those employed in the U.K. clothing industry are in Northern Ireland.

Scotland also has a heavy concentration of industries which appear to be at a comparative cost disadvantage—among them textiles, clothing (especially hosiery), glass, watches and clocks, scientific instruments, and shipbuilding. In turn, over one-fifth of those employed in the shipbuilding and marine-engineering industries are in northern England, and nearly 10 per cent of those engaged in locomotive and railway equipment. Nearly 13 per cent of those employed in chemical industries are also in this region, but the branches where concentration is heaviest (synthetic resins, plastic materials, and coal tar products) are not among the more successful of the chemicals industry.

On the other hand, paints and pharmaceuticals which have (according to Table 5.4) a comparative advantage in the United Kingdom, are concentrated in the more prosperous regions. In fact, many of the commodity groups whose prospects are the most favorable are located in the Southeast and Midlands. Motor vehicles, paints, and explosives all account for a higher-than-average share of employment in these regions. Slightly under 20 per cent of the United Kingdom-employed labor force in 1958 was located in London and the southeastern region, and 13.6 per cent in the Midlands. At the same time, over 38 per cent of those engaged in motor-vehicle manufacture were in the Midlands, and 19.4 per cent in London and the southeastern region, while only 4.1 and 2.6 per cent respectively of the textile labor force were located in these regions.

Clearly, more detailed research is necessary to assess accurately the impact of freer trade upon the individual regions of the United Kingdom. Still it seems that on balance, trade liberalization is likely to worsen the prospects of regions with relatively high unemployment and brighten those where labor is scarce, thereby aggravating Britain's regional problem. Accordingly, the liberalization of trade would probably result in a further movement of labor towards the southeast, intensifying the already serious problem of providing social capital (especially houses and transport services) for this region, and causing further waste of social capital in the north and west.

As regards our second consideration, it has often been argued in Britain that industries close to the southeast ports would gain most in terms of wider export opportunities if the United Kingdom were more closely linked with Europe. In the event of participation in an Atlantic free trade area, the argument is less strong, since in transatlantic trade the western ports have an advantage over London and the south.

But the importance of transport costs in the British economy should not be exaggerated. A report on the regional problem in Scotland revealed nothing to support the view that transport costs were a substantial burden on the manufacturing industry in industrial Scotland.[14] The transport problem is perhaps of greater importance for firms which are established in Northern Ireland. But even here, a recent survey[15] has shown that of a sample of twenty-eight firms, (employing—

[14] *Inquiry into the Scottish Economy 1960–61*, Report of the Committee appointed by the Scottish Council ("The Toothill Report"), p. 75. Of a sample of representative firms, 26 per cent found the extra transport costs resulting from establishment in Scotland to amount to over 1 per cent of total costs; 37 per cent found that some increase in costs existed, but it amounted to less than 1 per cent of costs. Twenty-six per cent of the firms in the sample reported that location in Scotland made no difference to their transport costs; 11 per cent found that transport costs were actually lower in Scotland. Of a further sample of firms selected by the Transport Division of the Scottish Council because they might be expected to experience some transport hardship, about 85 per cent discounted the additional transport costs as a factor of importance.

[15] David Law, "Industrial Movement and Locational Advantage," *Manchester School*, May, 1964.

together—11,714 workers) which had set up factories in Northern Ireland, fourteen found that increased transport costs resulting from establishment there raised unit production costs by less than 2.5 per cent. At the same time, there was a general consensus that lower real wage costs and ease of physical expansion more than compensated these moderate increases in transport costs. None of the firms interviewed regretted their decision to start operations in Northern Ireland.

Looking Ahead

Dynamic aspects. Apart from the reallocative effect, the liberalization of trade is likely to have an impact upon the average size of British firms, since the widening of markets may justify the establishment of large, specialized plants. At the same time, large firms have better opportunities to engage in research, to introduce new products, and to incur selling expenditures abroad. A larger market would also intensify competition, whereas a small market often leads to monopoly.

In their study of British industry, Carter and Williams found a number of cases where the British market was apparently too small to encourage rapid industrial progress.[16] Apart from disadvantages of the relatively small size of many British firms, the authors argue that in a small national market, the prizes of success are less obvious and excuses for inaction are more readily made. Moreover, the growth of specialization would permit the production of more specialized equipment (e.g., machine tools), and this, in its turn, would create new opportunities of progress. Carter and Williams suggest that a larger market might create new prospects for progress in paper and rubber manufactures, as well as in the scientific instrument and aircraft industries.

There is little doubt that American industry enjoys many of the advantages of large-scale production and concentration denied to British producers. It is less known that in the majority of manufacturing industries, firms are larger in Germany than in the United Kingdom. Andrew Shonfield, in his study of

[16] C. F. Carter and B. R. Williams, *Industry and Technical Progress* (London, 1957).

modern capitalism, has pointed out that 100 of the biggest firms in Western Germany in 1960 were responsible for nearly 40 per cent of industrial output, and employed one out of every three workers in industry.[17] In turn, the largest 180 British firms account for 38 per cent of manufacturing output and one-third of employment. It would appear, then, that the degree of concentration in British manufacturing industry is lower than in Germany, although the data for the United Kingdom cover only the manufacturing industries, while those for Western Germany relate to all industries, including mining and power. The extent of concentration has increased in Britain in recent years; wider export outlets and increased foreign competition in the domestic market would accelerate this process.

At the time of the Brussels negotiations for entry into the Common Market, much attention was given to the favorable "demonstration effects" upon British industry which were believed to follow participation in the Community. It was assumed that the "salutary jolt" resulting from increased competition would rid British industry of much of its deadwood. Firms would have to modernize, to become efficient in their use of manpower, and use up-to-date marketing methods in order to survive. After 1962, there was some reaction from this view in Britain. It has been said that while the integration of the U.K. economy into some wider grouping *could* make of Britain a second Ruhr, it could also turn it into another Northern Ireland.

In the eyes of most British economists, however, the 1964–66 economic crisis has strengthened, rather than weakened, the "salutary jolt" argument for integration. To an increasingly large number of observers, it has become apparent that only the shock of some radical readjustment would provide the incentive for the readaptation of British industry which was so obviously necessary if growth were to be accelerated.

In this study, it has been argued that not only would the jolt of competition prove salutary to many British industries, but that there is scope for further specialization of production in

[17] *Modern Capitalism* (Oxford University Press, 1965), p. 241.

British industry. Much of the increase in trade between the partner countries of Benelux in the 1950s, and between EEC members in the early years of the Community, has taken the form of increases within particular commodity groups rather than between commodity groups; this suggests that increased specialization within industries is one of the advantages which Britain might derive from membership in a large grouping.[18] For example, in a regime of freer trade, the United Kingdom might well find that certain branches of—say the electrical engineering industry—would expand, while other branches would tend to suffer a relative decline, but that there would be little question of the decline of the *whole* electrical engineering industry. Moreover, if freer trade resulted in lower unit-production costs, British exports to nonparticipating countries as well as to member countries might be expected to expand. Thus, there would be an indirect gain to the U.K. balance of trade, of which no account has been taken in the quantitative estimates.

Alternatives for Britain. What are the merits of the various methods of reducing trade barriers? If the United Kingdom joined an Atlantic Free Trade Area, there would be substantial gains in certain sectors where the United States tariff is high. In the longer run, the United Kingdom is also likely to benefit from the demonstration effect of closer competition with highly efficient American firms. Probably, too, some of the problems which arise from the United Kingdom's role as an international banker would be most easily solved in an Atlantic framework.

But, many of the economic advantages of Atlantic integration would be secured if Britain joined a geographically more limited trading arrangement. On the other hand, the economic gains for the United Kingdom of joining an Atlantic grouping which excluded the EEC would be rather limited also. There would be a loss of close contact with the rapidly growing economies of the Common Market countries. Also, U.S. capital would tend to flow toward the EEC rather than the U.K. Even

[18] Cf. B. Balassa, "Tariff Reductions and Trade in Manufactures among the Industrial Countries," *American Economic Review* (June, 1966), pp. 466–73.

the recent successes of British exports to the EEC would be unlikely to continue as discrimination against the U.K. increased and as tariff barriers hardened.

From the political point of view, there is much in favor of Britain's joining a European, rather than a broader Atlantic, grouping. Within Western Europe, the U.K. could exercise a leading role; in an Atlantic community, she would be overshadowed by the political and economic power of the United States. The least attractive possibility would be for the U.K. to link itself with an Atlantic group which excluded the Common Market, since Britain would become a kind of junior partner to the United States, and her influence in relation to that of the Community would continue to decline. Thus, in terms of power politics, there is much to be said for working toward full membership in the EEC as a step towards the establishment of a European political union.

In this connection, it should also be added that while British ties with some countries in the Commonwealth remain strong, there is a tendency for Commonwealth nations to become less concerned with trade links with the United Kingdom. Many of these countries are now seeking trade arrangements which cut across Commonwealth ties or involve non-Commonwealth countries. A dramatic example is the case of Nigeria, which has concluded an association treaty with the Common Market, although it had earlier opposed British participation in the EEC.

Britain would further benefit from multilateral tariff reductions. However, it can be argued that tariff reductions which take place outside an institutional framework are less likely to have the salutary psychological impact of those secured in the framework of free trade area arrangements. There is nothing like a tight program of tariff reductions to be carried out in accordance with an agreed-upon timetable to convince businessmen that they must face up to the competition from abroad. Tariff negotiations in the GATT are often long drawn out, uncertain in their results, and subject to modifications and exception lists. For this reason, freer trade secured under these conditions is less likely to administer successfully the salutary jolt to British industry than would participation in a free trade area.

Fortunately, the alternatives discussed here are not mutually exclusive. Thus, the wisest course for Britain at the present time is to work for closer integration in Western Europe, and at the same time to give full support to multilateral trade liberalization. This course of action would combine the political and economic advantages of European integration with co-operation in the Atlantic area. Such a co-operation is necessary for strengthening the West in its dealings with Communist countries, as well as for helping the less developed countries. Only if the countries of the Atlantic area are prosperous, and their economies are growing rapidly will they be able to provide the capital and the trading opportunities necessary for harmonious political and economic progress in less developed areas.

CHAPTER VI

TRADE ARRANGEMENTS AMONG INDUSTRIAL COUNTRIES: EFFECTS ON SCANDINAVIA

Staffan B. Linder[1]

Historical Perspective

Among the Scandinavian countries, the decline of the mercantilist doctrines first affected the trade policy of Denmark. A liberal tariff law was adopted in this country in 1797; this law applied also to Norway that was, at the time, under Danish rule. On the other hand, trade policy in Sweden was characterized by protectionism until the middle of the nineteenth century. But trade barriers were reduced in subsequent decades; furthermore, in 1874, tariffs were eliminated between Sweden and Norway, which had formed a political union in 1814, although retaining autonomy in matters of trade policy.

Toward the end of the century, protectionist forces again gained strength in Sweden even though, by international standards, tariff levels were only moderate. Attitudes in Norway changed in the same direction. It is symptomatic that the break-up of the free trade area between Sweden and Norway in the 1890s was due not only to the political animosity that led to the dissolution of the political union in 1905, but also to the pressure of protectionism. A contributing reason was the fear of trade deflection in Sweden, which was assumed to take the form of the inflow of foreign goods via Norway which, at that time, had lower tariffs than Sweden.

The revival of protectionism was short-lived, however, and aside from the periods of war and the depression of the 1930s, the Scandinavian countries have followed liberal trade policies since the turn of the century. The reasons for the pursuance of these policies are easy to see. The Scandinavian countries are small, and their natural resource endowments show a

[1] The author is associate professor at the Stockholm School of Economics.

155

marked skewness; they can derive considerable benefits from the reallocation of resources through trade and from obtaining large-scale economies in their export industries. Thus, in formulating trade policies in these countries, the emphasis has been on long-term gains rather than on short-term expediency. At the same time, their foreign policy objectives have not conflicted with the liberal commercial policy dictated by economic considerations.

It is understandable, therefore, that the Scandinavian countries actively participated in the post-war efforts aimed at a liberalization of trade, and supported the creation of GATT and OEEC. Talks had also begun on the establishment of a Nordic Customs Union, but this plan encountered various obstacles, and after protracted discussions, the negotiations eventually broke down. The difficulties were due in particular to a certain hesitation in Norway, to expose its industries to the competition of the well-established Swedish manufacturing industry. Nevertheless, after the first attempt to create an all-European free trade area failed, Norway and Denmark, together with Sweden, decided to participate in the European Free Trade Association. Subsequently, Denmark, whose agricultural exports were threatened by the discriminatory affects of the agricultural policy of the EEC, joined the United Kingdom in applying for full membership in the Common Market. As the negotiations progressed, Norway also applied for full membership, and Sweden for association.

The subsequent breakdown of the Brussels negotiations on the enlargement of the Common Market gave new lease on life to EFTA. At the same time, the Scandinavian countries have continued to pursue their interests in multilateral trade liberalization. They are strong supporters of the Kennedy Round of tariff negotiations, and follow with interest the new British effort to gain entry into the EEC. In the present chapter, we will evaluate the trade policy alternatives which have been proposed in recent years from the point of view of the political and economic objectives of the Scandinavian countries. Political considerations will be examined first, and following a short section that provides an economic background, the static and dynamic benefits of trade liberalization will be analyzed. Finally, some suggestions will be offered concerning the choice among alternative arrangements for the Scandinavian countries.

Political Considerations

Aside from the requirement that the measures undertaken in the trade field should not lead to political commitments, the foreign policy objectives of the Scandinavian countries have rarely affected their trade policies. Due to the smallness of these countries, they have not attempted to gain influence in the affairs of other nations by means of trade policy. At the same time, their smallness has made them vulnerable to the possible attempts of other countries to use trade policy for such a purpose. It follows that the countries of the area have a special interest in multilateral trade liberalization, and that they would welcome the continuation of tariff reductions under the most-favored-nation clause. This is particularly true of Sweden whose policy has traditionally been one of neutrality and nonalignment.

However, the multilateral approach leads to trade connections of differing intensity between countries and country groups. There are several nations—of which the Soviet Union is the most important—that have stayed outside of GATT; furthermore, geographical distance and economic structure have an important influence on trade flows. Thus, we find that the Scandinavian countries, taken individually, carry out almost three-fourths of their trade within Western Europe, one-tenth with the other industrial nations, 5 per cent with Soviet-type economies, and the remainder with less developed countries (Table 6.1). Nevertheless, given the affinity of political views and interests, this dependence on trade ties with the West has been considered acceptable in Sweden. In turn, Denmark and Norway have joined NATO and—as noted above—they applied for full membership in the EEC on the occasion of the first British application for entry.

In Sweden, on the other hand, various objections have been raised against participation in the EEC. It has been argued that in such an event, Sweden would no longer be free to conclude trade agreements on her own with third countries, she would have difficulties in following independent economic policies aimed at preserving her neutrality in times of war;

TABLE 6.1. AREA DISTRIBUTION OF SCANDINAVIAN EXPORTS AND IMPORTS

(EXPORTS, F.O.B.; IMPORTS, C.I.F.)

	Denmark				Norway			
	Exports		Imports		Exports		Imports	
	million $	per cent	million $	per cent	million $	per cent	million $	per cent
U.S. and Canada	133	7.1	194	9.2	111	10.4	193	10.6
EEC	543	29.0	761	35.9	289	26.9	543	29.8
EFTA (incl. Finland)	852	45.5	757	35.7	455	42.4	804	44.2
of which Denmark	—	—	—	—	76	7.0	109	6.0
Norway	115	6.2	76	3.6	—	—	—	—
Sweden	199	10.6	254	12.0	147	13.7	349	19.1
Scandinavia	314	16.8	330	15.6	223	20.7	458	25.1
Finland	36	1.9	45	2.1	19	1.8	11	0.6
Japan	9	0.5	17	0.8	4	0.4	13	0.7
Other developed countries	63	3.3	41	2.0	51	4.8	42	2.3
Soviet-type economies	93	5.0	101	4.7	42	3.9	48	2.7
Developing countries	181	9.6	249	11.7	121	11.2	179	9.7
Total	1,874	100.0	2,120	100.0	1,073	100.0	1,822	100.0

TABLE 6. 1. (CONTINUED)

| | Sweden | | | | Scandinavia, consolidated | | | |
| | Exports | | Imports | | Exports | | Imports | |
	million $	per cent	million $	per cent	million $	per cent of total imports	million $	per cent of total imports
U.S. and Canada	206	6.4	368	10.9	450	9.0	755	12.2
EEC	1,026	32.0	1,319	38.9	1,858	37.1	2,623	42.3
EFTA (incl. Finland)	1,289	40.2	1,031	30.4	1,455	29.0	1,460	23.5
of which Denmark	246	7.7	191	5.6	—	—	—	—
Norway	358	11.2	153	4.5	—	—	—	—
Sweden	—	—	—	—	—	—	—	—
Scandinavia	604	18.9	344	10.1	193	3.9	113	1.8
Finland	138	4.3	57	1.7	29	0.6	66	1.1
Japan	16	0.5	36	1.0				
Other developed coun-tries	200	6.3	78	2.3	314	6.3	161	2.6
Soviet-type economies	138	4.3	162	4.8	273	5.4	311	5.0
Developing countries	328	10.3	399	11.7	630	12.6	827	13.3
Total	3,203	100.0	3,393	100.0	5,009	100.0	6,203	100.0

Source: National Statistics and OECD.

last, but not least, the supranational aspects of European integration have been said to come into conflict with Sweden's longstanding neutrality.

Some Swedish groups and commentators have suggested, however, that these specific reservations are of a somewhat legalistic nature, and that they have been used as a "cover" for other, more vague, objections against EEC membership. It would seem that in some quarters, opposition to full membership under the Rome Treaty is derived from a feeling of uncertainty concerning the possibility that commitments within the Common Market gradually would increase beyond what could now be foreseen, and that this process would change the whole basis of Sweden's economic and political identity. Fears that the EEC would develop into an inward-looking entity rather than furthering multilateral trade liberalization also have played a role. Some such misgivings have also made their appearance in Norway, although here their political weight has been considerably smaller.

The wider the integration area, the smaller the undertakings beyond the elimination of tariffs can possibly be. This means that the establishment of an Atlantic Free Trade Area would not give rise to any of the political reservations to full membership in the EEC. On the other hand, such an arrangement would have other political disadvantages. The wider the integration area, the more conspicuous is the discrimination against outsiders and the greater is the political affront to these countries. In the present case, the outsiders would be made up of two groups of nations, namely, the developing countries and Soviet-type economies.

Discrimination against the developing countries would conflict with the principles enunciated at the 1964 United Nations Conference on Trade and Development. The argument that not much of their present trade would be exposed to discrimination is politically weak, and its economic validity is reduced if the potentialities of expanding the exports of manufactured goods from less-developed areas are considered. Moreover, the Scandinavian countries which apply the most-favored-nation clause to their trade with the Soviet Union and other Eastern European countries would be under strong pressure to extend zero tariffs to these nations. This would be especially true for Sweden, which has a political interest in avoiding steps that might lead to Soviet retaliation against Finland. Although the nonapplication of zero tariff rates to Communist countries may be defended by reference to GATT provisions on customs unions and free trade areas, this argument is not likely to impress the Communist countries if the integration project embraced all industrial nations.

The political drawbacks of an Atlantic Free Trade Area could be reduced by extending tariff concessions at least to the developing countries. But, for practical purposes, this alternative would become undistinguishable from the elimination of trade obstacles under the most-favored-nation clause without requiring reciprocity on the part of the developing nations. At the same time, for reasons of political expediency, it seems easier to reach this goal through periodical tariff reductions than by establishing an Atlantic Free Trade Area.

Discrimination against less-developed countries and against the Communist bloc would be less conspicuous in case of a trade arrangement among the industrial countries that excluded the European Common Market. Such an arrangement could take the form of a free trade area or a preference system. Of the two, considerations of political feasibility would probably lead to the use of preferences—euphemistically called tariff reductions under the "conditional m.f.n."—that would apply only to countries which are prepared to offer reciprocal concessions. A system of preferences would, however, tend to antagonize the Common Market and to complicate trade arrangements within Western Europe. Moreover, it might easily lead to the breakup of GATT. These repercussions would be objectionable to the Scandinavian countries, for whom a weakly-knit preference area with the U.S., Canada, and Japan would not offer sufficient compensation for the risks such an arrangement would entail. In this connection, it should be noted that the obligations undertaken by the participating countries may be disregarded even more readily than has been the case in EFTA where the United Kingdom found it convenient to impose a surcharge on imports in the years 1964–66. At the same time, a U.S.–Canada–EFTA preferential arrangement may not withstand pressures even smaller than what produced the British breach of contract in EFTA.

This does not prevent, however, that increasing attention be given to the possibilities of creating some kind of preferential arrangement in the event that other avenues of trade liberalization appear blocked. Professor Bertil Ohlin, the leader of one of the opposition parties in Sweden, had at one time advocated such a scheme. Clearly, Ohlin's suggestions were based on a pessimistic appraisal of the chances for other types of trade arrangements. His recommendations have not been taken up by others, possibly because of differences in the evaluation of possible future events. At any rate, even though a preferential scheme excluding the EEC would not be instituted unless there was what would appear to be a definite breakdown in negotiations on European economic arrangements and multilateral trade liberalization, such a breakdown could only *seem* definite but it could never *be* definite. Circumstances may change and create new possibilities for the former alternatives. In the Scandinavian countries, and especially in Denmark, the particular merits of trade arrangements would tend to be evaluated in relation to their effects on trade arrangements in Western Europe. While there may be groups, particularly in Norway, that feel much more closely attached to the United Kingdom and the United States than to the European continent, in case of a renewed British application for entry into the EEC, these objections against European integration will lose in strength.

Economic Background

In order to evaluate the economic effects of alternative arrangements, it is necessary to provide some information about the structure of foreign trade in the Scandinavian coun-

TABLE 6.2. SHARE OF FOREIGN TRADE IN VALUE ADDED IN
THE PRODUCTION OF TRADED GOODS IN SCANDINAVIA

		Export Share		Import Share		Average Share	
		1953	1963	1953	1963	1953	1963
Denmark		49.3	56.9	52.9	64.4	51.1	60.7
Norway		45.3	58.7	81.3	99.7	63.3	79.2
Sweden		42.4	45.3	45.2	48.0	43.8	46.6
Scandinavia							
	Total	43.2	49.1	52.2	58.6	47.7	53.9
	Extra-area	37.8	40.0	46.6	49.5	42.2	48.8

Source: National and international trade statistics.

tries. Tables 6.1 to 6.3 bring together such material. In Table 6.2, the ratio of exports and imports to value added in the production of traded goods is shown for the individual countries, and for the three countries taken together. Further, Tables 6.1 and 6.3 indicate the geographical and the commodity composition of this trade.

The importance of foreign trade for each of the Scandinavian countries is evident from the data of Table 6.2. The consolidation of trade data for the Scandinavian countries entails the elimination of their mutual trade from the figures; still, the consolidated data on the ratio of exports and imports to value added in the production of traded goods is comparable to that of Sweden by itself. It is apparent, therefore, that trade with countries outside of the area is of considerable significance for Scandinavia. Finally, it should be noted that in the case of Norway, the large excess of imports over exports is explained by the fact that a substantial proportion of Norwegian export earnings is derived from shipping that comes under the service account in the balance-of-payments statistics.

The area distribution of foreign trade shown in Table 6.1 has implications for the relative attractiveness of trade policy alternatives under consideration. The European market is of dominating importance for all three Scandinavian countries. Trade with countries that belong to neither EEC nor EFTA hardly amounts to one-fourth of their total trade, and this proportion does not exceed one-third, even in the case that intra-Scandinavian exchange is excluded from the calculations.

As to the relative importance of the two European integration projects in the trade of the Scandinavian countries, EFTA leads in regard to both Norwegian and Danish exports and imports, while Sweden's trade with the two areas is of approximately equal value. Trade between the EEC and EFTA in 1963 has been affected by discrimination against members of the opposing group, due to tariff reductions undertaken within each area. Hence, comparisons provide a somewhat distorted picture. Still, the 1963 figures indicate the great importance of EEC as compared to the United States and Canada in the trade of the Scandinavian countries. Despite the discriminatory effects of the Common Market's establishment, in 1963 exports to, and imports from, the EEC countries exceeded by four times trade with the United States and Canada.

Trade with the developing countries is of comparable magnitude to that with North America. Much of this consists of exports of manufactures and imports of primary products; in this respect, hardly any differences are shown among the three countries. On the other hand, Soviet-type economies are more important as trading partners for Denmark and Sweden than for Norway, and trade with Japan is the largest in the case of Sweden. Interestingly, while Swedish industrialists often complain about Japanese competition, exports to Japan exceed imports by one-and-one-half.

As regards the commodity composition of trade, the large share of manufactures in both exports and imports is characteristic of the pattern of specialization among the industrial countries. But at least in the case of Denmark and Norway, the large export share of manufactured goods is a relatively recent phenomenon; between 1953 and 1963, the relevant proportions increased from 21.7 to 40.2 per cent in Denmark, and from 38.0 to 50.6 per cent in Norway. The restructuring of exports is of especial interest to Denmark, where agricultural exports have fallen back from their commanding position within a short period of time. This change reflects not so much the restrictions applied to Danish food exports in the Common Market as to the expansion of manufacturing industries in Denmark. Machinery and instruments, ships, and furniture are leading exports among manufactured products, while livestock, meat, butter, cheese, and eggs predominate in the agricultural group. Nevertheless, the value of agricultural exports still exceeds that of manufactured goods in Denmark.

In turn, paper, ships, pig iron, and fertilizers loom large in the manufactured exports of Norway, with industrial materials—chiefly wood pulp and unwrought aluminum and nickel—occupying second place. Among agricultural commodities, fish and fish preparations are of importance. Finally, Sweden exports a large variety of manufactured goods, among which the most noteworthy are engineering products, automobiles, ships, paper, and special steels. Swedish exports of agricultural commodities are negligible, but sales of shaped wood,

TABLE 6.3. COMMODITY DISTRIBUTION OF SCANDINAVIAN FOREIGN TRADE

Exports (in f.o.b. prices)

SITC categories	Denmark 1953		Denmark 1963		Norway 1953		Norway 1963		Sweden 1953		Sweden 1963	
	mil-lion $	per cent	mil-lion $	per cent	mil-lion $	per cent	mil-lion $	per cent	mil-lion $	per cent	mil-lion $	per cent
Food and beverages, 0+1	647	71.5	958	51.3	102	20.1	159	15.0	80	5.4	105	3.3
Industrial materials, 2+4 + unwrought metals	61	6.7	145	7.7	211	41.5	334	31.5	690	46.6	888	27.8
Fuels, 3	1	0.1	12	0.7	2	0.4	31	2.9	1	—	15	0.5
Manufactured goods, 5+6+7+8 − un-wrought metals	197	21.7	750	40.2	193	38.0	538	50.6	710	48.0	2,183	68.4
Total	912	100.0	1,874	100.0	508	100.0	1,073	100.0	1,480	100.0	3,203	100.0

Imports (in c.i.f. prices)

SITC categories	Denmark 1953		Denmark 1963		Norway 1953		Norway 1963		Sweden 1953		Sweden 1963	
	mil-lion $	per cent	mil-lion $	per cent	mil-lion $	per cent	mil-lion $	per cent	mil-lion $	per cent	mil-lion $	per cent
Food and beverages, 0+1	158	15.6	283	13.5	133	14.6	199	10.9	240	15.2	409	12.1
Industrial materials, 2+4 + unwrought metals	147	14.5	225	10.6	111	12.2	192	10.5	218	13.8	342	10.1
Fuels, 3	172	16.9	275	13.0	86	9.4	159	8.7	272	17.2	459	13.6
Manufactured goods, 5+6+7+8 − un-wrought metals	538	53.0	1,330	62.9	582	63.8	1,268	69.9	850	53.8	2,166	64.2
Total	1,015	100.0	2,113	100.0	912	100.0	1,818	100.0	1,580	100.0	3,376	100.0

Source: National statistics.

wood pulp and iron ore continue to provide a substantial proportion of foreign exchange earnings.

Economic Effects of Alternative Trade Arrangements

Against the background of the data provided in the third section, we will now consider the economic effects of the various trade policy alternatives. We will separately examine the effects of tariff reductions on (1) trade flows; (2) balance of payments; (3) industrial structure; (4) welfare; and (5) growth. Since equal attention cannot be given to all alternatives, one of these—the establishment of an Atlantic Free Trade Area—has been singled out for detailed discussion. At a later point, some remarks will also be made regarding the other trade arrangements under consideration.

Effects on trade flows. In Table 6.4 an attempt has been made to estimate, under the assumption of unchanged production methods, the effects on the manufactured trade of the Scandinavian countries of the removal of tariffs in the framework of an Atlantic Free Trade Area. Since among member countries of EFTA tariffs will be eliminated irrespective of the success of multilateral trade liberalization, the calculations have been restricted to trade with the Common Market, the United States, Canada, and Japan. At the same time, no effort has been made to estimate the impact of the removal of discrimination in the EEC and EFTA, associated with the over-all elimination of tariffs on imports into the two areas.

Assuming that 1 per cent reduction in import prices would lead to a 4.1 per cent increase in imports to North America, and a 3.1 per cent rise in the Common Market and Japan, and that export prices would not be affected by tariff reductions, we have concluded that the elimination of duties would lead to a 45 per cent increase in Scandinavian exports of manufactured goods to the industrial countries while the corresponding increase in imports would be 25 per cent. The relevant figures are 36 and 20 per cent if supply conditions in Western Europe were to lead to an increase in export prices by one-third of the reduction in tariffs.

The differences in the results are in a large part explained by the disparities shown in regard to tariffs. In all the Scandinavian countries, duties on manufactured goods are generally lower than in any other industrial country. The higher import

TABLE 6.4. EXPANSION OF MANUFACTURED TRADE OF THE SCANDINAVIAN COUNTRIES IN AN ATLANTIC FREE TRADE AREA

	Exports					Imports				
	Actual, 1960 million $	Estimated increase Variant I million $	Variant I per cent	Estimated increase Variant II million $	Variant II per cent	Actual, 1960 million $	Estimated increase Variant I million $	Variant I per cent	Estimated increase Variant II million $	Variant II per cent
Denmark in trade with:										
North America	44	16	36	21	48	68	11	16	18	26
Common Market	113	40	35	49	43	518	71	14	91	15
Japan	3	1	33	1	33	11	2	18	3	27
Together:	160	57	36	71	44	597	84	14	112	19
other countries:	360	—	—	—	—	407	—	—	—	—
Total	520	57	11	71	14	1,004	84	8	112	11
Norway in trade with:										
North America	22	8	36	10	45	62	19	31	27	44
Common Market	104	36	35	45	43	378	95	25	118	31
Japan	2	1	50	1	50	5	1	20	1	20
Together:	128	45	35	56	44	445	115	26	146	33
other countries:	284	—	—	—	—	457	—	—	—	—
Total	412	45	11	56	14	902	115	13	146	16
Sweden in trade with:										
North America	142	54	38	69	49	202	46	23	69	34
Common Market	365	128	35	159	44	833	153	18	197	24
Japan	8	3	38	4	50	28	5	18	7	25
Together:	515	185	36	232	45	1,063	204	19	273	26
other countries:	1,073	—	—	—	—	583	—	—	—	—
Total	1,588	185	12	232	15	1,646	204	12	273	17
Scandinavia in trade with:										
North America	208	78	38	100	48	332	76	23	114	34
Common Market	576	204	35	253	44	1,729	319	18	406	23
Japan	13	5	38	6	46	44	8	18	11	25
Together:	797	287	36	359	45	2,105	403	19	531	25
other countries:	1,723	—	—	—	—	1,444	—	—	—	—
Total	2,520	287	11	359	14	3,549	403	11	531	15

Note: On the procedure of estimation, see the Appendix to Chap. 1.
Source: OECD statistics.

demand elasticities assumed for the countries of North America would also benefit the exports of manufactures originating in Scandinavia. However, the absolute increase in the imports of manufactured goods would exceed that of exports. This result follows because the Scandinavian countries presently have a large import balance in manufactured trade with North America, the Common Market, and Japan. In Denmark, exports of agricultural products, in Norway earnings from shipping are largely responsible for this lopsided trade-pattern, while the Swedish import-surplus with the above-mentioned countries is balanced by an export-surplus with other areas, including the partner countries of EFTA.

Although we have not prepared estimates on the expansion of trade in industrial materials following the elimination of duties, some comments on prospective changes in these commodities are also given. Swedish exports of industrial materials to Canada and Japan are negligible, while exports of woodpulp to the United States amounted to $23 million in 1960. In the same year, the Common Market countries imported shaped wood in the value of $89 million; woodpulp, $150 million; and iron ore, $136 million, from Sweden. Woodpulp imports into the United States and iron ore imports into the Common Market are not subject to duty. On the other hand, the 6 per cent tariff on woodpulp and the 6 to 13 per cent duty on shaped wood present obstacles to Sweden's exports to the EEC.

Danish exports of industrial materials are relatively unimportant, while Norway exports a wide variety of materials. Among these, the Common Market took $22 million worth of woodpulp, $16 million of aluminum, and $12 million of nickel in 1960, while U.S. imports of aluminum amounted to $13 million. The removal of the 6 per cent U.S. and 8 per cent Common Market tariff would stimulate Norwegian exports of aluminum. The elimination of the 6 per cent duty on woodpulp would have a similar effect on exports to the Common Market, while unwrought nickel is not subject to duty. In turn, none of the Scandinavian countries import dutiable industrial materials in appreciable quantities from other industrial countries.

Among agricultural products, Danish sales of livestock, meat, dairy products, eggs, and fish to the European Common

Market are of importance. These exports totaled $214 million in 1960, of which $20 million were in fish products. Norway exported to the EEC fresh and preserved fish of the same value in that year. While high duties restrict the imports of preserved fish into EEC, in the case of livestock products the common agricultural policy of the Community is the main obstacle. This could be surmounted only if Denmark joined the Common Market since an Atlantic Free Trade Area is unlikely to contain provisions on agricultural trade.

Balance of payments effects. Despite the possible expansion of the exports of industrial materials, the establishment of an Atlantic Free Trade Area is likely to entail a deterioration of the balance of payments of Denmark and Norway, while the rise in exports and imports may balance in the case of Sweden. Even if we restricted our attention to trade in manufactured goods, the incremental import balance of $120–$150 million for the Scandinavian countries taken together appears to be rather small in comparison with total exports of over $4 billion and imports of $5 billion in 1960. Hence, balance-of-payments considerations would hardly influence the determination of these countries to liberalize their foreign trade.

Effects on industrial structure. The reallocation of existing resources following the creation of an Atlantic Free Trade Area would also affect the industrial structure of the Scandinavian countries. A simple way of analyzing this effect is to indicate the relative importance of estimated changes in exports and imports in particular industries. We have prepared such calculations for the Scandinavian countries, but the results do not show dramatic changes in the industrial structure of any of these countries. The explanation is that in the Scandinavian countries and in industrial countries in general the distinction between export industries and competing import industries is blurred. It appears that trade among these countries is characterized by intra-industry, rather than inter-industry, specialization; i.e., differentiated products are exchanged within each commodity category.

A further disaggregation of the results would not substantially affect these conclusions, while a consideration of the prospects for the exports and imports of individual commodities would be open to the objection that it disregards the pattern of reaction on the part of management. Thus, an aggressive response of enterprises whose products compete with imports will greatly influence the effects of tariff reductions on the production and trade of a particular commodity. While differences in the reaction pattern of individual firms may not affect the result for individual industries, it would make a statistical exercise on the commodity level highly precarious.

Another way of approaching the problem is to use information on "revealed" comparative advantage provided by data on the relative export performance and export-import ratios for seventy-four manufacturing industries. Among the Scandinavian countries, the relevant information is available only for Sweden. Thus, we shall deal with that country here.

From the data shown in Appendix Tables 1.2 and 1.3, it appears that Sweden possesses comparative advantages in regard to railway construction material, paper, ships, plumbing and heating fixtures, lead, copper, and rubber goods, and disadvantages in cotton and synthetic yarns, woolen fabrics, synthetic dyes, fertilizers, and photographic equipment. More detailed calculations reveal, however, that the pattern of comparative advantages is changing, with glass and glassware, pottery, motor vehicles, furniture and a variety of rubber and textile products gaining, and pig iron, as well as leather, chemicals, and dyestuffs, losing. In general, there appears to be a tendency for further diversification of Swedish exports, and a shift towards the exportation of commodities in a more highly processed form.

Static welfare effects. Although basic to an evaluation of the economic advantages and disadvantages of the various trade-policy alternatives, the welfare effects of trade liberalization are singularly elusive. While a number of attempts have been made to provide quantitative estimates on the *static* welfare effects of reallocation, these have been based on extreme simplifications with regard to both their assumptions and methods, and hence their practical usefulness is open to question. Further complications are introduced by the fact that welfare gains from freer trade the Scandinavian countries derive from the reallocation of resources in an Atlantic Free Trade Area would be affected by the elimination of discrimination due to the existence of the Common Market and the European Free Trade Association. Thus, in the event that AFTA is created, the exports of the Scandinavian countries would receive equal treatment with French producers in the German market where the French presently have a differential advantage, and discrimination against Common Market producers in the markets of the Scandinavian countries would also be eliminated. Accordingly, existing trade diversion due to the establishment of EEC and EFTA would disappear in the framework of an Atlantic Free Trade Area, while there would be trade diversion against nonparticipating countries.

But whatever the method of calculation, the static welfare gains would appear to be rather small, hardly exceeding one-half of 1 per cent of the gross domestic product of the Scandinavian countries. Still, these benefits should not be underestimated since, as we will see below, they would favorably affect the rate of growth of national income by improving the allocation of future increments in resources, and increasing the amount available for investment. It should be added that in the case of the Scandinavian countries, much of the gains from the reallocation of resources would be derived from trade with the European Economic Community. The Common Market accounts for three-fourths of estimated increases in exports and imports, to which the expansion of trade due to the elimination of EEC and EFTA discrimination should be added.

Growth effects. While a consensus seems to be developing among economists that the dynamic effects of trade liberalization exceed in importance the static effects, there is little chance that these could be quantified in any way. Nevertheless, it is of interest to note some of the influences that might affect the rate of economic growth. These include the increase in the amount available for investment, the improvement in the allocation of the increment in resources, economies of scale, technological progress, the impact of increased competitive pressures on production methods, and the international movement of productive factors.

1. To begin with, by increasing the gross domestic product—i.e., the base to which the growth rate is applied—static allocation gains would make future additions to income larger in absolute terms and permit an increase in the rate of investment.

2. Aside from the greater amount available for investment, the growth rate itself would increase because the annual increment in resources would be allocated in a more efficient fashion. It should be added, however, that this change would be rather small: in the most favorable case, a growth rate of 4 per cent would increase to 4.04 per cent if the gains from resource reallocation amounted to 1 per cent of national income. It is a different question that their rate of economic growth would increase if the Scandinavian countries succeeded in expanding exports in industries where world demand is rising at a rapid rate.

3. The exploitation of economies of scale in wider markets would provide important gains in many of the industrial countries. These benefits would be especially pronounced in Scandinavia where national markets are small.

4. Additional improvements can be obtained through the dissemination of technological progress that is expected to become more rapid if tariff barriers are eliminated. This would mean a higher return on investment, which in turn may call forth additional savings, at least out of profits.

5. Production methods may also improve as a result of intensified competition. There may be more intensive efforts to reduce costs and to adopt new methods in response to the encroachment of foreign producers on domestic markets. The gains from increased competition are likely to be smaller in the Scandinavian countries than in other areas, however, since the low tariffs of the former have permitted foreign competition to exert its influence on domestic economic activity.

6. Finally, the amount of resources would be influenced through international factor movements. Among productive factors, the inflow of capital has been subject to restrictions in the Scandinavian countries, and these countries have made a number of exceptions to the OECD code of liberalization of capital movements. But while the relevant laws are quite similar in the three countries, their application has in some respects been different. Thus, direct investment in Denmark and Norway encounters few limitations and permits have been easily granted, although the attitude toward such investment is less favorable in Sweden. At the same time, there are limitations in all of the Scandinavian countries on the pur-

chase by foreigners of natural resources, and of real estate in general. Similar considerations apply to the purchase of securities and the granting of loans.

Foreigners may not purchase Scandinavian securities in excess of the amount of such assets already held abroad, and cannot borrow in Scandinavian capital markets. Nor can Scandinavians acquire foreign securities in excess of amounts already held, or float loans on foreign markets without permission. In the latter respect, however, again there is an important difference among these countries since in Denmark and Norway—but not in Sweden—it has been relatively easy to obtain permission to float loans abroad.

In Sweden, the restrictive attitude toward international capital movements which in practice has meant an isolation of the domestic capital market, is partly influenced by the desire to facilitate the task of domestic stabilization policy which concerns both the domestic economic situation and the balance of payments. Also, there has been the feeling that foreign interests might easily acquire dominating positions in the key industries of small countries and that they would possibly not pay attention to what—rightly or wrongly—is considered to be the national interest. One aspect of this problem that has attracted considerable attention is the internal arrangement that international concerns may make for tax purposes so that profits can be taxed in countries where tax rates are low. It has been argued also that the present prices of industrial assets in Sweden are relatively low, and that such assets would be acquired by foreign buyers in the case of freedom of capital movements. True enough, international bidding on industrial assets would force up these prices, but for reasons of internal income distribution, such changes in asset values are considered to be undesirable. In Denmark and Norway, on the other hand, it has been answered that the building of modern industry could not be accomplished without having recourse to international capital markets. But direct foreign investment comes under limitations in these countries, too.

Since capital is more fluid than labor, and since the elimination of controls on capital movements in an Atlantic Free Trade Area is likely to go farther than the elimination of controls on labor movements, it is probable that the creation of an AFTA would have more noticeable effects on capital movements than on labor movements. As to the *direction* of this capital flow, there will in all probability be substantial movements in both directions, i.e., both to and away from Scandinavia. But, even if there were to be no *net* capital movements, the gross movements would tend to favorably affect the rate of growth, since capital is a vehicle for know-how and entrepreneurship. At the same time, the present net inflow of capital into Denmark and Norway might be accelerated in such an event.

The Choice among Alternatives

The Scandinavian countries are primarily interested in the economic effects of their trade policies. Political considerations only enter in the form of a desire to avoid trade arrangements that would be discriminatory against outsiders, or—in the case of Sweden—give rise to political commitments conflicting with neutrality and nonalignment. As to economic effects, the Scandinavian countries—contrary to the case of the United Kingdom—are not interested primarily in improving the balance of payments, or "shaking up" a slow-moving economy through freer trade and intensified competition. Rather, there is a wish to provide the most suitable circumstances for the economy to prosper from freer trade that would, among other things, permit the exploitation of large-scale economies.

Against this background, both political and economic considerations support continued multilateral reductions of tariffs. However, the attractiveness of this approach will, in the end, depend upon the extent to which trade barriers are lowered. If, as a result of periodical tariff reductions, obstacles to trade were eliminated within a reasonable time, this would represent the optimum solution to the trade policy problems of the Scandinavian countries. But in the event that tariff reductions are less than complete, other alternatives will demand attention.

From the economic viewpoint, the establishment of an Atlantic Free Trade Area would provide a near-optimum. But this alternative possibly would have decisive political drawbacks due to the discrimination against less developed countries and Soviet-type economies it would entail. In turn, the merger of the European Common Market and the European

Free Trade Association would offer virtually the same economic attractions to the Scandinavian countries as an Atlantic Free Trade Area, while its political disadvantages in the form of discrimination against nonindustrial countries would be less pronounced. This alternative would create, however, certain political problems in the case of Sweden.

Finally, a trade arrangement encompassing the United States, Canada, the European Free Trade Association, and Japan would bring few economic advantages to the countries of Scandinavia, while it could easily lead to a permanent division within Western Europe. Given the interest of the Scandinavian countries in trading with the European Common Market, this alternative would provide little attraction for them. In case of hesitation on the part of other nations to carry out tariff reductions in the near future, the countries of the area would therefore be better off if they waited for the opportunity to pursue the objective of trade liberalization through multilateral tariff reductions and an accommodation between the EEC and EFTA.

CHAPTER VII

TRADE ARRANGEMENTS AMONG INDUSTRIAL COUNTRIES: EFFECTS ON JAPAN

Kiyoshi Kojima[1]

Japan's Position in World Trade

Changing patterns in Japanese trade. Japan is a small country, with a high population density and an unfavorable resource endowment.[2] Consequently, the Japanese have had to concentrate on the development of manufacturing industries in order to attain a steady growth of income, and specialization in manufacturing is associated with heavy dependence on foreign trade. In the past, the commodity and the geographical composition of Japan's exports have undergone successive changes in response to rapid shifts in world demand. This, in turn, has required a continuous process of transformation and modernization in the Japanese economy. Continuation of this process will be necessary for reducing the gap between Western and Japanese levels of industrialization and per capita income.

In which commodities and with what countries shall Japan's trade be expanded? These are the questions to which the present study seeks an answer. As an introduction to this inquiry, we shall provide information about changes in the pattern of Japan's trade, the transformation of her production structure, as well as the geographical and commodity composition of her exports and imports. In subsequent sections, we will examine Japan's comparative advantage in a multicountry set and will consider the potential impact of multilateral trade liberalization on her trade. Finally, alternative trade arrangements will be appraised from the point of view of Japan.

[1] The author is professor of economics at Hitotsubashi University.

[2] Japan consists of many small and mountainous islands. The total area is 370,000 square kilometers, less than one-twentieth the size of the United States or Australia, with a total population of more than 96 million.

177

The Japanese economy passed through three major stages of growth between the opening of Japan to foreign influences and World War II: the first period was from the 1870's to 1900; the second, 1900 to 1931; the third, 1932 to 1942. In each period, the economy underwent successive transformation through the development of some leading sectors: agriculture and mining in the first period; silk and cotton textiles in the second; heavy industries in the third. The development of heavy industries was not completed during the interwar years, however, and has continued until the present time.[3] The rate of growth of Japanese exports was high throughout the period: 7.5 per cent a year during the years 1881–85 and 1911–13, and 5.1 per cent during 1911–13 and 1938. This high rate of growth was accompanied by shifts in the structure of exports. After the Meiji Restoration of 1868, Japan was an exporter of primary products and importer of manufactures, like most of the presently developing economies. However, between the 1870s and World War II, the composition of Japanese exports changed from reliance on food (especially tea) and raw materials, to semi-manufactured goods (mainly raw silk and cotton yarns), and subsequently to finished manufactures.

World War II disrupted Japanese trade to a considerable extent. In 1950, exports were only 32 per cent of their prewar level which was not attained again until 1958. Exports grew at an average annual rate of 14.8 per cent between 1950 and 1963—a growth rate 2.7 times higher than that of world trade, and 1.7 times higher than that of world manufactured exports. Nevertheless, despite rapid recovery and expansion since the second World War, Japan's share in world trade was only 3.6 per cent in 1963—still lower than the share she enjoyed before the war (which was 4.6 per cent in 1938).

The postwar period may also be divided into three stages: the first was the wake of war devastation between 1946 and 1953; the second, a period of recovery between 1953 and 1959; and the third, a period of normalization from 1959 onwards. In 1948, exports were only $145 million, but they increased markedly during the Korean War and reached

[3] See Kiyoshi Kojima, "Capital Accumulation and the Course of Industrialization, with Special Reference to Japan." *Economic Journal,* December, 1960, pp. 757–68.

$1,273 million in 1953. During this period, about four-fifths of the exports were traditional products such as raw silk, silk fabrics, cotton yarn, and cotton fabrics. Manufacturing industries recovered in the second period, however, and provided an increasing share of exports. Total exports grew at an annual rate of 17.4 per cent between 1953 and 1959, and surpassed $3.6 billion in the latter year.

The growth of exports slowed down somewhat after 1959, but the 11.7 per cent annual rate of increase between 1959 and 1963 was still more than double the growth rate of world exports. By the end of this period, manufactured goods accounted for nine-tenths of Japanese exports, and within this category the share of heavy manufactured goods and chemicals increased to a considerable extent. Parallel with these developments, the severe import restrictions in effect throughout the postwar period were progressively liberalized.

As to the dependence of the Japanese economy on foreign trade, we find that imports as a percentage of national income expressed in terms of 1913 prices increased steadily from 6 per cent in the 1880s to 21 per cent in the 1920s. After 1930, this ratio declined to 17 per cent, in a large part because of the fall in world market prices of primary products. The expansion of heavy industries may also have contributed to this result since, as we shall see below, the import content of production is considerably smaller in heavy than in light industries.[4]

Following the decline in the volume of trade during World War II, the growth of foreign trade has led income growth in Japan. The ratio of imports to national income, expressed in terms of 1958 prices, increased from the low level of 7.3 per cent in 1950 to 18.5 per cent in 1963. During the same period, the share of exports rose from 7.2 per cent to 14.6 per cent. Finally, in 1963, the average ratio of exports and imports to value added to the production of traded goods was 27.5 per cent in Japan (see Appendix Table 1.1).

Despite the rapid increase of foreign trade in the postwar period, the share of imports in Japan's national income remained well below the interwar level. Among the factors contributing to this result, the shift from light to heavy manufac-

[4] Kiyoshi Kojima, "Economic Development and Import Dependence in Japan," *Hitotsubashi Journal of Economics* (October, 1960).

tures in Japanese production and exports should first be mentioned. The import content of exported goods is 26 per cent in the case of textiles, as compared to 16 per cent for chemicals and 6 per cent for machinery.[5] As the share of textiles in exports and in the gross domestic product declined and that of machinery increased, the import content of exports fell from 23 per cent in 1954 to 15 per cent in 1963, and the import/national income ratio also decreased. The increased self-sufficiency in staple food, the shift from consumption of natural fibers to the use of synthetic fibers, and other technical changes of a material-saving character have had a similar influence, while the rapid rise in imports of mineral fuels has been an offsetting factor.

Transformation of the structure of production. Shifts in the pattern of trade have been associated with changes in the structure of production in Japan. In the last decade, the transformation of the Japanese industrial structure was more rapid than anywhere else in the world. Between 1954 and 1961, the share of agricultural output in the gross domestic product decreased by 7.5 percentage points, the share of mining output fell by 0.9 percentage points, and transport, communications, commerce, and banking by 0.8 percentage points, whereas the share of manufacturing output increased by 6.6 percentage points, construction by 1.5 percentage points, and electricity, gas, and water supply by 1.1 percentage points. The sum of these negative and positive movements in sectoral shares was 18.4 percentage points, as compared to 14.3 for Italy, 9.1 for the United Kingdom, 7.0 for the Federal Republic of Germany, 5.6 for the United States, and 5.4 for France. Similar results are reached if we consider changes in the shares of thirteen major industries within the manufacturing sector. The sum of percentage changes are 43.8 for Japan, 20.8 for Italy, 16.0 for France, 11.9 for the Federal Republic of Germany, 8.8 for the United Kingdom, and 4.0 for the United States.[6] During this period, Japanese labor productivity rose more rapidly than money wages, and the reduction in

[5] These estimates were made for the year 1963 by the Economic Planning Agency. Only direct inputs of imported materials are included in the figures.

[6] Calculated from United Nations *Yearbook of National Accounts Statistics and the Growth of World Industry,* (New York, 1963).

labor costs has been accompanied by a rate of increase of exports far exceeding that of any other industrial country. One of the important factors contributing to the growth of labor productivity has been a high rate of investment and capital accumulation in the Japanese economy. With the ratio of savings to the gross domestic product exceeding 30 per cent, fixed capital per worker approximately doubled between 1955 and 1963. The importation of foreign technological know-how has also played a part in these developments, while the availability of an ample labor supply has supported the rapid expansion. Investments, as well as increases in productivity, have been concentrated in heavy and chemical industries: between 1950 and 1960, labor productivity in heavy manufacturing and chemicals increased at an annual rate of 13.4 per cent, as compared to 7.6 per cent for light manufacturing.

By now, the Japanese economy has attained a level of industrialization comparable to that of Italy, although it still lags behind the United States and the more developed European countries. While the share of heavy manufactures and chemicals in total value added in manufacturing in Japan approaches that in advanced industrial countries, these industries comprise a much smaller share of manufacturing exports in Japan than in other major industrial countries. In 1960, the relevant figures were 46 per cent for Japan, 60 per cent for Italy, 77 per cent for the United Kingdom, 80 per cent for the United States, and 81 per cent for Germany.

The expansion of heavy manufacturing and chemical industries has followed roughly the same course of development in the larger industrial countries. Domestic demand, first satisfied by imports, encouraged the expansion of domestic production. The expansion of production, then, led to the exploitation of economies in scale, increases in productivity, improvements in quality, and reductions in costs. As domestic costs reached the international comparative cost threshold, foreign markets were developed, the scale of production was extended further, and costs were reduced again. Thus, the expansion of exports that had originally been made possible by the growth of domestic demand has, in its turn, provided a stimulus to industrial development.

The production of heavy manufactures and chemicals was

increasing rapidly during the interwar period in Japan but exports remained insignificant. After the war, the expansion of domestic demand for industrial equipment and durable consumer goods stimulated the further development of these industries, and also led to increases in exports. First iron and steel, ships and boats, and light machinery, then radio and television sets, automobiles and motorcycles, as well as heavy machinery, came to be exported. The importance of new commodities in Japanese exports is indicated by the fact that goods whose share in total exports has risen above 0.2 per cent between 1951 and 1963 accounted for 26 per cent of the total increase in exports during the period.

Structure of Japanese trade. Data on the commodity composition of Japanese exports show the increasing importance of heavy manufactures and chemicals. With an annual growth rate of 20.2 per cent, the share of these commodities in the total exports of Japan rose from 33.9 per cent in 1953 to 49.9 per cent in 1963 (see Table 7.1). Despite a rate of growth of

TABLE 7.1. JAPAN'S TRADE: COMMODITY COMPOSITION AND
ANNUAL RATE OF GROWTH: 1953–63

(PER CENT)

Commodity group[a]	Exports			Imports		
	Commodity composition		Annual rate of growth 1953–1963	Commodity composition		Annual rate of growth 1953–1963
	1953	1963		1953	1963	
1. Food, beverages, tobacco	9.4	5.3	9.2	25.9	16.2	5.7
2. Industrial materials	8.1	3.8	7.3	49.6	43.2	9.2
2a Agricultural raw materials	6.2	3.5	9.1	38.7	28.3	7.4
2b Minerals and metals	1.8	0.3	−3.2	10.9	14.2	13.7
3. Fuels	0.7	0.3	6.1	12.0	18.0	15.4
4. Manufactured goods	80.9	90.0	16.9	12.4	22.6	17.5
4a Light manufactures	47.0	40.1	13.8	1.4	3.7	22.4
4b Heavy manufactures and chemicals	33.9	49.9	20.2	11.1	18.9	16.8
Total	100.0	100.0	15.6	100.0	100.0	10.8

Source: Japanese Department of Finance, *Japan's Foreign Trade Returns.*
Note: [a] The commodity classification follows the revised SITC as indicated in Chap. 1. Light manufactures have been defined to include Sections 6 (less 67, 68, and 69) and 8.

13.8 per cent, the proportion of exports supplied by light manufactures declined from 47.0 to 40.1 per cent during the same period. In particular, machinery and transport equipment have replaced textiles as the leading export group. Between 1953 and 1963, the share of the former increased from 16.0 per cent to 29.6 per cent, while that of latter fell from 36.1 per cent to 22.9 per cent.

Much of Japanese imports are industrial materials (43.2 per cent in 1963). Fuels account for another 18.0 per cent, and food for 16.2 per cent, bringing the imports of primary products to nearly four-fifths of the total. Japan's industrial development depends upon her ability to import cheap primary products, since almost 100 per cent of her demand for a number of basic materials—such as wool, cotton, petroleum, iron ore, and various nonferrous metals—is supplied by imports. On the other hand, despite rapid increases since 1953, the share of manufacturing imports remains relatively small (22.6 per cent in 1963). The increase in imports of manufactured goods has been concentrated in machinery that is necessary for the modernization of manufacturing industries.

The geographical distribution of Japan's exports has also undergone considerable changes in the postwar period (see Table 7.2). Developed countries (North America, Western

TABLE 7.2. JAPAN'S TRADE: MARKET COMPOSITION
AND ANNUAL RATE OF GROWTH: 1953–63

(PER CENT)

	Exports			Imports		
	Market Composition		Annual rate of growth	Market Composition		Annual rate of growth
	1953	1963	1953–63	1953	1963	1953–63
I. Developed countries	30.4	47.2	20.9	53.3	54.4	11.9
North America	19.5	29.9	20.3	36.8	35.6	10.9
Oceania	1.6	4.1	26.0	8.4	8.8	13.5
Western Europe	9.3	13.1	19.6	8.1	10.0	15.1
II. Developing countries	69.2	48.2	10.4	45.1	41.5	10.0
Southeast Asia	47.0	29.5	9.0	26.3	18.0	6.7
Latin America	8.5	6.6	11.0	11.0	8.4	7.0
Africa	10.1	8.7	10.9	2.3	3.9	17.9
Middle East	3.5	3.4	13.4	5.5	11.2	18.9
III. Communist countries	0.4	4.6	32.4	1.6	4.1	19.2
Total	100.0	100.0	14.7	100.0	100.0	11.3

Source: Japanese Ministry of International Trade and Industry.

Europe, and Oceania) took 47.2 per cent of Japan's exports in 1963 as compared with 30.4 per cent in 1953, while the share of developing countries fell from 69.2 per cent in 1953 to 48.2 per cent in 1963. Within the developed country group, the importance of North America as a market for Japanese exports further increased (the North American share rose from 19.5 per cent in 1953 to 29.9 per cent in 1963). Despite a rapid expansion of trade, Western Europe's and Oceania's share has not surpassed 13.1 and 4.1 per cent, respectively. At the same time, Japan provides only 1 per cent of Western Europe's imports.

Changes in the geographical origin of Japanese imports have been less marked. Developed countries accounted for 53.3 per cent of Japanese imports in 1953 and 54.4 per cent in 1963, whereas underdeveloped countries supplied 45.1 per cent and 41.5 per cent respectively in the two years. However, the relative importance of the individual regions changed considerably. Increased imports of mineral fuels helped Middle Eastern countries to increase their share in Japanese imports from 5.5 per cent to 11.2 per cent, while the shares of Southeast Asia and Latin America (whose main exports are agricultural products) fell from 26.3 per cent to 18.0 per cent, and from 11.0 per cent to 8.4 per cent, respectively. These changes have resulted in part from a shift in the commodity composition of imports, increased domestic food production, and shifts in the Japanese diet from rice to noodles, bread, butter, and cheese. Further, the deficiency in the supply and the relatively high prices of primary products in developing countries with overvalued exchange rates have been contributing factors. This trend has been accentuated following the liberalization of imports in 1960, since previously quotas were allocated under bilateral agreements generally favoring less developed countries. Importers now prefer to buy from suppliers in developed countries that often provide cheaper, and higher quality products with reliable delivery dates. In particular, Japan's imports of iron ore, copper, soybeans, and sugar come increasingly from North America and Oceania.

Another way to approach the problem is to consider changes in the intensity of trade.[7] The intensity of Japan's export trade with another country is measured by the ratio of

<hr>

[7] The concept of "intensities of trade" was first used in A. J. Brown, *Applied Economics, Aspects of the World Economy in War and Peace* (London, 1947), pp. 212–26.

that country's share in Japanese exports to its share in total world trade less Japan's imports.[8] Similarly, the intensity of Japan's import trade with another country is measured by the ratio of Japan's share in that country's exports to Japan's share in total world trade less imports into the country in question.[9] Thus, an export intensity of more (or less) than 100 indicates that Japan is exporting more (or less) to a particular country than might be expected from that country's share in the world trade total. Likewise, the intensity of Japan's import trade indicates the extent to which Japan takes more (or less) imports from a particular country than might be expected from that country's share in world trade. The intensity of trade is affected, among other things, by geographical proximity, by economic complementarity, and by political and historical ties.

The intensity of Japan's trade with Southeast Asia has been declining in the period under consideration; it was 619 for exports and 383 for imports in the years 1956–58, while the corresponding figures are 291 and 272 in the years 1960–62 (Table 7.3). The intensity of export trade with the Middle East and Africa declined too, although a slight increase in imports intensities is shown in the case of these areas. Both exports and imports intensities increased in trade with Latin America, but the level of intensity remained low.

By contrast, the intensity of Japan's export and import trade with the United States and Australia is high and rising. Increases are shown also in the intensity of trade with Canada, although this has not yet reached the 100 level. In general, Japan's trade has shifted away from the developing countries of Southeast Asia to the developed countries of the Pacific area. Trade intensities with Western Europe, however, are the

---

[8] In symbols,
$$\frac{X_{ji}}{X_j} \Big/ \frac{M_i}{W - M_j}$$

where X_{ji} stands for Japanese exports to country i; X_j for total Japanese exports; M_i for total imports by country i; M_j for total imports by Japan; and W for total world trade.

[9] In symbols,
$$\frac{X_{ij}}{X_i} \Big/ \frac{M_j}{W - M_i}$$

where X_{ij} stands for Japanese imports from country i; X_i for total exports by country i; M_i, M_j and W are the same as in the preceding note.

TABLE 7.3. INTENSITY OF JAPAN'S TRADE[a]

	Japan's exports		Japan's imports	
	1956–58 average	1960–62 average	1956–58 average	1960–62 average
Japan—USA	191	218	180	183
Japan—Canada	48	58	83	94
Japan—Australia	102	160	411	427
Japan—Western Europe	26	26	14	12
Japan—Southeast Asia	619	291	383	272
Japan—Latin America	81	107	102	105
Japan—Middle East	158	127	245	253
Japan—Africa	231	123	48	64

Source: United Nations, Commodity Trade Statistics.
Note: [a] For definitions, see text.

lowest of all, and have not changed substantially during the period under consideration.

Japan's Comparative Advantage in the Multicountry Set

Comparative advantage in manufactured products. An examination of Japan's comparative advantage is necessary in order to evaluate the possible effects of trade liberalization among the industrial countries on the pattern of her trade. Professor Balassa suggests that information on relative export and import performance may be used as an indicator of comparative advantage, since these reflect revealed comparative advantage, or the extent of success (or failure) in exporting and importing different commodities. Such success or failure, it is argued, will be determined by relative costs as well as by nonprice factors.

Indices of relative export performance and export-import ratios have been calculated for the years 1953–55, as well as for 1960–62 in regard to 74 categories of manufactured goods. Moreover, composite indicators have been derived to reflect the level of these indices in the second period as well as changes over time (Appendix Tables 1.2 and 1.3).[10] The results show Japan to have relative advantages in exporting footwear, cotton yarn and fabrics, clothing, pottery, as well as buses and trucks, while she appears to be at a disadvantage in the manufacturing of aircraft, tractors, wrought nickel and zinc, essential oils, and chemical products.

[10] On the derivation of these indices, see the Appendix to Chap. 1.

But these indices do not tell the full story. In a country such as Japan where the structure of exports is rapidly changing, it is of interest also to compare the pattern of relative advantages between the two periods under consideration, and to indicate the direction of change. For this purpose, we have divided the 74 commodity categories into three broad groups: S = a strong advantage group (with an index of export performance over 150); M = a medium advantage group (with an index of 67 to 150); and W = a weak advantage group (with an index of 67 or less).[11]

In the first period, Japan had 19 commodities in the strong advantage group, 15 in the medium advantage group, and 40 in the weak advantage group. Between the first and second periods, 6 commodities moved down from the S group to either the M or W group, while 6 commodities moved up from the M group to the S group, so that 19 commodities remained in the S group in the second period. At the same time, the number of commodities in the M group increased from 15 to 20, and those in the W group declined from 40 to 35.[12] The industries which produce commodities that remained in the S group may be called *established export industries*. Except for ships and boats, and universals, plates, and sheets of steel, they produce light manufactures (textile products account for 9 of the 13 items) of the traditional kind. Within this category, a decline in relative export performance is shown for cotton fabrics, synthetic fabrics, blankets, special textile fabrics, clothing, made-up textile articles, pottery, jewelry, and

[11] The classification is somewhat arbitrary. After having taken 150 as the benchmark for the strong advantage group, the upper limit of the weak advantage group has been given as the reciprocal of 150, multiplied by 10,000. Only export performance indices have been considered because these appear to be more reliable than indices of export-import ratios which are greatly affected by the level of protection in individual industries.

[12] It will be perceived that the number of commodities which moved from a lower to a higher group exceeds the number for which the reverse is true. This may seem strange at first sight, since the weighted average of the export performance indices must necessarily equal 100. But the declining importance of commodities with a large relative share in trade has allowed for an upgrading of a greater number of commodities. These developments give expression to the transformation and diversification of Japan's manufactured exports, which is also reflected in the declining dispersion of the indices of export performance: the standard deviation of these indices fell from 127.7 in 1953–55 to 117.7 in 1960–62.

universals, plates, and sheets of steel, while the opposite conclusion holds for unbleached cotton yarn and thread, miscellaneous woven textile fabrics, floor coverings, as well as ships and boats.

The second group of *established but declining export industries* includes 6 product groups that moved down from the S group to the M or W groups between the two periods. These are wool yarn, synthetic yarn and thread, manufactured fertilizers, simple forms of steel, textile machinery, and glassware. All of these products except the last derive from old, established industries in Japan. The trend has been for exports of these commodities to give way to exports of more sophisticated manufactures in the same line, as in the case of special steel products, and to products at higher levels of fabrication, such as the export of wool and synthetic fabrics instead of yarn and thread.

There are 44 *developing export industries* that may, in turn, be subdivided into three groups. The *rapidly developing export industries* moved from the M (or even the W) group to the S group. Both heavy and light industries are represented in this group. Rubber tires and tubes, railway construction material, buses, lorries, and trucks, automobile parts, railway vehicles, electrical machinery other than electrical generators, as well as scientific, measuring, and controlling instruments are classified as the products of heavy industry. In turn, footwear, musical instruments and phonographs, travel goods and handbags, fur clothing, and bleached cotton yarn and thread are the products of light industry.

A second group of 15 *developing export industries* moved from the W to the M group. Most of these commodities come from heavy manufacturing and chemical industries: organic chemicals, plastic materials, a variety of forms of steel, electrical generators, sanitary, plumbing, and heating equipment, office machinery, motorcycles and bicycles, as well as explosives. They also included a few commodities from light industries: leather manufactures, materials and articles of rubber, paper articles, and woolen fabrics. Finally, a third group of *slowly developing export industries* improved their export performance but remained, nevertheless, in the W group. Of the 16 items in this category—inorganic chemicals, perfumes and cosmetics, medical and pharmaceutical products, leather, furskins, paper and paperboard, lead, tin, passenger motor cars, tractors, aircraft, power-generating machinery, metal-working machinery, agricultural machinery, furniture, and photographic supplies—the majority derive from the heavy and chemical industries.

Six commodities came from *unsuccessful export industries* that experienced a decline in their export performance. These include chemicals such as synthetic organic dyestuffs, pigments, paints and varnishes, miscellaneous chemical materials and products, and essential oils and perfume materials, as well as glass and machinery other than textile machinery. Finally, five other items which moved down to the W group represent a rather special case. They are all semi-processed metals—aluminum, copper, pig iron, zinc, and nickel—and, as industrialization progressed, the domestic demand for these products increased, and they are now exported in more sophisticated forms.

The data give some indication of the transformation and diversification in Japan's manufactured exports which is characterized by increased reliance on heavy manufactures and chemical products. Three important qualifications should be made to this observation. Firstly, Japan's strongest comparative advantage still lies in textiles and other traditional light manufactures, although there appears to be a shift from low quality to high quality products, as well as from lower to higher levels of fabrication within this category. Secondly, changes within the group of heavy manufactures and chemicals have been complicated and diverse. Shipbuilding was already an established export industry in the first period. A number of heavy and chemical products moved into the S group, others have expanded their exports but remained in the M or W groups, while some industries have experienced a deterioration in their export performance. Thirdly, it should be noted that most of the heavy industrial and chemical product groups are characterized by product differentiation, hence their exports and imports often increased in a parallel fashion. This is not the case for several light manufactures and for metals which are standardized commodities.[13]

[13] On this point see Bela Balassa, "Tariff Reductions and Trade in Manufactures among the Industrial Countries," *American Economic Review* (June, 1966), pp. 466–73.

Global comparative advantage. The preceding analysis was confined to a study of Japan's comparative advantage in manufacturing exports among ten major industrial countries. Since Japan's trade depends heavily upon imports of primary products and trade with developing countries, it is necessary to study Japan's comparative advantage over a much broader range—not only in manufactures, but also in primary products and not only commodity by commodity, but also country by country. To simplify the analysis, all commodities traded internationally were classified into four broad groups: the *A* group consists of agricultural products such as staple and processed foodstuffs, tobacco and agricultural raw materials; the *N* group includes natural-resource-intensive products outside of agriculture, such as minerals, metals, and fuels; the *L* group comprises labor-intensive manufactures, principally from light manufacturing industries but also from heavy and chemical industries (cameras, sewing machines, bicycles, precision equipment, medicine); finally, the *K* group encompasses capital-intensive heavy manufactures and chemicals.[14]

Chart 7.1 indicates the composition of exports and imports for the United States, Western Europe, Japan, Southeast Asia, and the entire world. The percentage share of each commodity group in total exports and imports is represented by the length of the blocked areas in each diagram. Exports are shown on the right and imports on the left of each vertical axis. The staircase shapes of these blocked areas reflect global comparative advantages in each region's trade with the rest of the world.

The simplest pattern on the export side is revealed in the case of Western Europe where the share of *N* goods in total exports is smallest, and this share increases for *A* goods, *L* goods, and *K* goods progressively to make a triangular pattern. If this is compared with that for world trade, it is easy to

---

[14] Using the revised SITC classification, the following products come into the four groups:

A group: Sections 0, 1, 2 (excluding 251, 266, 267, 27 and 28), 4 and subgroup 941.0.
N group: Divisions 27, 28, and Section 3.
L group: Sections 6 (excluding 67, 68, and 661–64) and 8, and groups 267, 541, and 733.
K group: Sections 5 (excluding 541) and 7 (excluding 733), divisions 67 and 68, and groups 251, 266 and 661–64.

discern the typical pattern of comparative advantage for highly industrial countries which have the strongest comparative advantage in K manufactures, a lesser advantage in L goods, and a comparative disadvantage in primary products.

The pattern of imports into developing countries is expected to be symmetrical with that of exports from advanced industrial countries. Aside from agricultural products, this is the

CHART 7.1. COMMODITY COMPOSITION OF TRADE, 1960–62 AVERAGE.
(SHOWN IN PER CENT)

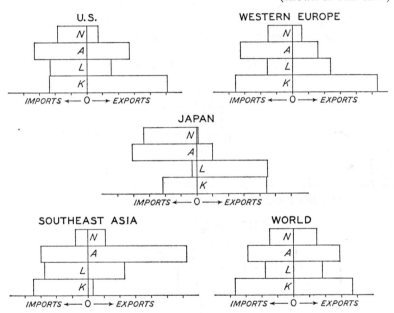

Source: Japanese Ministry of International Trade and Industry.

case in Southeast Asia, where the large share of agricultural imports is explained by American aid provided in the form of foodstuffs under the *P.L. 480* program. At the same time, the countries of Southeast Asia derive over 60 per cent of their export earnings from the sale of agricultural commodities, chiefly raw materials.

Some differences between United States and European trade patterns should next be noted. The United States exports more A goods in relation to L goods and imports more L goods in relation to K goods than does Western Europe. This reflects

CHART 7.2. COMMODITY COMPOSITION OF JAPAN'S TRADE WITH THE U.S. WESTERN EUROPE, AND SOUTHEAST ASIA, 1960–62 AVERAGE.
(SHOWN IN PER CENT)

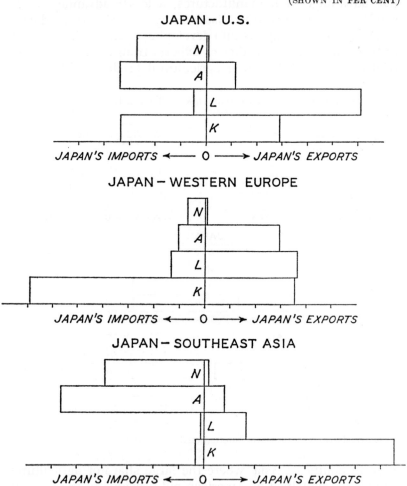

Source: Japanese Ministry of International Trade and Industry.

the United States' comparative advantage in agricultural and capital-intensive products, and Europe's relative advantage in labor-intensive and capital-intensive manufactures. In comparison with the United States and Western Europe, Japan's trade pattern reveals specialization in manufacturing industry, and the dominance of imports in N and A goods. L and K manufactures are of approximately equal importance in Japanese exports, while the latter predominate in the exports of the United States and Western Europe. But the share of K manufactures is increasing in both the exports and the imports of Japan, indicating the expansion of horizontal (competitive) trade. These goods constituted 35 per cent of exports in 1956–58 and 44 per cent in 1960–62, and 19 per cent and 22 per cent of imports for the same years.

The pattern of bilateral trade. We indicated earlier that Japan's over-all intensity of exports was large in the case of the United States and Southeast Asia, it was in the intermediate range in the case of Australia and Canada, and was quite low in the case of Western Europe. An examination of the intensity of Japan's exports of particular commodities into each trading region may now be undertaken.

Chart 7.2 shows the commodity composition of Japan's trade with the United States, Western Europe, and Southeast Asia. Further, export-import ratios were derived for Japan's bilateral and total trade in regard to four commodity groups (see Table 7.4). While the over-all ratio rose between

TABLE 7.4. EXPORT-IMPORT RATIOS IN JAPAN'S TRADE

(per cent)
Upper row = 1956–58 average
Lower row = 1960–62 average

	N goods	A goods	L goods	K goods	Total
Japan—USA	1	23	812	25	49
	1	21	836	56	66
Japan—Canada	3	9	14,467	51	45
	0.1	7	5,666	81	50
Japan—Australia	0.4	1	2,379	52	16
	0.4	2	1,871	151	31
Japan—Western Europe	14	250	312	40	101
	4	302	307	55	110
Japan—Southeast Asia	4	10	10,385	11,578	145
	4	15	1,394	2,208	107
Japan—World	1	19	1,462	141	76
	1	20	1,246	158	83

Source: United Nations, *The Commodity Trade Statistics.*

1956–58 and 1960–62,[15] Japan continued to run an import surplus in trade with the United States, Canada, and Australia, and an export surplus with Western Europe and with Southeast Asia.

In L goods, Japan has a substantial export surplus in trade with all regions. She also has an over-all export surplus in K goods, inasmuch as large exports to Southeast Asia more than counterbalance her import surplus in trade with the United States, Canada, and Western Europe. In turn, Japan has a large import surplus in N and A goods with all regions, the only exception being trade in A goods with Western Europe.

It is apparent that Japan's bilateral export-import ratios in regard to individual commodity groups tend to be either very large or small. This reflects the predominantly vertical (complementary) nature of Japanese trade. However, as noted above, horizontal (competitive) trade in K goods is on the increase in Japan.[16] Next, we may compare the right-hand side of Chart 7.2 with the left-hand side of Chart 7.1 to indicate the differences in the commodity composition of Japanese exports to particular regions and that of the over-all pattern of imports into these regions. More exactly, the index of the *commodity intensity of bilateral trade index,* calculated by dividing the share of a given commodity in Japan's exports to a particular country by the share the same commodity has in that country's over-all imports,[17] reveals the extent to which Japan's exports to a particular country meet the pattern of the latter's

[15] It should be added that the ratio of 83 for 1960–62 was due to a large extent to the high transport costs of primary goods which account for three-fourths of Japan's imports. Transportation costs are included in the c.i.f. price of imports, while exports are valued at f.o.b. prices. The ratio approaches 100 if both exports and imports are valued on an f.o.b. basis.

[16] Still, the degree of horizontal trade in K goods is smaller in the case of Japan than for any of the other industrial countries, and Japan has practically no horizontal trade in light manufactures, though such trade is substantial for other industrial countries. See Kiyoshi Kojima, "The Pattern of International Trade among Advanced Countries," *Hitotsubashi Journal of Economics* (June, 1964).

[17] In symbols:
$$\frac{X_{ji}^h}{X_{ji}} \bigg/ \frac{M_i^h}{M_i},$$

where X_{ji}^h is Japan's exports of commodity h to country i, X_{ji} is Japan's total exports to country i, M_i^h country i's imports of commodity h from all sources of supply, and M_i country i's total imports.

import demand. An index of 120, for example, indicates that Japan's exports of a given commodity have a 20 per cent larger share than the average in the imports of this commodity by a particular country.

As column (a) in Table 7.5 shows, Japanese *L* manufac-

TABLE 7.5. COMMODITY INTENSITY AND REGIONAL
BIAS OF JAPAN'S BILATERAL TRADE

Upper row = 1956–58 average
Lower row = 1960–62 average

	N goods (a)	N goods (b)	A goods (a)	A goods (b)	L goods (a)	L goods (b)	K goods (a)	K goods (b)
Japan–United States	2	95	53	153	401	126	53	44
	2	80	32	112	255	126	117	68
Japan–Canada	8	268	101	117	291	126	38	54
	7	16	49	81	303	146	44	52
Japan–Australia	2	58	54	65	266	144	38	46
	2	47	40	52	227	137	62	69
Japan–Western Europe	3	170	92	319	299	68	94	76
	2	49	87	300	233	74	96	83
Japan–Southeast Asia	26	200	21	40	194	95	90	126
	19	284	26	81	60	35	213	178

Source: United Nations, *Commodity Trade Statistics.*
Notes: (a) Commodity intensity of Japan's trade with particular regions.
(b) Regional bias of Japan's trade.
(For explanation, see text.)

tures had high export intensities in all markets in 1956–58. The index for these goods was highest in relation to the United States (401), and lowest in relation to Southeast Asia (194). Except in the case of Canada, the index for these goods had generally declined by 1960–62. The most notable decline was in the intensity of *L* exports to Southeast Asia, where, in contrast, the intensity of *K* exports increased markedly from 90 to 213. Light manufacturing industries have expanded in Southeast Asia over this period, while these countries required increasing imports of *K* goods. Incidentally, the intensity of exports in *K* goods increased in all markets, reaching 117 in the case of the United States. On the other hand, the intensity of exports in *N* and *A* goods remained low, the exception being the exports of *A* goods to Europe where, though declining, the index remained relatively high.

Then again we may compare the right hand side of Chart 7.2 with the right hand side of Chart 7.1 for Japan to indicate the differences in the commodity composition of Japanese exports to particular regions and that of Japan's total exports. An index of *the regional bias in Japan's trade* was also calculated by dividing the share of a given commodity in Japan's total exports to a particular country by the share of the same commodity in her total exports.[18] Since the commodity composition of Japan's total exports reflects her overall comparative advantage vis-à-vis the entire world, the resultant index reveals a bias which stems from the difference between Japan's comparative advantage vis-à-vis a particular trading partner and the whole world. If the index for exports of heavy manufactures to the United States is less than 100, for example, the U.S. can be said to be in a more advantageous position in exporting heavy manufactures than is Japan, even though both countries may enjoy a comparative advantage in these products vis-à-vis the whole world.

Column (b) in Table 7.5 shows that Japan's exports are biased toward L goods in relation to the United States, Canada, and Australia, and toward K goods in relation to the countries of Southeast Asia. It appears, then, that Japan has comparative advantage in exporting L goods to developed countries, and in selling K goods to less-developed areas. This conclusion is supported by the results of a survey undertaken in 1958, according to which the direct and indirect capital requirements per unit of labor input for Japanese exports to the United States were $677, to Western Europe $716, to Southeast Asia $927, and to other less-developed countries $1,543.[19]

Japan's policy objectives. The data indicate a duality in both the geographical and the commodity composition of Japanese trade. For one thing, Japan's exports and imports are roughly evenly divided between developed and developing countries.

[18] In symbols:

$$\frac{X_{ji}{}^h}{X_{ji}} \Bigg/ \frac{X_j{}^h}{X_j}$$

where $X_{ji}{}^h$ and X_{ji} are as explained in footnote (16) above; $X_j{}^h$ stands for Japan's exports of commodity h to the whole world and X_j is Japan's total exports.

[19] Cf. Japanese Ministry of International Trade and Industry, *Annual Report on Foreign Trade* (Tokyo, 1961).

For another, her trade with developed countries is characterized by the exchange of light manufactures for heavy manufactures and primary products, while she trades heavy machinery for primary products with the developing countries of
Southeast Asia. In the following, we will consider the implications of this duality for Japanese trade policy.

The importance of Japan's trade with developing countries
should be considered first. We noted that half of Japan's total
exports are destined for developing countries. This dependence on markets in less-developed areas is not a feature of the
trade patterns of other industrial countries. Common Market
countries sold only 17 per cent of their total exports to underdeveloped countries in 1963, the United Kingdom, 28 per cent,
and the United States, 32 per cent.

Japan's need for imports of primary products, and the developing countries' rapidly increasing demand for imports of
capital equipment, makes the further expansion of trade between them seem a most natural and profitable objective.
Markets in less-developed areas are particularly important for
Japanese exports of heavy manufactures and chemicals.
Around 66 per cent of Japan's machinery exports, 79 per cent
of her chemical exports, and 60 per cent of her steel exports
went to these areas in 1963. Exports to developing countries
enable new Japanese export industries to realize economies of
scale, reduce costs, improve quality, and ultimately gain access to more sophisticated markets. Moreover, increased Japanese imports from developing countries lead to a greater rise
in Japanese exports to these countries than is the case with
increases in imports from developed countries.[20] But there are
certain difficulties involved in the expansion of Japan's trade
with developing countries. To begin with, these countries are
competitive suppliers of primary imports such as iron ore,
coal, copper, soybeans, sugar, and cotton with the developed
countries of the Pacific area. We indicated that, because of

[20] Japan's exports appear to increase by 1.3039 for every unit increase
in her imports from Asian sterling area countries, the corresponding
figures being 1.4149 for other Asian countries, as against 0.7945 for the
United States and 0.9650 for the European Economic Community.
These "reflection ratios" calculated by the Japanese Economic Planning
Agency, show the sum of direct and indirect effects of a unit change in
imports, and are based upon an international trade matrix for an
average of 1960 and 1961.

lower prices and shorter delivery dates, Japanese imports of these products have increased more rapidly from developed than from developing countries after the import regulations were liberalized. Japan's trade liberalization has thus "turned its back" on less-developed countries. At the same time, these countries have encountered balance-of-payments difficulties and have been induced to seek bilateral reciprocity instead of the traditional triangular settlement. Thus, while Japan used her export surplus with developing countries to pay for her import surplus with developed economies in the past, she cannot expect to increase exports to the former group of countries without commensurate increases in her imports from them.

A further consideration is that the expansion of light industries in developing countries has increased their competitiveness with Japan's own exports. Accordingly, Japan has to continue to transform her industrial and export structure so as to make more room for light manufactures from developing countries in her own and in international markets. Aside from concentrating on the production of high-quality textiles, she has to further expand her production and exports of heavy manufactures and chemicals.

We noted that Japan's trade relations with developed countries are characterized by the exchange of labor-intensive manufactures for heavy manufactures and primary products. These observations apply especially to the countries of the Pacific area (the United States, Canada, Australia, and New Zealand) but have to be modified in respect to the countries of Western Europe. Although European import capacity is large (the combined imports of the EEC and EFTA countries were $61.7 billion in 1963) as compared with the United States ($16.5 million), the countries of Western Europe take only 1 per cent of their imports from Japan, while nearly one-tenth of U.S. imports originate in Japan. Japanese exports to Western Europe are confined to traditional speciality goods—canned fish, ceramics, whale oil, silk, toys, pearls, pottery, and so on—and her imports from Europe are predominantly capital-intensive manufactures and chemicals. Various influences have contributed to this situation.

Europe is geographically distant from Japan and there is

less opportunity for business communication and advertisement, personnel, or cultural exchange as there is in the case of the developed countries of the Pacific area. Also, Japanese and European trade patterns are largely competitive, and high trade barriers have restrained trade between them. Consequently, mutual trade liberalization is very desirable, and the Kennedy Round offers an opportunity for the pursuit of this objective. Since there is no complementary trade in primary products between Western Europe and Japan, and their exports of light manufactures are competitive, the expansion of horizontal trade in heavy manufactures and chemicals presents the most promising avenue for the expansion of trade between the two regions.

It appears, then, that trade expansion in both of these directions—to developing and developed countries—requires the acceleration of heavy industrialization, and the consolidation of competitive power in heavy manufactures and chemicals in Japan. This complicates her approach to trade liberalization. However, five or ten years should see her heavy industries and chemicals on a sound enough footing, and enable her to join in freer trade and successive tariff reductions without fear. International specialization within this sector must therefore be encouraged in advanced countries.

Continued heavy industrialization in Japan is desirable, it should be added, because: first, the growth rate in export demand for the products of heavy industry is highest; second, because labor intensive manufacturing is becoming increasingly less advantageous for Japan. In recent years, wage increases have begun to catch up with productivity increases, and the Japanese economy is now assuming many of the characteristics of a fully employed economy. The tighter labor market has not only resulted in a faster increase in wage levels, but it has also led to some narrowing of the wage differential between light manufacturing and heavy manufacturing industries, and between small and large scale firms.

Japan's 90 major export items may be classified into 5 commodity groups according to wage levels prevailing in each group. Exports from industries in lower wage groups (I and II) increased by 61 per cent during the period 1954–58, and by 37 per cent during the period 1958–62, while exports from industries in higher wage groups (IV and V) increased by 117 per cent in the first period, 275 per cent in the second.[21] The lower wage groups include light manufacturing industries such as textiles, clothing, canned food, toys, ceramics and the like. The wage level in the lower wage groups increased more rapidly than that in the higher wage groups, and the wage differential between the two categories narrowed. Between 1958 and 1962, wages in the first category increased by 25 per cent, compared with an average wage increase of 10 per cent for all manufacturing industry.

As a result, Japanese light manufacturing industries are losing some of their advantages to other exporters. Japanese textiles, for example, have recently encountered difficulty in third markets from increasing competition by exporters from Hong Kong, Singapore, Taiwan, India, Pakistan and mainland China. Expansion of exports of light manufactures from developing countries, however, is of paramount importance in Japan's own expansion of heavy manufactured and chemical exports to those regions.

The opportunity for improvement in technology and cost reduction is also smaller in light industries than in heavy industries and chemicals. Finally, the lower import-content of exports in heavy manufactures and chemicals relative to light manufactures would facilitate accelerated economic growth in Japan by reducing the import/Gross National Product ratio, thereby lessening balance-of-payments difficulties.

Impact of Multilateral Trade Liberalization on Japan's Exports and Imports

Effects of tariff reductions on Japanese trade. In the following, we will present some estimates regarding the possible effects on Japanese trade of multilateral tariff reductions undertaken by the industrial countries. We will examine first the case of an Atlantic Free Trade Area that would entail the elimination of tariffs in trade among the countries of North America, Western Europe, and Japan, while maintaining tariff barriers against all other suppliers. Subsequently, consideration will be given to a 50 per cent tariff reduction undertaken by

[21] Economic Planning Agency, *Japan's Economic Survey for 1962*, pp. 435–36.

these countries that would be extended to other nations under the most-favored-nation clause.[22]

The effects of tariff reductions on trade in the individual countries will depend on the height of the original tariff, changes in tariff rates, the composition of exports and imports, and the responsiveness of demand and supply to price changes associated with reductions in duties. Tariffs are higher in Japan than in any other industrial country. Tariff averages for manufactured goods and industrial materials, respectively, were estimated at 17.1 and 4.2 per cent in Japan as compared to 13.2 and 2.6 per cent for the United States, 14.6 and 1.6 per cent for Canada, 12.2 and 1.3 per cent for the Common Market, 16.5 and 3.3 per cent for the United Kingdom, 9.1 and 1.0 per cent for the countries of Continental EFTA.

However, from the point of view of the potential expansion of exports following reductions in duties, the commodity and the country composition of her trade provide important advantages for Japan. In trade with industrial economies, the share of manufactured goods is greater in Japan's exports (86 per cent), and smaller in her imports (43 per cent), than is the average proportion for the industrial country group (64 per cent). Now, since tariffs on manufactures are considerably higher than on industrial materials, Japanese exports will tend to rise more than imports.

Within the manufactured goods category, the exports of Japan are concentrated in textiles and other products of light industry which are generally subject to high duties, while machinery and chemicals bear heavily on her imports. Moreover, the United States predominates in Japan's trade with the industrial countries, and by reason of the small share of imports in domestic production, U.S. import demand is greatly responsive to price changes. In 1960, over 70 per cent of Japanese exports of industrial materials and manufactured

[22] On the assumptions underlying the calculations, see the Appendix to Chap. 1. However, by reason of the relative unimportance of Japan's trade with Western Europe, no account was taken of the possibility that European export prices would rise following the liberalization of trade. Neither did we consider the discriminatory effects of the two European trade groupings—the EEC and EFTA—on Japanese exports that were estimated to entail only a $26 million reduction in imports from 1960 levels.

goods, destined for the industrial nations, found markets in the United States.

These considerations largely explain the differences in the estimated expansion of Japanese exports and imports in an Atlantic Free Trade Area. The data of Table 7.6 show an

TABLE 7.6. TRADE CONSEQUENCES OF ESTABLISHING
A FREE TRADE AREA FOR JAPAN

(MILLION $)

Trading partner	Product group	1960 value of trade		Estimated expansion of trade	
		Exports	Imports	Exports	Imports
United States	IM	47	667	1	12
	MG	976	448	527	168
Canada	IM	2	65	0	2
	MG	105	12	34	3
Common Market	IM	34	17	1	1
	MG	84	162	28	56
United Kingdom	IM	17	17	1	0
	MG	35	67	14	25
Continental EFTA	IM	11	5	0	0
	MG	71	47	14	20
Industrial countries, Total	IM	111	771	3	15
	MG	1,271	736	617	272

Source: See Appendix to Chap. 1.

increase of 3 per cent in Japan's exports of industrial materials, 48 per cent in her exports of manufactured goods, and 45 per cent in her combined exports of the two commodity categories to the industrial countries. The corresponding figures are 2 per cent for imports of industrial materials, 37 per cent for imports of manufactured goods, and 19 per cent for the two categories, taken together. All in all, Japan's balance of trade would improve by $333 million in an Atlantic Free Trade Area.

As expected, light manufactures would account for the bulk of the expansion of Japanese exports (about 70 per cent) and heavy manufactures and chemicals of that of imports (80 per cent). At the same time, the estimates indicate an increasing geographical concentration in Japan's trade: the United States would absorb about 85 per cent of the increase in her exports and supply over 65 per cent of the rise in imports. The United States would also account for much of the improvement in the Japanese trade balance. On the other hand, Japan's balance of trade with European countries would tend to deteriorate, in part because she presently has an import surplus in her trade with these countries, and in part because tariffs are higher in Japan than in Western Europe.

A 50 per cent reduction in duties would bring about an expansion in trade among the industrial countries amounting to one-half of that shown for an Atlantic Free Trade Area. But, trade with the other developed countries (chiefly Australia and New Zealand) and with the developing countries of Latin America, Africa, the Middle East, and Asia would also expand if tariff reductions were undertaken under the most-favored-nation clause. Nevertheless, as a result of the feed-back-effect in the form of increased purchases, Japan's exports to these countries are expected to rise more than her imports. We have assumed that nonindustrial countries spend the entire increment in their foreign exchange earnings; at the same time, Japan would derive a benefit from the concentration of her exports in Southeast Asia and Oceania.

Evaluation of the effects of tariff reductions. The estimated increase in Japan's trade in an Atlantic Free Trade Area would amount to 16.0 per cent of her total exports, and 7.6 per cent of total imports in the base year 1960. The expansion of exports would reach 2.5 per cent, and that of imports 1.1 per cent of Japan's gross domestic product in the same year. These results are subject to various qualifications, however.

First, there are a number of marginal imports whose trade may expand considerably following reductions in tariffs, although reliable estimates can hardly be prepared. Japan's success in introducing new export items in the postwar period indicates that her exports of such commodities may be stimulated by reductions in duties. In turn, these changes are likely to be of lesser importance in the countries of North America and Western Europe that are established producers of manufactures.

A related consideration is that in conjunction with the shift in exports from the products of light to those of heavy industry, tariff reductions would lead to a larger expansion of Japan's exports of heavy manufactures and chemicals than we have estimated on the basis of the 1960 composition of trade. In this connection, note that according to the Medium Term

Economic Plan for 1964–68, the share of these commodities in Japanese exports would reach 57.4 per cent in 1968 as compared to 43.2 per cent in 1960.

Excepted items in the Kennedy Round of tariff negotiations would also affect the expansion of trade. From available information, it appears that the exception lists of the other industrial countries would include several products of interest to Japan, among them textiles. Correspondingly, excepted items would account for a much larger proportion of imports from Japan (perhaps 30–40 per cent in the United States, 20–30 per cent in the Common Market and the United Kingdom) than in total imports into the major industrial countries (15–20 per cent in the United States and the Common Market, and 5–10 per cent in the United Kingdom). Altogether, these exceptions may affect 30 per cent of Japanese exports of light manufactures, and 10 per cent of her exports of heavy manufactures. In turn, it has been reported that the Japanese exception list includes some 40 per cent of imports into Japan.

Finally, attention should be given to the dynamic effects of tariff reductions which are not amenable to numerical measurement. Dynamic effects are related to market size and technological change. The reduction or the elimination of tariffs is expected to give rise to technological improvements by increasing the effective size of the market, as well as through the effects of competition in a larger area. In an economy as large as that of the United States, economies of scale are easily exploited, but the expansion of markets through trade liberalization is necessary for their wide Japanese exploitation. Although Japan's population is 96 million, per capita incomes are still low in relation to the more advanced industrial countries (less than half of those in Germany and the United Kingdom). Hence, the need for the development of overseas markets if economies of scale are to be fully realized, especially in heavy manufactures and chemical products.

Trade liberalization and foreign investment. The exploitation of economies of scale and technological improvements following the liberalization of trade would necessitate the merger of small firms, investment in new facilities, and the introduction of modern techniques in Japan. These developments in turn can be furthered by the inflow of capital and technology.

Japan provides an attractive outlet for foreign investment since her labor costs are relatively low and the educational level of the labor force is high.

According to an unpublished survey of the Ministry of International Trade and Industry in the period 1950 to 1964, Japanese firms negotiated 2,786 technological assistance agreements of varying importance. In the same period, capital inflow amounted to $3,642 million, nearly 80 per cent of which took the form of loans. Portfolio investment other than loans amounted to $687 million, and direct investment to merely $218 million. Direct investment has been relatively insignificant because of Japan's reluctance to permit direct investment, except in cases when this entailed the importation of new and advanced technology which could not otherwise be obtained. This Japanese attitude stems from fear of the superior financial power of American firms, and a desire to protect domestic industries from domination by foreign firms.

Foreign capital inflow taken together accounted for only 0.7 per cent of total private investment in the period 1955–59 and 1.9 per cent in the period 1960–63. While the amount was not considerable, technological asistance obtained from abroad as well as foreign capital inflow played an important role in the rapid development of specific activities, particularly in heavy and chemical industries. The import of know-how has been instrumental in lessening the gap between techniques in other advanced countries and those in Japan in the manufacture of motor vehicles and industrial machinery, as well as to initiate the expansion of new industries such as petrochemicals, plastics, synthetic fibers, and electronics. Most of the technological assistance came from the United States, which also accounted for 70 per cent of direct investment.

Production which in a large part depends on foreign technology expanded 3.5 times as rapidly as total manufacturing output in this period, and accounted for 90 per cent of the production of heavy and chemical industries. It also contributed to the expansion of exports, and accounted for about 15 per cent of total exports in recent years. In turn, payments for patents, royalties, and technological assistance in general have increased rapidly, and amounted to $623 million in the fifteen-year period.

Japan is still a capital-scarce economy in relation to her

capacity for growth, and might well take a more liberal attitude toward direct foreign investment of a productive kind. Foreign investment of this kind would bring with it advanced technical and managerial know-how, useful foreign ideas and business practices, and would assist in the transformation and rationalization of Japanese industry. United States' firms are especially likely to increase their investment in Japan, and this would promote horizontal trade between the two nations. Japanese firms, on the other hand, could profitably increase investment in Australia, New Zealand, and in less developed areas.

Nontariff restrictions. The use of nontariff restrictions in Japan and in other industrial countries is of particular concern for the liberalization of trade. Nontariff restrictions make multilateral tariff concessions ineffective as they represent a much more direct and far stronger means for restricting international trade. In trade among industrial countries, these restrictions are of special importance for the exports and imports of Japan. Prior to 1960, all Japanese imports were subject to license. While licenses for the imports of many commodities were easy to come by, they often gave rise to irrational decisions on the part of business and affected, to a lesser or greater degree, the structure of imports.

The liberalization of these restrictions took place in two stages: the first stage lasted from early 1960 through June, 1961; the second, from July, 1961 to October, 1964, by which time 93 per cent of imports were liberalized.[23] Japan accepted full obligations for the elimination of quantitative restrictions under Article XI of GATT in February, 1963; shifted to so-called 'Article VIII status' of the International Monetary Fund on April 1, 1964; and became a member of the Organization for Economic Co-operation and Development in April, 1964.

In the first stage, Japan eliminated restrictions mainly on (1) imports of raw materials and semi-manufactured materials used in domestic manufacturing industries and non-competitive with domestic production, and (2) imports of some machinery and steel in which Japan's competitive power was strong. The share of these items in total imports was 27.3

---

[23] This ratio indicates the percentage of liberalized items in the total value of imports in 1959, excluding governmental imports.

per cent in 1959. It increased to 28.4 per cent in 1960, and fell successively to 27.9 per cent in 1961, and 25.9 per cent in 1962. While it is not easy to isolate the effects of liberalization since the behavior of imports is influenced by the pattern of economic growth and by the business cycle, it would appear that the removal of restrictions has not appreciably affected the imports of raw materials and semi-manufactures in Japan. Nevertheless, the removal of restrictions brought benefits to Japanese importers. Before liberalization, businessmen were forced to acquire import licenses whenever they had the opportunity to do so, and they often failed to give sufficient consideration to price fluctuations and geographical price differentials. Since then, they have more been able to "shop around" for imported materials in search of lower prices. In the second stage, import liberalization was extended to (1) foodstuffs, (2) manufactured consumer goods, and (3) capital goods, most of which compete with domestic industries. The share of these items in total imports was 14.0 per cent in 1961; it increased to 16.4 per cent in 1962, and to 18.3 per cent in 1963. Thus, following the removal of restrictions, the imports of these items increased more rapidly than did total imports, although it is difficult to evaluate as yet the full impact of the liberalization of quotas.

Nevertheless, some estimation of the effect of liberalization may be worth attempting. For this purpose, we have compared the income elasticity of imports for liberalized and restricted items in five commodity categories on a half-yearly basis.[24] In regard to raw materials and mineral fuels, average elasticities for seven semi-annual periods are 0.92 for liberalized items, and 0.98 for restricted items. The corresponding elasticities for semi-manufactured materials (covering nine periods) are 2.00 and 1.99, respectively. Thus, in the case of these commodities whose imports were liberalized first, there is practically no difference in income elasticities between liberalized and restricted items.

For foodstuffs, too, the elasticity for liberalized items (3.84) is only slightly larger than that for restricted items (3.40). On the other hand, there is a large difference between the two elasticities in the case of capital goods (covering five

[24] The time period covered for each commodity group varies, since the imports were liberalized at varying intervals.

periods), and for manufactured consumer goods (covering three periods). The elasticity is 5.60 for liberalized items and 0.72 for restricted items in the former category, as compared to 6.08 and − 0.25 in the latter. But the income elasticities for liberalized items have been declining over time. The relevant elasticities for the first three half-year periods immediately after decontrol are: 4.77, 13.30, and 4.06 for capital goods; 11.26, 7.88, and 1.63 for manufactured consumer goods. Similar changes are not observed in elasticities for restricted imports.

Although our survey is tentative, since the time period covered is very short, we find some noticeable differences in the pattern of income elasticities. In the case of imports that compete with domestic production, the average elasticities are shown to be much larger for liberalized than for restricted items, indicating that the quantitative restrictions worked rather strictly and that their removal induced some substitution of liberalized for restricted items. At the same time, it appears that the impact of liberalization is particularly large in the early period after decontrol but tapers off as the process of adjustment proceeds.

Aside from some pressures upon the balance of payments, the recent stage of liberalization has apparently had beneficial effects on the Japanese economy. There has been minimal disruption in domestic industries, and the new heavy and chemical industries have been stimulated by the impetus provided by quota liberalization. In particular, it has made businessmen more confident of their ability to survive international competition, and has also led to the rationalization of production.

Japan is now proceeding to the third and final stage of liberalization. Import quotas still remain in effect on 162 items of the Brussels Tariff Nomenclature. Among these 162 items, 38 items are generally excepted items under Article XX of GATT, and security exceptions under Article XXI include items such as arms, ammunition, anesthetics, and so on. The remaining restricted items accounted for 10.7 per cent of total imports in 1963. Of these, 1.9 per cent are agricultural products, 5.5 per cent minerals and fuels, 2.4 per cent heavy manufactures and chemicals, and 0.9 per cent other commodities. The principal items are: (1) agricultural products (75 items), including rice, wheat, butter, cheese, and meat; (2) minerals and fuels (12 items), of which the most sensitive items are gas, oil, and heavy fuel oil; (3) heavy manufactures and chemicals (52 items), of which the most sensitive items are heavy electrical machinery, electronic computers, and machine tools.

Restrictions on the importation of foodstuffs present difficult policy problems for Japan, just as they do for other advanced countries. Abolition of restrictions remains politically difficult since a large number of small farmers would be adversely affected if these restrictions were removed. An economist cannot but conclude, however, that Japan will find it difficult to catch up with Western standards of per capita income unless she liberalizes imports of foodstuffs, in particular imports of dairy products, meat, and fruits. This is a necessary task, but should be undertaken gradually over a ten-year period (or more). While about 3 per cent of the agricultural working force is being transferred to the manufacturing sector annually, it would be desirable to accelerate this trend.

Similar considerations apply to the restriction of coal and oil imports. The domestic production of petroleum is rather limited, and quota restrictions have been maintained largely to prevent the rapid substitution of oil for coal. However, the protection of coal is hardly justified since this industry produces at high costs in Japan.

Restrictions on the importation of motor vehicles and machines have been maintained for a quite different reason. Business leaders assert that these are still weak and internationally uncompetitive industries, despite the increasing flow of exports from them. The government remains concerned that liberalization would lead to a rapid substitution of the foreign for the domestic product, since there is some tendency for the Japanese consumer to prefer the foreign merchandise. It is also assumed that imports would increase rapidly in the future because of the high income elasticity of demand for these commodities. However, the international competitiveness of these industries has greatly increased in recent years, and there is little doubt that quotas could be removed[25] in

[25] Quantitative import restriction of automobiles was abolished, in fact, in September, 1965.

exchange for similar concessions on the part of Japan's trading partners.

Of the 62 member nations of GATT, 27 use their right under Article XXXV to refuse the application of the Agreement to Japan. As most of these are developing countries, this discrimination does not have substantial adverse effects upon Japanese trade at the present. Japan's most serious concern is the application of quotas against Japanese exports by industrial countries. So called "voluntary export quotas" are a special form of quantitative restrictions which grew out of difficulties encountered in the rapid increase in exports of a few products (particularly cotton textiles) to the United States in the mid-1950s, and spread to Japan's trade with Canada and Western Europe. The importing countries claimed that the interests of "orderly marketing" demanded export restraint on the part of Japan, and Japan accepted these demands because she feared the imposition of more stringent trade restrictions. In November, 1964, there were 67 items under voluntary quotas in the United States, 28 in Canada, 65 in the United Kingdom, 24 in Denmark, 7 in Switzerland, 5 in West Germany, 1 item in both France and Norway.

In addition to voluntary quotas, ordinary quota restrictions are imposed in Western Europe against Japanese exports, although successive rounds of negotiations have reduced their importance in recent years. There are such controls on 382 items of the Brussels Trade Nomenclature in Austria, 119 in Italy, 91 in France, 88 in Norway, 33 in Benelux, 28 in West Germany, and 18 in the United Kingdom. It is estimated that in 1962 these restrictions, including voluntary quotas, affected 14 per cent of Japanese exports to the United States, 23 per cent of exports to Canada, 20 per cent of exports to the Common Market countries, 6 per cent of those to the United Kingdom, and 40 per cent of those to Norway. In Sweden, Denmark, and Portugal, all imports from Japan enter under government license.

The principal items affected by voluntary quota restrictions and other nontariff measures are: (1) textile products, including clothing (woolen and cotton), synthetic yarn and fabrics, tableware, carpets, as well as footwear; (2) miscellaneous light manufactures of a labor-intensive type, including canned vegetables, fruits, and sea foods, buttons, toys, hand-

tools, plywood, tile products, china and ceramic ware, etc.;
(3) equipment of a labor-intensive type, including electric
bulbs, binocular, bicycles, sewing machines, radios, transistor
radios, cameras, insulated electric wire, etc. These commodities can often be produced by Japan at lower cost than they
can be supplied by other developed countries.

It should be emphasized that restrictions against many of
these imports in developed countries are reserved exclusively
or mostly for Japan, while the import restrictions imposed by
Japan are global in character. Because of the existence of
nontariff restrictions which operate in a discriminatory fashion against Japan, tariff reductions on certain light-industry
products would be quite ineffective in stimulating her trade.
In these cases, any gains in trade would accrue to competing
suppliers as long as Japanese exports are voluntarily restrained. As mentioned before, items subject to nontariff restrictions more or less overlap excepted items under Kennedy
Round negotiations. This double protection is surely unreasonable. The occasion provided by the Kennedy Round should be
used to abolish quantitative restrictions in Japan as well as in
the other developed countries.

The Choice for Japan

The best choice for Japan is to expand and free her trade
with every trading region. The present stage of her industrialization, her dual pattern of trade with developed and developing countries, and her geographical location dictate such a
choice. The continuation of Kennedy Round type tariff reductions on a multilateral basis would serve this objective reasonably well. Aside from the static benefits of trade liberalization,
a rapidly growing economy in the process of industrial transformation like Japan has much to gain from the dynamic
effects of freer trade and capital flows. At the same time,
multilateral tariff reductions and the elimination of quantitative restrictions would tend to improve Japan's trade balance
vis-à-vis the industrial countries.

But Japan has to give attention to two important problems
in promoting trade liberalization. First, the comparative advantage of Japanese production, and the structure of her trade
vis-à-vis developed countries suggests that tariff reductions
would stimulate the growth of light industries more than that

of heavy and chemical industries. At the same time, Japan is pledged to heavy industrialization and aims to develop her heavy and chemical industries more rapidly than her light industries. Nevertheless, although it may be legitimately feared that hasty tariff reductions, as well as decontrol, would stifle the expansion of some immature heavy and chemical industries, in so far as tariff reductions in the Kennedy Round would not become fully effective until the early 1970s, Japan should be able to make the necessary adjustments. Indeed, heavy industrialization is likely to be accelerated by the creation of larger markets and the freer inflow of foreign capital and know-how. Multilateral tariff reductions may then contribute to increased horizontal trade in heavy manufactures and chemicals with industrial countries.

Second, Japan cannot disregard the interests of developing countries, especially in Southeast Asia. The question is often raised: should Japan rely on the rapidly increasing but competitive markets in developed countries, or on the complementary but more slowly expanding markets in developing countries? She has, in fact, to expand trade in both directions. Tariff reductions of the Kennedy Round type would not be contrary to the interests of developing countries, since they would benefit from tariff reductions under the most-favored-nation clause. But in order to reduce the gap in growth rates between the two groups of countries, tariff reductions will have to be supplemented by the application of other measures, such as the liberalization of quotas and foreign aid.

At the same time, multilateral tariff reductions among advanced countries would present no political problems for Japan. Internally, they should produce a minimal disturbance—as noted above, heavy and chemical industries would have sufficient time for adjustment—and externally, they fit into the pattern of her established international alliances. Moreover, such an arrangement would not be objectionable to Japan's Asian trade partners who would automatically benefit from tariff reductions under m.f.n.

However, proposals for an Atlantic Free Trade Area comprising the United States, Canada, the EEC, EFTA, and Japan seem quite premature. Japan considers it necessary to maintain tariffs for the sake of developing her heavy and chemical industries. Moreover, the establishment of a "richman's club" in the form of AFTA would have particularly adverse effects for the developing countries. Given Japan's special position vis-à-vis Asian countries, the price of her membership in an Atlantic free trade area would be particularly high. The trade diverting effects of an AFTA on Japanese imports from Asia would make the expansion of her exports to that area more difficult, and the political disadvantages of turning her back to Asia would be considerable.

Japan's interests in trade with the countries of the Pacific region should next be noted. The countries of this region have intensive and complementary patterns of trade which could be expanded further in the framework of a free trade area. Japan would benefit through the cheaper imports of raw materials and other primary products, the expansion of her exports of light manufactures, and the promotion of horizontal trade in heavy manufactures and chemicals. Given the possibilities of expanding trade with Australia and New Zealand, Japan may indeed prefer a Pacific Free Trade Area to an AFTA which did not include the latter two countries. A related consideration is that Japan has greater bargaining power in Oceania than in Western Europe, and that she is destined by geography to participate in political and economic arrangements in the Pacific rather than in the Atlantic region. The establishment of the Common Market and Britain's desire to join the EEC have led both Australia and New Zealand to look increasingly toward neighboring countries, and especially toward Japan. However, Japanese markets alone are too small for primary produce from Oceania, and the markets of Oceania alone are too small for Japanese manufactures. Hence, the usefulness of a Pacific Free Trade Area would be greatly increased if the United States and Canada also participated in it.

To date, the United States has been more interested in Atlantic arrangements. However, European integration through a fusion of the EEC and EFTA could well produce an "inward looking" Europe, whereupon the United States might find closer integration in the Pacific region desirable. And while for the time being the political and economic integration a free trade area entails is not feasible in the Pacific area, economic co-operation among the advanced countries in the region could be profitably fostered. Collective measures by the group are especially desirable for assisting economic development and trade growth in Southeast Asian countries.

It has also been suggested that Japan should consider some form of integration among developing countries of Southeast Asia. The ECAFE Secretariat has studied a number of proposals for integration in this area. But, compared with Europe or advanced countries in the Pacific area, countries in Southeast Asia are less homogeneous, trade less with each other, and are less disciplined financially; also, there exists considerable political enmity and nationalistic antagonism among them. All this makes regional integration quite unworkable. Co-operation in the form of specific projects in irrigation, transportation, and/or subregional integration seem feasible. But even if integration were possible among the less developed countries of the area, Japan's participation would be neither possible nor desirable. Her superior competitiveness in manufacturing industries would tend to stifle the development of competing industries in the less developed countries of Southeast Asia. Moreover, Japan alone could not bear the financial burdens that her membership would entail. It would seem far better for Japan, in co-operation with other developed countries, to promote economic development in the region through collective assistance.[26]

Japan is also interested in expanding her trade with socialist countries (of the Soviet Union, Red China, and Eastern Europe) that provide a marginal, though growing, outlet. The share of these countries in Japanese exports increased from 0.4 per cent in 1953 to 4.6 per cent in 1963; on the import side, the relevant figures are 1.6 and 4.1 per cent. While tariff reductions of the Kennedy Round type would not hurt the interests of socialist countries if these multilateral tariff reductions were extended to them, the establishment of and Japan's membership in an AFTA would not fail to provoke adverse political and economic reactions.

In short, as Professor Haberler said a decade ago, "Japanese trade interests are worldwide. They do not fit into any regional arrangement. The problem must be solved on a global basis."[27]

---

[26] See Kiyoshi Kojima, "A Proposal for International Aid," *The Developing Economies* (December, 1964), pp. 337–57.
[27] Gottfried Haberler, "Defects in the Concept of Regionalism to Solve Trading Problems," *The Indian Journal of Economics* (July, 1957), p. 29.

Multilateral tariff reductions and the promotion of freer trade among developed countries should be among Japan's foremost policy objectives in the coming decade. At the same time, she must join and encourage collective action by developed countries for fostering the growth and trade of developing economies which need special consideration in the process of trade liberalization.

CHAPTER VIII

FISCAL AND SOCIAL BARRIERS TO ECONOMIC

INTEGRATION IN THE ATLANTIC AREA

Douglas Dosser[1]

Introduction

The country studies of this volume deal with obstacles to international trade arising from tariffs. But even if all tariffs were removed, there would remain distortions affecting trade and the international flow of capital and labor due to nontariff barriers and differences in fiscal and social regulations between countries. Distortions due to differences in these regulations are generally more complex than in the case of tariffs. While tariffs are a specific charge levied on imports, fiscal and social policies involve a vast complex of charges which have only an indirect influence on trade. Moreover, tariffs restrict trade which would be desirable, but taxes often encourage trade, as well as labor and capital, to move in undesirable directions.

Out of the complex of fiscal and social regulations, some selection has to be made. The measures studied here are the ones which appear to be of greatest importance for trade and factor movements: direct and indirect taxes, government expenditures, and social security schemes.[2] The purpose of the present study is to provide a quantitative assessment of the

---

[1] The author is professor of economics at the University of York. He acknowledges the help of Mr. G. Heerkens, a senior economist on the staff of the commission of the EEC, in his capacity as a consultant to the study. Much of the statistical work was carried out by Mr. S. S. Han of the University of York, the scope of whose assistance virtually rates him a joint contributor.
[2] Nontariff barriers to trade will be discussed in Chap. 9 of this volume.

217

differences in fiscal and social regulations in eleven major industrial countries (the United States, Canada, the Common Market countries, the United Kingdom, Sweden and Japan) and a qualitative appraisal of the effects of these differences on trade and on the movement of labor and capital. Each type of tax (or social security scheme or government expenditure) will be studied for its effect on one or more classes of decision-making units—consumers, owners of capital, and owners of labor.

If we look at tax laws and take them at their face value, our task seems to be fairly easy. We can read off the effect of corporate income tax on capital owners, the effect of personal income tax on the owners of capital and labor, the effect of indirect taxes on consumers, and so on. But the final amount of tax paid by a firm or a person will differ from these *nominal* (statutory) rates because of various legislative provisions on levying taxes: depreciation provisions in the case of direct business taxes, and personal allowances in the case of direct personal taxes. We attempt to take account of such provisions by calculating *effective* rates of taxes. Needless to say, one cannot account for all possible exceptions and qualifications but only for the major ones.

The next and final step is to calculate *incident* rates which take account of the possibility of corporations or persons shifting the burden of the tax to other firms or individuals. This is a very difficult matter; we have to rely on economic theory since there is little empirical evidence that would enable us to choose among alternative hypotheses. The situation regarding nominal, effective, and incident rates could then be summarized by saying that, as we move through these steps, the figures become more significant economically but less significant statistically.

It may be argued that the nominal rate of tax gives so little indication of the true impact of the tax that it is hardly worth considering. However, differences in nominal rates may well influence the movement of productive factors, since information on effective or incident rates is incomplete or not available. Thus, while it is possible that the movement of labor or capital induced by differences in nominal rates would be reversed if the effective or incident rates were known to those concerned, some of the decision-makers may not take cognizance of differences between nominal and effective rates.

In attempting to obtain the three sets of rates, there are two approaches one may take, a "micro" or a "macro" approach. The micro figures are derived from legislation and administrative regulations on taxes, subsidies, and social security, while the macro figures come from national accounts statistics. By necessity, nominal rates are obtained entirely from micro sources, but both approaches can be employed in calculating effective rates. On the micro side, a "standard" firm or taxpayer can be set up, and average allowances applied to calculate effective rates. On the macro side, the effective rate of a particular tax is, simply, the receipts from the tax over the tax base. Both approaches, micro and macro, could also come into play in dealing with incident rates.

Our aim is to derive a set of nominal, effective and incident rates for each tax, for certain government subsidies, and for social security. However, our tables will have to be more complex than it would seem on first sight. For one thing, depending on the country of destination, trade or income flows from a given country may carry different rates, either statutorily (nominal rates) or due to special provisions (effective rates), or due to different incidence (incident rates). For another, we need separate tables for each class of decision-making units: consumers, capital owners, labor owners. Thus, we have nominal rates on consumers (NC), on capital income (NK), and on labor income (NL); effective rates on consumers (EC), on capital income (EK), and on labor income (EL); finally incident rates on consumers (IC), on capital income (IK), and on labor incomes (IL).

The letters in parentheses indicate the symbol system of tables used throughout; these initials are followed by the designation of the tax or subsidy in question, e.g., IL—Social Security Benefits. We will not have a complete set of tables for each tax or subsidy, however. One reason for this lies simply in the nature of the individual cases. For example, the nominal rates of corporate income tax bear only on capital income, so there is an NK table, but no NL or NC tables. The second reason is the lack of information; while this does not affect the nominal and effective rate tables very much, it creates considerable uncertainty in the case of incident rates.

It is apparent that the major effort involved in our work is the actual statement of tax differentials on particular income claims in the various countries. This differs from the tariff work since the actual levels and incidence of tariffs are known or can be relatively easily ascertained. Hence, what is a minor part of the tariff study—the statement of rates—is a major task in the fiscal study. Conversely, what is a major preoccupation in a tariff study, namely the impact of tariff changes on trade, is not given the same prominence in the fiscal work because, as we shall see in the final chapter, there is much less basis to judge the likely or desirable directions of changes in fiscal policy.

It is customary to relate the "burden" of each form of tax—and of all taxes taken together—to national income.[3] But this is quite inappropriate in a study of the effects of fiscal differences on trade and factor movements. The impact on particular firms, on particular forms of investment, and on labor cannot be inferred from the total amount of taxes which affect them. The tax burden must therefore, be related to the correct base, like profits or the average manufacturing wage, rather than to total national income. Additionally, account should be taken of special provisions, such as tax treaties, depreciation allowances, personal income tax allowances, which are obscured by the global data. Thus, the figures presented in subsequent tables do not compare with the usual investigations of fiscal burdens which are on a national income basis, but at the same time, they provide a more realistic picture of fiscal differences affecting trade and the movement of the factors of production.[4]

Direct Taxes

Under this heading, we will consider the corporation tax and the personal income tax, both of which affect the international movement of capital, either as corporate or as individ-

---

[3] A recent example is O. Eckstein and V. Tanzi, "Comparison of European and U.S. Tax Structures and Growth Implications," in *The Role of Direct and Indirect Taxes in the Federal Reserve System* (Princeton, N.J.: Princeton University Press, 1965), pp. 217–93.

[4] The following sections are a blend of statistics, economic theory, and policy discussion. For a detailed treatment of the theoretical issues involved, see my contribution in C. Shoup (ed.), *Fiscal Harmonization in Common Markets* (New York: Columbia University Press, 1966), Chap. 1. This volume contains several other papers complementary to this one.

ual investment.[5] The personal income tax will also affect the movement of labor across national borders. Moreover, there may possibly be effects on international trade if these taxes are shifted to consumers in the form of increases in prices.

The effects of taxes on the flow of capital and labor involve some major differences. Capital usually moves without its owner also moving. Thus, a distinction arises between the country of source of income earned and the country of residence of the income-receiver. While allowances are usually made to avoid two tax burdens cumulating on a dollar of profit, such arrangements vary from country to country. And since the rates applied differ in the individual countries, the final tax rate will be different for each pair of countries. Moreover, the net rate payable will vary even for a given pair of countries according to which of the two is the source of earnings and which is the country of receipt. Hence, we have a rather complicated table stating the net tax rates on "emigrant" and "immigrant" capital.

The situation is much simpler in the case of labor. Necessarily, the owner of labor will move with the labor services, and he will often establish residence in the new country of work. Of course, there may be temporary flows, daily or seasonal, across national borders, but such movements are of importance only within the European area and rarely occur between Western Europe and North America. Now, since the tax rate of the new country applies to mobile labor, it is the personal income tax differentials in the individual countries which will affect labor mobility.

Taxes on capital. Much of our discussion will relate to corporation investment. In the majority of the industrial countries, this involves only a corporation tax. In others, the tax on corporate profits is partly a corporation or profits tax, and partly a personal income tax (there is usually a "standard" rate to be applied to profit income) or, alternatively, a special national tax is added to the corporation tax.

With corporate investment, distinction is made between home investment (the source of profits and the country of

[5] While in most countries the corporate income tax applies to the income of corporations, the income of unincorporated business is subject to the personal income tax.

residence or incorporation are one and the same country),
branch investment (the corporation is a part of a foreign
concern and is not incorporated in the country of operation),
subsidiary investment (the corporation is part of a foreign
concern but incorporated in the country of operation), and
corporate portfolio investment (the securities are owned by
firms outside the country of the corporation). Nominal tax
rates on these four forms of investment are shown in Appendix Table 8.1.

But as noted earlier, differences in nominal rates between
countries rarely represent differences between relative burdens. To give expression to the latter, we have calculated
effective rates by adjusting for the system of depreciation
allowances which is the most important cause of discrepancies between nominal and effective rates. Following P. Richman Musgrave's method,[6] we have adopted a standard in-
come-earning asset—standard as regards rate of return, period of depreciable life, and rate of discount applied to income
arising in the future—and estimated the tax relief (reduction
in the nominal amount of tax) due to the depreciation provisions of each country. The standards assumed[7] are a 20 per
cent annual rate of return for 10 years with a rate of interest
of 5 per cent. Given these assumptions, we can adjust the
nominal tax rate (t_n) to yield the effective rate (t_e) as far as
depreciation is concerned.[8] The result is that, with the excep-

---

[6] The taxes included, and indeed the figures, for the EEC countries
and the United Kingdom are from Peggy Richman Musgrave, "Direct
Business Taxation in EEC and UK," *Fiscal Harmonization in Common
Markets* (New York: Columbia University Press, 1966), Chap. 2. We
have extended her pioneering methods of estimating nominal and
effective rates for direct business taxes in these countries to the United
States, Canada, Sweden, and Japan.

[7] For comparability, these are the standards used by Richman Musgrave. However, the resulting effective rates are not very sensitive to
moderate changes in standards.

[8] The formula used is

$$t_e = t_n \left[1 - \frac{\text{Discounted Present Value of Depreciation Stream}}{\begin{array}{c}\text{Discounted Present Value of Income Stream} - \\ \text{Discounted Present Value of Cost of Asset}\end{array}} \right]$$

as in P. Richman Musgrave, "Direct Business Taxation in EEC and UK,"
and as explained in R. A. Musgrave, *Theory of Public Finance* (New
York: McGraw-Hill Book Co., Inc., 1959), Chap. 14, pp. 336–44.

tion of Belgium, the rate of tax on capital income in the individual countries is reduced. The reduction for home investment is: Belgium, 0 per cent; France, 8 per cent; Germany, 6 per cent; Italy, 12 per cent; Luxembourg, 29 per cent; Netherlands, 8 per cent; United States, 5 per cent; Canada, 6 per cent, United Kingdom, 27 per cent; Sweden, 12 per cent; Japan, 2 per cent. In deriving effective rates on international investment, account has been taken of the reduction in nominal rates on home investment due to depreciation allowances. This procedure reflects the fact that depreciation is allowed against corporate profits in the country of source of income, but not by the country of residence. (The estimated effective rates are shown in Appendix Table 8.2.)

A study of the figures in Appendix Table 8.2 reveals many points of interest. There are two guiding principles in their study. First, a corporation may seek the lowest-taxed form of investment when a decision to invest rather than to export to a given country has been made. Secondly, a corporation may seek the country with the lowest tax rate when making a particular form of investment. Following the first principle, the choices for the corporation in entering a particular foreign market are between setting up a branch, when the tax rate in square *A* of the table applies, setting up a subsidiary, when rates in *B* or *C* apply, according to whether profits are left in the foreign country or brought back to the home country, or finally the purchase of securities in a corporation indigenous to the foreign country, square *D*.

The general pattern within the Common Market is that income from branch investment bears lower taxes than subsidiary investment with incomes remitted home. Outside the EEC, the situation varies and it is sometimes reversed, as in the United Kingdom and Sweden. It should be remembered, however, that the typical situation with subsidiary investment is that some earned income will be remitted to the parent company, and some ploughed back into the country of source. In such cases, a rate in between *B* and *C* will apply. Now, since *B* is generally the lowest rate of all, subsidiary investment with part of the earnings remitted often will be preferred to the establishment of branches abroad. Finally, corporate portfolio investment is nearly always the most heavily taxes form of investment.

Following the second guiding principle for the corporate investor—the ranking of the least-tax countries for a given form of investment—we find that while some countries favor home investment over foreign, elsewhere the opposite is the case. In France, Germany, and the Netherlands, for example, branch investment by a foreign corporation is taxed less than home investment. As regards subsidiary investment, especially without remittance, a few non-EEC countries also come into this category, including Canada and the United Kingdom.[9] Note finally that in absolute terms, Belgium, Italy, Luxembourg, and Sweden offer the most favorable tax treatment to foreign investors, while foreign income bears the highest tax burden in France, Germany, the United States, Canada, the United Kingdom, and Japan.

We have also calculated effective rates from macroeconomic data, i.e., from the national income accounts of the individual countries (see Appendix Table 8.3). But it is not possible to differentiate in governmental accounts between levies on firms operating in different countries, nor between different types of such operations, such as branch and subsidiary investment. Accordingly, the table contains information on taxes of home investment, expressed as a percentage of corporate tax receipts on corporate income.

A further problem is that only five of the eleven countries under study state profits separately from other items of property income (interest and rent), and for Italy not even property income figures could be derived. It is then for only five countries—Belgium, France, the United States, Canada, and Japan—that taxes on corporate profits as a percentage of profits could be calculated. Thus, the micro and the macro figures on effective taxes can be compared for these five countries, but not for the other six.

If we compare effective rates of corporate taxes derived by the use of the micro and the macro approaches, we find that the two are practically identical in the cases of Belgium and the United States, they differ little for Canada, while considerable differences are observed in France and Japan. In the latter cases, the micro rates substantially exceed the macro rates, indicating that special provisions and/or tax evasion

---

[9] In the United States, the situation has changed in recent years, inasmuch as the fiscal advantages earlier accorded to investment in the other industrial countries have been removed.

greatly reduce the burden of taxes on corporate profits as compared to the nominal rates.

But will companies not shift at least part of the incidence of corporate taxation to consumers in the form of higher prices? The traditional theory of taxation gives a negative answer to this question: if one assumes competitive markets and profit maximization, optimum output is unaffected by the taxation of profits, and hence firms cannot "force" consumer prices higher by restricting output. But the introduction of monopoly elements and/or objectives other than profit maximization would modify the conclusions. It is hardly surprising, therefore, that in recent years there has been much empirical work on the shifting of the burden of corporate taxation.[10] Unfortunately for the present work, the two major efforts have led to opposite conclusions, however. While the results put forward by Kryzaniack and Musgrave indicated more than 100 per cent shifting (i.e., firms would raise their prices to more than compensate for an increase in corporate taxation), Hall's work suggests that no shifting occurs.

Except for technical evaluation and criticism, the contradiction in the findings remains unresolved. Thus, available evidence does not permit us to derive incident rates for taxes on capital in the United States. And, even if we had unambiguous results on the shifting of corporate taxes for the United States, these could not necessarily be applied to the other industrial countries, chiefly because of differences in the share of foreign trade among these countries. Thus, it may be assumed that there is less possibility for shifting the corporate income tax in the more "open" economies of Western Europe than there is in the United States. Accordingly, should shifting occur at all, this would raise U.S. prices more than prices in Western Europe.

Finally, in assessing the relevance of differences in tax rates for the movement of capital, account has to be taken of formal or informal restrictions on foreign investment. In this respect, the major difference is between the United States, Canada, the United Kingdom, and the Common Market on the

[10] The main contributions are M. Kryzaniack and R. A. Musgrave, *The Shifting of the Corporation Income Tax* (Baltimore: The Johns Hopkins Press, 1963) and C. A. Hall, "Direct Shifting of the Corporation Income Tax in Manufacturing," *American Economic Review*, Papers and Proceedings, May, 1964.

one hand, and Sweden and Japan on the other. While the French policy has been changing over time, in the first group of countries permission to foreign investors has generally been granted (permission is not even required in the United States and Canada). On the other hand, Sweden and Japan permit foreign investment only in special circumstances, chiefly when the importation of foreign know-how is not otherwise ensured.

Taxation of labor income. We now turn to labor income and the personal income tax. In the case of corporate income, it was possible to calculate a flat rate of tax on a dollar of profits in the individual countries, because tax rates generally do not vary with the amount of corporate profits. This is quite different with labor income, since in most countries a progressive personal income tax is applied. Accordingly, we can bring tax rates in different countries into comparison only for given incomes.

One possible method is to adopt some norm derived for a particular country, such as the average manufacturing wage, and convert it to the currency of other countries. If the actual rate of exchange of currencies is thought to be a poor guide to relative purchasing powers in the different countries, purchasing power parities can be used. The latter method has been applied in Appendix Table 8.4, where the U.S. manufacturing wage has been used as a standard of comparison.

But, is this the appropriate comparison when our interest is in the influence of tax differences on the movement of labor? The norm adopted for the "base" country has meaning there, but less in the other countries. For if labor moves from one country to another, it is likely to move from one income to the other. We have, therefore, compared also the tax payable on the average manufacturing wage in each country.[11]

As in the case of capital income, either the nominal rates or the effective rates may be analyzed. We have chosen to do this

[11] It might be interesting to do the same thing for the average executive salary in each country. But no average or typical figures for average executive salaries are available. Also, it may be claimed that tax matters are less significant here, since corporations sending executives abroad tend to pay them at the higher salary level—the home or the foreign country's—taking into account any major tax differences between the two countries.

for effective rates, just as we have done it in the case of capital incomes. The main factors intervening between nominal and effective rates are the various allowances in the personal tax system. Effective rates of tax have been calculated for standard incomes by deducting the allowances which would accrue to an ordinary two-child family in the particular national tax systems.

The highest-to-lowest taxed countries on the average manufacturing wage of the individual countries are the United States, Belgium, Sweden, Canada, Germany, the Netherlands, Italy, Luxembourg, Japan, France, and the United Kingdom. But the results change to a considerable extent if taxes levied on an income equivalent to the average U.S. wage are compared. Now, because of the progressivity of her tax system and the effects of family allowances at low income levels, the United Kingdom occupies the first rather than the last place. Britain is followed by Sweden, the Netherlands, and Belgium, while effective rates are the lowest in France. It must be remembered however, that a high tax rate may be compensated by welfare services, and in some countries income taxes in part represent a contribution to social security which in other countries are levied as such. Thus, net burdens on labor shown in the fourth section are better guides of the position of labor in the different fiscal systems than is a comparison of income taxes.

We turn finally to incident rates on labor. In the case of taxation of capital income, we have assumed that the tax might be shifted to product prices but not to labor. In the case of labor income, it has been suggested that part of the tax is shifted forward, since its imposition will affect the amount of labor supplied. But empirical evidence does not support this proposition. Though scanty, it points to the conclusion that the degree of progressivity in the tax system makes little difference to the supply of work.[12] It would appear then, that the incidence of the personal income tax is fully borne by labor.

Indirect Taxes

In the section on direct taxes, we examined the corporation tax and the personal income tax. Since social security contri-

---

[12] See e.g., A. R. Prest, *Public Finance in Theory and Practice* (London: Weidenfeld and Nicholson, 1960), Chap. 4.

butions are dealt with separately, all other principal taxes (other than those on wealth) will be included in the category of indirect taxes.[13] This is, indeed, quite a large group of taxes, but they have a common characteristic in being levied on a product basis. The major types of indirect taxes are as follows:

1. *Turnover, single stage taxes:* These *ad valorem* taxes are levied at the manufacturing, wholesale, or retail stage.
2. *Gross turnover, multi-stage taxes:* These cumulative or "cascade" taxes are levied on transaction value at every stage of the production and distribution process.
3. *Net turnover, multi-stage taxes:* The so-called turnover value added (TVA) tax differs from the preceding in being levied on transaction value net of material costs (value added) at each stage of production and distribution.
4. *Excises:* These are single-stage taxes on single products, levied on an ad valorem or unit (e.g., weight or volume) basis. They can be defined by the product involved: tobacco, beer, wines and spirits, and gasoline ("traditional" excises).

A major difference in this section compared with that on direct taxes relates to the differentiation of indirect taxes by product which does not enable us to present in a simple table the indirect taxes falling on consumers. Thus, type (1) taxes are of importance in Belgium, Italy, the United States, Canada, Sweden, and Japan, but there is no uniformity as regards type of article taxed, point of assessment, or rate. In general, the industrial countries outside the Common Market raise all or most of their indirect tax revenue from varied rates on relatively small classes of products. In contrast, type (2) and (3) taxes are dominant in the EEC, with the cascade system operating in Belgium (at a rate of 6 per cent), the Netherlands (5 per cent), Germany (4 per cent), Italy (3.3 per cent), and Luxembourg (2 per cent). The only country that applies value-added taxation is France, where the rate is 20 per cent. Finally, all eleven countries levy type (4) traditional excises (usually alcoholic beverages, tobacco, and fuel oils), including both federal and state governments in the United States, as well as federal and provincial governments in Canada.

---

[13] This method of treating indirect taxes as a residual category avoids the extensive discussion of the definition of an indirect tax.

The question arises, then, whether indirect taxes involve hidden tariffs that affect the flow of international trade. In examining this question, note should be taken of two alternative principles for levying indirect taxes on internationally-traded products—the origin and the destination principle. If the origin principle is applied, goods traded internationally carry the tax of the country of source or production. Conversely, under the destination principle, taxes are levied according to the rates existing in the country of receipt or consumption. It follows that under the origin principle, exporters pay a tax to their own government but the goods are exempt from indirect taxes when they enter the country of destination. In turn, with the destination principle, the exporter receives a rebate for domestic taxes paid, and his product is taxed in the importing country. At present, all of the countries included in this study employ the destination principle for indirect taxes, but in the Common Market a decision has been reached to change to the origin principle on the basis of a recommendation made by the Neumark Committee.[14] Much discussion has centered recently on the problem of whether the administrative arrangements for the destination principle, i.e., rebating the producing country's tax and imposing the consumer country's tax, actually leave the product tax-free as it crosses a border, and put it on the same basis as competitive products produced in the country of consumption. If not, this is equivalent to a competitive advantage or disadvantage for an imported product over its home-produced counterpart and is in effect a hidden tariff on, or a subsidy to, imports.

The situation varies with the type of tax (1) to (4), and with the administrative arrangements employed. Taking the arrangements generally employed in the industrial countries, an investigation conducted by the OECD[15] has concluded that products leaving countries where tax types (1) and (3) are dominant, are generally undercompensated. In other words, the tax charged in the producing country is not fully rebated to exports, and the product goes forward at some competitive disadvantage that can be called a quasi-tariff. Countries using type (2) taxes also undercompensate, probably to a greater

[14] European Economic Community Commission, *Report of the Fiscal and Financial Committee* [Neumark Report], Brussels, 1963.
[15] Organization for Economic Co-operation and Development, *Report on Border Tax Adjustments* (Paris, 1964), mimeographed.

degree than in the case of types (1) and (3). This is particularly the case in Belgium and the Netherlands. But since, with the cascade system, the amount of tax paid in manufacturing a given product differs greatly from one corporation to another, depending on the degree of vertical integration, the situation is much more variable—firms will be undercompensated to different degrees and some may even be overcompensated.

Thus, exports often enter the country of destination with a quasi-tariff due to the incomplete compensation of taxes in the producing country. However, if they are charged less in the importing country than are that country's comparable home products, the quasi-tariff will be neutralized. This is thought to occur in countries who employ type (2) taxes, but not in countries using tax systems (1) and (3). Taking account of extended under- and over-compensation in exporting and importing countries, we can then express, for various pairs of countries, the net effect of indirect taxes. This is done in Table 8.1.

As regards effective taxes, only tables for the impact on the consumer will appear. Since there is no direct link between nominal and effective rates on the micro level, we swing over entirely to national accounts data, and relate indirect taxes to consumer expenditure on the products in question (Appendix Table 8.5). The procedure has the advantage of indicating the general level of indirect taxation in a country summed up in a few figures, and the disadvantage that the great diversity in rates in any one country is lost.

Appendix Table 8.5 shows the ratio of both turnover taxes and traditional excises to total consumer expenditure as well as to the relevant tax base. It is apparent that the Common Market countries make greater use of indirect taxes than do other industrial nations. Effective rates are especially high in France and Italy where the proportion of turnover taxes to consumer expenditure exceeds 20 per cent as against only 3.7 per cent for the United Kingdom. In turn, excise taxes appear to be the most important in the United Kingdom, followed by Canada, Sweden and Japan.

We turn now to the incidence of indirect taxes. Let us consider first the effects of indirect taxes levied under the origin principle on consumers. If imports carry a different indirect tax than the same product manufactured in the home country, there is substitution between the imported and home-produced variety of a particular product. Since the indirect tax load on imported products may be lower or higher than that in the receiving country, it will be equivalent to positive or negative tariff protection for the domestic merchandise. This conclusion applies chiefly to specific taxes,

TABLE 8.1. QUASI-TARIFFS DUE TO THE UNDERCOMPENSATION OF INDIRECT TAXES IN THE MAJOR INDUSTRIAL COUNTRIES

Country of origin \ Country of destination	France U.S. Canada U.K. Sweden Japan	Belgium Germany Netherlands Italy Luxembourg
France United States Canada United Kingdom Sweden Japan	Some quasi-tariff	No quasi-tariff
Belgium Germany Italy Luxembourg Netherlands	Heavier quasi-tariff	Some quasi-tariff

Source: Organization for Economic Co-operation and Development, *Report on Border-Tax Adjustments* (Paris, 1964), mimeographed.

while the effects of a general tax may be compensated, to a lesser or greater extent, by variations in the exchange rate.[16]

While intercountry as well as intercommodity substitution may occur if the origin principle is applied, the use of the

[16] It has been argued that international differences in general turnover taxes are fully compensated by historical changes in exchange rates. See European Coal and Steel Community, *Report on Turnover Tax Problems in a Common Market* [Tinbergen Report], Luxembourg, 1958. But not even a general turnover tax will change all prices proportionately so they can be compensated simply by an exchange rate adjustment; furthermore, under the present-day system of fixed exchange rates, a compensating change in exchange rates might not have taken place. Cf. C. Cosciani, "Problèmes fiscaux de la Communauté économique européenne," *Public Finance* (1958), pp. 1–20, for an example of views opposed to Tinbergen's.

destination principle can give rise only to intercommodity substitution. For example, if in Germany taxes on liquor, both home produced and imported, are high, the demand for liquor as a whole is reduced and other alcoholic beverages are substituted for it. Accordingly, trade flows will be affected, not by substitution of one country for another, but by the substitution of one product (of whatever country) for another. Some degree of substitution may be observed even if a general indirect tax is applied, since such a tax applies neither to savings nor much of services. As a result, industrial products which are usually subjected to general indirect taxes, will be discriminated against in favor of other uses of personal incomes.[17]

But what assumptions to make about incidence? In the country studies, it has been assumed that in the event of the elimination of tariffs, producers in the United States, Canada, and Japan could increase exports at constant prices. In turn, for Western Europe calculations have been made under the alternative assumptions of constant prices and a rise in prices by one-third of the tariff reduction.

On first sight, there seems to be an analogy between the shifting of tariffs and taxes. However, it should not be forgotten that the postulated increases in export prices reflect the assumption that inducements would have to be provided for resources to move to the export sector from other sectors of the economy. This argument does not apply to general taxes which are levied on most or all commodities, although there may be some shifting between goods and services and between consumption and saving, and some degree of backward shifting is not excluded in the case of specific taxes.

Correspondingly, we have assumed 100 per cent forward

---

[17] We have emphasized here the trade effects, that is the consumer rather than the factor side, because indirect taxes are traditionally thought to be shifted onto product prices, and therefore have direct effects only on consumers. They would also affect factor movements, however, if the indirect tax was passed back to the factors of production. It should be added that the choice between the origin and destination principle does not make any difference in this case; the net-of-tax receipts by factors which have gone into the making of the product would be reduced by the amount of the tax, irrespective of whether this was levied in the country of destination or of origin. Thus, while the difference in the principle of levying indirect taxes matters for trade, it would be of no significance were indirect taxes to affect factor movements.

shifting of indirect taxes, which causes effective and incident rates to be identical. Still, it may be of interest to indicate the implications of the alternative assumption of less than full forward shifting. The calculations of Appendix Table 8.6 indicate the burden on capital, labor, and consumers if prices increase by two-thirds of the indirect tax, while the remainder is shifted back to capital and labor, each bearing one-half. This illustrative case is of some interest, inasmuch as it indicates that in several countries such a backward shifting of an indirect tax would impose a burden larger than the corporate income tax on profits, while this would be much smaller than the personal income tax in the case of labor.

Government Expenditures

It is difficult to evaluate the fiscal benefits accruing to different groups of individuals from government expenditures. This is due to conceptual difficulties as well as to the paucity of investigations into the incidence of these expenditures. While the classification of taxes into personal, corporation, and indirect taxes corresponds to our economic decision-making groups for factor movements and trade, the usual classification of government expenditures—an administrative (ministry or agency) classification and/or a functional classification—does not correspond to this division. Accordingly, it is difficult to determine whether a particular item of expenditure benefits one group of individuals or another. Moreover, there is a large class of government expenditure, such as defense spending or foreign aid, whose benefits are viewed as accruing to the entire population.

The decision as to where to stop on the ladder from the specific to the general must be based on the problem at hand. Ours must be rooted, on the products side, as to which government benefits are specific enough to reduce enterprise costs, and on the factors side, as to which government expenditures will influence factor movement. Of course, a considerable degree of arbitrariness in making a choice still remains.

Note further that there are hardly any statutory rates of subsidy or expenditure as there are statutory tax rates; the "rate" of benefit is mostly determined by year-to-year political decisions. Hence, all of our calculations are based on the macro rather than the micro approach, and the benefits received by capital, labor, and consumers give rise directly to effective rates. Furthermore, since the effective rates are an attempt to relate expenditure items to their ultimate beneficiary, these are at the same time incident rates, too.

1. *Housing:* Housing expenditures are related to labor-income, in view of the fact that housing subsidies go to poorer households whose income is almost entirely derived from labor.

2. *Education:* Spending on education is also ascribed to labor income. Thus, it is assumed that education benefits are spread among all income receivers in proportion to the labor element in their income.

3. *Industry and commerce, research and development expenditures:* These expenditures include both direct cash subsidies to enterprises and the provision of public goods which are assumed to be cost-reducing services to enterprises. Accordingly, the whole of expenditure is considered as accruing to capital.

4. *Transport:* Some transport services, for example part of road expenditure over and above charges to users, provide cost-reducing benefits to enterprises, while others, including part of spending on roads, will be more of a consumer service. By necessity, any division of these expenditures will be arbitrary. We ascribe one-half of government spending on transportation to capital, and one-half to consumers.

A further problem is whether government expenditures should be defined to also include expenditures on the state and the local level. This choice is not an easy matter. If local expenditures are included, it is problematic where to stop, for in many countries there are several tiers of local authorities. Also, the statistical sources become less reliable as we proceed to local expenditure. Finally, it may be realistic to assume that factor movements are motivated by national differences in government expenditure rather than by expenditures at lower levels.

We have decided to include national (federal) expenditures and "middle-level" public expenditure in the calculations for those of the industrial countries that are highly decentralized: Germany (Länder), U.S. (states), Canada (provinces); for all others, only the expenditures of central government have been considered. However, we have made an exception for expenditures on education and housing where we have also provided data on the entire public sector, including local authorities. This solution has been chosen because the division of responsibilities in these fields differs from country to country.

It appears, then, that the benefits to labor provided by public expenditures on education and housing amount to about 10 per cent of the wage bill, with the Netherlands well above this norm, and the countries of North America slightly below (Appendix Table 8.7). The conclusion hardly changes if benefits to consumers are added to the above figures. Direct government benefits to the consumer are small; the relevant proportions are between 1.2 and 2.3 per cent, the exceptions being Luxembourg (3.5 per cent) and Japan (0.1 per cent).

Comparisons are more difficult in regard to expenditures benefiting capital, in part because profit figures are available for five countries only. Among these, France leads with a ratio of 39.4 per cent, followed by Belgium, 35.1 per cent; the United States, 24.2; Canada, 20.8 per cent; and Japan 9.0 per cent (Appendix Table 8.8). Moreover, the results are affected to a considerable extent by the assumptions made in regard to the allocation of transport expenditure; also, the comparisons are distorted by reason of the fact that expenditures on research and development financed from the military budget have not been included. This omission leads to a considerable degree of underestimation of the benefits to capital in the case of the United States. Finally, the figures for Japan are understated because only a small part of transport expenditures is financed directly from the government budget in that country.

Social Security

Social Security arrangements simultaneously affect the cost and the benefit side of our calculations of the net fiscal burden on consumers, labor, and capital. Employee contributions appear as taxes on labor, employer contributions as taxes on capital (direct burden), while the government contribution to the financing of social security represents taxes on various economic units, calculated in proportion to their total tax bill (indirect burden). On the benefit side, the system can be viewed to benefit one class of economic units only—labor.

Social security is defined to include national insurance (retirement pensions and unemployment), family allowances, public assistance, war pensions and benefits, national health services, employment-injury insurance, and special schemes for public employees.[18] As regards the cost of social security, there are nominal rates of taxes on labor and capital, while only effective rates are shown for consumers, corresponding to the use of general government revenue for financing social security from taxes on consumption.[19] Effective rates differ from nominal rates in the case of capital, since the basis of the tax (payroll of an enterprise) differs from our focus of interest, corporate profit. Incident rates, too, appear for all three classes. Finally, on the benefit side, there will be nominal rates for labor only that also equal effective and incident rates.

The system is simplified by having fewer international complications than are present under direct taxes. In the case of capital and consumers, national tables only are required as the social security law is the same for all enterprises operating in a particular country. But, in the case of labor, note should be taken of the "portability" of social security rights, though we cannot express these in terms of rates of benefits for migrant labor.

Table 8.2 provides information on the size and the financing of social security in the major industrial countries. It appears that the relative importance of social security in national income is considerably greater in the Common Market than in the other industrial countries. The relevant proportions are between 16 and 23 per cent for the former group of nations, as compared to 18 per cent in the United States, 14 per cent in the United Kingdom and Sweden, 13 per cent in Canada, and only 8 per cent in Japan. Considerable differences are shown also in the mode of financing; while the EEC countries, the United States, and Japan derive about two-thirds of financing social security from employer and employee contributions, in Canada, the United Kingdom, and

[18] This is the classification adopted by the International Labor Office, *The Cost of Social Security, 1958–60* (Geneva, 1964).

[19] It is true that the "burden" from this source has already been counted under direct and indirect taxation. But we include it under the finance of social security through taxation to obtain the full picture. We shall avoid double-counting in our summation tables later.

TABLE 8.2. SIZE AND FINANCING OF SOCIAL SECURITY IN THE MAJOR INDUSTRIAL COUNTRIES, 1960.

(PER CENT)

Item	Belgium	France	Germany	Italy	Luxem-bourg	Nether-lands	U.S.	Canada	U.K.	Sweden	Japan
Proportion of social security contributions to national income	19	18	23	19	22	16	18	13	14	14	8
Percentage breakdown:											
Employee contributions	19	15	25	12	20	40	24	12	19	21	26
Employer contributions	42	62	41	59	46	39	38	12	17	11	42
Government contributions	31	20	26	23	24	12	33	71	59	67	25
Other sources[a]	9	3	8	6	11	8	6	6	5	2	7

Sources: ILO, *The Cost of Social Security, 1958–1960* (Geneva, 1964). OECD, *Statistics of National Accounts, 1950–1961* (Paris, 1964). U.N., *Statistical Yearbook, 1963* (New York, 1964). U.N., *Yearbook of National Accounts Statistics, 1963* (New York, 1964).
Notes: [a] Includes income from capital, transfers from other schemes, etc.

Sweden the same proportion comes from general government revenue.

In turn, Appendix Tables 8.9 and 8.10 show nominal, effective, and incident rates on social security contributions, and the social security benefits accruing to labor. The direct contribution of capital and labor to social security is shown on a micro as well as on a macro basis: it is the latter which is used in further calculations since the micro figures are somewhat tenuous, having been obtained as an average of a multiplicity of rates. In turn, indirect contributions to social security have been calculated by applying the relative proportions in total government revenue derived from taxes on capital, labor, and consumers to the amount of government contribution to social security.

Whether we need to go from nominal to effective rates depends on whether the base of nominal rates is different from that on which we want to estimate the burden of social security for comparisons with tax burdens discussed in earlier sections. The base is the appropriate one for labor and consumers, namely labor earnings and consumer expenditure, but not so for capital. Since the burden on corporate profits is relevant for capital movements, it has been necessary to relate capital's contribution to social security to this basis. It is easy to see that the result depends on the labor-intensiveness of the production process and it differs from enterprise to enterprise within a given country.

But how about incidence? Will the employer's contribution indeed burden corporation earnings and will the employees' contribution be borne by labor? It is customary to assume that employee contributions fall on labor. Thus, in UN and OECD statistics, they are classified with direct personal taxes. This is not an entirely comfortable procedure, since an increase in social security contributions may conceivably lead to a wage demand. However, in the absence of evidence as to whether any part of the direct employee contribution is passed forward, we assume that labor does bear it.

Direct employer contributions are a more controversial area. Most observers consider them a burden on labor under the assumption that higher wages or higher social security contributions are alternative ways of increasing labor's share in national income. For employers, in fact, social security contributions appear as a part of labor costs, while workers are said to regard employer contributions as additions to labor income.[20] Thus, we have accepted the majority opinion here that the employer's contribution is fully shifted to labor. In the incidence tables, therefore, only the indirect contribution via government revenue raised by corporation tax falls on capital, with labor bearing its own, as well as capital's, direct contribution.

On the benefits side of social security, only labor is concerned. In conformity with our earlier discussion, we have used the average manufacturing wage as a basis in the calculations. But if the test is to be the size of benefits in different countries, other characteristics of the recipient should also be standardized. Some benefits are supplied on a per capita basis, and it is relatively easy to standardize family size for the purpose of comparing family allowances. This is not the case for health and accident insurance and for old age pensions, however. By taking average per capita payments as our guide, we implicitly assume that low and high income earners in a particular country receive the same absolute benefits.

There are two over-riding features of social security in the eleven countries, as revealed by Appendix Tables 8.9 and 8.10. First, a considerable redistribution of income to labor occurs in this way in all of the industrial countries. Second, social security is generally on a much larger scale in the Common Market than in the other industrial countries. The statistical results are discussed in more detail in the next section. This is because a proper evaluation can only be made in relation to the personal income tax that may compensate for the redistributive features of the social security system.

We turn finally to the international aspect of social security. When labor moves, it may be put to disadvantage by its inability to carry social security rights acquired in the home country. In such a case, say, the benefits a worker newly arrived from Italy will receive in France are less than those the resident French worker receives. Further, temporary labor movement may be hampered by differential benefits for aliens versus indigenous Frenchmen.

[20] On this point, see e.g., Bela Balassa, *The Theory of Economic Integration* (Homewood, Ill.: Richard D. Irwin, 1961), Chaps. 10 and 11.

Even complete uniformity of social security benefits among the industrial countries would not entirely solve the problem, since differing claims against the old systems would go back several decades. Further, international differences in social security systems (e.g., France's emphasis on family allowances) reflect deep cultural and religious differences. So the problem is approached by treaty arrangements rather similar to those for taxation of income crossing national boundaries. According to the International Labor Union's "Convention Concerning Equality of Treatment of Nationals and Non-nationals in Social Security," a national from another country should be granted the same benefits in the country of work as the nationals of the latter. In this way, international differences in social security could be maintained while the movement of labor would not be impeded by discrimination between aliens and nationals in the country of destination. But even if the Convention were to be implemented, differences in social security systems would remain a factor affecting labor movements.[21]

Present Differences in Fiscal and Social Security Systems in the Atlantic Area

In previous sections, the discussion of charges and benefits arising from national fiscal and social security systems were confined to the particular item the section dealt with. We will now take an over-all view, and sum up the relevant rates to indicate the total or over-all differences in the various countries of the impact of the fiscal and social security systems as a whole on capital, labor, and consumers. (This is done in Table 8.3.)

In principle, all tables indicating nominal, effective, and incidence rates can be brought together to yield the total net burden (benefit) for capital owners, labor, and consumers. But we have seen that the assumptions on incidence have, at present, little empirical foundation. In turn, data on nominal rates do not always conform to the purposes of this study: the consideration of the effects of fiscal and social security sys-

---

[21] A full account of the implication of this solution and of others is found in N. Andel, "Social Security and International Economic Integration," *Fiscal Harmonization in Common Markets* (New York: Columbia University Press, 1966).

TABLE 8.3. SUM OF EFFECTIVE BURDENS AND BENEFITS ON CAPITAL, LABOR, AND CONSUMERS

(PER CENT)

	Belgium	France	Germany	Italy	Luxembourg	Netherlands	U.S.	Canada	U.K.	Sweden	Japan
I. Capital[a]											
1. Corporate tax	27.9 (4.4)	32.7 (7.4)	(10.7)	n.a.	(18.4)	(9.1)	47.0 (17.0)	55.4 (18.1)	(11.2)	(8.5)	34.3 (10.9)
2. Government expenditure (benefit)	35.1 (5.0)	39.4 (8.8)	(5.4)		(12.4)	(3.5)	24.1 (8.4)	20.8 (7.3)	(16.6)	(7.0)	9.0 (2.4)
3. Net benefit (+) or burden (−)	+7.2 +(0.6)	+6.7 +(1.4)	−(5.3)		−(6.0)	−(5.6)	−22.9 −(8.6)	−34.6 −(10.8)	+(5.4)	−(1.5)	−25.3 −(8.5)
II. Labor											
4. Personal income tax	7.3	0.0	4.0	3.3	2.5	3.5	8.7	5.2	0.0	6.8	0.1
5. Social Security contributions[b]	19.8	23.8	25.0	25.9	24.7	22.7	7.3	4.4	6.8	6.6	10.8
6. Social Security benefit	13.0	15.2	12.0	9.7	11.4	8.2	3.5	5.2	7.8	8.3	2.7
7. Government expenditure (benefit)	10.5	12.0	12.2	9.6	9.4	18.5	7.6	7.4	9.1	11.3	3.6
8. Net benefit (+) or burden (−)	−3.6	+3.4	−4.8	−9.9	−6.4	+0.5	−4.9	+3.0	+10.1	+6.2	−4.6
III. Consumers											
9. Indirect taxes	12.0	17.9	16.0	16.4	8.7	12.5	14.8	13.8	12.9	14.6	9.9
10. Government expenditure (benefit)	1.9	1.2	1.6	1.4	3.5	1.4	1.3	2.3	1.7	1.5	0.1
11. Net benefit (+) or burden (−)	−10.1	−16.7	−14.4	−15.0	−5.2	−11.1	−13.5	−11.5	−11.2	−13.1	−9.8

Sources: Appendix Tables 8.1—8.10.
Notes: [a] The nonparenthesized figures are related to corporate profits, and those in parentheses to property income.
[b] Includes employer and employee contributions to Social Security. Excludes the indirect burden through general taxation since this is already accounted for under particular taxes.

tems on trade and factor movements. Correspondingly, the summary tables have been restricted to effective rates. An exception has been made in the case of social security contributions paid by employers since it is fairly well established that these contributions are shifted to labor.

For capital, corporate tax rates shown in the micro EK table on home investment range from 30 to 54 per cent; this result is generally confirmed by the macro EK tables. But, as indicated above, corporate tax rates have to be related to property income in order to permit comparisons among ten of the eleven major industrial countries. Assuming that social security contributions are fully shifted to labor, and taking account of the benefits capital derives from government expenditure, the fiscal systems of most major industrial countries seem to burden property incomes to the tune of 0 to 10 per cent. The highest figures are shown for Canada (10.8 per cent), the United States (8.6 per cent), and Japan (8.5 per cent). In turn, three industrial countries, the United Kingdom, France, and Belgium, show net benefits of 5.4, 1.4, and 0.6 per cent, respectively.

These considerations relate to the taxation of domestic incomes that will influence the flow of capital if the owner also moves. However, as indicated in the previous section, this is the exception rather than the rule. Appendix Table 8.2 shows the tax treatment of various forms of investment for all pairs of the eleven industrial countries. As we have noted earlier, tax considerations would favor investment in Belgium, Italy, and Luxembourg, while foreign investors bear the highest tax burden in France, Germany, and the United States. At the same time, subsidiary investment with earnings retained in the country of operation receives the most favorable treatment, generally followed by branch investment.

We turn now to intercountry differences in taxes, social security charges, and benefits on labor. Personal tax rates vary to a considerable extent among countries: nominal rates on the average manufacturing wage range from 9 to 31 per cent, and effective rates from 0 to 9 per cent. But there are also differences in social security charges and benefits as well as in the effects of government expenditures on labor. Taken together, the net impact of taxes and social security charges and benefits ranges from a burden of 9.9 per cent in Italy to a gain

tions in financing social security while the general government budget plays a major part in the latter. Note finally that differences in regard to indirect taxes are also greater within the Atlantic area than within the Common Market.

It appears, then, that the problem of harmonization starts from a more difficult initial situation in the Atlantic area than in the Common Market. The largest net fiscal differences are found in the case of labor, followed by capital, while relatively small differences are shown in regard to the net tax burden on consumers. However, in the latter case, general sales and traditional excise taxes have been aggregated, and differences in regard to the two types of taxes utilized are greater within the Atlantic area than in the EEC.

In this and in the previous sections, we have examined some of the main quantitative differences in taxes and social security charges and benefits bearing on capital, labor, and consumers in eleven industrial countries. The remaining two sections are devoted to a discussion of the economic and political significance of these differences. In this connection, two questions are to be raised: to what extent do existing differences in fiscal and social security systems distort competitive patterns and lead to undesirable trade and factor movements? And, is it desirable and feasible to attempt reducing or eliminating these differences? In this connection, we will first examine how the two existing trade groupings—the EEC and EFTA—have approached these questions.

Policy on Fiscal and Social Security Systems in the EEC and EFTA

The European Common Market. In the Treaty of Rome, various provisions were made for reducing differences in fiscal and social security systems among the EEC countries. In the field of taxation, emphasis was given to indirect taxation, while direct taxes were not dealt with specifically in the Treaty. Nevertheless, it is thought that there are implicit grounds for harmonizing direct taxes in Articles 100–102 on Approximation of Laws, for these articles state that any legislative provisions which distort the conditions of competition in the Common Market should be eliminated. Further, one might interpret the general articles on the free movement of workers, services, and capital and on the right of establishment that if direct taxes or any taxes impaired free movement, the need would arise for co-ordinated action. In turn, Article 51 asks the EEC Commission to prepare any measures in the field of social security which appear necessary for the free movement of workers, but in particular to ensure the maintenance of accumulated social security rights for migrant workers.

Actually, the discussion of the harmonization of indirect taxes had started well before the signing of the Treaty of Rome; it began in connection with the establishment of the European Coal and Steel Community. Many of the problems examined in connection with the Common Market were anticipated by the Tinbergen Committee, appointed in 1953 to consider the problems of taxation in the ECSC.[23] The main question then was whether the origin or the destination principle should apply to indirect taxes. It was recommended that the origin principle be used in regard to general turnover taxes, and the destination principle in regard to excises and specific taxes on particular products. Also, the difficulties arising from the application of two different types of indirect tax—the cascade type and the value-added type—became evident already at that time.

Following the establishment of the EEC, a special committee was set up to consider the implementation of the tax harmonization provision in the Treaty. This was the Neumark Committee, whose report was made public in 1962.[24] The Neumark Committee endorsed the earlier conclusions of the Tinbergen Committee on the origin versus the destination principle—the origin principle ought to be applied to general turnover taxes, and the destination principle could be retained for specific excises. The Committee further recommended that the origin principle be applied in intra-EEC trade only, while the destination principle should continue to be used in regard to trade between the Common Market and third countries. Finally, suggestions were made for the employment of a value-added tax by all member states.

The implementation of the Rome Treaty and of the Neu-

---

[23] European Coal and Steel Community, *Report on Turnover Tax Problems in a Common Market* [Tinbergen Report], Luxembourg, 1957.
[24] European Economic Community, *Report of the Fiscal and Financial Committee* [Neumark Report], Brussels, 1962.

mark Committee recommendations on indirect tax harmonization have made some progress in recent years. In a revised draft of a 1962 Directive presented in 1964, provision is made for a value-added system of taxation throughout the Community that will come into effect by 1970. However, the member states may add a national retail sales tax if they so desire. The abolition of border adjustments remains to be accomplished, and proposals to this effect will be submitted at a later date. This second step would involve the substitution of the origin principle for the destination principle, followed by an equalization of rates.

We see that thus far the emphasis of fiscal harmonization in the Common Market has been on indirect taxes. This is something of a paradox since the destination principle is supposed to minimize the distorting effects of differences in indirect taxes among the member countries. Why, then, has the emphasis fallen here? A number of reasons can be given. Nearly all of the actions in the early stages of the establishment of a Common Market relate to trade and tariff impediments to trade. It is therefore logical, once tariffs are out of the way, to look for the most nearly equivalent charges which may differ from country to country, and these are of course indirect rather than direct. But perhaps the most powerful reason has been the desire to do away with fiscal frontiers. The existing situation involves rebates of indirect taxes on exports and the imposition of such taxes on imports at national boundaries, so that checks and control over trade would continue to be necessary even after all tariff barriers are removed. On top of this, the predominance of the cascade system means that it is difficult to make these border adjustments correctly.

More recently, attention has also been given to direct taxes, though action is confined to preliminary discussions; directives by the Commission of the EEC have not been prepared. It is recognized that direct taxes must be acted upon in some way, both because of the provisions of the Rome Treaty concerning impediments to the free movement of labor, capital, and enterprises, and because the harmonization of types and rates of indirect tax has budgetary consequences in member states which will require offsetting changes in direct taxation.

Current thinking on direct tax harmonization is that it will occur in regard to corporate, rather than personal, taxation. The reasons for this choice are four-fold. In the first place, it is felt that capital is mobile, while labor is generally immobile; thus, differences in taxation bearing on capital influence its movement, but differences in taxation bearing mainly on labor, namely personal income taxes, have little effect on the movement of this factor. Second, it is thought that profit taxes might affect prices in some degree through shifting the incidence of the tax, and therefore come as the third item in the "logical chain of attention": tariffs, indirect taxes, and direct taxes on corporate profits. In the third place, it is felt that the citizens of some member states may desire a higher level of government services than others, so that there must be one class of taxation which would permit differences in levels of government revenue. The least important tax to harmonize on the preceding arguments is the personal income tax, and so it is through this tax that differences in the size of the public sector in member states might be continued. Last but not least, it is difficult to conceive of harmonizing the highly idiosyncratic personal tax structures of the EEC countries, reflecting as they do national and cultural characteristics.

It is interesting to note that in the case of corporate profit taxes the same general procedure is being followed as in regards to indirect taxation, namely type or structure harmonization precedes the harmonization of rates. But this harmonization is more complicated in the case of corporate than in the case of indirect taxes, since there exist differences in provisions for depreciation, valuation of stocks, treatment of losses, etc. Still, the Directorate on Competition in the EEC Commission considers that the differences in depreciation and valuation of stocks are not very severe, but that the variations in incentives provided by the tax treatment of foreign invesment in the member countries are a matter of concern.[25]

Perhaps the most interesting feature of direct tax harmonization in the EEC is what may be called "induced harmonization." This is a process whereby—with the many contacts and discussions between politicians and officials of the EEC countries—national reforms of the tax systems tend to conform to

[25] "Statement by P. Verloren von Themaat to the Commission on Taxation of the International Chamber of Commerce," Appendix to EEC Document 180/87 (Brussels, 1964).

a European norm. For example, in 1957, only three of the six countries had a corporation tax in the usual sense of the word. Belgium, France, and Italy still used the so-called schedular income tax system, applying different income taxes to different types of income, of which corporate profits was one. In 1958 France had done away with such schedular taxes, and in 1962, Belgium also changed over to a general progressive income tax for private persons and a single corporation tax for companies. Italy still has a schedular tax system, but within a few years she is expected to change to the predominant system of corporate and income taxes. By 1970, all six will have the same basic structure of income taxes, a progressive personal income tax, and a separate corporation tax.

We turn now to the harmonization of social security systems in the EEC. In this respect, not much progress has been made so far. In December, 1962, there was a European conference on social security which led to the drafting of a proposal for effecting such a harmonization. There appeared two avenues of progress. First, specific areas of social security might be brought into harmony, e.g., industrial accident and occupational disease benefits are being studied. Second, a number of bills on social security prepared by individual member governments have been sent to the Commission, thus giving rise to some expectation of "induced harmonization" in this field also. It seems, however, that there is less likelihood for the harmonization of social security systems than is the case in the fields of indirect taxes and corporate taxation. The differences in the social security systems of the member countries are considerable, and harmonization looks nearly as difficult to achieve as in the case of personal income taxation.

So much for the harmonization of fiscal and social security systems in the Common Market. In addition, actions have been taken to facilitate the movement of capital, enterprises, and persons, pursuant to relevant articles of the Rome Treaty. The first Directive on capital movements was issued in May, 1963, but among direct investments this freed only investments in fixed property and capital movements of a personal nature. However, member states could still limit the freedom of residents to deal in foreign securities and to issue securities on foreign stock exchanges. Regarding short term movements of funds, they remained completely free to retain controls. In the second Directive of December, 1962, liberalization was taken a step further. The most important advance was the granting of total freedom from exchange restrictions for transactions in quoted securities. The succeeding stage is likely to be unconditional liberalization of stock issues on any stock exchange in a member country, and the opening up of national financial markets to issues by the individual states themselves.

Freedom of establishment has been subject to many directives, as a piecemeal approach has been adopted—sometimes a sector at a time like agriculture or cinematography, sometimes specific questions to do with entry or residence or transfer of payments across borders. This program takes longer than expected because of the intricate differences of company law in the different states which are eventually to be coordinated.

The European Free Trade Association. In regard to the harmonization of fiscal and social security systems, EFTA offers quite a contrast to the EEC. Compared with the progress made in reducing differences in tax systems in the Common Market, there appears to be a lack of will and action in EFTA. This subsection will therefore be much briefer than the one on the EEC. It will nevertheless be of interest for purposes of the present study since it illustrates certain differences between a common market and a free trade area in regard to policy harmonization, and points to the difficulties that may arise in an Atlantic Free Trade Area.

The Stockholm Convention on the establishment of EFTA concerns chiefly tariffs, and there are only a few provisions relating to fiscal and social legislation. The only explicit consideration of taxation comes in Article 6, which covers revenue tariffs as well as internal taxes. Naturally, in view of the preoccupation of EFTA with commodity trade, the taxes referred to are indirect taxes. It seems fair to say that if this Article has had any effect, it has only been in discouraging the raising of indirect taxes to counteract the loss of tariff protection, rather than action on indirect taxes as they stand. This miniscule effect is about the only one on the internal tax system of the member states that the Stockholm Convention has produced.

This is a negative report on co-ordination of fiscal or other internal economic policy in EFTA. But a certain amount of discussion on these problems is taking place under the aegis of OECD. On the question of tax harmonization, there was an interesting exchange of views at the end of 1963. The "demonstration effect" of EEC developments in this field and tax reforms carried out in Sweden led the Swedish delegate to propose a study of differences in tax systems in the EFTA countries by a special committee or by the Economic Development Committee. But the proposal met only with indifference. And, in subsequent changes in her tax system, the most powerful member—Britain—has paid little regard to the types of tax systems existing in other EFTA countries.

Policy on Fiscal and Social Security Regulations in the Atlantic Area

In the preceding two sections, we examined the differences in regard to fiscal and social security systems within EEC and within the wider group of Atlantic countries, as well as the policies adopted in the EEC and EFTA. The question arises, then, what actions may be taken in the event of Atlantic integration? The answer to this question will largely depend on whether particular fiscal problems are worse in the Atlantic area then in EEC or EFTA. "Worse" is to be understood in an economic as well as in a political sense: are the initial differences regarding fiscal and social security regulations greater, or less, in the Atlantic region than in EEC or EFTA? Do these differences greatly distort the flow of commodities and productive factors? Are the political difficulties of reducing these more, or less, difficult in the Atlantic area?

The answer will partly depend on the degree and type of Atlantic integration under consideration. We shall consider two alternative developments: an Atlantic Free Trade Area, or continuing tariff reductions under the most-favored-nation clause—the Kennedy Round approach. The list of the relevant measures and their economic effects should now be clear: indirect taxes and trade, corporation taxes and capital movements, social security *cum* personal income tax, and labor migration. The order does not follow that of our statistical sections, but rather the "chain of attention" we find in regard to the EEC. We shall review each of these below.

Differences in the indirect taxes are greater, both as regards type of indirect tax and rates, in the Atlantic area than in the Common Market. The differences in regard to types of taxes put into focus the problem of harmonization in the Atlantic area, for we have seen that the EEC countries considered it necessary to get the structure of indirect taxes into line before harmonizing rates. But is the emphasis that the Common Market has placed on eliminating the differences in indirect taxes equally applicable to the Atlantic region? The EEC has followed this objective for two main reasons. First, it is difficult to make exact border tax adjustments under the destination principle; and second, there is a desire to remove "fiscal frontiers" within the Common Market.

The latter consideration does not appear to be of much importance in the Atlantic area. And even if differences in indirect taxes produce some quasi-tariff, the trade effects will be of lesser significance than in the EEC because of geographical factors. While differences in indirect taxes may greatly affect the movement of commodities in a close-knit union like the EEC, they become less important in a widely dispersed area. In fact, the cost of transportation between Japan, North America, and Western Europe will often make differences in taxes seem trivial by comparison.

Geography is of little importance for corporate taxes, and we may expect differences in corporate tax rates to cause similar distortions in capital flows in the Atlantic area, as within the EEC. There is little difference between the EEC and the Atlantic area as regards the type of corporate taxation (with the exception of Italy, all countries have a single corporate tax) and the pattern of rates is also broadly similar in the two cases. Thus, political obstacles apart, the problems of equalizing competitive conditions for investment would not be much different.

We come now to the question of labor movements. The impact of fiscal and social security systems on labor differs greatly within the Atlantic area. But we have seen that in the case of EEC these differences do not inhibit international labor movements, nor would their harmonization contribute much to such movement. This conclusion applies *a fortiori* to the Atlantic region, where geographical, linguistic, and cultural differences inhibit migration. Thus, equalizing the burdens on labor is not called for.

From our discussion, it appears that while the harmonization of indirect taxes and corporate taxation is economically desirable in the Atlantic area, social security and personal income tax harmonization can be largely ruled out. But there are political difficulties with regard to the former two which create obstacles in the way of tax harmonization. To begin with, in the Atlantic area there are greater differences in the structure of states and their levels of economic development than in the EEC. There are more federal states involved, and the harmonization of tax systems is more difficult to achieve in cases where a large part of the tax burden is imposed at a lower level, as in the states of the U.S. and the provinces of Canada, or the cantons of Switzerland.

A further consideration is the manner in which integration proceeds: whether it takes the form of a free trade area or a common market. In this connection, it should be emphasized that the difference between the two forms of integration is much more than that indicated by their tariff position—the common external tariff versus individually-determined tariffs. The difference is symptomatic of a will to co-ordinate economic policies versus the insistence on maintaining national sovereignty over internal economic affairs. It leads one to doubt whether an organization like a free trade area will ever take effective action in regard to fiscal and social regulations. It might also be argued that an Atlantic Free Trade Area would be an even weaker form of free trade area than EFTA, and our conclusions apply even more if tariffs are reduced only partially through a series of Kennedy Rounds. It is difficult, therefore, to expect actions similar to those taken by the EEC on internal economic policies in an AFTA because of an unwillingness to surrender national sovereignty. Rather, one might expect a situation just as in EFTA: piecemeal efforts to co-ordinate on questions of lesser importance such as double taxation, which is taking place already through OECD.

But will the EEC move towards a fiscal structure similar to that of the United States that would make harmonization at some future date much easier? This is indeed happening in the case of corporate taxation where all Common Market countries and Britain are adopting a single tax instead of the old schedular systems of taxation. On the other hand, the basic federal-member state split in the fiscal system that EEC is moving to is utterly different from the U.S. system. The federal tax of Europe is likely to be the value-added turnover tax, while for the reasons stated earlier, personal income taxation will remain the prerogative of the member states. Finally, there are considerable differences between the Common Market and the United States in regard to the types and rate of indirect taxation.

As things are going, therefore, in a future EEC–U.S. negotiation, one might find it relatively easy to harmonize corporation tax, more difficult to harmonize indirect tax, and very difficult to harmonize personal income taxes and social security systems. This might be viewed as a not too disagreeable prospect if it is recalled that capital movements, rather than trade or labor movements, are the least inhibited by geographical and other problems discussed earlier. Thus, corporate tax harmonization is economically desirable and politically possible, indirect tax harmonization economically desirable but—with either kind of Atlantic integration—politically difficult. Harmonization of taxes falling on labor can be largely dismissed from both economic and political points of view.

The most helpful preparatory work on the eventual diminution of differences in fiscal and social security systems in the Atlantic area would be in these countries moving towards common norms on structure, because then harmonization can easily be implemented by a political decision. Such harmonization is evident in EEC, although it does not necessarily move in the direction of the U.S. tax system. There is also some conformity in tax changes in other countries—the introduction of a value-added tax in Sweden, the transformation of the corporation tax in Britain—but the single corporation tax is the only true Atlantic norm at present. However, consultation and agreement on specific issues in the framework of the OECD may be helpful for further harmonization.

APPENDIX TABLE 8.1. NK–DIRECT TAXES—CORPORATE INVESTOR, 1963[a]

(TAX RATE, PER CENT)

Each cell contains four figures arranged in a 2×2 square: top‑left (A) top‑right (B) / bottom‑left (C) bottom‑right (D).

Receipt	Belgium	France	Germany	Italy	Luxembourg	Netherlands	U.S.[b]	Canada	U.K.	Sweden	Japan
Belgium	30 / 46 46	58 50 / 62 62	64 57 / 60 60	46 38 / 63 63	53 45 / 62 62	53 45 / 62 62	56 48 / 66 66	58 50 / 65 65	62 54 / 63 63	48 40 / 52 52	58 50 / 61 61
France	35 30 / 43 58	50 50 / 67 69	56 57 / 50 58	38 38 / 57 57	45 45 / 53 68	45 45 / 58 72	48 48 / 56 75	50 50 / 58 75	54 54 / 54 54	40 40 / 40 70	50 50 / 52 76
Germany	51 30 / 42 30	50 57 / 55 50	57 71 / 60 57	38 73 / 57 38	45 45 / 51 76	45 45 / 51 76	48 48 / 56 75	50 50 / 58 79	54 80 / 59 59	40 40 / 49 74	51 50 / 57 74
Italy	43 43 / 35 30	62 62 / 69 69	60 60 / 56 57	44 44 / 42 38	51 45 / 51 61	51 51 / 51 45	53 56 / 56 56	62 62 / 50 50	54 54 / 72 72	46 40 / 46 46	55 50 / 57 57
Luxembourg	50 66 / 35 30	50 50 / 50 72	62 66 / 56 57	74 74 / 38 38	45 45 / 45 67	75 75 / 45 45	48 48 / 78 78	50 75 / 50 50	54 54 / 54 75	43 40 / 75 75	71 71 / 50 50
Netherlands	43 69 / 48 30	50 50 / 57 78	50 68 / 56 57	38 76 / 48 38	45 45 / 53 73	45 70 / 48 45	48 48 / 51 73	50 77 / 58 78	54 54 / 54 76	40 40 / 40 70	53 74 / 48 48
U.S.[b]	48 70 / 50 30	62 81 / 54 50	48 74 / 56 57	48 78 / 50 38	48 45 / 48 73	48 71 / 50 45	48 48 / 51 52	58 50 / 50 50	54 54 / 54 77	48 48 / 49 73	52 76 / 54 54
Canada	43 72 / 54 30	55 77 / 50 50	50 75 / 56 57	57 79 / 54 38	50 45 / 53 77	53 77 / 54 45	48 48 / 56 78	54 54 / 50 50	54 54 / 54 54	50 40 / 43 75	54 72 / 50 50
U.K.	54 68 / 35 30	50 50 / 50 50	54 54 / 50 50	54 54 / 38 38	54 45 / 54 75	54 75 / 45 45	54 48 / 54 54	58 58 / 58 50	54 54 / 54 54	54 54 / 54 54	50 50 / 49 49
Sweden	43 66 / 50 71	50 50 / 50 50	56 60 / 50 75	57 68 / 57 78	69 45 / 72 72	72 67 / 50 45	48 48 / 53 53	58 58 / 58 50	54 54 / 54 77	40 40 / 40 40	50 50 / 50 50
Japan	50 50 / 50 71	62 81 / 50 50	50 50 / 56 60	57 78 / 57 78	50 45 / 53 77	50 45 / 53 77	48 48 / 56 74	58 50 / 58 79	54 54 / 54 77	50 40 / 50 75	50 50 / 50 50

Sources: P. Richman-Musgrave, "Direct Business Taxes in EEC and UK," in *Fiscal Harmonization in Common Markets* (New York: Columbia University Press, 1965). Chap. 2. "The International Bureau of Fiscal Documentation, *The Taxation of Patent Royalties, Dividends, and Interest in Europe* (Amsterdam, 1963). F.B.I., *Taxation in Western Europe* (London, 1962). Commerce Clearing House, *U.S. Master Tax Guide* (Chicago, 1964). Commerce Clearing House, *Canadian Master Tax Guide* (Montreal, 1964). M. Norr and C. Sandels, *The Corporate Income Tax in Sweden* (Stockholm, 1960). Tax Bureau, Ministry of Finance, *An Outline of Japanese Tax* (Tokyo, 1963). Okura Zaimu Kyokai, *Tax Agreements with Japan* (Tokyo, 1963). Harvard Law School, *Taxation in Sweden* (Commerce Clearing House, Boston, 1959). Harvard Law School, *Taxation in U.S.A.* (Commerce Clearing House, Boston, 1963).

Notes: [a] Nominal tax rates on corporate incomes. The figures in each cell represent:

top left (square A) = tax rate on branch investment.

top right (square B) = tax rate on subsidiary investment when retained in country of source.

bottom left (square C) = tax rate on subsidiary investment when income remitted home.

bottom right (square D) = tax rate on portfolio investment by a corporation.

[b] In the case of the United States, the Interest Equalization Tax, which came into operation in July, 1963, is not incorporated in the figures for it is a tax on the *value* of foreign securities acquired by American owners (at 15 per cent of the value for long term securities.) and so it is not an *income* tax commensurable with the taxes included in these figures. However, to take account of the reduction in the corporation tax which has taken place since 1963, the appropriate 1965 tax rate has been submitted for the rate applicable in 1963.

APPENDIX TABLE 8.2. EK—DIRECT TAXES—CORPORATE INVESTOR, 1963[a]

(TAX RATE, PER CENT)

Receipt	Belgium		France		Germany		Italy		Luxembourg		Netherlands		U.S.[b]		Canada		U.K.		Sweden		Japan	
Belgium	30	30	58	46	64	54	46	33	53	32	53	41	56	46	58	47	62	50	48	35	58	49
	46	46	59	59	58	58	62	62	53	53	60	60	64	64	62	62	60	60	50	50	60	60
France	35	30	46	46	56	54	38	33	45	32	45	41	48	46	50	47	54	50	40	35	50	49
	43	58	64	67	48	57	53	53	45	58	55	71	54	73	55	74	50	50	35	68	51	76
Germany	51	30	50	46	54	54	38	33	42	32	45	41	48	46	50	47	54	50	40	35	51	49
	59	70	54	77	54	70	53	69	58	71	49	76	54	76	55	77	50	79	45	72	57	79
Italy	42	30	55	46	60	55	33	36	51	32	51	46	53	46	73	47	59	50	46	35	55	49
	43	43	59	59	55	55	36	36	48	49	47	47	54	54	73	73	55	55	42	42	56	56
Luxembourg	35	30	62	46	56	54	42	33	32	32	45	41	48	46	50	47	54	50	43	35	50	49
	50	66	50	62	60	65	72	72	32	63	70	70	77	76	60	60	70	70	73	73	71	71
Netherlands	35	30	50	46	56	54	38	33	45	32	41	41	48	46	50	47	54	50	40	35	50	49
	43	69	46	70	48	54	33	33	48	67	41	41	46	46	50	47	50	73	35	68	51	73
U.S.[b]	48	30	50	46	56	54	48	74	48	32	48	69	46	46	55	75	50	74	49	35	49	74
	48	71	54	76	48	68	48	33	48	67	48	41	50	50	55	47	54	50	48	71	50	49
Canada	50	30	50	46	56	54	50	76	50	32	50	75	48	50	47	76	50	75	50	35	50	76
	43	72	59	79	48	73	53	77	42	71	50	41	54	46	54	47	54	50	38	73	51	73
U.K.	54	30	54	46	56	54	54	33	54	32	54	41	54	77	54	47	54	50	54	35	54	49
	54	68	51	75	54	74	54	54	54	73	54	73	54	54	54	54	50	50	54	54	54	72
Sweden	35	30	50	46	56	54	38	33	69	32	45	41	48	46	50	47	54	50	35	35	54	49
	43	66	46	46	48	59	53	64	66	65	41	65	51	51	55	55	50	50	35	35	48	48
Japan	50	30	50	46	56	54	50	33	50	32	50	41	48	46	50	47	54	50	50	35	49	49
	50	71	59	80	50	74	53	77	50	71	50	75	54	73	55	78	50	75	50	68	49	49

Sources: See Appendix Table 8.1.
Notes: [a] Effective tax rates on corporate incomes. On the meaning of the individual cells, see Appendix Table 8.1.
[b] Data refer to 1965.

APPENDIX TABLE 8.3. EK—DIRECT TAXES, 1960[1]

(MILLIONS OF LOCAL CURRENCY AND PER CENT)

	Belgium	France	Germany	Italy	Luxem-bourg	Nether-lands	U.S.	Canada	U.K.	Sweden	Japan
1. Property income	208,900	97,230	81,680		7,549	15,100	131,668	8,729	6,285	17,890	5,714,200
2. Profits	33,000	22,090					47,708	2,853			1,814,700
3. Tax on corporate profits	9,200	7,230	8,770		1,386	1,370	22,435	1,581	705	1,517	622,100
4. Tax rate on property income base (%)	4.4	7.4	10.7		18.4	9.1	17.0	18.1	11.2	8.5	10.9
5. Tax rate on corporate profits base (%)	27.9	32.7					47.0	55.4			34.3

Sources: OECD, *Statistics of National Accounts, 1950–1961* (Paris, 1964). UN, *Yearbook of National Account Statistics, 1963* (New York, 1964).

Notes: [1] For five countries, comparable profits figures are available and are used above; for all eleven, comparisons are only possible on a broad basis of property income.

APPENDIX TABLE 8.4. N.L. AND E.L.—DIRECT TAXES, 1963[a]

	Average annual income U.S. Dollars		Nominal rate of tax per cent		Effective rate of tax per cent[b]	
	A	B	A	B	A	B
Belgium	1,362	4,155	9.3	19.7	7.3	10.9
France	1,381	4,000	13.5	27.7	0.0	2.3
Germany	1,995	4,026	14.9	20.3	4.0	11.9
Italy	1,116	3,623	3.3	10.6	3.3	8.4
Luxembourg	1,966	4,155	13.3	23.2	2.5	9.4
Netherlands	1,577	3,442	12.5	23.0	3.5	12.7
United States[c]	5,168	5,168	22.1	22.1	8.7	8.7
Canada	3,819	4,796	17.6	18.3	5.2	6.8
United Kingdom	1,920	4,258	30.6	35.1	0.0	14.6
Sweden	2,700	4,651	11.4	19.7	6.8	12.8
Japan	1,007	3,235	11.7	18.4	0.1	9.3

Sources: I.L.O., *Yearbook of Labour Statistics* (Geneva, 1964); F.B.I., *Taxation in Western Europe* (London, 1962); Commerce Clearing House, *U.S. Master Tax Guide* (Chicago, 1964); Commerce Clearing House, *Canadian Master Tax Guide* (Montreal, 1964); Tax Bureau, Ministry of Finance, *Outline of Japanese Taxes;* B. Balassa, "The Purchasing Power Parity Doctrine: A Reappraisal," *Journal of Political Economy,* December 1964.

Notes: [a] Nominal and effective taxes on labor income. Figures in column (A) are based on the average annual wage in the manufacturing industries of the individual countries; figures in column (B) are based on the average U.S. wage converted to the incomes of the other countries by using purchasing power parities.

[b] Based on the allowances under national tax laws for a married income earner with a family of two children.

[c] The data do not account for reductions in U.S. taxes that have taken place since 1963. The relevant nominal rate of tax was reduced from 22.1 per cent in 1963 to 19.6 per cent in 1963 and to 18.3 per cent in 1965. In turn, the effective rate was lowered from 8.7 per cent in 1963 to 7.6 per cent in 1964 and to 6.9 per cent in 1965.

APPENDIX TABLE 8.5. EC—INDIRECT TAXES, 1960[a]

(MILLIONS OF LOCAL CURRENCY AND PER CENT)

Item	Belgium	France	Germany	Italy[d]	Luxembourg	Netherlands	U.S.	Canada	U.K.	Sweden	Japan[d]
1. Turnover taxes	31,244	24,165	17,733	1,151	806	1,876	35,000	1,247	523	2,435	187
2. Traditional excises	15,516	9,554	7,953	861	417[b]	1,135	12,698	1,975[b]	1,618	3,023	558
3. Consumer expenditure	391,700	189,350	160,520	12,235	14,133	24,150	322,504	23,366	16,654	37,327	7,515
4. Expenditure on traditional excise goods[c]	155,900	83,940	66,301	7,057	6,077	10,509	97,678	8,162	7,651	15,487	3,787
5. Consumer expenditure other than (4)	235,800	105,410	94,219	5,178	8,057	13,641	224,826	15,204	9,003	21,850	3,728
6. (1):(3), per cent of	8.0	12.8	11.0	9.4	5.7	7.8	10.9	5.3	3.2	6.5	2.5
7. (2):(3), per cent	4.0	5.1	5.0	7.0	3.0	4.7	3.9	8.5	9.7	8.1	7.4
8. (1):(5), per cent	13.3	22.9	18.8	22.2	10.0	13.8	15.6	8.2	5.8	11.1	5.0
9. (2):(4), per cent	10.0	11.4	12.0	12.2	6.9	10.8	13.0	24.2	21.1	19.5	14.7

Sources: OECD, Report on Border Tax Adjustment (Paris, 1964), mimeographed. OECD, Statistics of National Accounts 1950–1961 (Paris, 1964). U.N. Yearbook of National Account Statistics, 1963 (New York, 1964). EEC, General Statistics Bulletin No. 11 (Brussels, 1964). Central Statistical Office, National Income and Expenditure, 1964 (Her Majesty's Stationery, London, 1964). U.S. Bureau of the Census, Statistical Abstract of the United States, 1963 (Washington, D.C., 1964).

Notes: [a] Effective rates of indirect taxes on consumer expenditure.
[b] Includes taxes on nontraditional excise goods.
[c] Includes expenditure on food, nonalcoholic beverages, gas and electricity, as well as on alcoholic beverages, tobacco, and fuel.
[d] In terms of billions of local currency.

APPENDIX TABLE 8.6. IK, IL, AND IC—INDIRECT TAXES, 1960[a]

(PER CENT)

	IK[b]	IL[c]	IC[d]
Belgium	23.6 (3.7)[e]	2.9	8.0
France	25.4 (5.8)	4.2	11.9
Germany	(5.2)	3.2	10.7
Italy		4.1	10.9
Luxembourg	(2.7)	1.8	5.8
Netherlands	(3.3)	2.5	8.3
U.S.	16.7 (6.1)	2.7	9.9
Canada	18.8 (6.2)	2.9	9.2
U.K.	(5.6)	2.4	8.6
Sweden	(5.4)	2.5	10.3
Japan	6.8 (2.2)	2.2	6.6

Sources: Appendix Tables 8.3 and 8.5.

Notes: [a] Incident rates of indirect taxes on capital labor and consumers under the assumption of some backward shifting.

[b] One-sixth of indirect taxes as a proportion of corporate profits (property income).

[c] One-sixth of indirect taxes as a proportion of compensation of employees.

[d] Two-thirds of indirect taxes on a proportion of consumer expenditure.

[e] Parenthesized figures relate to property income, nonparenthesized to corporate profits.

APPENDIX TABLE 8.7. EL—GOVERNMENT EXPENDITURE, 1959[a]

(MILLIONS OF LOCAL CURRENCY)

	Belgium	France	Germany	Italy	Luxem-bourg	Nether-lands	U.S.[b]	Canada	U.K.	Sweden	Japan
Expenditure on education and housing	21,326 (25,796)	13,217 (14,435)	11,075 (14,210)	594,000 (713,000)	610 (1,000)	2,237 (3,290)	5,424 (24,515)	674 (1,333)	344 (1,283)	2,720 (3,899)	178,369 (n.a.)
Education	19,381 (23,380)	8,436 (9,342)	6,885 (9,125)	529,000 (640,000)	545 (860)	1,330 (1,994)	4,868 (22,814)	672 (1,331)	247 (845)	1,907 (3,086)	165,074 (n.a.)
Housing	1,945 (2,416)	4,781 (5,093)	4,190 (5,085)	65,000 (73,000)	65 (140)	907 (1,296)	556 (1,701)	2 (n.a.)	97 (438)	813 (n.a.)	13,295 (n.a.)
Compensation of employees	246,600	120,710	116,690	7,415,000	10,629	17,824	324,531	17,959	14,049	34,449	4,934,700
Benefits to labor per cent	8.6 (10.5)	11.0 (12.0)	9.5 (12.2)	8.0 (9.6)	5.7 (9.4)	12.6 (18.5)	1.7 (7.6)	3.8 (7.4)	2.5 (9.1)	7.9 (11.3)	3.6 (n.a.)

Sources: See Table 8.4 in text.
Notes: [a] The nonparenthetical figures relate to central government expenditures, while figures in parentheses cover the whole public sector: central government, local authorities, and other public authorities.
[b] Data refer to 1962.

APPENDIX TABLE 8.8. EK AND EC—GOVERNMENT EXPENDITURE, 1959[a]

(MILLIONS OF LOCAL CURRENCY)

	Belgium	France	Germany	Italy	Luxembourg	Netherlands	U.S.[c]	Canada	U.K.	Sweden	Japan[d]
1. Expenditure on commerce, industry, technology and research	2,522	5,311	1,514	140,000	350	160	7,535	117	663	709	107,777
2. Expenditure on transport[b]	14,613	4,192	4,685	309,000	960	628	8,717	1,028	552	1,073	11,025
3. (50 per cent of 2)	7,307	2,096	2,343	154,500	480	314	4,359	514	276	537	5,513
4. (1 + 3)	9,829	7,407	3,857	294,500	830	477	11,894	631	939	1,246	113,290
5. Profits before tax	28,000 (197,500)	18,810 (84,540)	(71,490)		(6,684)	(13,732)	49,399 (141,114)	3,034 (8,690)	(5,651)	(17,753)	1,259,300 (4,725,600)
6. Benefits to capital (4); (5) per cent	35.1 (5.0)	39.4 (8.8)	(5.4)		(12.4)	(3.5)	24.1 (8.4)	20.8 (7.3)	(16.6)	(7.0)	9.0 (2.4)
7. Consumer expenditure	378,700	173,600	144,160	11,356,000	13,687	22,237	348,822	22,489	15,911	35,360	6,704,900
8. Benefits to consumers (3); (7) per cent	1.9	1.2	1.6	1.4	3.5	1.4	1.3	2.3	1.7	1.5	0.1

Sources: See Table 8.4 in text.

Notes: [a] Parenthesized figures relate to property income, nonparenthesized to corporate profits.
[b] Figures include expenditure on communication in the EEC countries, the United Kingdom, Sweden, and Japan.
[c] Data refer to 1962.
[d] The Japanese system of special accounts makes comparison very difficult; only the general account is included above.

APPENDIX TABLE 8.9. NK, NL (EL), EK, IK, IL, IC—SOCIAL SECURITY CONTRIBUTIONS[a]

(per cent)

	Bel-gium	France	Germany	Italy	Luxem-bourg	Nether-lands	U.S.	Canada	U.K.	Sweden	Japan
Nominal burden on capital owners (per cent of payroll)	22[c] 15[c]	31 19	15 17	47 24	15 19	18 11	7[c] 6	3[c] 3	4[c] 4	9[c] 3	11 8
Nominal and effective burden on labor (per cent of payroll)	11 11	6 7	12[c] 13	7 6[c]	8 11	15 13	5[c] 5	4[c] 4	5[c] 8	5[c] 11	6[c] 5
Effective burden on capital (per cent of profits)[b]	115.4 (18.2)	116.1 (26.4)	(26.7)		(28.2)	(14.9)	31.0 (11.3)	23.6 (7.8)	(10.1)	(7.0)	24.1 (7.4)
Effective burden on consumers (per cent of consumers' expenditure)[b]											
Incident burden on capital (per cent of profits)[b]	3.1 5.0 (0.8)	2.3 2.2 (0.5)	4.0 (1.2)	3.0	2.1 (2.3)	1.0 (0.5)	1.2 3.7 (1.3)	6.4 9.0 (3.0)	5.0 (2.4)	5.0 (2.1)	1.4 2.7 (0.6)
Incident burden on labor (per cent of payroll)	19.8	23.8	25.0	25.9	24.7	22.7	7.3	4.4	6.8	6.6	10.8
Incident burden on consumers (per cent of consumers' expenditure)	3.1	2.3	4.0	3.0	2.1	1.0	1.2	6.4	5.0	5.0	1.4

Sources: See Table 8.2, and U.S. Department of Health, Education, and Welfare, *Social Security Programmes Throughout the World, 1964* (Washington, D.C.,: U.S. Government Printing Office, 1964). Also, for calculation of indirect burdens and use of correct bases, Appendix Tables 8.3, 8.6, and 8.7.

Notes: [a] For NK and NL entries, the upper figure arises from micro, the lower from macro sources. The rest of the table provides macro figures. Micro figures relate to 1964 (mainly from U.S. Department of Health, Education, and Welfare, see above), macro for 1960 (from I.L.O. work in *The Cost of Social Security*, 1958–60).

[b] Parenthetical figures relate to property income; nonparenthesized to corporate profits.

[c] Figures include direct and indirect social security contributions (see text).

APPENDIX TABLE 8.10. EL—SOCIAL SECURITY BENEFITS, 1960

	Per capita benefits U.S. $[a]	Average annual income U.S. $[b]	Benefits per cent
Belgium	169	1,299	13.0
France	168	1,104	15.2
Germany	187	1,553	12.0
Italy	75	775	9.7
Luxembourg	213	1,866	11.4
Netherlands	101	1,240	8.2
United States	163	4,665	3.5
Canada	180	3,462	5.2
United Kingdom	140	1,804	7.8
Sweden	199	2,399	8.3
Japan	20	754	2.7

Sources: ILO, *The Cost of Social Security, 1958–1960* (Geneva, 1964). ILO, *Yearbook of Labour Statistics, 1964* (Geneva, 1965).

Notes: [a] Calculated by dividing total benefits by the population.
[b] Average wage in the manufacturing industries of the individual countries.

CHAPTER IX

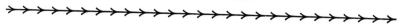

NONTARIFF BARRIERS

William B. Kelly, Jr.[1]

Introduction

Apart from eliminating virtually all quantitative restrictions on nonagricultural products, postwar trade negotiations among the industrial countries have primarily concerned tariffs. The 1947 GATT agreement did establish international rules on a number of nontariff barriers; and in tariff negotiations, nontariff barriers were considered in evaluating the benefits to be gained from tariff concessions. But because of the height of tariff levels, it was generally not thought essential to deal directly with nontariff barriers. Also, their negotiation is much more complex and difficult. However, with further reductions in tariffs, whether they be accomplished through establishing a free trade area, or through multilateral trade negotiations, such as the Kennedy Round, nontariff measures will become increasingly important barriers to trade and will demand greater attention. Such lowering of tariffs would be analogous to a lowering of the water level of the Atlantic Ocean—the mountains of the ocean floor that had hitherto been submerged would now become navigation hazards.

Existing nontariff measures that may only marginally affect trade when coupled with tariff protection could become formidable obstacles if tariffs were eliminated or further reduced. More important, in order to compensate domestic producers for loss of tariff protection, it is likely that many nontariff measures, now dormant, would be rigorously applied, new measures introduced, and old ones amended to make them more effective in restricting trade. Consequently, the improvement sought in the flow of international trade would not fully materialize.

[1] When this chapter was written, the author was a member of the U.S. delegation to the Kennedy Round trade negotiations. (The views expressed here are his own, and not those of the U.S. government.)

It is already recognized that nontariff restrictions are not merely residual obstacles to trade that would have to be negotiated after the successful reduction or elimination of tariffs, but that they are an integral part of liberalizing trade. In both the European Economic Community (EEC) and the European Free Trade Association (EFTA), they are taken up in one form or another. They are an important part of the Kennedy Round negotiations, where in some instances countries have conditioned their tariff cuts on other countries' actions on nontariff barriers. The EEC, the United Kingdom, and Switzerland, for example, have linked their tariff cuts on chemicals to U.S. action on the American selling price basis of customs valuation.

In the broadest sense, a nontariff barrier is any law, regulation, policy, or practice of a government, other than an import duty, that has a restrictive effect on trade.[2] Usually, however, only government actions that have the purpose and/or effect of protecting particular domestic producers from foreign competition are regarded as nontariff barriers.[3] The nontariff barriers with which this chapter is concerned are as follows: quantitative restrictions and state trading, government procurement, customs classification and valuation, antidumping legislation and practices, and various internal and other measures that restrict trade. These are the nontariff barriers relating to nonagricultural products that have been the principal subject of complaints among Atlantic area countries in recent years, and in the Kennedy Round trade negotiations. Other nontariff measures exist, but they have not been the subject of complaints and it may be assumed that they do not restrict trade to an appreciable extent. However, the space devoted to particular nontariff barriers does not necessarily reflect their trade importance; lengthy treatment is given some restrictions only because of their complexity or because of the publicity that they have received.

[2] This definition does not include restrictive private business practices or such "natural" barriers as language differences and cultural affinities, which may be quite important.

[3] Governments' monetary and fiscal policies, for example, can have restrictive trade effects, but they are not usually regarded as nontariff trade barriers. Also, nontariff measures imposed by governments to protect public health, morals, national security, and for other reasons unrelated to protection from foreign competition are not regarded as nontariff barriers unless they are abused.

Nontariff barriers on agricultural products[4] are omitted from this discussion but not because they lack importance; in fact, they limit trade much more than those on industrial products. However, in the Atlantic area, nontariff restrictions on agricultural products are largely a by-product of domestic agricultural policies. They cannot be abolished or modified unless these policies are abandoned or changed. While domestic agricultural systems are central to any discussion of nontariff barriers on agricultural products, such a discussion requires separate treatment that is beyond the scope of this chapter.[5]

There are many misconceptions and some misleading information about nontariff barriers that, on the one hand, overstate their importance and, on the other, understate it. In large part, this is due to the difficulties in estimating the trade effects of nontariff as opposed to tariff restrictions. While price comparisons can be made to estimate the tariff equivalent of some nontariff barriers on standardized products that have comparable world market and domestic prices, such estimates are possible chiefly with respect to fuels, raw materials, and agricultural products. Furthermore, "world" and "domestic" price comparisons can usually be made only in relation to a few nontariff barriers, such as import quotas, that are imposed on particular products. Such comparisons are virtually impossible to make for nontariff barriers that apply to all imports, such as complex customs regulations.

Estimates of the trade effects of nontariff barriers must be based in most instances on the educated guesses of commodity or other specialists who have a "feel" for the subject.[6] In some cases, even guesses are not possible. For example, a "guesstimate" can be made of how much coal might be im-

---

[4] Most items in Chaps. 1 to 24 of the Brussels Tariff Nomenclature are treated here as agricultural products. However, some of these products, such as whiskey and cigarettes, are regarded as industrial.

[5] See, for example, John O. Coppock, *North Atlantic Policy—The Agricultural Gap* (New York: The Twentieth Century Fund, 1963).

[6] An example of a study based on such estimates is Howard S. Piquet, *Aid, Trade, and the Tariff* (New York: Thomas Y. Crowell Co., 1953), particularly Chap. 8. See, also, Robert M. Stern, "The U.S. Tariff and the Efficiency of the U.S. Economy," *The American Economic Review*, LIV, No. 3 (May, 1964), pp. 459–70. This article, which relates to Piquet's estimates, evaluates the economic significance of U.S. tariffs and import quotas.

ported into the United Kingdom if the embargo on imports were removed. However, any reliable estimate of the trade-restrictive effect of the Canadian antidumping law is impossible. Like similar measures that apply to all or most imports, its restrictive effect cannot be estimated by commodity specialists—not because of the range of commodities involved, but because the principal restrictive effect of such a nontariff barrier is its uncertainty and consequent discouragement of imports.

The importance of this element of uncertainty, inherent in most nontariff barriers, should not be underestimated. In fact, it is the most restrictive aspect of some nontariff measures. Traders must know where they stand if goods are to be exchanged. Unlike tariffs, the effects of nontariff measures on importers' and exporters' sales and profits may not be calculable. Because of such open-ended risks, the effort necessary to develop a foreign market may never be made.

Another source of misunderstanding about nontariff barriers is a fundamental difference between U.S. and other countries' restrictions that make the latter much more difficult to evaluate. In general, U.S. restrictions are specifically stated in legislation and in detailed regulations, and officials are given relatively little discretion in their administration. In most other countries, legislation tends to be less specific, and administrative regulations, if any, may be very general, making it much more difficult to identify nontariff restrictions and to evaluate their effects. Such nontariff measures are not, thereby, less restrictive; indeed, their lack of specificity may increase their trade-inhibiting effect.

This difference between U.S. and other countries' nontariff restrictions has resulted in much more attention being given to the former. Because it is easier to identify and to cite U.S. nontariff restrictions, most publications tend to emphasize them and unavoidably to give the impression that they are more important than those of other countries.[7] This is true in some instances but is not a valid generalization. In this connection, it may be noted that the EEC and EFTA are dealing

[7] Several publications deal specifically with U.S. nontariff barriers. See, for example, Craig Mathews, "Non-Tariff Import Restrictions: Remedies Available in United States Law," *Michigan Law Review*, Vol. 62, No. 8 (June, 1964), pp. 1295–1356; and Noel Hemmendinger,

with nontariff problems among member countries within these regional trade arrangements, and presumably will continue to do so until these barriers are eliminated or substantially reduced. However, in the absence of common EEC and EFTA policies on nontariff barriers, third countries continue to have nontariff problems with the individual member states.

Quantitative Restrictions and State Trading

Quantitative restrictions usually apply to specific products and are the most easily identifiable of all nontariff barriers. They range from a complete prohibition of trade to a system under which licenses, although required, are granted liberally.

Quantitative restrictions are absolute limitations on the quantity or value of imports (or exports). Restrictions that permit stipulated amounts to be imported during a given period of time are called *quotas*. Those that do not provide for stipulated amounts may grant special permission to import specified amounts through the issuance of *licenses*. Licenses may also be required for individual transactions even though a quota is established.

During the postwar period when balance-of-payments difficulties were experienced by almost all nondollar countries, quantitative restrictions were used widely to restrict imports. After the Marshall Plan became effective, the Organization for European Economic Cooperation (OEEC) initiated a program to reduce and eliminate these restrictions among Western European countries, and then later between them and the dollar

Non-Tariff Trade Barriers of the United States (Washington, D.C.: United States-Japan Trade Council, 1964). Even when publications do not directly relate to U.S. nontariff restrictions, they frequently focus on them because of their ease in identification. See, for example, Mark S. Massel, "Non-Tariff Barriers as an Obstacle to World Trade," Reprint of The Brookings Institution, June, 1965.

U.S. and Canadian nontariff barriers are treated in several publications, some of which are cited below, n. 71.

A discussion of U.S. and European nontariff barriers is contained in two articles in the April 22 and 29, 1965 issues of *Opera Mundi Europe*, published by the Times Publishing Co., Ltd. Excerpts from these articles are reprinted in the July and August, 1965 issues of *European Community*, a publication of the European Community Information Service. Neither of these articles, however, is very accurate. *Le Comité Européen pour le Progrès Economique et Social* (CEPES), an organization of French, German, and Italian businessmen that is affiliated with the U.S. Committee on Economic Development (CED), plans future publication of a study of North American and European nontariff barriers.

area. Similar efforts were made by the GATT and the International Monetary Fund. Gradually these restrictions were reduced, and they have been practically eliminated on industrial products. Except for coal and restrictions relating to Japan, which are discussed separately, remaining quantitative restrictions among Atlantic area countries on nonagricultural products are of minor importance, because import licenses are usually granted freely when they are required.

Under the Treaty of Rome, all quantitative restrictions among EEC countries are to be abolished and, in fact, have virtually disappeared. However, licenses and quotas still apply to a few industrial imports of individual member states from other countries of the Atlantic area.[8] But these restrictions are relatively minor trade deterrents. Of some importance are French licensing controls on transistor assemblies, transistors, and parts, and on helicopters and light aircraft, which primarily affect the United States. Penicillin and penicillin products are subject to quotas in Benelux. Italy embargoes all imports of sulphur, even from other EEC countries. Imports into Italy of tetraethyl lead and "anti-knock" preparations are licensed automatically to EEC countries, but a quota applies to imports from the United States and the United Kingdom. Italian licensing controls on citric acid, crude calcium citrate, and essential citrus oils also have a restrictive trade effect.[9]

Pursuant to the Stockholm Convention, quantitative restrictions among EFTA countries on industrial products have been virtually eliminated, and remaining restrictions on third-country imports are of relatively little trade importance. In the United Kingdom, imports of airplanes from the dollar area are

[8] As part of the contemplated EEC common commercial policy, national quantitative restrictions are to be replaced by Community measures by the end of the transitional period. However, little progress has been made in establishing a common commercial policy because member states, particularly France, have been reluctant to relinquish independence in this area. Even a modest proposal by the EEC Commission for the gradual introduction of common procedures for the administration of import quotas is still being studied by the Council.

[9] For a listing of quantitative restrictions maintained by EEC countries, see the following GATT documents: L/2740/Add. 8, April 25, 1967 (Germany); Add. 6, April 6, 1967, and Corr. 1, May 17, 1967 (Benelux); Add. 2, March 15, 1967 (Italy); and L/2336, February 26, 1965, pp. 40–63 (France).

subject to discretionary individual licensing. Quantitative restrictions are still maintained by Austria on lignite, penicillin and other antibiotics, and motion picture films. Restrictions by other EFTA countries on nonagricultural products are either nil or negligible.[10] Canada prohibits the importation of used automobiles and used aircraft.[11] Although both restrictions are nondiscriminatory, they have their greatest impact on the United States. In addition, Canada restricts exports of logs and pulpwood by licensing controls.[12] Their purpose and effect is to furnish protection to Canadian saw mills and pulp and paper producers by restricting the raw material supplies of competing producers, primarily U.S. producers located along the U.S.–Canadian border. Japan is also adversely affected by export restrictions on logs.

The United States maintains quantitative restrictions on imports of petroleum and petroleum products. However, except for Canada, the only industrial country that is an important supplier of petroleum, the effect of these restrictions on the exports of countries in the Atlantic area is negligible.[13]

The most important quantitative restrictions on nonagricultural products among countries of the Atlantic area relate to coal. Although fuels are not discussed elsewhere in this volume,

---

[10] See the following GATT documents: L/2740/Add. 9, April 21, 1967 (United Kingdom); Add. 10, May 11, 1967 (Sweden); Add. 5, March 29, 1967, and Corr. 1, April 28, 1967 (Austria); Add 3, March 30, 1967 (Denmark); L/2568/Add. 11, July 20, 1966, and L/2675/Add. 2, January 16, 1967 (Norway); and L/1862, October 17, 1962 (Switzerland).

[11] See GATT document L/2740/Add. 7, April 14, 1967.

[12] These restrictions, which are of long standing, are administered by Federal authorities in co-operation with Canadian provinces, which have jurisdiction over Crown lands on which most forests are located. For example, under present regulations in British Columbia, a permit issued by the British Columbia Forest Service is required for all log exports. Such permits are not usually given unless the applicant can present three letters from prospective Canadian purchasers indicating that they have no need for the logs. See article in *The Financial Post,* Toronto, April 9, 1966. See also, U.S. Tariff Commission, transcript of hearings on softwood lumber, Investigation No. 7–116 (TEA-1-4), October, 1962, pp. 908–11.

[13] The United States also prohibits the importation of more than 1,500 copies of most books in the English language for which the U.S. copyright is obtained. This restriction affords protection to the U.S. publishing industry by virtually requiring that books with a U.S. copyright be manufactured in the United States. See GATT document L/2568/Add. 6, March 22, 1966.

an exception is made in this instance because of the importance of restrictions on coal and because of the part they have played in the Kennedy Round discussions of nontariff barriers.

Within the EEC, only Italy has no restrictions on coal imports. Germany imposes a prohibitive tariff of 20 DM ($5) per ton on all coal imports in excess of a duty-free global quota, which has averaged about 6 million metric tons annually. Because no imports enter at this prohibitive rate, this tariff quota is comparable to an absolute limitation of imports.[14] Belgium imposes quotas on coal that are administered through the issuance of licenses. Imports into the Netherlands are also licensed, and imports of anthracite are subject to a quota that discriminates against the United States in favor of the United Kingdom and the U.S.S.R., the traditional suppliers. In France, a de facto state-trading company, Association Technique de l'Importation Charbonnière (ATIC), has a monopoly on the importation of non-EEC coal. Imported coal is then sold at a price fixed by the French government that limits the competition of foreign coal.[15]

The United Kingdom prohibits imports of coal from Atlantic area countries. At the same time, the United Kingdom is an important coal exporter.[16] The National Coal Board, established in 1946 when the coal industry was nationalized, prices exports so that they can compete in world markets. Because export prices are related to prevailing world prices rather than to domestic prices, such a pricing policy constitutes a subsidy.[17] Instead of quantitative restrictions, Canada

[14] Germany also prohibits all imports of non-EEC coal south of the Mittelland Kanal, where most of the German steel industry is located. The effect of this geographical restriction is to limit the use of imported coal under the duty-free quota to the production of coal gas, the generation of power, and other non-steelmaking purposes. Germany also grants tax advantages and cash subsidies to power plants that use Community instead of third-country coal.

[15] All EEC producing countries subsidize domestic production in some form. In 1965, indirect and direct subsidies ranged from $.80 per ton in the Netherlands to $6.20 per ton in Belgium. See Bulletin de la Communauté Européenne du Charbon et de l'Acier Haute Autorité, No. 61 (Luxembourg: April, 1966), p. 21.

[16] In 1964, the United Kingdom exported 6.0 million metric tons of coal, of which 4.9 million tons were exported to Atlantic area countries. The Netherlands, France, Denmark, Germany, and Belgium were the principal purchasers.

[17] See GATT document L/2593/Add. 6, May 20, 1966, pp. 2 and 3.

subsidizes the transportation of coal, which enables coal mined in Nova Scotia and the other maritime provinces to compete with imported U.S. coal in eastern and central Canada.[18] A similar subsidy is paid to enable coal mined in western Canada, primarily Alberta, to compete with U.S. and other coal exports to Japan.[19]

Japan licenses imports of coal, which consist largely of low-volatile metallurgical coking coal necessary for blending with high and medium volatile coals from domestic sources to meet the requirements of the steel industry.

The United States, as the world's largest producer and exporter of coal, has been most affected by these various restrictions. U.S. commercial exports of coal in 1964 totaled 44.9 million metric tons, valued at $463.3 million. Of this total, 40.3 million tons, valued at $413.1 million, were exported to industrial countries. Canada was the most important purchaser, followed by Italy and Japan.

U.S. exports in 1964 to those industrial countries that restrict imports totalled 32.0 million metric tons valued at $324.8 million. It has been estimated that if restrictions were liberalized, U.S. coal exports to these countries in 1970 could increase by 50 to 200 per cent and earn an additional $180 to $740 million of foreign exchange depending on the extent to which import barriers and other protective measures were relaxed.[20] These estimates include normal growth of exports, as well as growth resulting from the relaxation of restrictions. On the other hand, they assume continued protection of indig-

[18] The amount of the subsidy depends upon the delivered cost of Canadian as compared with imported coal to the same market. The total cost of subventions in 1963 was C$15.2 million and averaged C$5.49 per short ton. This assistance provided a market for 2.8 million tons of Canadian coal, most of which, in the absence of the subsidy, would have been supplied by the United States. See GATT document L/2326, January 13, 1965, pp. 31 and 32.

[19] In 1963 such subventions totaled C$2.3 million and averaged C$3.24 per short ton and enabled 0.7 million tons of Canadian coal to be exported to Japan. See *ibid.*, p. 33. Canada also pays a subsidy of C$.495 per ton on bituminous coal mined in Canada and converted into coke to be used in the manufacture in Canada of iron or steel. This subsidy, which is paid to the coke producers, totaled C$239 thousand in 1963. See *ibid.*, pp. 34–35.

[20] These estimates are derived from forecasts contained in Robert R. Nathan Associates, Inc., *The Foreign Market Potential for United States Coal,* Report to the U.S. Department of the Interior, 4 Vols. (Washington, D.C.: U.S. Government Printing Office, 1963).

enous coal production but at a lower level. If this protection were removed entirely, estimated U.S. export potential would be considerably greater than indicated.

Apart from coal, the major application of quantitative restrictions on trade among industrial countries relates to Japan. When Japan became a member of the GATT in 1955, France, Belgium, Luxembourg, the Netherlands, the United Kingdom, and Austria (and some nonindustrial countries) invoked Article XXXV of the GATT, thereby declining to apply the most-favored-nation clause and other obligations under GATT to Japanese exports. Of these countries, only Austria continues to invoke Article XXXV against Japan, but as a price for disinvocation, the other countries usually obtained commitments from Japan that permit discrimination against certain Japanese products. Although Italy, Germany, and the Scandinavian countries never formally invoked Article XXXV against Japan, they, too, impose discriminatory quantitative restrictions on many Japanese products.[21]

Japanese exports to the industrial countries are also limited by "voluntary" export controls, which are usually imposed at the specific request of an importing country and are frequently included in negotiated bilateral agreements. Thus, although neither Canada nor the United States applies discriminatory quantitative restrictions to imports from Japan, they, along with other industrial countries, have formally and informally pressured Japan to control exports of a number of products. These controls have the same purpose and effect as discriminatory import restrictions.[22] Under the "Long-Term Ar-

[21] Actions under Article 115 of the Rome Treaty have resulted in still more restrictions against Japan. Under this article, which is a transitional measure to be used until the adoption of an EEC common commercial policy, member countries may deviate from intra-community free trade to deal with trade disruption caused by a third country because of a different commercial policy of another member country. For example, if France limits imports of a product from Japan and Germany does not, France may apply to the EEC Commission for authority to limit imports of the product that are transshipped through Germany. At the beginning of 1964, there were 138 EEC tariff positions subject to Article 115 actions. Most of these actions stemmed from differences in member-country commercial policies toward Japan or the Soviet bloc.

[22] Export controls, however, permit the realization of "quota profits" (higher prices resulting from the imposition of quotas) by traders in the exporting country instead of by those in the importing country.

rangement Regarding International Trade in Cotton Textiles," all EEC countries and Austria, Denmark, Norway, and Sweden impose quotas on imports from Japan of cotton yarns, piece goods, made-up articles, garments, and other cotton-textile manufactured products.[23] In turn, under bilateral arrangements concluded under this agreement with the United Kingdom, the United States, and Canada, Japan limits exports of cotton textiles to these countries.[24]

Under the cotton textiles agreement, import and export restrictions have been applied to the trade of a number of less developed countries as well as to that of Japan. However, between 1961, the year before the agreement entered into force, and 1964, exports of the cotton textiles covered by this agreement of the thirteen participating less developed countries increased from $485 to $675 million or by 39 per cent. Exports of the fifteen participating developed countries (excluding Japan) increased by 9 per cent from $1,360 to $1,480 million. Japanese exports, however, declined by 2 per cent from $465 to $455 million.[25] It would appear, therefore, that this agreement has had its most significant impact on Japan. However, under the agreement's bilaterally negotiated quotas, Japanese exports may now be larger than if they competed with the exports of the less developed countries under a global quota.

Japan, on its part, maintains quantitative restrictions on imports, both to protect certain domestic industries and to bargain for the removal of other countries' restrictions against Japan. Japanese restrictions apply to products that constituted

---

[23] See GATT, *Long-Term Arrangement Regarding International Trade in Cotton Textiles* (Geneva, 1963). Twenty-nine countries, including all industrial countries except Switzerland, are signatories of this agreement, which entered into force on October 1, 1962. For the products subject to quotas and the size of these quotas, see GATT document COT/W/51, December 6, 1965, pp. 20–24.

[24] See GATT documents COT/53, September 23, 1965, p. 7 (United Kingdom); COT/11, November 21, 1963, Add. 1, August 30, 1965, and Add. 2, May 18, 1966 (United States); and COT/51, July 28, 1965 (Canada). The only other restrictions among industrial countries applied to cotton textiles under the long-term agreement are limitations by Italy on exports of cotton velveteens to the United States (see GATT document COT/39, November 18, 1964) and quotas by Italy on imports of grey and bleached cotton fabrics from the United States (see GATT document COT/46, February 10, 1965, and Add. 1, April 28, 1965).

[25] GATT, *A Study on Cotton Textiles* (Geneva: July, 1966), p. 21.

about 7 per cent of the value of all imports in 1959.[26] Quotas on nonagricultural products apply to all or part of 86 tariff items.[27] Because quotas are usually imposed on categories of products rather than on individual items, licensing officials have wide discretionary authority, which creates uncertainty for imports of particular products. These Japanese import restrictions, as well as the restrictions applied by the other industrial countries on Japanese exports, are discussed further in Chapter VII of this volume.

Closely related to quantitative restrictions and sometimes almost inseparable from them is the problem of state trading. When a government agency (or monopoly) is given the exclusive right to import a product for resale domestically, its decisions relating to purchases and domestic resale may have the same trade effects as quantitative restrictions (or tariffs). Only if the state-trading agency bases these decisions on commercial considerations would they have a neutral effect on trade. But even with the best intentions, it may be very difficult, if not impossible, for a state-trading agency to act as if it were a private trader.

No industrial country conducts all or most of its foreign trade through state-trading agencies as do countries of the Soviet Bloc and a few others, such as the United Arab Republic. Nevertheless, some of them resort to state trading in such nonagricultural products as ethyl alcohol and alcoholic beverages, salt, manufactured tobacco, matches, and coal.

Apart from coal, which, as indicated above, is state-traded

[26] Thus, it is alleged that Japan has liberalized 93 per cent of its imports. Although such a liberalization standard has been widely used, particularly by OEEC countries, to measure the liberalization of postwar balance-of-payments restrictions, it is obviously unsatisfactory, because imports in the base period were subject to restrictions. Under this standard, little or no liberalization credit is given for the elimination of restrictions that permitted little or no trade in 1959, but much credit is given for the elimination of restrictions that allowed a large volume of trade.

[27] Restricted items are heavily concentrated in machinery and include machine tools (mostly used), industrial sewing machines, large computers, outboard motors, boilers, and typewriters. Other items are sulphur, graphite, iron pyrites, tungsten ores, coal, petroleum, soda ash, menthol, sodium glutamate, certain antibiotics, flavors, cosmetics, starches and glues, color film, leather, certain textiles, footwear, glass, alloy tool steel, electric generators, telephone switchboards, and thermionic tubes. See GATT document L/2740/Add. 1, February 9, 1967.

in France, the protective effect of state trading in the EEC is important on petroleum products, including lubricants and waxes, in France and on cigarettes in Italy and France. State trading in most other products is largely for fiscal and social reasons and has relatively little effect on trade.[28]

Under Article 37 of the Treaty of Rome, EEC member states are progressively to adjust state monopolies so that all discrimination between nationals of member states in the marketing of state-traded products will be eliminated. In effect, this means that state-trading activities by member countries must be given up or include all of the Community; but relatively little progress has been made toward this objective.

The most important state-trading restriction in the EFTA countries relates to coal in the United Kingdom. Technically, the U.K. National Coal Board has no legal monopoly on the importation of coal but, in practice, only the Coal Board has imported quantities of any importance. However, as indicated above, imports from industrial countries are embargoed.[29] Except for tobacco products in Austria and pharmaceutical products and fishing equipment in Norway, state trading in nonagricultural products by other EFTA countries has little importance for international trade.[30] In Japan only imports of manufactured tobacco appear to be restricted by state-trading

[28] Imports into France of petroleum, coal and petroleum gases, electric current, newsprint and paper for periodicals, potash, matches, and propellant powders and explosives are also state-traded. Ethyl alcohol, spirits, brandy, and matches and other inflammables are state-traded in Germany. State-trading enterprises exist in Italy for salt, cigarette paper, lighter flints, matches, and tobacco products. For a description of state-trading enterprises in Germany and Italy, see GATT documents L/2741/Add. 5, April 27, 1967 (Germany); and L/2593/Add. 16, February 27, 1967 (Italy). France has never reported its state-trading enterprises to the GATT.

[29] State trading, which also applies to jute goods, protects the jute industry in Dundee against imports from India and Pakistan, but it has no significance for trade among industrial countries. See GATT documents L/2741/Add. 4, April 6, 1967, and L/2593/Add. 6, May 20, 1966.

[30] Austria also conducts state trading in salt, ethyl alcohol, spirits, and brandy; Norway and Sweden in alcoholic beverages; and Switzerland in ethyl alcohol, spirits, and brandy. See GATT documents L/2741/Add. 2, March 29, 1967, L/2593/Add. 10, June 8, 1966, Add. 13, July 7, 1966 and L/1949/Add. 21, June 12, 1963 (Austria); L/2593/Add. 3, April 27, 1966, L/2313/Add. 10, May 6, 1965, and L/1949/Add. 17, April 17, 1963 (Norway); L/2593/Add. 7, May 18, 1966 (Sweden); and L/2313/Add. 8, March 25, 1965, and L/1949/Add. 23, October 23, 1963 (Switzerland).

practices.[31] Neither Canada nor the United States engages in state trading in nonagricultural products.[32]

Government Procurement

Somewhat analogous to state trading is government procurement. However, while in state trading the government acts as a middleman between producer and consumer, in the case of procurement the government purchases goods and services for its own use.

Government procurement, like state trading, is not a nontariff barrier, *per se*. Trade is restricted only when governments favor domestic over foreign sources of supply. Such favoritism is so widespread, however, that the term "government procurement" has acquired the connotation of a trade restriction.

Preferences to domestic producers, in addition to normal tariffs, are a common practice in government procurement. This distinction between purchases for government and private purposes is even reflected in the GATT, which specifically exempts goods imported for government use from the national-treatment rules relating to internal taxes and regulations that apply to imports for private consumption.

The means by which domestic producers are favored over foreign producers are numerous. Preferences may be specifically provided for in legislation and administered according to detailed regulations. Alternatively, preferences may be granted under general legislation and/or administrative procedures in which procuring authorities are given much discretionary power. But the absence of legislation or regulations does not necessarily constitute liberality; it may afford the widest possible latitude for restricting trade.

The United States is the outstanding example of specific preferences to domestic producers in government procurement. The well-known "Buy American" Act of March 3, 1933 requires that goods of domestic origin[33] be purchased by fed-

[31] Salt and ethyl alcohol are also state-traded in Japan. See GATT document L/2593/Add. 12, June 28, 1966.

[32] The Canadian provinces, however, have a monopoly on the sale of alcoholic beverages, and provincial authorities have exclusive authority to import.

[33] Goods are considered to be of domestic origin if the cost of their domestic components exceeds 50 per cent of the cost of all components.

eral agencies for use in the United States except when domestic cost is unreasonable, domestic materials are not available in sufficient quantity or satisfactory quality, or domestic procurement is inconsistent with the public interest.[34]

The unreasonable-cost exception has given rise to much controversy. Executive Order 10582 of December 17, 1954, which implements the "Buy American" Act, provides that domestic cost shall be considered unreasonable if it exceeds by 6 per cent the foreign bid price, including applicable duty. An additional 6 per cent or a total of 12 per cent applies if the domestic product is produced in an area of substantial unemployment or by a small business firm.

U.S. procuring agencies have generally used the 6/12 per cent differential. However, since July, 1962, the Defense Department has utilized a "national-interest" exception in the Executive Order and has applied higher differentials (50 per cent is used as a "bench mark") in order to lessen expenditures affecting the U.S. balance of payments.[35]

As indicated above, the "Buy American" Act applies only to procurement for use in the United States. Procurement for use outside the United States in connection with military forces abroad and foreign aid programs has been more closely linked to U.S. purchases.[36] Other countries resort to the same practice. France, for example, ties substantially all of its foreign aid loans and grants to procurement within France. The EEC European Development Fund ties its assistance to procurement from Community sources.

Most industrial countries other than the United States are more subtle in granting preferences to domestic producers in

[34] Under international agreements the "Buy American" Act does not apply to certain military supplies when procured from Canada or to procurement in Panama for use in the Canal Zone.

[35] For a discussion of the "Buy American" Act and its early administration, see Laurence A. Knapp, "The Buy American Act: A Review and Assessment," *Columbia Law Review*, LXI (March, 1961).

[36] Most procurement for use outside the United States is by the Defense Department and the Agency for International Development (AID). In July, 1962, as part of the U.S. balance-of-payments program, the Defense Department increased the price preference given domestic producers in procurement for use overseas from 25 to 50 per cent. Subject to exceptions, AID requires that commodity procurement financed by loans under its assistance programs be made in the United States. Foreign procurement of commodities financed by AID grants is restricted to the United States and developing countries.

government procurement. These preferences most often result from the exercise of broad administrative discretion because there are usually no specific "buy national" laws or regulations. In addition to administrative discretion, practices that limit or deny the opportunity to compete for government contracts include little or no advance publicity, eligibility and other regulations that preclude foreign bidding, and closed lists of suppliers.

Specific cases of preferential treatment are difficult to cite because, given the broad administrative discretion that is so common, disappointed foreign bidders are reluctant to complain publicly lest such complaint be held against them in future bidding. Also, after a few such disappointments, foreign exporters may be discouraged from seeking such government business. The following discussion illustrates a few of these preferential policies.

As part of the common commercial policy envisaged in the Treaty of Rome, government procurement policies of the EEC countries are to be harmonized. As a first step, the EEC Commission has proposed to the Council two draft directives on the awarding of contracts for public works and is preparing directives relating to contracts for supplies. The purpose of these directives is to eliminate discrimination in government procurement among member countries.

Perhaps the best evidence of restrictive government procurement policies in the EEC countries is a report[37] of the European Parliament commenting on the Commission's draft directives and explaining why Community rules are needed. This report says that in the EEC member states "many discriminations to be found in legislative or statutory texts or even in administrative provisions or practices" result from the "universal tendency to keep public funds 'within the country' " and points out that "almost all public work contracts have so far been assigned to national contractors."

The report then comments on various EEC country practices. It notes that the procedure in France of inviting certain contractors to submit their bids "gives almost exclusive preference to contractors known by the administration; in other

---

[37] *Parlement Européen, Documents de Séance,* 1965–66, Document 1, March 22, 1965. The quotations cited in the following paragraphs are translated from pp. 3 and 4 of this report.

words, to French contractors, and that foreign applicants are usually not invited to bid." In Italy, "theoretically, foreign contractors may always participate in public call for bids," but there is "a provision by virtue of which the contractors to be taken into consideration must figure on so-called trusted firms lists." Although the purpose of such lists is to prevent awards to contractors who are not technically and professionally qualified, "these lists may only include Italian contractors or foreign firms established in Italy." In the Netherlands, "only persons domiciled in the Netherlands may be admitted as contractors." In Belgium, a January 1, 1965 law on public works contracts permits procedures under which bidding is limited to "Belgian companies or to companies whose capital is two-thirds in the hands of Belgian contractors." In 1960, Germany guaranteed equal terms to foreign and national applicants in regard to public works contracts. However, this guarantee "includes a clause under which it may be immediately suspended in case the economic situation should change." Moreover, "the procedure applied in Germany leaves the adjudicating authority much freedom."

The report also cites several examples of discrimination, but the EEC countries involved are not identified. It indicates that "in one Member State, the general administrative provisions of the Minister of Postal and Telegraph Services prescribe, in particular, that all persons or companies of foreign origin shall be excluded from the assignment of public works contracts." A letter to "a large public company by the competent minister of a Member State" is cited as an example of broad administrative discretion. The minister explains that "due to the difficulties presently faced by our national electric construction industry, I decided not to approve, as a rule, the import of electrical equipment, since the latter can be manufactured in our country. However, an exception is being made for orders of an exceptional nature. I therefore ask you to submit your case to me prior to taking any other steps." A letter to a Belgian contractor from the Minister of Public Works of another member state advised: "I am in a position to let you know that, on principle, foreign contractors are authorized to submit offers in my country; however, the administration of public works does not take any foreign firm into consideration."

Under Article 14 of the Stockholm Convention, discrimination among EFTA countries in government procurement (and in state-trading practices) was to be abolished by the end of 1966. However, after a two-year EFTA study by a committee of experts, it was found that "in many cases" changes would have to be made in the practices of some member states "in order to fulfil the obligation of reciprocal non-discrimination." Subsequently, agreement was reached at a ministerial meeting in October, 1966, on how Article 14 was to be interpreted and implemented so that competition among EFTA countries could be increased "by removing protection."[38]

The United Kingdom furnishes a few publicized examples of preferential procurement practices. Under the policy of allowing government departments virtually full discretion to follow whatever purchasing practices best suit their needs, the Post Office purchases most of its telephone apparatus and exchange equipment from a group of eight U.K. suppliers, which share the orders between them on a noncompetitive basis.[39] In another case, where no discretion was allowed, British European Airways (BEA) was required by the U.K. government to purchase British instead of U.S. aircraft. In a statement on this decision, the Minister of Aviation explained that BEA "would have preferred on purely commercial grounds to buy American aircraft."[40] Since 1965, the U.K. government has followed a similar policy with respect to computers, provided that "there is no undue price differential" and that "the United Kingdom-produced model is technically suitable and no undue delay would be involved."[41]

Canadian procurement policy is reflected in a report of the

[38] *EFTA Bulletin,* March–April, 1967, pp. 2 and 6.

[39] See *The Financial Times,* February 22, 1965. Another example of a discriminatory purchasing policy by the Post Office appears to be reflected in the following excerpt from an advertisement that appeared on the front page of the April 4, 1966 edition of *The Times* (London): "The Postmaster General invites offers forthwith for the supply of telegraph poles . . . from the following *home-grown* species of timber: scots pine, larch, Douglas fir, Japanese larch and/or hybrid larch." (Emphasis provided.)

[40] Statement by the Minister of Aviation in the House of Commons, August 2, 1966. See also, *The Economist,* August 6, 1966, p. 574.

[41] OECD, *Government Purchasing* (Paris: 1966), p. 105. This publication is a compilation of all OECD countries' procurement regulations and procedures.

Tariff Board, which states that "in making government purchases it is customary to grant a preference to domestically produced goods." Though "the nature and the extent of such preferences varies from time to time and from one department to another," a 10 per cent margin is the norm for defense equipment. Preferences are given "especially to Canadian suppliers who offer higher proportions of Canadian content."[42]

A "Buy Japan" policy is contained in a Japanese Cabinet Order of September 25, 1963 that permits the chief of any ministry or agency "for the purpose of encouraging the use of domestic products" to resort to "limited competition" in the procurement of certain designated goods. The "designated" goods comprise fourteen categories of equipment that include automobiles, computers, office machines, air conditioners, measuring instruments, construction machinery, communication apparatus, aircraft, electric generators, pumps, printing machines, and machine tools.[43]

The above discussion relates to procurement by central government authorities, but preferences are also granted to national and/or local producers by provinces, municipalities, and other government bodies. For example, according to a 1963 survey, fourteen states in the United States restricted some or all foreign purchases.[44] Canadian provinces have similar practices.[45]

[42] *Report by the Tariff Board,* Radio, Television, and Related Products, Reference No. 123 (Ottawa: 1965), pp. 28–29.

[43] See U.S. *Congressional Record,* House, August 12, 1965, pp. 19566–19567. This issue of the *Congressional Record* contains 68 pages of material (inserted by Congressman Saylor) on the laws, regulations, and practices of foreign countries relating to government procurement.

[44] The states reporting restrictions on foreign purchases were Alabama, California, Colorado, Connecticut, Indiana, Maine, Massachusetts, Montana, New Jersey, New Mexico, Oklahoma, Pennsylvania, Virginia, and West Virginia. Puerto Rico restricts all foreign (non-U.S.) purchases. This survey was conducted by The National Association of State Purchasing Officials of The Council of State Governments. See also, United States-Japan Trade Council, *State "Buy American" Restrictions,* Council Report No. 75, December 6, 1965.

[45] The Canadian province of Quebec provides a good example. Under its "Buy Quebec" policy, the Hydro-Electric Commission, a semi-autonomous government organization that controls virtually all production and distribution of electricity in the province, will pay up to 10 per cent more for a product made in Quebec than for the equivalent item manufactured elsewhere in Canada, and up to 15 per cent more than

It is extremely difficult to evaluate the restrictive trade effects of preferential government procurement policies, particularly because, as is so often the case with nontariff barriers, the most significant effect is to deter potential trade rather than to restrict existing trade. A possible method of measuring such effects would be to compare foreign procurement as a percentage of total government procurement with commercial imports of similar goods as a percentage of total domestic production of such goods. Unless additional protection is afforded domestic producers in preferential procurement policies, there should be a reasonably close relationship between these ratios. As part of its examination of member countries' procurement practices, initiated in 1963, the OECD attempted to make a similar comparison, but was unable to obtain the necessary information.

Customs Classification and Valuation

Before a tariff can be imposed, an imported product must be classified under a tariff nomenclature so that the rate of duty can be determined. If this rate of duty is either an *ad valorem* or a combination of *ad valorem* and specific duty, the product must be valued before the duty can be calculated.[46] Legislation or regulations relating to classification and valuation become nontariff barriers when they create uncertainty, necessitate costly and time-consuming litigation, or otherwise have a restrictive effect on trade. Such restrictions are sometimes referred to as paratariff barriers, because they are directly related to tariffs.

All EEC and EFTA countries are signatories to the "Convention on Nomenclature for the Classification of Goods in Cus-

---

for a foreign product. Furthermore, when the article cannot be obtained in Quebec, the Commission favors firms in other provinces with a 5 per cent differential over foreign suppliers. The Provincial Purchasing Service follows essentially the same guidelines as the Commission.

A private Montreal organization would go even further. This organization, the Quebec Council for Economic Expansion, has sponsored a campaign to induce Quebeckers to buy only from firms with at least 51 per cent French-Canadian ownership. For additional examples of provincial preferential practices, see U.S. *Congressional Record*, House, August 12, 1965, p. 19561.

[46] Valuation may also be necessary if classification is in terms of value brackets. For example, in the United States, pocket knives are subject to six different rates of duty, depending upon their value per dozen.

toms Tariffs," usually referred to as the Brussels Tariff Nomenclature (BTN) and to the "Convention on the Valuation of Goods for Customs Purposes," widely known as the Brussels Definition. These countries and Japan are also members of the Customs Co-operation Council, which was established to maintain uniformity in the application of these conventions. Although Japan is not a signatory of either convention, it has adopted the BTN, and its valuation system is not very different from that of the EEC or the EFTA.[47]

Tariff classification problems among the countries that have adopted the BTN have been greatly reduced. A common nomenclature has also facilitated international comparisons of tariff levels and trade statistics. This is not to say that these countries have identical tariff classifications, since they often use different subdivisions under the same general headings.

Tariff classification differences among the countries applying the BTN are minor, however, as compared with the United States and Canada. The "Tariff Schedules of the United States" (TSUS), a major nomenclature revision, became effective in September, 1963. Although this revision was influenced by the BTN, it is markedly different from it.[48] The Canadian classification system differs from both the BTN and the TSUS.[49]

---

[47] In Japan, valuation is normally on the basis of c.i.f. invoice prices and presents few problems. If value cannot be determined on the basis of invoice prices, it is based on the wholesale price of similar Japanese goods minus customs duties that would be imposed on such goods and expenses incidental to delivery from the port of entry to the domestic wholesale market.

[48] For a report on this revision, see U.S. Tariff Commission, *Tariff Classification Study* (Washington, D.C.: U.S. Government Printing Office, 1960).

[49] A complicating factor in Canadian classification is the determination of whether certain imports are of a "class or kind made in Canada." If 10 per cent of Canadian consumption of a product is supplied from Canadian sources, it is regarded as "made in Canada," and imports are assessed higher rates of duty. For example, the most-favored-nation rate on machinery is 22.5 per cent for items "made in Canada" and 7.5 per cent for items "not made in Canada."

For a discussion of problems involved in the administration of provisions relating to "class or kind made in Canada," see Francis Masson and H. Edward English, *Invisible Trade Barriers Between Canada and the United States* (Canadian-American Committee of the National Planning Association [U.S.A.] and the Private Planning Association of Canada, 1963), pp. 18–22.

These differences in tariff classification systems among countries of the Atlantic area do not restrict trade, *per se,* but they do increase uncertainty. Even uniform systems would not eliminate uncertainty, because disagreements between customs officials and traders over the classification of imports will exist as long as there are tariff schedules. However, if decisions in such disputes are time consuming, involve expensive legal proceedings, or otherwise inhibit trade, which is sometimes the case, particularly in the United States, this administrative aspect of customs classification constitutes a nontariff barrier.

A basic difference in valuation of imports among Atlantic area countries is that the EEC, the EFTA, and Japan include insurance and freight as part of the value of imports (c.i.f. system), while the United States and Canada do not (f.o.b. system). This means that *ad valorem* tariff rates in the countries using a c.i.f. system are applied to higher valuations, resulting in import duties that on the average are about 10 per cent higher than the same rates on identical products in countries using an f.o.b. system. But such differences in valuation systems do not constitute nontariff trade barriers and tariff levels can be compared by expressing duties on a common basis. Other aspects of these countries' valuation systems, however, may act as trade impediments.

As already indicated, the EEC and EFTA countries adhere to the Brussels Definition of valuation, which uses "normal price" as the basis for levying *ad valorem* duties. "Normal price" is defined as "the price which they [imports] would fetch at the time when the duty becomes payable on a sale in the open market between buyer and seller independent of each other."[50] This is a theoretical value, but in most cases, it corresponds to the c.i.f. invoice price.

The principal problem of the Brussels Definition stems from trade transactions between related parties, i.e., buyers and sellers that are not independent of each other. When the importer is a subsidiary, branch, sole distributor, or exclusive agent of a foreign firm, customs officials assume that invoice prices understate the dutiable value, because of discounts

---

[50] Customs Co-operation Council, *The Brussels Definition of Value for Customs Purposes* (Brussels: April, 1964), p. 41.

granted the importer for advertising, warranty, and other selling expenses. Consequently, an "uplift" or percentage increase in the invoice price is applied for valuation purposes. This "uplift" ranges between 1 and 10 per cent and varies among countries; it is sometimes negotiated between customs authorities and traders, and it may be arbitrary.[51]

Customs valuation in the United States is more complex than in any of the industrial countries. The United States has two sets of valuation provisions containing nine different bases of valuation, and their complexity undoubtedly has a restrictive effect on trade.[52] According to a 1961 study,[53] approximately 91 per cent of U.S. import invoices were appraised under the new set of valuation provisions introduced in 1958. More than 96 per cent of these invoices, or 87 per cent of all invoices, were appraised on the basis of "export value," which is very similar to "normal price" under the Brussels Definition, as both contemplate transactions between independent buyers and sellers for export to the country concerned. In transactions between related parties, "export value" may be adjusted in a manner similar to uplifts applied under the Brussels Definition. The principal difference between the two is that "normal price" includes all charges to the port of importation (c.i.f.), but "export value" is the ex-factory or port-of-shipment price in the country of exportation (f.o.b.).

[51] Arbitrary valuation is particularly true in cases of the "sole buyer," i.e., cases where a related firm is the only importer of a product. In such cases, the customs appraiser has no other transactions to guide his determination of "normal price." The International Chamber of Commerce has concluded that "of all the difficulties created by the Brussels Definition of Value, the most widespread and important is that of its application [uplift] to goods imported by 'sole buyers.'" See International Chamber of Commerce, *The Brussels Definition of Value, The Case of the "Sole Buyer"* (February, 1963), p. 5. See also, International Chamber of Commerce documents 131/128 and 131/129, March 4 and 20, 1964, which contain the Customs Co-operation Council's criticism of this brochure, and the reply of Marcel Dreyfus of the International Chamber of Commerce. For a critical discussion of other aspects of the Brussels Definition, see International Chamber of Commerce, *Customs Valuation of Imported Goods*, a Review of the Brussels Definition and of its Application (February, 1959).

[52] For an explanation of U.S. valuation and other customs provisions, see U.S. Treasury Department, Bureau of Customs, *Exporting to the United States* (Washington, D.C.: U.S. Government Printing Office, March, 1965).

[53] See U.S. Treasury Department, Bureau of Customs, *An Evaluation of: Mission, Organization, Management* (December, 1964), p. VI–24.

If "export value" cannot be determined, because goods are sold on consignment or for other reasons, "United States value" and "constructed value" are alternative valuation bases. These little used alternatives prescribe methods designed to approximate "export value."[54]

Pursuant to the Customs Simplification Act of 1956, a list of products comprising about 9 per cent of U.S. import invoices in 1961 are appraised under the old set of valuation provisions, which were applicable to all products prior to February 27, 1958. This "final list" of products, as it is generally known, consists of 1,015 tariff items whose dutiable value would have been reduced by 5 per cent or more under the new valuation provisions. The "final list" contains a wide variety of articles, including coal-tar and other chemicals, certain machinery and parts, automobiles and other vehicles, and various textiles.[55]

Among the alternative bases of valuation under the old provisions, "foreign value" is the most frequently used. The principal difference between "foreign value" and "export value" is that the former is the price for home consumption in the country of exportation instead of the price for export. "Foreign value" is usually higher than "export value," because it includes internal producer taxes, such as turnover taxes, from which exports are exempted. It is this feature of "foreign value," in addition to difficulties in its determination, about which traders have complained. The other old valuation bases, less frequently used, are "export value," "United States value," and "cost of production." They often result in dutiable values that are higher than their counterparts in the new provisions.

The U.S. method of valuation that has received the most attention and that has become a *cause célèbre* in the Kennedy Round negotiations is the American selling price (ASP).[56] ASP

---

[54] "United States value" is the wholesale price of the imported product in the United States less commissions, profits, customs duty, transportation costs, insurance, and other expenses from place of shipment to place of delivery. "Constructed value" is the estimated cost of production in the exporting country.

[55] A complete list of these products is contained in U.S. Treasury, *Exporting to the United States*, March, 1965, pp. 65–77.

[56] For an indication of European views on ASP in relation to the Kennedy Round negotiations, see the pamphlet, *Trade Expansion*

is defined under both the new and old valuation provisions with relatively minor differences. Unlike the other bases of valuation, it is not the f.o.b. price (or equivalent) of the imported article but the wholesale price of a comparable U.S.-produced article. It is not an alternative to other bases of valuation, but it is applicable to two categories of imports: (1) competitive benzenoid chemicals and certain products of these chemicals, which have been subject to ASP by statute since 1922, and (2) competitive rubber footwear, canned clams, and low-value knit wool gloves, which have been subject to ASP under Presidential proclamations issued during the 1930's under the cost-equalizing provisions of the 1930 Tariff Act (see Table 9.1).

TABLE 9.1. U.S. TARIFF ITEMS SUBJECT TO ASP VALUATION

Product	Number of tariff items	TSUS numbers	Value of 1964 imports[a] (thousand $)
Benzenoid chemicals			
intermediates	17	403.02–403.09	9,206
finished products	53	405.05–409.00	13,559
Rubber-soled footwear	1	700.60	13,416
Canned clams	1	114.05	223
Knit wool gloves and mittens valued at $1.75 or less per dozen pairs	1	704.55	0
Total	73		36,404

[a] Imports of benzenoid chemicals and of rubber footwear are foreign invoice values, and they include only competitive imports to which ASP applied. Imports of canned clams are estimated foreign export values of competitive imports to which ASP applied.

Sources: U.S. Tariff Commission, Imports of Benzenoid Chemicals and Products, 1964, TC Publication 159 (Washington, D.C.: July, 1965); U.S. Bureau of the Census, U.S. Imports, Tariff Schedules Annotated by Country, 1964 Annual (Washington, D.C.: July, 1965); and U.S. Tariff Commission, Products Subject to Duty on the American Selling Price Basis of Valuation; Conversion of Rates of Duty on Such Products to Rates Based on Values Determined by Conventional Valuation Methods (Including corrections to August 15, 1966), TC Publication 181 (Washington, D.C.: July, 1966).

Act—Yes, American Selling Price System—No, prepared by Verband der Chemischen Industrie e. V. in September, 1963. The Synthetic Organic Chemical Manufacturers Association of the United States has published two pamphlets giving the U.S. industry's views: The Case for American Selling Price and The Future of the American Dye Industry.

ASP was made applicable to benzenoid chemicals after World War I to give additional protection to the coal-tar sector of the war-born U.S. chemical industry. It is applied to imports of benzenoid intermediates and to certain finished products, such as dyes and pigments, medicinals and pharmaceuticals, flavor and perfume materials, synthetic rubbers, pesticides, and plastics and resin materials, when they are competitive with domestic production.[57] Determining the competitive status of imports is another problem, in addition to ascertaining the American selling price. Although imports are regarded as competitive whenever there is domestic production of similar articles, uncertainty still exists because it is not uncommon for articles to change from competitive to noncompetitive status and vice versa within short periods of time.

In 1964, the foreign invoice value of imports of benzenoid chemicals was $49 million, of which $23 million were competitive and therefore subject to ASP. Imports came almost exclusively from industrial countries, with the EEC supplying the largest quantity and Germany being the principal exporter.[58]

The $23 million of competitive benzenoid chemical imports to which ASP applied amounted to 3.2 per cent of total U.S. chemical imports of $710 million and to about 0.7 per cent of U.S. sales of benzenoid chemicals of around $3,400 million. Because of the trade-inhibiting effect of ASP resulting from high duties and uncertainty, such comparisons are not a good index of restrictiveness. Better perspective may be gained from the fact that sales of benzenoid chemicals are around 10 per cent of total sales of the U.S. chemical industry—ASP, therefore, relates to about this proportion of the U.S. chemical industry.

The effect of ASP valuation on duties collected varies widely. For example, a 40 per cent tariff rate applying to the American selling price of a particular group of dyes results in a duty that has an average *ad valorem* equivalent of 172 per

---

[57] If imports of benzenoid chemicals are not competitive with domestic production, "United States value" applies. If this is not ascertainable, then the other alternative bases of valuation under the applicable new or old valuation provisions apply.

[58] See U.S. Tariff Commission, *Imports of Benzenoid Chemicals and Products*, 1964, TC Publication 159 (Washington, D.C.: July, 1965).

cent when compared with conventional appraisement of these dyes. On the other hand, in a few instances the application of ASP results in a lower duty, because foreign prices are higher than U.S. prices.[59] But neither of these examples is typical. On the average, ASP about doubles the duties that would normally be collected.[60]

Under Section 336 of the U.S. Tariff Act of 1930, the President is authorized after an investigation by the Tariff Commission to raise or lower a statutory rate of duty by up to 50 per cent in order to equalize foreign and domestic production costs.[61] If a 50 per cent increase is not sufficient to equalize such costs, then imports may be valued on the basis of ASP.

The trade-agreements legislation exempts articles upon which tariff concessions have been negotiated from the applicability of Section 336. Beginning in 1934, the United States

[59] See U.S. Tariff Commission, *Products Subject to Duty on the American Selling Price Basis of Valuation; Conversion of Rates of Duty on Such Products to Rates Based on Values Determined by Conventional Valuation Methods* (Including corrections to August 15, 1966), TC Publication 181 (Washington, D.C.: July, 1966). Most of the conversions made in this report lump competitive and noncompetitive items, i.e., items that are, and are not, subject to ASP valuation. Consequently, this report does not usually indicate the *ad valorem* equivalent, based on conventional valuation, of rates that are actually applied to ASP. However, some of these *ad valorem* equivalents can be calculated on the basis of information relating to the competitive status of items that is contained in the Commission's report on *Imports of Benzenoid Chemicals.*

[60] According to official U.S. trade statistics, dutiable values (both conventional and ASP) of imports of benzenoid chemicals in 1964 totaled $79 million. The U.S. Tariff Commission has calculated that conventional valuation of these imports would have been $53 million, of which $28 million was noncompetitive and $25 million was competitive. Consequently, the ASP value of the $25 million of competitive imports was $51 million ($79 million minus $28 million) or approximately double conventional valuation. See U.S. Bureau of the Census, *U.S. Imports,* Tariff Schedules Annotated by Country, 1964 Annual (Washington, D.C.: July, 1965); and U.S. Tariff Commission, *Products Subject to ASP; Conversion of Rates, ibid.*

[61] The principle of equalizing production costs as a basis for tariff making and the practical difficulties of ascertaining "foreign" and "domestic" costs of production are beyond the scope of this study. However, because trade is based in great part on cost differences, the effect of equalizing costs would be to end much trade. Also, even if the terms "foreign" and "domestic" production costs are satisfactorily defined, obtaining such cost information is extremely difficult, if not impossible.

progressively extended the coverage of its trade-agreement concessions to include most tariff items. Consequently, in recent years there have been very few investigations under Section 336, and even fewer involving ASP. Only three cases in which ASP valuation is applied remain in effect: rubber-soled footwear with fabric uppers, canned clams, and knit wool gloves and mittens valued at $1.75 or less per dozen pairs. These cases date from 1933, 1934, and 1936, respectively.

In 1964, the foreign invoice value of U.S. imports of rubber-soled footwear was $16.9 million, of which $13.4 million was competitive and valued on the basis of ASP.[62] Imports of competitive footwear, more than 80 per cent of which was supplied by Japan, constituted less than 5 per cent of U.S. production of approximately $285 million. The duty on rubber footwear of 20 per cent applied to ASP valuation has an average *ad valorem* equivalent of 58 per cent when compared with conventional appraisement.[63] The estimated foreign export value of 1964 imports of canned clams, almost all of which came from Japan, was $0.4 million, of which $0.2 million was competitive and valued on the basis of ASP. The 20 per cent duty on these clams has an average *ad valorem* equivalent of 57 per cent of conventional valuation.[64] In recent years there have been no imports of the knit wool gloves that are subject to ASP valuation. Both imports and domestic production have been insignificant since the mid-1930s, because the increased price of wool and other production costs have made it uneconomical to produce gloves in this low-value category.

While tariff rates applied to ASP usually result in much higher duties than would normally be the case, these higher duties do not constitute nontariff barriers. The aspect of customs valuation that constitutes a nontariff barrier is uncertainty, which in the case of ASP is considerable. Domestic producers may influence the extent of their tariff protection

[62] During most of 1964, other rubber footwear was also subject to ASP valuation. However, the Tariff Schedules Technical Amendments Act of 1965 substituted higher duties for ASP valuation of certain rubber footwear. Only imports of rubber footwear that remain subject to ASP valuation are included in the statistics cited above.

[63] See U.S. Tariff Commission, *Products Subject to ASP; Conversion of Rates*, TC Publication 181.

[64] See *ibid.*

both by going into competitive production with imports and thus making ASP applicable and by adjusting their prices and thus changing the amount of duty collected. On the other hand, changes in export prices by foreign suppliers have no effect on the duty.

Related to the application of ASP to benzenoid chemicals is the standard-of-strength provision applied to imports of certain colors, dyes, and stains. Under this provision[65] specific duties are based on the actual strength of these products as compared with an established standard of strength. For example, the standard concentration or standard of strength of the dye vat blue 1 is 20 per cent. A shipment of this dye that had a concentration greater than 20 per cent would be dutiable on the computed weight of a 20 per cent concentration rather than on its actual weight. In practice, this provision applies to only three tariff items, two of which have negligible imports.[66]

Of greater importance is the application of the standard-of-strength principle to the valuation of all benzenoid chemicals. Under U.S. customs regulations ASP is adjusted in proportion to the comparative strengths of the imported and competitive domestic article.[67] Although it would seem reasonable that duties should vary according to the potency of an imported item, such an adjustment is inequitable if, as is sometimes the case, the prices of benzenoid chemicals increase less than proportionately with their strength.

Canadian valuation practices are almost as complex as those of the United States. The usual basis of valuation is "fair market value," which is the price in the country of export of like goods sold for home consumption, and is similar to "foreign value" under U.S. practices.[68] If the quality, quantity, or

[65] See *Tariff Schedules of the United States Annotated* (1965), Schedule 4, P. 1, Subpart C, headnote 6.

[66] In 1964, imports of vat blue 1 (*TSUS* 406.04) totaled $798 thousand. Imports of sulfur black (*TSUS* 406.02) and of natural alizarin and indigo colors, dyes, and stains (*TSUS* 406.60) were negligible.

[67] See *Code of Federal Regulations*, Title 19, 14.5 (f). For an example of such an adjustment, see R. Elberton Smith, *Customs Valuation in the United States* (Chicago, Ill.: University of Chicago Press, 1948), pp. 229–30.

[68] However, "fair market value" excludes internal taxes that are not borne by exported merchandise while, as indicated above, "foreign value" includes such internal taxes.

conditions of sale of the exported goods differ from those for like goods sold for home consumption, appropriate adjustments are made. However, dutiable values may be higher but not lower than f.o.b. prices to Canadian importers. Adjustments for differences in conditions of sale are very important because of the large volume of Canadian imports, particularly from the United States, that result from intra-company and similar shipments.

Although seldom used, some Canadian valuation provisions resemble escape clauses from tariff concessions. If imported goods "prejudicially or injuriously" affect the interests of Canadian producers, even though sold at "fair market value," the Minister of National Revenue may determine the value of such goods for duty purposes.[69] Furthermore, if, because of end-of-season sales, the market price of any manufactured good in the country of export declines to a level that the Minister does not regard as "normal," he determines dutiable value on the basis of average prices during a previous period. Similarly, if the same circumstances apply to any fresh fruit or vegetable of a class or kind produced in Canada, the Minister determines valuation on the basis of average export prices to Canada during the previous three years.

The possibility of dutiable values established by the Minister of National Revenue creates uncertainty because they can be arbitrary, and at very high levels. Style fabrics, dresses, and other garments are goods that have received higher valuations under these provisions. Such revaluations have also applied to strawberries, peas, potatoes, and cut flowers. In 1962, the valuation of potatoes received international consideration when the United States successfully protested to the GATT.[70]

Canadian valuation not only affects *ad valorem* import duties but, as discussed in the next section, determines whether and to what extent antidumping duties are levied. Consequently, for purposes of this antidumping legislation, dutiable

---

[69] This provision does not apply to goods entitled to entry under the British preferential tariff.

[70] See GATT, *Basic Instruments and Selected Documents*, 11th Supplement (Geneva: March, 1963), pp. 55 and 88–94. Potatoes were again revalued during the summer of 1966. See GATT document L/2682, August 5, 1966.

values may be determined for imports, even when they are subject to specific duties or are duty-free.[71]

Antidumping Legislation and Practices

Dumping, or international price discrimination, is the practice of selling abroad at a price lower than that charged domestically (or selling in different export markets at different prices). In the real world of imperfect price competition, many exporters in developed countries, particularly of chemicals, metals, and other standardized products, try to maximize their profits by charging different prices in markets with different demand elasticities. When, as is frequently the case, demand abroad is more price elastic than demand at home, a lower price is charged on foreign sales. On the supply side, once a firm has covered its overhead costs in one market, it can then sell profitably in another market at any price above marginal costs.

Although there is no consensus among economists, the argument has been made that the economic advantages of dumping may outweigh the disadvantages.[72] Consumers of dumped goods benefit by the lower prices paid for imports. Consumers in the exporting country are discriminated against, but the prices they pay may be higher, the same, or lower than if dumping had not occurred.[73] Even if prices are higher, they must be weighed against the increased profits of producers. Only in the rare case of predatory dumping, where the purpose is to drive a competitor out of business, does the economic balance appear to weigh clearly against this practice.

---

[71] For a comparison of Canadian and U.S. valuation practices and other nontariff barriers, see Masson and English, *Invisible Trade Barriers*. Other useful sources of Canadian and U.S. nontariff barriers published by the Canadian-American Committee are Constant Southworth and W. W. Buchanan, *Changes in Trade Restrictions Between Canada and the United States*, 1960; and Francis Masson and J. B. Whitely, *Barriers to Trade between Canada and the United States*, 1960.

[72] There is no recent comprehensive treatment of dumping. The standard work is Jacob Viner, *Dumping: A Problem in International Trade* (Chicago, Ill.: University of Chicago Press, 1923).

[73] See Gottfried von Haberler, *The Theory of International Trade*, translated by Alfred Stonier and Frederic Benham (London: William Hodge and Co., Ltd., 1936), pp. 302–17.

The economic objection to dumping (and to other discriminatory pricing) is not dumping *per se* but to the monopoly conditions that enable and encourage it. Dumping can only occur when there are monopoly or oligopoly conditions in the home market accompanied by tariffs and/or transportation costs that prevent dumped goods from being shipped back again. Dumping is the result of, not the cause of, such conditions. It appears that effective antitrust legislation and lower tariffs are better ways to combat monopoly practices than are antidumping measures.

Governments' concern with dumping has been the low prices of dumped imports rather than the discriminatory high prices to home consumers of dumped exports. Also, the term "dumping" has an emotional, anticompetitive, and "unfair" connotation. Consequently, many countries have legislation or regulations that authorize the imposition of antidumping duties to compensate for the lower export prices of dumped imports. This legislation is somewhat comparable to resale price maintenance or "fair trade" laws, which regulate domestic sales prices.

Under the GATT, countries may impose antidumping duties on imports of dumped products if such imports cause or threaten material injury to a domestic industry (or retard the establishment of an industry). Until recently, however, antidumping legislation in most European countries has been fragmentary or nonexistent. Canada is the only industrial country that has frequently used antidumping duties. But if tariffs are substantially lowered in the Kennedy Round negotiations, countries may be tempted to use antidumping duties to partially compensate for the loss of protection. Furthermore, if the introduction of duty-free treatment for producers within the EEC and the EFTA leads to increased incidences of dumping by third-country exporters in order to meet the prices of these internal producers, greater resort to antidumping measures may be anticipated.

In Canada, antidumping duties are imposed on imported goods, if they are of a class or kind produced in Canada, and the export price of such goods is less than their "fair market" or other value that is established for duty purposes. As indicated in the previous section, these dutiable values can be higher than invoice prices. Also, Canada is the only country in the Atlantic area that does not require that dumped goods cause or threaten injury to a domestic industry as a condition for imposing antidumping duties.[74] While goods may be exempted and the duty itself may not exceed 50 per cent of the "fair market value," an antidumping duty, equal to the difference between export price and dutiable value, is automatically imposed. Although Canada does not maintain separate customs records on antidumping actions, it is estimated that around $2 million of antidumping duties are levied annually.[75] About two-thirds of these duties are levied against imports from the United States. However, the trade-inhibiting effect of antidumping restrictions is far more important than the incidence of duties actually imposed.

U.S. antidumping legislation and regulations are the most specific and detailed of any of the Atlantic area countries. They have also been subject to the most complaints. In most instances, the complaints have concerned administrative practices and the time consumed in investigations rather than the imposition of antidumping duties.

U.S. antidumping legislation conforms with the GATT rules that both price discrimination and injury must be present before antidumping duties may be imposed.[76] Since 1954, the Treasury Department has made the determinations with respect to price discrimination or sales at less than "fair value," and if price discrimination is found, the Tariff Commission

[74] Although Canadian antidumping legislation is inconsistent with GATT provisions, it is not in legal violation of the GATT because it predates Canada's obligations under the GATT. For a discussion of this point, see below, p. 307.

[75] According to a study of the Canadian-American Committee, "in 1959 and 1960, $1.8 million and $1.6 million, respectively, were paid in dumping duties, which result from arbitrary valuations on goods of a class or kind made in Canada." However, it is not possible to estimate the number of cases, the products, or the value of trade involved. See Masson and English, *Invisible Trade Barriers*, p. 59.

[76] Unlike most countries, the United States has separate legislation relating to antidumping duties and to countervailing duties to offset the subsidization of exports. There is no injury requirement in Section 303 of the U.S. tariff act relating to countervailing duties. But countervailing duties have been imposed infrequently and, when imposed, have usually applied to agricultural products. However, the desire to avoid the imposition of countervailing duties on imports of automobile parts from Canada led to the 1965 U.S.–Canadian automotive agreement. For a list of the products to which countervailing duties apply, see U.S. Treasury, *Exporting to the United States*, pp. 16–17.

TABLE 9.2. U.S. ANTIDUMPING CASES

Calendar year	Number of cases	No price discrimination	Price revision	No injury	Injury	Appraisement withheld
1959	37	23	13	1	0	15
1960	29	19	7	2	1	24
1961	38	25	5	5	3	10
1962	23	9	12	2	0	11
1963	30	19	4	6	1	16
1964	37	13	12	9	3	13
Total	194	108	53	25	8	89

Source: Derived from tables, based on data supplied by the U.S. Treasury Department, published in the U.S. Congressional Record, June 1, 1965.

then finds whether or not such discrimination is causing or threatening injury to a domestic industry.[77]

Table 9.2 shows that between 1958, when the legislation was last amended, and 1965 there were 194 antidumping investigations. However, in only 8 instances, or 4 per cent of the cases, were antidumping duties imposed as the result of a finding of injury or likelihood of injury by the Tariff Commission.[78] In the remaining 186 cases, Treasury found no price discrimination in 108; 53 were terminated because the foreign exporter adjusted his prices; and the Tariff Commission found no injury in 25.

The restrictive element in U.S. antidumping practices is not the imposition of duties but the possibility that antidumping procedures will be instituted, the large number of cases actually initiated, and the withholding of appraisement in almost half of these cases. Apart from costs incurred by foreign exporters and domestic importers in an antidumping investigation, the uncertainties inherent in the initiation of an investigation are bound to have some trade-deterrent effects. These effects are enhanced by the practice of withholding ap-

[77] Between 1921 (when the U.S. Antidumping Act was legislated) and 1954, the Treasury Department made both the price discrimination and injury determinations.

[78] The eight cases in which antidumping duties were imposed and the countries affected were as follows: bicycles (Czechoslovakia, 1960), Portland cement (Sweden, 1961), Portland cement (Belgium, 1961), Portland gray cement (Portugal, 1961), Portland cement (Dominican Republic, 1963), chromic acid (Australia, 1964), steel reinforcing bars (Canada, 1964), and carbon steel bars and shapes (Canada, 1964). In April, 1965, the Tariff Commission also found injury in the case of azobisformamide (Japan), and subsequently, antidumping duties were imposed.

praisement, i.e., final determination of customs duties, whenever price discrimination is suspected during the course of an investigation. After appraisement is withheld, imported merchandise may be released under bond from Customs' custody, but importers do not know their profits on sales, or whether there will be profits, until after the antidumping investigation is completed. Furthermore, in a withholding action, no consideration is given to whether or not suspected price discrimination might cause or threaten injury. As indicated in Table 9.2, appraisement was withheld in 89 cases or eleven times the number in which antidumping duties were imposed.

It might be expected that because of profit uncertainty, imports would decline after the withholding of appraisement. However, this is not always the case; while imports often decrease and even stop, there are instances when imports have not declined. Nevertheless, traders may be adversely affected because of the failure of imports to increase and because of the time consumed in investigations, which averages well over a year. One case took more than three years. Under the law, the Tariff Commission must make injury determinations within 90 days, but there is no time limit on Treasury determinations relating to price discrimination.[79]

A GATT study in 1957 found that, except for Canada and the United States, industrial countries made little use of antidumping measures.[80] In recent years, however, several countries have enacted or revised antidumping legislation and have initiated a number of antidumping actions. For example, in the United Kingdom, the most active of these countries, there

[79] In January, 1965, after consultations in 1964 with domestic interests and with other OECD countries, the U.S. Treasury Department revised its antidumping regulations. But these revisions only partly satisfied the complaints of foreign exporters and domestic importers, on the one hand, and domestic producers, on the other.

For a comprehensive account of the administration of U.S. antidumping legislation, see Alexis C. Coudert, "The Application of the United States Antidumping Law in the Light of a Liberal Trade Policy," *Columbia Law Review*, Vol. 65, No. 2 (February, 1965), pp. 189–231. See also James Pomeroy Hendrick, "The United States Antidumping Act," *The American Journal of International Law*, Vol. 58, No. 4 (October, 1964), pp. 914–34.

[80] GATT, *Anti-Dumping and Countervailing Duties* (Geneva: July, 1958). GATT document MGT (59) 122, November, 1959, updates this publication somewhat. See also, GATT, *Anti-Dumping and Countervailing Duties, Report of Group of Experts* (Geneva: March, 1961).

were 29 antidumping cases during calendar years 1961 through 1964. In 23 of these cases, full investigations were instituted, 4 of which were pending at the end of 1964. Of the remaining 19, 11 were dismissed, exporters agreed to adjust their prices in 3, and antidumping duties were imposed in 5.

As part of the EEC common commercial policy, the Commission has proposed to the Council a draft Community antidumping regulation to deal with third-country dumping. After duties are eliminated within the EEC, a Community antidumping policy will be necessary if the dumping of third-country exports from one member state to another is to be regulated effectively. Because duty-free treatment within EFTA countries applies only to goods of EFTA origin, no similar problem arises.[81]

Antidumping legislation in these countries and the proposed Community regulation conform with the GATT principles of price discrimination and injury, but administrative procedures do not adequately assure that these principles will be followed. In the absence of specific legislation and/or detailed regulations, antidumping actions sometimes resemble star-chamber proceedings in which exporters are pressured to adjust their prices under threat of antidumping duties. A determination of whether dumping prices are injurious may not play a prominent part in such proceedings—injury is often assumed.[82]

---

[81] Unlike government procurement, dumping among countries of the EEC and of the EFTA is not treated differently from third-country dumping. However, both the Treaty of Rome (Article 91) and the Stockholm Convention (Article 17) provide that prior to completion of the customs union and free trade area, no duties or quotas will be applied to goods upon reimportation from another member state. Such free reimportation is often an effective deterrent against dumping because, if transportation and other costs do not exceed the dumping margin, dumped goods can be shipped back again into the dumping country.

[82] A recent antidumping action by the United Kingdom is illustrative. On March 25, 1966, the Board of Trade imposed an antidumping duty of £ 114 per ton on imports of a chemical mixture of diphenyl ether and diphenyl exported from the United States by the Dow Chemical Company. This action, which was based on a "threat of injury," resulted from a complaint on March 10 by Imperial Chemical Industries, the only U.K. producer, which was expanding its production facilities. The case was never discussed with the U.K. importer or the U.S. exporter before the antidumping duties were imposed. The duties were rescinded two months later, when Dow agreed to cease all exports of the mixture

Other Nontariff Barriers

There are a number of other nontariff barriers that do not lend themselves to easy classification. They relate to certain internal taxes and regulations, safety and other standards, marks of origin, labeling requirements, and other measures that can and often do have a restrictive effect on trade. Only those that have been the subject of recent complaints will be discussed in any detail.

The possible trade effects of differences in taxation policies among Atlantic area countries are discussed in Chapter VIII. However, it should be reiterated here that border taxes imposed on imported goods to compensate for indirect taxes borne by domestic products are not necessarily trade-neutral, nor are the rebates of indirect taxes when products are exported. Such border tax adjustments can have trade-distorting effects that are comparable to those of tariffs and export subsidies. This is particularly true with respect to *changes* in border tax adjustments, whether or not accompanied by changes in internal taxes.[83]

Another problem relating to internal taxes is annual automobile road-use taxes imposed by France, Belgium, Italy, and Austria. The effect of these taxes, which are sharply progressive and are assessed on the basis of certain physical characteristics rather than on the value of the vehicles, is to discriminate against larger automobiles, principally those of U.S. manufacture.

France, Belgium, and Italy assess road taxes according to fiscal horsepower, which is calculated from a tax formula that differs in each country but relates to such vehicle characteristics as number of cylinders, cylinder capacity, and weight. Austria imposes a road tax based on cylinder capacity. French, Belgian, and Austrian taxes decline with the age of the car, but the Italian tax is collected every year without any diminution.

The following schedule of road taxes in France is illustrative of the discriminatory effects of these countries' taxes. The

---

to the United Kingdom. See U.K. Board of Trade press release, March 24, 1966.

[83] The EEC objective of harmonizing tax policies and border tax adjustments will involve far-reaching changes in both the method of assessing taxes and the tax rates.

Fiscal horsepower	French francs	U.S. dollars
4 h.p. or less	60	12
5 to 7 h.p.	90	18
8 to 11 h.p.	120	24
12 to 16 h.p.	150	30
Over 16 h.p.	1,000	200

French tax is gradually progressive, but it jumps by 567 per cent on automobiles over 16 fiscal horsepower. This much higher tax on larger-engined vehicles applies principally to imported U.S. automobiles; it does not apply to any French production-line vehicle, nor does it apply to most other European cars.[84] The progressive nature of this tax is defended on the grounds that larger, more expensive cars should bear higher taxes. However, because fiscal horsepower has no necessary relationship to value, larger-engined U.S. cars bear a higher tax than smaller-engined European cars, even though the latter may be more expensive. For example, a Porsche 356 C/*Carrera* (retailing in France for 45,000 francs, with a rating of 11 h.p.) bears a road tax of 120 francs, while a Chevrolet *Chevelle* (retailing at 22,490 francs, with a rating of 18 h.p.) bears a road tax of 1,000 francs.[85] The Chevrolet, costing half as much as the Porsche, is subject to a tax more than eight times greater.

Japan imposes a commodity tax, payable only once, that is levied on the manufacturer's sales price of domestically produced cars and on the c.i.f. duty-paid value of imported vehicles. The tax rates are 40, 30, and 15 per cent, depending on engine capacity, wheelbase, and body width of the vehicle. All standard-size U.S. cars are subject to the 40 per cent rate; almost all Japanese cars fall in the 15 per cent rate category.[86]

It is not possible to estimate the trade-deterrent effects of these taxes, because they cannot be isolated from other factors

[84] France also imposes a registration fee based on fiscal horsepower. On January 1, 1967, this fee was to be increased from 13.2 to 20.0 francs per unit of fiscal horsepower on automobiles having a horsepower rating of 13 or more. There is no French production of automobiles that will be subject to the increased fee.

[85] These prices are taken from L'Argus de l'Automobile, May 28, 1964.

[86] In addition to the commodity tax, Japanese prefectures levy an annual automobile tax graduated on the basis of cylinder capacity and wheelbase.

that have discouraged sales of imported U.S. automobiles. For example, increased automobile production in Europe and Japan and higher gas consumption of larger-engined U.S. automobiles, coupled with high taxes on gasoline, have also been very important. Nevertheless, the basis for the assessment of these European road taxes and the Japanese commodity tax has a discriminatory effect on imports of U.S. automobiles.

The method of assessment acts as a nontariff restriction in the case of United States internal revenue taxes and import duties on distilled spirits. Both the excise tax and import duty are assessed on a proof-gallon basis when the distilled spirits are 100 proof (50 per cent alcohol) or more but on a wine-gallon basis when less than 100 proof. This distinction means that the excise tax and duty on distilled spirits of 100 proof or more vary proportionately with the alcoholic strength of the spirits but that distilled spirits of less than 100 proof are treated for tax and duty purposes as if they were 100 proof.

Most distilled spirits imported into the United States are bottled abroad at less than 100 proof, and consequently, they pay excise tax and duty on a wine-gallon basis. Almost all spirits produced domestically are taxed on a proof-gallon basis when they are withdrawn from bond at 100 proof or above before dilution and bottling. This results in a tax differential in favor of the domestic product. For example, a gallon of imported Scotch whiskey bottled at 86 proof pays an excise tax of $10.50 (based on wine-gallon assessment). A gallon of Bourbon whiskey bottled after dilution to 86 proof bears a tax of $9.03 (based on proof-gallon assessment). In addition, the imported whiskey pays a duty of $1.02 (based on wine-gallon assessment) that is $ .14 higher than if the duty were based on proof-gallon assessment. In effect, the wine-gallon basis of assessment for the excise tax and duty results in a levy on the water contained in the imported product of $1.61. It is estimated on the basis of 1965 imports that the additional revenue to the U.S. Treasury resulting from the wine-gallon basis of assessment is around $70 million.

The tax and duty differential resulting from wine-gallon assessment can be avoided by importing distilled spirits in bulk at 100 proof or above, paying the tax and duty at the proof-gallon rate, and bottling the spirits in the United States at whatever proof desired. In recent years, there has been a shift from bottled to bulk imports largely for this reason. For example, between 1960 and 1965 bulk imports of Scotch more than quadrupled in value and increased from less than 4 per cent to almost 11 per cent of imports. Foreign exporters, however, prefer not to ship in bulk, because there is prestige value in foreign bottling, and because they are better able to control quality if the bottling is done abroad. Furthermore, the value added in the bottling and labeling of the spirits abroad is lost in bulk exports. The wine-gallon system, therefore, affords protection not only to domestic producers of distilled spirits but also to domestic bottlers of spirits in bulk.[87]

The countries most affected by the wine-gallon system are the United Kingdom, Canada, and France. In 1965, U.S. imports from the United Kingdom of bottled Scotch whiskey were $165 million and imports of gin were $10 million; imports of bottled Canadian whiskey were $99 million; and imports of bottled brandy from France were $9 million. Bottled liqueurs were also imported at less than 100 proof from the United Kingdom ($4.6 million), France ($4.3 million), Italy ($2.9 million), and Denmark ($1.4 million).

Various nontariff restrictions on motion picture films and recorded television (TV) programs are of a unique character, because such films and programs, although subject to duties, are normally rented. Tariffs do not afford the same kind of protection as for products that do not generate invisible transfers. For both economic and cultural reasons many industrial countries require that a certain proportion of theater and TV screen time (screen quotas) be used for films and programs of national origin. Also, production is often subsidized or monopolized by governments, and requirements for domestic dubbing, subtitling, and printing are sometimes employed. Restrictions relating to TV programs tend to be more severe, probably because the viewer does not buy a ticket, and therefore, consumer preference has a less direct effect upon decisions of exhibitors.

Among industrial countries screen quotas for motion pic-

---

[87] Most other industrial countries afford similar protection to domestic bottlers by charging a higher duty on bottled imports. For example, the EEC imposes an additional duty of $10.00 per hectoliter on bottled spirits, which for 100 proof whiskey increases the total duty by 20 per cent.

ture films are not very restrictive, because they tend to approximate the commercial demand for foreign and domestic films. In addition to screen quotas, France requires a special permit for films dubbed in the French language and requires that the dubbing be done in France. Italy, the other EEC country that maintains screen quotas, rebates part of the theater admission tax to exhibitors when they show films of Italian origin.[88]

U.K. screen quotas on motion picture films are of little or no trade importance, but similar quotas on TV programs are both important and discriminatory. Under the Television Act of 1964, the Independent Television Authority (ITA), which, unlike the British Broadcasting Corporation (BBC), operates a national television service on a commercial basis, must assure that "proper proportions" of the material included in television programs are of British origin. Accordingly, the ITA requires that 86 per cent of TV screen time be reserved for domestic material. Thus, imported material has access to only 14 per cent of ITA screen time, or about 8 hours per week.[89] Further restrictions relate to the prime evening time period during which no more than two of five programs shown between 8:00 and 8:55 P.M. on weekday evenings may be of U.S. origin, and no more than three of these five may relate to crime or Western subjects regardless of national origin.[90] The United States is the only country on which the U.K. quota on recorded TV programs has any practical effect. The 86/14 ratio of domestic to imported material not only reduces the quantity of U.S. sales to the United Kingdom but also depresses the prices of the material sold; the discriminatory restriction on the showing of U.S. material during prime evening time enhances the price-depressing effects.

Requirements by industrial countries for marks of origin or

[88] Under the EEC Commission's proposed common policy for the film industry, films produced by other EEC countries are to be treated like national films under the French and Italian screen quotas. Similarly, other film restrictions by France and Italy were no longer to be applied to EEC countries after December 31, 1966.

[89] Material of Commonwealth origin and certain other material do not apply against the 14 per cent quota for imported material. No similar legislation or regulations apply to the BBC. In fact, however, BBC purchases of imported material have not exceeded 14 per cent of screen time.

[90] Press statement of the Independent Television Authority, August 18, 1965.

labeling of imported products become nontariff barriers when compliance is difficult or excessively costly. For example, Japan requires that the labels on canned goods contain *only* metric weights, and that imported products indicate the name of the importer and the date of importation. In order to meet these requirements, importers apply stickers containing this information over the avoirdupois weight on the can label. Similarly, Canadian restrictions on can sizes for fruits and vegetables prohibit the use of the standard vegetable can employed in the United States. Furthermore, certain can sizes may be used only for asparagus and corn; other sizes are allowed for general use but not for asparagus.

Safety and other standards and regulations relating to foods and drugs have an unavoidable deterrent effect on trade, which is increased when standards and regulations differ among countries. But, they become nontariff barriers only when trade is unnecessarily restricted. For example, differences among countries of electrical current voltages and equipment, such as two- and three-pronged plugs, are natural trade barriers. These barriers are enhanced by differences in electrical safety standards, which may even differ among states and provinces. However, only when such standards or other regulations become impossible or unreasonably difficult or expensive to comply with do they become nontariff barriers. For example, in the United States imports of boilers and pressure vessels are effectively excluded from some states and local communities by requirements that they be stamped with the seal of the American Society of Mechanical Engineers, which is not issued to manufacturers located outside the United States and Canada. Imports of gas cylinders are similarly excluded by a requirement of the Interstate Commerce Commission that they be inspected in the United States.

Among a number of miscellaneous nontariff restrictions, France prohibits the advertising of spirits distilled from grain but permits the advertising of spirits distilled from fruit. This prohibition is justified on health grounds, but protects French production of brandy from imports of whiskies and gin. In Germany, unless beer is made only from malt, yeast, hops, and water, it cannot be sold as "beer." This restriction effectively excludes imports of beer made from corn or rice. Canada prohibits imports of regional or "split run" editions of periodicals containing advertising directed primarily to the Canadian market, and imports of periodicals of which more than 5 per cent of advertising space indicates Canadian sources of supply. The purpose of this prohibition is to divert advertising revenue from foreign (primarily U.S.) to Canadian publications and thereby to encourage publication in Canada.[91]

Conclusions

As already suggested, the reduction or elimination of tariffs among industrial countries will increase the importance of nontariff barriers as obstacles to trade. But the problems that nontariff barriers present are so diversified that no single solution is possible.

Efforts being made in the GATT, the OECD, and the Kennedy Round negotiations are only beginning to deal effectively with nontariff barriers. Although the GATT prohibits many nontariff barriers, it is generally less effective in dealing with them than with tariffs. Under the Protocol of Provisional Application and subsequent protocols under which countries apply the GATT to their commercial policy, legislation existing prior to a country's membership is exempt from its provisions. Because many nontariff barriers are embodied in legislation of long standing, they are legally maintained under the GATT even though they are inconsistent with its provisions. In the OECD, countries have few legal obligations in regard to nontariff barriers, but through a series of confrontations an effort has been made to remove or reduce them, with relatively little success in recent years. A major attempt is being made in the Kennedy Round to negotiate on nontariff barriers. However, many of them cannot be easily negotiated, and the Kennedy Round is already burdened with difficult tariff issues. In this section, possible ways of dealing with nontariff barriers will be examined.

As already indicated, quantitative restrictions among industrial countries on nonagricultural products are a minor problem except those relating to coal and to Japan. GATT prohibits their imposition except for balance-of-payments and a few

---

[91] *Time* and *Reader's Digest* magazines, whose Canadian editions are published entirely in Canada, are exempt from this prohibition.

other purposes. Consequently, the few remaining restrictions that can no longer be justified on balance-of-payments grounds are illegal and should be dealt with under appropriate GATT provisions.

However, irrespective of their legal status, quantitative and other nontariff restrictions on coal could not, realistically, be handled in the same way. Restrictions on coal are similar in nature to those on agricultural products, because they reflect deep-rooted economic and social problems affecting politically important segments of the population. In all countries maintaining nontariff restrictions, efforts are being made to solve these problems, which are becoming smaller as the number of mines and miners declines.

The problem of coal restrictions is further complicated by its relationship to competing fuels and sources of energy. Domestic coal not only competes with imported coal but with petroleum, natural gas, hydroelectric power, and nuclear energy. One of the objectives of the Common Market is to develop a common energy policy that would allocate Community energy requirements among competing energy sources and between domestic and foreign suppliers. Such a policy has been under consideration since 1957, but it is unlikely to develop before the merger of the three communities.[92] In varying degrees other industrial countries have energy policies that determine or influence the tariff and nontariff restrictions on coal and competing energy sources.[93] Consequently, restrictions on coal can probably be handled effectively only within the context of countries' energy policies in which the comparative economic and social costs of alternative imported and domestic energy sources are considered. Any removal of coal restrictions would have to be undertaken gradually so as to provide an opportunity for adjustments, particularly on the part of affected miners.

[92] The European Coal and Steel Community is responsible for coal; the EEC for petroleum, gas, and hydroelectric power; and the European Atomic Energy Community for nuclear energy. For a discussion of developments in the Communities' common energy policy, see European Coal and Steel Community, 13th General Report, March, 1965, pp. 74–92.

[93] See, for example, the United Kingdom White Paper on *Fuel Policy*, published by the Ministry of Power, October 21, 1965 (Command 2798). This paper outlines energy policy for the next five to ten years.

The problem of quantitative import restrictions by Japan on the one hand and restrictions (including Japanese voluntary export controls) by industrial countries vis-à-vis Japan on the other suggests the need for a negotiated settlement. Japan maintains import restrictions in part as a bargaining lever against the discriminatory restrictions of other countries. In any Atlantic free trade area that included Japan, such a settlement would have to be made on the basis either of mutual elimination of these restrictions or agreed exceptions to free-trade treatment. Mutual elimination would necessitate a willingness on the part of the other industrial countries to adjust to increased competition from Japanese exports, which might involve assistance to affected factors of production. However, most industrial countries already have legislation to help in the adaptation or relocation of factors adversely affected by imports.

Although state trading is not a major problem among industrial countries, it would nevertheless have to be considered in any free trade area or a substantial reduction of tariffs. In a free trade area, national state-trading regimes would probably have to be eliminated or extended to include all industrial countries, just as the EEC envisages such elimination or extension. However, if tariffs were only reduced rather than eliminated, state trading could be treated in the same way as in GATT tariff negotiations. Unless otherwise agreed by the parties to the negotiation, a GATT tariff concession on a state-traded product limits the markup that may be charged by the state-trading agency (exclusive of expenses incurred and a reasonable profit) over the landed price of the imported goods. Such a commitment may be supplemented by agreement of the state-trading agency to purchase stipulated amounts of imports.[94]

Preferences to domestic producers in government procure-

---

[94] For example, in 1947 France granted the United States a concession on wheat, stipulating that the resale price should not exceed by more than 15 per cent the average duty-paid value of the imported grain. Italy made the same concession in 1949 on both wheat and rye. Also, in 1947 France agreed to purchase minimum annual quantities of cigarettes and leaf tobacco and to charge a price on imported cigarettes that would preserve the prewar ratio between the selling prices of foreign cigarettes and the best French brands sold by the state monopoly.

ment often result in restricting trade to a considerable extent. In the event of substantial reductions in tariffs, such preferences may become more restrictive to compensate domestic producers for loss of protection in the private sector. Because there are virtually no international rules relating to government procurement, this is an area where an international agreement or code might be successfully concluded. Such an agreement appears to be negotiable, because all industrial countries grant preferences to domestic producers in one form or another.

The purpose of an international agreement would be to eliminate these preferences or to make them uniform. Any effective arrangement would have to provide for standard procedures relating to publicity, submission of bids, awarding of contracts, and similar matters.[95] Unless this were done, the varying preferences inherent in the present procedures of many countries would continue. Any favoritism to domestic producers should be granted through margins of preference clearly stated in percentage terms. Such preferences could then be made uniform among countries and could be reduced over a period of time or in subsequent negotiations.

It might be too ambitious to include all government procurement in one agreement; nonmilitary, military, and foreign aid procurement could be dealt with separately. For example, the United States and Canada have mutually eliminated preferences on certain military supplies. This arrangement logically could be extended to include all NATO countries and Japan. Similarly, efforts now being made in the OECD to co-ordinate member countries' foreign aid programs might include an agreement under which this aid would be progressively untied so that recipient developing countries could purchase on a global basis from the most economical sources.

Preferences in procurement by provinces, municipalities, and other government bodies are more difficult to deal with, particularly because of the federal systems of some industrial countries. However, national governments could make efforts to standardize procedures and to eliminate such preferences.

In an Atlantic Free Trade Area, customs classification and

---

[95] Work on the possible harmonization of government procurement procedures is now taking place in the OECD.

valuation would disappear with tariffs. Correspondingly, the greater the tariff reduction the less important are the consequences of classification and valuation.

As indicated earlier, even though there is no uniform customs nomenclature among the industrial countries, this is not, by itself, an obstacle to trade. It would be desirable, however, if the United States and Canada were to adopt the BTN and to join the Customs Co-operation Council.[96] Also, procedures in the United States for making classification decisions and for handling disputes could be expedited.

Valuation is not a serious problem among those countries subscribing to the Brussels Definition. As in the case of tariff classification, there are always valuation problems relating to individual shipments, particularly in transactions between related parties. Any general problems can be worked out within the Customs Co-operation Council. U.S. and Canadian valuation practices, however, are out of line with those of other industrial countries. Their complexity, uncertainty, and in some instances opportunity for arbitrary valuation undoubtedly deter trade. Adoption of the Brussels Definition is a possible solution to such valuation problems. The U.S. Tariff Commission is now investigating the methods of valuation used by the United States and other countries, and the feasibility and desirability of U.S. adoption of the Brussels Definition.[97] A Treasury Department study has recommended elimination of the "final list,"[98] and ASP is under consideration in the Kennedy Round.

Adoption of the Brussels Definition by the United States and Canada would result in a higher c.i.f. system of valuation, so that rates bound in tariff negotiations would have to be lowered in order to compensate for the higher valuations. But

[96] Because of the introduction of a new tariff nomenclature in 1963, it may be some years before the United States is ready to make the considerable effort necessary to adopt the BTN. Separate negotiations with twenty-nine countries to compensate them for any impairment of previous tariff concessions caused by the 1963 nomenclature revision are still not completed.

[97] A preliminary report has already been published. See U.S. Tariff Commission, *Customs Valuation*, Preliminary Report to the Committee on Finance of the United States Senate, TC Publication 180 (Washington, D.C.: July, 1966).

[98] See U.S. Treasury, *An Evaluation*, p. VI–24.

since insurance and freight costs to the many U.S. and Canadian ports of entry vary considerably among countries, lower rates that would afford the same degree of protection to domestic producers would favor nearby countries and penalize distant ones.

Dumping and antidumping measures are becoming increasingly important problems in international trade. Antidumping measures may become more extensive as European countries introduce and amend legislation and regulations. However, multilateral tariff reductions as well as a free trade area would deter dumping by making it easier for dumped goods to be shipped back again into the dumping country. But even in a free trade area, transportation costs among many of the industrial countries are large enough to make this a limited deterrent. Furthermore, governments might be hard pressed to use antidumping measures to compensate domestic producers for the elimination or reduction of tariff protection.

Although the GATT requires that both price discrimination and injury be established before antidumping duties are imposed, it does not define what is meant by injury nor does it prescribe procedures to be followed in antidumping determinations. Consequently, GATT is not now adequate to regulate antidumping measures. As in the case of government procurement, an international agreement or code appears to be an appropriate and negotiable solution. Logically, a code would implement the GATT by including criteria for injury determinations and procedures for insuring that antidumping investigations would not inhibit trade and would treat all interested parties equitably. Such a code, which was discussed in the OECD and which is now being explored in the Kennedy Round, should eliminate the present and future nontariff barrier aspects of antidumping measures.

The elimination of such miscellaneous nontariff barriers as European and Japanese road and commodity taxes that have a discriminatory effect on imported automobiles, the U.S. wine-gallon method of assessing excise taxes and import duties, and the U.K. screen quota on recorded TV programs might be possible as part of a free trade area arrangement. If tariffs were only reduced, these and similar restrictions might best be handled through negotiations. Whatever their justification, unilateral complaints seldom result in satisfaction when difficult or important issues are involved.[99] Bilateral negotiations on such nontariff barriers may be impracticable when there is no basis for reciprocity. For example, the United States is interested in Austrian action on automobile road taxes, but Austria has no particular interest in any U.S. nontariff restrictions. Consequently, a multilateral package to which all countries contribute might be the best way to negotiate on such miscellaneous nontariff barriers. But even a multilateral package would be unbalanced for certain countries and, therefore, would not be reciprocal. Such a package would most easily be concluded within the framework of a general tariff reduction, such as the Kennedy Round, so that deficiencies in some countries' contributions could be made up by tariff concessions.[100] Short of a general trade negotiation, both tariff and nontariff barriers affecting trade in a particular industry might be negotiated. In chemicals, for example, an effort has been made in the Kennedy Round to exchange tariff concessions for elimination of the American selling price basis of customs valuation.

The misuse of standards and similar measures designed to regulate trade can best be treated within various international organizations dealing with these matters. The International Organization for Standardization and the International Electrotechnical Commission are ideally suited for this purpose with respect to industrial products. The *Codex Alimentarius*, which is being developed under the auspices of the Food and Agriculture Organization and the World Health Organization, is designed to cope with problems relating to agricultural products. The *Codex Alimentarius* will not only include health standards for food but also the standardization of can and other container sizes.

As indicated in the introductory section, this discussion

[99] For example, a U.S. complaint on European road taxes was considered by the OECD Trade Committee in 1963, but no changes in these countries' tax measures resulted.

[100] It might be possible to negotiate satisfactorily on recorded TV programs in connection with the OECD Code of Liberalization of Current Invisible Operations, part of which relates to liberalizing international transactions in motion picture films and recorded TV programs. However, neither the OECD code nor the GATT, which contains somewhat similar provisions, applies specifically to TV screen quotas, and their applicability to such quotas is a matter of contention that has not been resolved.

does not presume to encompass all nontariff barriers among industrial countries, but it does include the principal restrictions on nonagricultural products that have been the subject of recent international complaints. It is evident that in any elimination or further substantial reduction of tariffs the problems relating to these nontariff restrictions would be considerable. However, it is unlikely that any Atlantic free trade area or significant multilateral reduction of tariffs will develop until after the question of U.K. and other EFTA countries' entrance into the EEC is settled one way or the other. This key question to the future of Atlantic commercial policy may not be resolved for another few years. In the meantime, much greater attention is likely to be given to nontariff restrictions.

METHODOLOGICAL APPENDICES

As noted in Chapter I, the contributors have utilized estimates prepared by the project director concerning the potential impact of tariff reductions on trade flows, and the "revealed" comparative advantage of the industrial countries. A short discussion of the approach utilized in deriving these estimates was given in Chapter I; the Appendix to this chapter provides a detailed description of the methodology applied.

We have also indicated that the assumptions made in the U.S. study are partly different from those underlying the above estimates. These assumptions are explained in the Appendix to Chapter II. In order to maintain the continuity of the discussion, no effort has been made to eliminate duplication in these Appendices. Finally, in the Appendix to Chapter III, a short discussion of the methods applied in the Canadian study is given.

Appendix to Chapter I

Bela Balassa

Direct effects of tariff reductions. The direct effects of trade liberalization were defined to include changes in exports and imports that would result from multilateral reductions in duties if no account were taken of the potential discriminatory effects of the EEC and EFTA. The magnitude of direct effects is determined by the height of the original tariff rates, changes in these rates, and the responsiveness of the demand for, and the supply of, traded commodities to price changes in the individual countries. In turn, the elasticities of import demand and export supply will depend on the underlying elasticities of domestic demand and supply, the share of imports (exports) in domestic consumption (production), the substitutability of domestic and foreign goods, and the length of the period of adjustment.

1. *Tariffs.* In classifying tariffs, we have used the Brussels Tariff Nomenclature (BTN) which is employed by all of the countries under consideration except for the United States and Canada. For these two countries, tariffs have been reclassified according to the BTN, and expressed in terms of c.i.f. prices. Since the BTN headings largely correspond to the four- and five-digit items of the Standard International Trade Classification (SITC), tariff averages have been calculated by using the combined imports of individual items into all the industrial countries as weights.

315

2. *Import demand elasticities.* To indicate the responsiveness of import demand to decreases in import prices that result from reductions in tariffs, one may utilize estimates of price elasticities of import demand derived from past periods. Among time-series estimates of U.S. import demand elasticities, the recent calculations of Ball and Marwah appear to be the most reliable. These authors applied regression analysis to quarterly data covering eleven postwar years and estimated elasticities for five commodity groups, three of which are relevant for our discussion: −0.26 for crude materials, −1.38 for semimanufactures, and −3.50 for finished manufactures.[1] But, as the authors note, by reason of the downward bias associated with the statistical method applied, these figures provide lower limits of possible values.[2] As "upper bounds," they suggest the use of −0.53 or −0.65 for crude materials, −1.89 or −2.15 for semimanufactures, and −4.74 or −5.28 for finished manufactures—obtained by adding two and three standard errors, respectively, to the least squares estimates.

Ball and Marwah's estimates are purported to measure the effects of changes in relative prices on imports over time. Measured changes in prices, however, in part reflect changes in quality since import price indices are calculated by dividing an index of import values by an index of import volumes. Quality changes, then, contribute to the errors of observation, when errors in the independent variable are known to cause a downward bias in the estimated coefficients. This source of bias can be avoided if we consider the relationship between changes in tariffs and in imports because the rates of duties applied are known without error. Further sources of bias can be removed if cross-section comparisons are made.

This procedure has been applied by M. E. Kreinin and L. B. Krause. Kreinin compared data for two groups of commodi-

---

[1] R. J. Ball and K. Marwah, "The U.S. Demand for Imports, 1948–1958," *Review of Economics and Statistics*, November, 1962, pp. 395–401.

[2] On the error possibilities of least-square estimation from time-series data, see Guy H. Orcutt, "Measurement of Price Elasticities in International Trade," *Review of Economics and Statistics*, May, 1950, pp. 117–32, and Arnold C. Harberger, "A Structural Approach to the Problem of Import Demand," *American Economic Review*, May, 1953, pp. 148–59.

ties, classified according to whether or not they have been subject to tariff reductions. The elasticities implicit in his results are −5 for commodities excluding textiles in the period 1954–56 and −6 for finished manufactures in the period 1955–59.[3] In a cross-section analysis of 91 categories of manufactured goods, Krause obtained "tariff" elasticity estimates of −5.6 for the period 1947–54, and −4.5 for 1947–58. For both periods, the elasticity of demand for imports calculated with respect to the tariff change was considerably higher than the elasticities calculated with respect to price.[4]

Kreinin's and Krause's results point to the conclusion that a reduction in tariffs is likely to have a larger effect on imports than an equivalent change in import prices—a phenomenon which requires explanation. Aside from the downward bias in least-squares estimates of price elasticities, a possible explanation is that importers regard tariff changes as permanent and reallocate their purchases accordingly, while changes in import prices are often considered transitory. Also, a ratchet-effect may be operative in the second case: once purchases are accommodated to a lower import price, habit formation or simply the acquired knowledge of foreign goods would limit the shift back to domestic commodities if import prices rose again. On the other hand, we have but few instances when tariffs were raised in the postwar period.

Further evidence on the responsiveness of imports to changes in tariffs is provided in a study by B. A. deVries. DeVries calculated implicit "tariff" elasticities for 176 products on the basis of projections made by commodity experts regarding the possible long-term effects on American imports

---

[3] M. E. Kreinin, "The Effects of Tariff Changes on the Prices and Volume of Imports," *American Economic Review*, June, 1961, pp. 310–24.

[4] Elasticities calculated for the years 1954–58 provide an exception, but tariff changes were relatively small during this period, and the tariff elasticity was not statistically significant:

	Price elasticity		Tariff elasticity	
1947–58	−1.77	(0.32)	−5.64	(2.11)
1947–54	−1.54	(0.31)	−4.49	(1.83)
1954–58	−1.32	(0.21)	−0.52	(0.28)

(L. B. Krause, "United States Imports, 1947–1958," *Econometrica*, April, 1962, pp. 221–38).

of an assumed 50 per cent reduction—or increase—in the 1939 U.S. tariffs. For all commodities, taken together, the weighted average of elasticities is −2.2 for a reduction and −2.7 for an increase in duties. For the three product groups of the Ball-Marwah study, the following elasticities were obtained: crude materials, −1.3; semimanufactures −3.1; and finished manufactures −3.9.[5]

These results suggest that, for the purpose of estimating the possible effects of tariff reductions on U.S. imports, the elasticities calculated by Ball and Marwah need to be adjusted upwards. Although available information does not provide a precise indication for selecting appropriate values within the range indicated, the addition of one standard deviation to the estimates may provide a reasonable compromise. This adjustment is also in conformity with deVries' results for the commodity group that has primary importance for the present study—finished manufactures. The corresponding elasticities are: crude materials −0.39, semimanufactures −1.63, and finished manufactures −4.12.[6] In making calculations on the possible expansion of imports following reductions in tariffs, we have assigned an elasticity value to each three-digit SITC commodity category, depending on whether it contained crude materials, semimanufactures, or finished manufactures. In regard to commodity categories that comprise products classified in two or three of the above groups, an average elasticity has been estimated, using United States imports of each product as weights.

Estimates on import demand elasticities for Western Europe, Canada, and Japan are few and far between. Among available calculations, Harberger's[7] results are subject to a

---

[5] B. A. deVries, "Price Elasticities of Demand for Individual Commodities Imported into the United States," *International Monetary Fund Staff Papers*, April, 1951, pp. 397–419.

[6] Estimates utilizing "lower limit" elasticities can be derived from our results by reducing the latter by 15 per cent—the percentage difference between the two elasticities in the case of semifinished and finished manufactures. (The difference in the elasticities is larger in regard to crude materials, but this complication can be readily overlooked since most crude materials bear low duties or are imported duty free into the industrial countries.)

[7] A. C. Harberger found elasticities of a round unity for total imports into various European countries, although higher values obtain if agricultural products are excluded. See his "Some Evidence on the Interna-

substantial downward bias while the figures provided by Scott[8] for the United Kingdom, and by Wemelsfelder[9] for Germany are sensitive to conditions of capacity utilization during the periods under study. At any rate, estimates are not available for all of the major industrial countries, nor for the appropriate commodity categories. Hence, we have chosen to derive the elasticity coefficients used for these countries from estimates pertaining to the United States.

Under the assumption of identical domestic demand and supply elasticities in all areas, import demand elasticities would be negatively correlated with the share of imports in domestic consumption. Empirical evidence on this a priori relationship is provided in deVries' study. According to the latter, U.S. import demand elasticities average about −2.0 for commodities in the case of which the ratio of imports to domestic consumption exceeds 27 per cent (the average for all 176 products) while the corresponding figure is −3.4 for products where the import/consumption ratio is below the average.[10] Since the share of imports in domestic consumption is considerably smaller in the United States than elsewhere, import demand elasticities are expected to be lower abroad than in the U.S.

The ratio of the imports of manufactured goods to value added in the manufacturing sector in the year 1960 was estimated at 4.6 per cent in the United States, 50.9 per cent for Canada, 8.4 per cent for the European Common Market, 12.5 per cent for the United Kingdom, 34.7 per cent for Continental EFTA, and 9.3 per cent for Japan.[11] However, these esti-

---

tional Price Mechanism," *Journal of Political Economy,* December, 1957, pp. 506–21.

[8] According to Scott's results, in the 1931–32 period, a one percentage point rise in tariffs was accompanied by a 4.3 per cent fall in the U.K. imports of manufactured goods. (M. F. G. Scott, *A Study of United Kingdom Imports,* Cambridge University Press, 1962, pp. 168–69).

[9] In a study of the effects of unilateral tariff reductions undertaken by Germany in 1956 and 1957, J. Wemelsfelder derived an import demand elasticity of −9. See his "The Short-run Effects of the Lowering of Import Duties in Germany," *Economic Journal,* March, 1960, pp. 94–105.

[10] B. A. deVries, "Price Elasticities of Demand for Individual Commodities Imported into the United States," p. 413.

[11] Organization for Economic Co-operation and Development, *General Statistics,* January, 1965, and United Nations, *Commodity Trade Statistics, 1960,* New York, 1961. In the case of the EEC and EFTA countries, only extra-area trade has been considered.

mates need to be adjusted downwards because the relevant comparison is not between the value of imports and value added in manufacturing, but between the value of imports and the value of the domestic consumption (production) of manufactures.[12] In turn, various factors, including transportation costs, product differentiation, imperfect information, and intercountry differences in tastes tend to restrict the substitutability of imports for domestic production and necessitate a substantial *upward* adjustment.

The latter factors are of especial importance in the United States, and we have followed J. E. Floyd in assuming the ratio of the consumption of competing goods to imports to be 4 in this country (an import share of 25 per cent).[13] We have taken the corresponding ratio to be 2 for Canada, under the assumption that the factors necessitating downward and upward adjustments in the proportion of imports to value-added approximately balance in this case. Accordingly, in deriving import-demand elasticities for Canada, we have divided the U.S. import-demand elasticities by the United States consumption-import ratio, and multiplied the results by the comparable Canadian figure. This procedure reflects the assumptions that consumption-import and production-import ratios are the same within each country, and that domestic demand and supply elasticities are identical internationally. The underlying formula is:

(1)
$$\eta_m = \eta C/M + \epsilon P/M,$$

when C denotes domestic consumption, P domestic production, and M imports, η and ϵ are the domestic elasticities of demand and supply, and η_m is the import-demand elasticity.

The estimates so obtained are roughly in conformity with the Canadian import-demand elasticity of -1.75 calculated by Chang for the interwar period.[14] In turn, on the basis of the data on import shares and the considerations noted in an earlier paper of the author, we have assumed consumption-import

[12] In addition to value added in manufacturing, the latter also includes the value of nonindustrial inputs, and that of imports used as inputs.

[13] J. E. Floyd, "The Overvaluation of the Dollar," *American Economic Review*, March, 1965, pp. 95–109.

[14] Cited in R. E. Caves and R. H. Holton, *The Canadian Economy— Prospect and Retrospect* (Cambridge, Mass.: Harvard University Press, 1959), p. 86. Note that Canada hardly imports any foodstuffs and crude materials.

ratios of 3 for the European Common Market and Japan, 2.6 for the United Kingdom, and 2.2 for Continental EFTA.[15] The import-demand elasticities calculated by the use of these ratios are:

	United States	Canada	Common Market	United Kingdom	Continental EFTA	Japan
Finished manufactures	−4.12	−2.06	−3.09	−2.68	−2.27	−3.09
Semi-finished manufactures	−1.63	−0.82	−1.42	−1.06	−0.90	−1.42
Crude materials	−0.39	−0.20	−0.29	−0.25	−0.22	−0.29

3. *Export-supply elasticities.* In most contributions dealing with the effects of tariff reductions on trade, it has been explicitly or implicitly assumed that the elasticities of export supply are infinite; i.e., every country can expand production at constant costs, and hence import prices will fall by the full amount of the cut in tariffs.[16] Kreinin's calculations on the impact of multilateral tariff reductions on the prices of commodities exported to the United States in the years 1954–56 and 1955–59 have led him to different conclusions, however. In his view, "it appears plausible that close to half of the benefit from tariff concessions granted by the United States accrued to foreign exporters in the form of increased export prices."[17]

This empirical result suggests the conclusion that export supply elasticities in the countries that provide the bulk of U.S. imports are less than infinite. In general, the size of these elasticities will depend on the share of exports in domestic production, as well as on the conditions prevailing in the labor market. For one thing, export supply elasticities will tend to be negatively correlated with the share of exports in domestic production; for another, in a tight labor market, wages in the export industries will have to be raised in order to attract labor from other sectors of the economy. However, the elasticities

---

[15] Bela Balassa, "Tariff Protection in Industrial Countries: An Evaluation," *Journal of Political Economy*, December, 1965, pp. 592–93.

[16] Cf. e.g., H. G. Johnson, "The Gains from Freer Trade with Europe: an Estimate," *Manchester School*, September, 1958, pp. 247–55; L. B. Krause, "United States Imports and the Tariff," *American Economic Review*, Papers and Proceedings, May, 1959, pp. 542–51, and Robert M. Stern, "The U.S. Tariff and the Efficiency of the U.S. Economy," *American Economic Review*, Papers and Proceedings, May, 1964, pp. 459–70.

[17] M. E. Kreinin, "Effects of Tariff Changes on the Prices and Volume of Imports," p. 317.

will be higher, the longer the time period considered. For despite the observed rigidity in prices and wages in the industrial countries, increases in productive capacity and in the labor force permit a certain degree of reversibility in relative prices in the long run.

These considerations can be applied to United States–Western Europe relationships. Given the small share of exports in production, and the anticipated rapid rate of increase in the labor force, we may assume that an expansion of exports will not necessitate price increases in the United States. On the other hand, in Western Europe exports account for a large proportion of output, and future increases in the labor force will hardly remedy the tightness of the labor market. The reallocation of resources following multilateral reductions in duties may, then, lead to higher wages in European export industries. However, in the process of long-term adjustment the ensuing price increases will be mitigated, and hence the rise in export prices can be expected to be smaller than Kreinin's short-term results suggest.[18]

4. *Estimated changes in imports.* In the present study we have prepared two sets of estimates. Variant I assumes that the export prices of manufactured goods in Western Europe would rise by one-third of the tariff reduction, while Variant II is calculated with unchanged European export prices. In all other exporting areas constant export prices have been assumed throughout, and the same assumption has been made in regard to industrial materials irrespective of their origin.

If the original tariff rate, expressed as a fraction of the c.i.f. price exclusive of duty, is denoted by t, and the rate of tariff reduction by s, the price of imports would decline by $st/1+t$ in the event that export prices remained unchanged (Variant II); on the alternative assumption, import prices would fall by two-thirds and export prices increase by one-third of this magnitude. Correspondingly, in calculating increases in the imports of individual commodities in constant prices under Variant II, we have used the formula:

(1) $$dM = \eta_m M st/1 + t$$

[18] In this connection, note that according to a study carried out by the EFTA Secretariat, it appears that a large part of the tariff cuts have been passed on in prices lower than would otherwise have been charged. See *The Effect on Prices of Tariff Dismantling in EFTA* (Geneva, 1966), p. 7.

In turn, equation (1) has been multiplied by two-thirds, and the amount of new imports ($M+dM$) has been adjusted for the assumed increases in European export prices of manufactured goods in the case of Variant I.[19]

Discrimination against non-member countries in the EEC and EFTA. An across-the-board tariff reduction in the framework of the Kennedy Round would also diminish the extent of discrimination by the European Common Market and the European Free Trade Association against each other's members as well as against third countries. The effects of this reduction in the extent of discrimination on exports can be estimated by measuring the potential impact of discrimination on trade flows. In this connection, note should first be taken of the possibilities of expanding the exports of manufactured goods in the partner countries.

For the event of a balanced expansion of trade, we have concluded that some increases in prices may be expected to occur in Western Europe. Pressures for cost-and-price increases will be stronger in a union encompassing only some of the industrial countries, since trade diversion resulting from tariff discrimination is equivalent to an *unbalanced* expansion of trade, and, correspondingly, excess demand is created on the national economy (union) level.

But even substantial price increases may not permit member country producers to replace imports from third countries if the former are small producers and exporters. It would make little sense, for example, to estimate the extent of discrimination against the United States in a Benelux union without taking account of capacity limitations in the latter. Given the present industrial structure of the member countries, this observation is of considerable importance for the European Free Trade Association, and with respect to a number of industrial materials, it pertains also to the European Common Market.

We have dealt with this problem by assuming that the possibility of replacing foreign suppliers depends on the share of member country suppliers in each other's market. Accord-

---

[19] A different procedure has been followed in regard to Britain's trade under the Commonwealth preference system, where we have estimated the shift in the sources of supply that would follow the elimination of, or reductions in, preferences.

ingly, the rate of discrimination has been taken to be the following fractions of the tariff levied on products imported from nonmember countries (the common external tariff for the EEC and the national tariffs for EFTA): two-thirds, in cases where the share of internal suppliers in total (intra-and extra-area) imports exceeded 30 per cent;[20] one-third, where this share was between 10 and 30 per cent; zero, whenever the share of internal suppliers was less than 10 per cent.

Assuming that third-country exporters do not reduce their prices, the decrease in their sales due to the establishment of the Common Market and EFTA can be estimated by utilizing substitution elasticities between commodities exported by the partner countries on the one hand, and by nonmember countries on the other. It has been shown that substitution elasticities are generally higher than demand elasticities.[21] However, we have used the latter in the calculations in order to give expression to the fact that, as a result of increases in their export prices, member countries are bound to lose some foreign markets.

Indirect effects and the feedback mechanism. In the event that the industrial nations were to undertake tariff reductions under the most-favored-nation clause, their imports from nonindustrial countries would also rise, and the latter would further benefit from the lessening of EEC and EFTA discrimination. Now, assuming that industrial countries and Soviet-type economies accumulate (decumulate) reserves while nonindustrial economies spend all increases in their foreign exchange earnings, there will be a feedback in the form of higher imports from the industrial countries. Taking account of the cumulative effects of purchases by nonindustrial economies, it would appear that ultimately 95 per cent of the foreign exchange spent in these areas would return to the industrial nations in the form of higher exports. The remainder is assumed to "leak out" to Communist countries.[22]

[20] In other words, the export prices of competing member-country suppliers have been assumed to rise by one-third of the external tariff.

[21] Cf. A. C. Harberger, "Some Evidence on the International Price Mechanism," *American Economic Review*, May, 1965.

[22] The results have been obtained through an inversion of a trade matrix for 1960. For a description of the method of calculation, see W. W. Hicks, "Estimating the Foreign Exchange Cost of Untied Aid," *Southern Economic Journal*, October, 1963, pp. 168–74.

Evaluation of comparative advantage. As noted in Chapter 1 of this volume, we have used indicators of export performance and export-import ratios to indicate the "revealed" comparative advantage of the industrial countries in their trade in manufactured goods. In conformity with the definition used elsewhere in this volume, manufactured goods have been defined to include the products classified in commodity categories 5 to 8 of the Standard International Trade Classification other than unwrought metals. With respect to these products, we have attempted to establish a commodity classification based on substitution possibilities in production. The point of departure has been the three-digit breakdown of the SITC; this has been supplemented by a four-digit breakdown whenever it appeared necessary and was made possible by the availability of statistical information.

Altogether, we have distinguished 74 commodity categories, having excluded from the investigation commodities that are not easily transportable, such as lime, cement and fabricated building materials (SITC 661), clay construction materials (662), and mineral manufactures n.e.s. (663), as well as commodities where the countries under consideration, taken together, have an import surplus. This solution has been chosen because in such instances other exporters are likely to benefit from an over-all tariff reduction; less-developed countries in regard to mineral tar and crude chemicals (521), dyeing and tanning extracts (532), wood and cork manufactures (631), jute fabrics (653.4), pearls and precious stones (667), silver (681), and miscellaneous metals (688.9), and Switzerland in the case of watches and clocks (864). Further, for obvious reasons we have excluded developed cinematographic film (863), printed matter (892), as well as the motley collection of other miscellaneous manufactured articles, n.e.s. (893–896, 898).

We have first calculated the relative shares of individual countries in the world exports of the different commodity categories for the periods 1953–55 and 1960–62 that have been taken as representative of the mid-fifties and the early sixties. In both instances, the data have been made comparable through appropriate "normalization." This has been accomplished by dividing a country's share in the exports of a given commodity by its share in the combined exports of manufactured goods of the ten industrial countries under consideration, and expressing the result in index number form. Thus, for a given export commodity of a particular country, an index number of 110 will mean that the country's share in this commodity's exports is 10 per cent higher than its share in the total exports of manufactured goods. Further calculations have been made with regard to changes in shares between the two periods in order to provide an indication of developments over time.

Correspondingly, we have calculated (1) the relative share of country i's exports of commodity j in the years 1953–55; (2) the relative share of country i's exports of commodity j in the years 1960–62; (3) the ratio of the relative share of country i's exports of commodity j in the second period to that in the first period. In all cases, the expression "relative share" refers to the ratio of the share of country i in the exports of commodity j to the share of country i in the exports of all manufactured goods.

In symbols,[23]

$$(3) \qquad \left. \frac{X_{ij}^{o}}{X_{nj}^{o}} \middle| \frac{X_{it}^{o}}{X_{nt}^{o}} \right. = \frac{x_{ij}^{o}}{x_{i}^{o}}$$

$$(4) \qquad \left. \frac{X_{ij}^{l}}{X_{nj}^{l}} \middle| \frac{X_{it}^{l}}{X_{nt}^{l}} \right. = \frac{x_{ij}^{l}}{x_{j}^{l}}$$

$$(5) \qquad \left. \frac{x_{ij}^{l}}{x_{i}^{l}} \middle| \frac{x_{ij}^{o}}{x_{j}^{o}} \right.$$

In evaluating relative advantages in the export of manufactured goods, various assumptions may be made. One may assume, for example, that relative shares observed in the most recent period will pertain also to the future, or one may take

[23] Explanation of symbols:

X = exports
x = relative share of exports
o = average for the years 1953–55
l = average for the years 1960–62
i = country i
n = ten industrial countries taken together
j = product j

relative growth rates as an indicator. Both of these methods have their advantages and disadvantages. On the one hand, in considering relative export performance in a certain year, or an average of several years, we neglect the trend factor; on the other, relative growth rates can give a misleading impression of comparative advantage, since high growth rates are compatible with small exports in absolute terms, while a country that has a large segment of the export market in a given commodity can hardly be expected to further increase its share.

These considerations point to the need for using some combination of the two indicators to express comparative advantage. One possible solution would be to project the continuation of past trends in relative shares by multiplying equations (4) and (5) to obtain equation (6). We have decided against using this formula since it involves the questionable assumption that changes in relative shares take the form of a geometrical progression which can be extrapolated into the future. Instead, a compromise solution has been chosen by calculating the arithmetical average of equations (4) and (6).

$$(6) \qquad \frac{x_{ij}{}^l}{x_i{}^l} \cdot \frac{x_{ij}{}^l}{x_i{}^l} \; \middle| \; \frac{x_{ij}{}^o}{x_j{}^o}$$

$$(7) \qquad \frac{1}{2} \left[\frac{x_{ij}{}^l}{x_i{}^l} + \frac{x_{ij}{}^l}{x_i{}^l} \cdot \frac{x_{ij}{}^l}{x_i{}^l} \; \middle| \; \frac{x_{ij}{}^o}{x_j{}^o} \right]$$

This choice reflects the presumption that while past trends in relative shares can be expected to contine, they will do so at a declining pace. The results of the calculations are shown in Appendix Table 1.2.[24] In the case of export-import ratios, too, indices of relative level and relative growth have been calculated, while the procedure of "normalization" has taken the form of dividing the export-import ratio of a country for a given commodity by that of the ten countries, taken together. The calculations have been carried out on the basis of considerations simi-

---

[24] The reader will observe that any other average of the two figures could have been taken, and our choice is based on the assumption that it is appropriate to give equal weights to the two indicators.

lar to those relating to export shares, and are shown in Appendix Table 1.3.[25]

[25] The formula corresponding to equation (7) in the case of export-import ratios is:

$$\frac{1}{2}\left[\frac{x_{ij}{}^{l}}{m_{ij}{}^{l}} + \frac{x_{ij}{}^{l}}{m_{ij}{}^{l}} \cdot \frac{x_{ij}{}^{l}}{m_{ij}{}^{l}} \mid \frac{x_{ij}{}^{o}}{m_{ij}{}^{o}}\right]$$

(In the equation, m stands for relative export-import ratios.)

Appendix to Chapter II

M. E. Kreinin

Direct effects of tariff reductions. The possible changes in U.S. exports and imports due to the establishment of an Atlantic Free Trade Area were estimated in two parts: the direct effects of trade liberalization, and the expansion of trade due to the elimination of EEC and EFTA discrimination. The direct effects will depend largely on the height of tariffs and the elasticities of import demand and export supply in the individual countries. These factors will be considered in succession.

1. *Tariffs.* The United States tariff schedule covers about six-thousand commodities, of which 38 per cent are imported duty free. The distribution of these tariffs shows a considerable degree of dispersion. Of the 3,760 duties on nonagricultural commodities examined by the EEC Commission, tariff rates exceeding 40 per cent are levied on 325 items in the United States, while there are 62 such items in the United Kingdom, and none in the Common Market.[1] In this connection, note that the averaging of national tariffs has reduced the number of very high—and very low—duties in the EEC. It has often been shown that tariff averages, weighted by a country's own imports, have a substantial downward bias, because highly restrictive duties receive little weight while low duties that hardly restrict imports have large weight. In the present chapter, we used unweighted averages of duties calculated for the 1,100 headings of the Brussels Tariff Classification,[2] and aggregated for each three-digit SITC commodity category. In

[1] European Economic Community, *Disparate Aspects of Selected Tariff Structures*, Brussels, 1962, mimeographed.
[2] Political and Economic Planning, *Atlantic Tariffs and Trade* (London: Allen & Unwin, 1962).

the case of the United States, the estimates have been adjusted to express tariffs on a c.i.f. basis.[3]

2. *Import Prices.* How would the removal of tariffs affect import prices? Two extreme views may be noted in this regard. Some argue that import prices in the United States would not be affected at all. Most industrial imports have close domestic substitutes, and in most cases the imports constitute a very small portion of total new supply. Consequently, import prices would fall under the "umbrella" of domestic prices, and if tariffs were eliminated, the foreign supplier rather than the domestic consumer would reap the benefit. This view, which is consistent with the "charging what the traffic would bear" philosophy, may be valid for some standardized products where quality, brand names, and other features of product differentiation are absent or immaterial. But manufactures are highly differentiated commodities that differ in quality, specifications, and the like. And even identical goods produced here and abroad are not considered perfect substitutes for each other. It would appear, then, that the umbrella price argument applies only to isolated cases.

The opposite view is that import prices fully reflect the tariff, and in an Atlantic Free Trade Area they would be reduced by the amount of the tariff.[4] This approach would be valid only if foreign supply elasticities were infinite. But considering the fact that the European and Japanese economies have been operating at, or near, full capacity for the past fifteen years and may continue to experience excessive aggregate demand at least through 1968,[5] the validity of this proposition is open to question.[6]

Where between these two extremes the actual outcome is

[3] Cf. F. K. Topping, *Comparative Tariffs and Trade*, Washington, 1963, p. xiii.

[4] See for example Robert Stern, "The U.S. Tariff and the Efficiency of the U.S. Economy," *American Economic Review*, Papers and Proceedings, May, 1964, p. 463.

[5] See Walter Salant, *et al.*, *The United States Balance of Payments, in 1968* [The Brookings Report] (Washington, D.C.: The Brookings Institution, 1963) pp. 50–53.

[6] The assumption also conflicts with the idea of the optimum tariff. According to international trade theory, a country can improve its terms of trade in imposing a tariff by shifting part of the tax to foreign suppliers, if it faces a less than perfectly elastic reciprocal demand curve. The United States, which accounts for a large share of world trade is able, more than any other industrial country, to so affect its terms of trade.

likely to be depends on the relative elasticities of export supply and import demand. In studying the effects of the tariff concessions granted by the United States during the 1955 and 1956 GATT negotiations, I estimated that between one-third and one-half of the tariff cuts averaging 15 per cent were passed on to the American consumer in the form of reduced import prices.[7] The remaining gain was reaped by the foreign exporters through an increase in export prices. For the complete elimination of duties contemplated here leading to a larger increase in demand for foreign products, the cut in import prices may be even smaller. On the other hand, pressures on the European productive capacity may abate somewhat at some future time. Moreover, the results referred to above are of a short-term character, and increases in European export prices are likely to be mitigated in the process of long term adjustment. In making estimates, we assumed that one-half of the decline in duties would be reflected in lower import prices.[8] An alternative calculation was also prepared under the supposition that export prices would not change at all.

With respect to U.S. export prices, a different assumption was made. Since exports occupy a very small share of total production in almost all industries, it was assumed that increases in exports would not necessitate a rise in prices. Finally, in regard to industrial materials, export prices were assumed to remain constant, irrespective of their origin.

3. *The elasticity of demand for imports.* The effects of reductions in prices on the volume of imports will depend on the price elasticity of import demand in the individual countries. For the United States, if has been decided to use the elasticity estimates constructed by Ball and Marwah[9] that were based on quarterly data for eleven postwar years. The results of the calculations for the relevant commodity groups are: crude materials, -0.26; semimanufactures, -1.38; and finished manufactures -3.50.

[7] See M. E. Kreinin, "Effect of Tariff Changes on the Value and Volume of Imports," *American Economic Review*, June, 1961, pp. 310–14.

[8] When converting the volume to value figures, account was taken of the increase in export prices in the country of origin.

[9] R. J. Ball and K. Marwah, "The U.S. Demand for Imports, 1948–1958," *Review of Economics and Statistics*, November, 1962, pp. 395–401.

For various reasons, however, those estimates are subject to a downward bias. For one thing, the application of the least-squares method to time series data has been shown to underestimate the price elasticities of import demand;[10] for another, the statistical calculations do not appropriately take account of the existence of prohibitive rates. The reductions in prohibitive rates of tariffs are neglected in the data, since there are no observations on imports. Nevertheless, if we consider that the U.S. tariff of today is the outcome of two decades of tariff reductions, this drawback does not appear to be too severe. The problem is of even lesser importance in European countries where we find few instances of excessively high rates.

A further limitation on the application of elasticity estimates to price changes arises from the possibility of price response. Domestic producers in individual industries may react to the tariff cut by lowering their prices in order to meet foreign competition, thereby barring—or a least moderating—any increase in imports. This, however, is unlikely to occur in the case of the United States, since imports account for too small a share of total production in most industries. In the very few industries where imports play a major role, some price reduction may be expected. But even here it is constrained by cost considerations, since these tend to be labor-intensive industries. With respect to American exports, this possibility can also be largely discounted on the ground that in most cases, the industries of the countries in question are operating at full capacity and would not be inclined to reduce prices.

The deficiencies of time-series estimation of import demand elasticities do not apply to projections made by commodity experts, although these are subject to error due to the limitation of human capacity to foresee future events. Such estimates were prepared by B. A. deVries concerning the long-run impact on American imports of a 50 per cent reduction ($\bar{e}_1$), and a 50 per cent increase ($\bar{e}_2$) in the tariff levied on individual commodities. The unweighted averages of elasticity for the 176 commodities (including 27 raw materials) are: $\bar{e}_1 = -2.23$

---

[10] Guy H. Orcutt, "Measurement of Price Elasticities in International Trade," *Review of Economics and Statistics*, May, 1950, pp. 117–32.

and $\bar{e}_2 = -2.74$. For 20 manufactured products imported from the United Kingdom (whiskey is excluded for special considerations), deVries obtained $\bar{e}_1 = -4.8$ and $\bar{e}_2 = -3.5$, while the corresponding figures for the United States' imports from other industrial countries are: Belgium -3.4; Austria -4.6; Denmark -4.3; France -4.2; and Italy -3.4.

While these considerations indicate the existence of a downward bias in the Ball-Marwah results, they do not provide a clue to the magnitude of this bias. In the present chapter we made calculations using the elasticities obtained by these authors. In addition, "upper bound" elasticities were derived by adding two standard deviations to the results shown by regression analysis which involves an approximately 30 per cent upward adjustment in the estimates. Separate calculations were made for 118 commodity groups, corresponding to the three (and in some cases four) digit SITC categories of which 85 groups comprised manufactured goods and the remainder industrial materials. Using the Ball-Marwah estimates, an elasticity value was assigned to each commodity category depending on whether the products contained in it were crude materials, semimanufactures or finished manufactures, or any combination of these.

There is reason to believe that the elasticity of demand for U.S. exports is smaller than U.S. import demand elasticity. The United States produces close substitutes for virtually all industrial imports, and imports occupy a small proportion in the consumption of each product. This supposition is corroborated in deVries' study[11] of American imports of individual products. He found that "commodities whose imports supply a relatively large share of the U.S. market tend to have a relatively low elasticity of import demand; while commodities whose imports supply a relatively small share of the market have relatively high elasticity." For commodities in which the import/consumption ratio was above the average for all 176 commodities studied, his two elasticities were: $\bar{e}_1 = -1.77$; $\bar{e}_2 = -2.33$. For those in which the import/consumption ratio was below the average, the elasticities were much higher; $\bar{e}_1 = -3.13$, $\bar{e}_2 = -3.64$. In the case of tariff reduction ($\bar{e}_1$) the difference is

[11] B. A. deVries, "Price Elasticities of Demand for Individual Commodities Imported into the United States," *IMF* Staff Paper, p. 419.

about 80 per cent. Since estimates on import-demand elasticities in a comparable breakdown are not available for Canada, Western Europe, and Japan, we relied on the results of Arnold Harberger who put the elasticity of demand for United States manufacturing exports at about −2.[12] In conformity with the method used for estimating changes in imports, an alternative calculation was made by using an elasticity of −2.6. Finally, by applying a method similar to that described in regard to U.S. imports, a demand elasticity of −0.6 was derived for U.S. exports of industrial materials to the other countries of the Atlantic Area.

Discriminatory effects. The possible decrease in U.S. exports due to tariff discrimination in the European Common Market was estimated by Lawrence B. Krause in the Brookings Report on the basis of 1960 trade data.[13] For 61 categories of U.S. exports of manufactured goods, Krause calculated the additional protection accorded by the common external tariff to the low cost producers within the Community. Then, applying a substitution elasticity of −2, the potential decline of American manufacturing exports was estimated at $200 million.

I have two reservations concerning this result. First, the method employed in deriving the estimates assumes that low-cost producers in the Community could increase their exports to the partner countries at constant prices. To the extent that the EEC members are operating at capacity, and even suffer from shortages of capacity, this is not likely to be the case. At the very least, the discriminatory tariff may cause them to divert some of their exports from external to internal destinations. That would relieve some competitive pressure against American exports in third markets, and perhaps even cause some reduction in the EEC exports to the United States. The Brookings Report does not consider the possibility of

[12] A. Harberger, "Some Evidence on the International Price Mechanism," *Journal of Political Economy,* December, 1957, pp. 506–21. This is also the figure used in the Brookings Report to estimate the impact of the European Economic Community on American exports. *The United States Balance of Payments in 1968,* p. 104. In another context, however, the Brookings Report employed an elasticity estimate for U.S. exports of −2.5 (p. 82).

[13] L. B. Krause, "The European Economic Community and the United States Balance of Payments," in Salant *et al., The United States Balance of Payments in 1968,* pp. 95–118.

such export retardation. Rather, it is assumed that "in an industrially advanced country, output usually can be increased; the door is rarely slammed in the face of willing customers."[14] But the door need not be "slammed" for exports to be retarded. The effect would usually take the form of longer waiting periods for European products and less aggressive sales efforts outside the Community on the part of European producers. These are highly probable results for an economy characterized by shortages in capacity, to which the Brookings Report alludes in a different context.[15] At the same time, the statistics used in the Report to support the contention that no retardation has taken place relate to 1961 when there was still no significant discrimination against outsiders either. It would appear, then, that tariff discrimination would lead to at least some retardation of exports in the EEC. In order to account for this factor, we assume that one-half of the European price advantage imparted through the EEC discrimination would be wiped out by domestic price increases.

On the other hand, the elasticity figure of −2 used in the Brookings Report appears to be on the low side. To the extent that the change in relative prices applies to the national market of the competitor because the common external tariff differs from the original national tariff, the elasticity of demand for American exports (−2) may be used in the calculations. But the country's own tariff may move in either direction, while discrimination will result in replacing imports from nonparticipating countries by the products of the low-cost producers favored by the external tariff. Accordingly, the relevant figure is the elasticity of substitution between the goods produced in the United States and in the partner (EEC) countries. On the basis of Harberger's[16] work, we assumed this substitution elasticity to be −2.5.

In order to estimate the potential diversionary impact of the Common Market on U.S. exports of manufactured goods, we selected 26 three- and four-digit SITC categories in the case of which American exports to the EEC exceeded $10 million in

[14] *Ibid.*, p. 113.
[15] *Ibid.*, p. 130.
[16] Arnold Harberger, "Some Evidence on the International Price Mechanism," *American Economic Review*, p. 516.

1960. These commodity groups cover 91 per cent of U.S. manufacturing exports to the Common Market. Taking one-half of the level of the common external tariff as the measure of discrimination, and assuming a substitution elasticity of −2.5, we arrived at a figure of $238 million.[17] Further, we accepted the estimates of the Brookings Report in regard to industrial materials, ($100 million) and on the indirect effects of EEC discrimination. The latter is due to the fact that the EEC members would discriminate in favor of their associated African territories and against Latin American countries which are traditional customers of the United States.[18]

A similar procedure was followed in estimating the diversionary effect of the European Free Trade Association, except that in the absence of a common external tariff the degree of discrimination against outsiders varies from one member to another. In 1960, there were 25 SITC categories of manufactured goods for which U.S. exports to EFTA exceeded $10 million, accounting for 88 per cent of U.S. exports of manufactures to EFTA. In 2 of these categories, the United States faces virtually no competition within EFTA, and the degree of discrimination is assumed to be nil. In 9 industries, there is one major competitor; in 15 industries, two major competitors; and in 2 industries, three competitors. The United Kingdom occupies a predominant position in almost all industries: she is the first, or (in some cases) second, major competitor in 21 of the 23 industries. Consequently, in a large measure EFTA would involve discrimination against American exports competing with similar British products.

Since EFTA does not call for a common external tariff, and it involves only the elimination of duties on the intra-area trade, the degree of discrimination against outsiders can be measured in each country by its external duty. If the U.S. and

---

[17] The main industries so affected are: organic chemicals (SITC 512), $25 million; miscellaneous chemicals (SITC 599), $20 million; office machinery (SITC 714), $10 million; metal-working machinery (SITC 715), $10 million; industrial machinery n.e.s. (SITC 716), $34 million; electrical machinery (SITC 721) $17 million; road motor vehicles (SITC 732), $17 million; aircraft (SITC 734) $37 million.

[18] *The United States Balance of Payments in 1968*, pp. 111–12. It is not made clear how these figures have been derived in the Brookings Report. Observation indicates that they exaggerate the effect of the Common Market on trade flows. We included them for want of other estimates.

the U.K. are major competitors in the Austrian market in a given commodity, on which the Austrian tariff is 22 per cent, then the creation of EFTA would favor the British over the American exporter by 11 per cent under the assumption that U.K. export prices would rise by one-half of the tariff. Assuming again substitution elasticities of a 2.5, U.S. exports would fall by 27.5 per cent. Similar calculations were performed for each industry and for each EFTA country with the exception of industries 533, 734, and 862 where the U.K. is the only intra-EFTA exporter. That means that in the British market itself there would be no discrimination against American exports as a result of EFTA.

Summing up the results for all countries and for the products involved, we obtained $138 million as the decline in U.S. exports due to discrimination in EFTA.[19] On the other hand, given that the tariffs of EFTA countries on industrial materials tend to be low, we assumed that the extent of trade diversion would be nil. A similar assumption was made with regard to the indirect effects of EFTA's establishment.

Discriminatory effects of an Atlantic Free Trade Area excluding the Common Market. An AFTA without the EEC would involve trade discrimination on both sides. The EEC would discriminate against the United States, causing a loss of $438 million in exports. On the other hand, American exports would benefit from discrimination against the EEC in other AFTA countries. To estimate the magnitude of this benefit, we selected 50 industries in which the United States and the EEC compete in the markets of Japan, Canada, and "Other Europe." The tariff rates levied by third countries on each article would constitute the measure of discrimination against the EEC. Given the high elasticity of supply in the United States, it may be assumed that no increase in export prices would take place. Thus by multiplying the elasticity of substitution of -2.5 by the degree of discrimination on each manufactured article in the non-EEC countries, we obtained the percentage reduction in EEC exports resulting from the discrimination. These percentages were then applied to the 1960 EEC export

[19] The main industries affected are: miscellaneous chemicals (SITC 598), $11 million; iron and steel (SITC 681), $14 million; metal working machinery (SITC 715), $12 million; industrial machinery, n.e.s. (SITC 716), $24 million; electrical machinery (SITC 721), $11 million; road motor vehicles (SITC 732), $10 million.

figures to each country, to derive dollar estimates of their prospective decline. The decline in each case is equal to the export gain of the non-EEC countries, part of which would accrue to the United States. The allocation of that part was based on the share of United States exports in the total exports of the non-EEC countries (all trade data pertaining to 1960), and the assignment was made separately for each product and country. The gain amounted to $0.6 million, with various machinery items accounting for over 40 per cent of the total.

Appendix to Chapter III

R. J. Wonnacott

Effect of AFTA on Canada's trade in industrial products. The formula used for the price elasticity of demand (η_m) for imports takes into account the fact that the total quantity demanded and sold in its domestic market (Q_d) consists of the following parts: the quantity domestically supplied (Q_s), the quantity of dutiable imports (Q_m) and the quantity of duty-free imports (Q_f). Accordingly, the formula becomes:

$$(9) \qquad \eta_m = \frac{Q_d}{Q_m} \eta_d - \frac{Q_s}{Q_m} \epsilon_s - \frac{Q_f}{Q_m} \epsilon_f,$$

where η_d is the price elasticity of demand for the commodity, ϵ_s is the price elasticity of domestic supply, and ϵ_f is the price elasticity of supply of duty-free imports.

If there is no necessity to distinguish between dutiable and duty-free imports, then the following formula may be used:

$$(10) \qquad \eta_m = \frac{Q_d}{Q_m} \eta_d - \frac{Q_s}{Q_m} \epsilon_s$$

in which η_m and Q_m represent demand elasticity and quantity respectively of total imports, including both those that are dutiable and duty-free. This was the formula used by Robert Stern[1] to measure the total net change in imports into the United States following the assumed elimination of tariffs. We have used equation (10) to estimate prospective changes in Canadian imports in an Atlantic Free Trade Area. However, to esti-

[1] R. M. Stern, "The U.S. Tariff and the Efficiency of the U.S. Economy," *American Economic Review*, Papers and Proceedings, May, 1964.

mate changes in Canadian exports, it was necessary to apply equation (9) to the import patterns of the major countries to which Canada exports. This is because dutiable and duty-free imports must be handled separately—for two reasons. The first is that the United Kingdom admits many Canadian exports duty free under the Commonwealth preference system; the second reason is because of the mix of dutiable and duty-free goods that may make up an export category.

For example, suppose that the U.K. has a 10 per cent m.f.n. duty on a product and a 4 per cent tariff on exports originating in the Commonwealth. The first 4 per cent of the U.K. tariff reduction will apply to all countries exporting to the U.K. (Commonwealth and non-Commonwealth alike). The resulting increase in U.K. imports is computed from equation (10), and is allocated to exporting countries according to their present share of the U.K. market. At this point, Commonwealth countries have achieved duty-free treatment, and the final 6 per cent of U.K. tariff reductions applies only to non-Commonwealth countries. The trade-creating effects of this change can be evaluated by the use of equation (9), but there will also be a shift in the source of supply from Canada to non-Commonwealth countries because of the removal of preferences accorded to Canada.

A reduction in the U.S. tariff could also result in a *decrease* in Canadian exports to the United States in the industry concerned. Assume, for example, that the United States imports $10 million worth of dutiable fresh fish, $1 million of which comes from Canada; suppose also that the U.S. imports $2 million of fresh fish duty free—all of which comes from Canada. The effect of eliminating the U.S. tariff would be to increase U.S. imports of fresh fish which previously were subject to duty, while reducing U.S. imports of fish which previously paid no duty. Because Canada's exports are so heavily concentrated in the latter category, it is quite possible that Canadian exports of the latter type might fall by more than the increase of Canadian exports of the former type.[2]

[2] Sources of calculations: Canadian and U.S. trade statistics: Industry reports of the Dominion Bureau of Statistics; Committee for Economic Development, *Comparative Tariffs and Trade* (Washington, 1964); Political and Economic Planning, *Atlantic Tariffs and Trade* (London, 1962).

INDEX

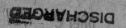